THE CONSTITUTION AFTER SCOTT

THE CONSTITUTION AFTER SCOTT

Government Unwrapped

ADAM TOMKINS

School of Law
King's College, London

CLARENDON PRESS · OXFORD
1998

Oxford University Press, Great Clarendon Street, Oxford OX2 6DP

Oxford New York

Athens Auckland Bangkok Bogota Bombay
Buenos Aires Calcutta Cape Town Dar es Salaam
Delhi Florence Hong Kong Istanbul Karachi
Kuala Lumpur Madras Madrid Melbourne
Mexico City Nairobi Paris Singapore
Taipei Tokyo Toronto Warsaw
and associated companies in
Berlin Ibadan

Oxford is a trade mark of Oxford University Press

Published in the United States
by Oxford University Press Inc., New York

British Library Cataloguing in Publication Data
Data available

Library of Congress Cataloging in Publication Data
Tomkins, Adam.
The constitution after Scott: government unwrapped / Adam Tomkins.
p. cm.
Includes bibliographical references and index.
1. Constitutional law—Great Britain. 2. Scott Inquiry, Great Britain, 1992–1997.
3. Great Britain—Politics and government—1979–1997. I. Title.
KD3989.3.T66 1998 342.41'02—dc21 97–44982
ISBN 0–19–826291–4
ISBN 0–19–826290–6 (Pbk)

1 3 5 7 9 10 8 6 4 2

Typeset by Hope Services (Abingdon) Ltd.
Printed in Great Britain
on acid-free paper by
Bookcraft Ltd., Midsomer Norton, Somerset

To Chloé

Preface

THIS book is about the British constitution, seen through the lens of the Scott report. I hope that it has been written in a sufficiently accessible style so as to allow both lawyers and non-lawyers, and those who know nothing of Scott as well as those who are already quite familiar with it, to be able to read and use it. It has been written not only with only academics and university students in mind. Anybody who is interested in British parliamentary government, whether from journalism, politics, academia or anywhere else, should if I have done my job properly, be able to get something out of this book.

There is already a quite extensive literature on the Scott report, but I believe that there are two things which make this book distinct. First, the focus here is on the longer term constitutional implications of Scott rather than solely on reacting to the report itself. Although this book does explain the Scott story in a reasonably comprehensive manner, this is done more with a view to setting the scene for the constitutional analysis which follows, rather than for its own sake. Secondly, this book compares the Scott story with its American equivalent: the Iraqgate scandal, which has thus far been an under-explored (yet revealing) aspect of the Scott story.

Some of the chapters of this book have drawn on previously published work, and I am grateful to the editors of *Public Law, Legal Studies*, and *Parliamentary Affairs* for permission to reproduce some paragraphs from my articles: 'Public Interest Immunity after Matrix Churchill' [1993] *Public Law* 650; 'A Right to Mislead Parliament?' (1996) 16 *Legal Studies* 63; 'Government Information and Parliament: Misleading by Design or by Default?' [1996] *Public Law* 472; and 'Intelligence and Government' (1997) 50 *Parliamentary Affairs* 109.

I have been fortunate during both my research for and my writing of this book. First, King's College London generously provided me with financial support for the research I undertook on US constitutional and national security law, research which formed the basis of chapters six and seven. I am also grateful to all those at Pace University School of Law (in 1993) and at Quinnipiac College School of Law and at the National Law Center at George Washington University (in 1997) who provided me with facilities during my two research trips to the US. The School of Law at King's College London provided me with sabbatical leave in 1997 to enable me to write the book.

A number of people have helped me enormously by reading and commenting on numerous drafts of various parts of the book. They include Malcolm Anderson, Anthony Barker, Rodney Brazier, Keith Ewing, Conor Gearty, Geoffrey Marshall, Peter Oliver, and Mark Tushnet. In addition, four special friends read the whole book and generally kept me going when things got boring: without Lionel Bently, Brian Bix, Chloé MacEwen, and Victor Tadros, writing this book would not have been anything like as much fun. Lastly, I would like to acknowledge the support of my parents. My Dad read the book while it was in preparation and always had useful things to say about it, and both my parents have supported me throughout my education, even if they have not always understood what I was trying to say, and I owe them a great deal. Most of all, however, I thank Chloé MacEwen for putting up with me when the obsession was getting too much and for reeling me in when things threatened to get too wild.

A.T.

Summary of Contents

Contents

Introduction:
the Constitutional Importance of Scott

THE Scott report[1] was the most important constitutional event of the long Conservative period in office. Although that era dramatically ended on 1 May 1997, the New Labour government and its overwhelmingly New Parliament have much to learn from the old story from which this book has developed. The three-year Scott inquiry and the 1,806 page Scott report penetrated more deeply into the heart of British parliamentary government than any other public inquiry has ever done. For that reason alone its constitutional importance is unprecedented. The layers of government secrecy have never before been so thoroughly peeled back. Scott allowed us a unique glimpse of the murky depths of British central government. When we gaze at the picture Scott revealed, what do we see? What does the normally shrouded British government look like when it has been so publicly—and so reluctantly—unwrapped?

The sight is not a pretty one. Lies, deceit, double standards, disregard for legal authority, ignorance, amateurism, and complacency all feature prominently. It is little wonder that British government prefers secrecy to accountability and opts to keep itself under wraps as much as possible—it would be indecent to expose such an ugly scene to the unprotected public. But it is the job of a constitution to blow these covers, and that is why the Scott story is such an important *constitutional* story. It allows us to evaluate how well the British constitution manages its essential task of holding the government to account. Before Scott we could guess that all was not well, but now we know. Before Scott we could guess that ministers were not answering questions in Parliament as fully or as accurately as they might, but we lacked the materials and the information to know for sure. Before Scott we might have suspected that Britain's security and secret intelligence services were not being used as efficiently as they might be, but again, we could not tell for sure. Now we can, and now that Scott has filled in some of the gaps, we are for the first time in a position to know a little more about what we can actually do about it. The Scott story might be one from a previous political age, but the lessons it has to teach us about constitutional practice and its reform are as immediately topical and contemporary as ever.

---

[1] *Report of the Inquiry into the Export of Defence Equipment and Dual-Use Goods to Iraq and Related Prosecutions*, chaired by Rt. Hon. Sir Richard Scott, VC: published as HC (1995–96) 115. All footnote references in this book which cite only a paragraph number are references to the Scott report.

There is another factor which helps to make the Scott story more than just another political scandal. A hitherto neglected aspect of the Scott inquiry is that it was an affair which did not only affect Britain. The scandals which Scott investigated were not the domestic trivia of sexual affairs or financial impropriety which are the more usual ingredients of political scandal. Rather, Scott was concerned with a major plank of foreign policy of not only the British government, but of a number of western governments, most notably the USA. Britain was not alone in being scandalized by having a government which was apparently prepared to do business with Saddam Hussein's Iraq, even at the cost of lying to its electors. In America, just as in Britain, there was a constitutional investigation into the role played by the government in Iraq's arms procurement network. In the US, the investigation was conducted by a congressional committee chaired by one Henry Gonzalez; in Britain, by the judicial inquiry chaired by Scott. The comparison between the work of Scott and that of Gonzalez is a revealing one, as is the comparison between the constitutional implications which arise out of this multinational scandal in both the USA and in Britain. The constitutional lessons to be learnt from Scott and from Gonzalez are no more comfortable for those who have dominated the constitutional reform debate in Britain than they are for the former administrations of John Major and George Bush. This book seeks to understand exactly what those constitutional lessons are. What is it that we have to learn about the strengths and limitations of the British constitution from the events which Scott investigated and from the conclusions which the Scott report drew, when we look at those conclusions in the light of the work of congressman Gonzalez? These are the questions which this book seeks to answer.

The comparative constitutional focus of this book distinguishes it from much of the other academic and journalistic literature which the Scott report has already spawned.[2] This book seeks to serve two main purposes: first, to provide an authoritative account of what happened—of what the Scott report said—hopefully in a way which is more readable and more accessible than the

---

[2] Two distinguished collections of essays serve the purpose of providing a first reaction to Scott: see the special issues of *Public Law* (autumn 1996) and of *Parliamentary Affairs* (January 1997). The latter was republished in book form as B. Thompson and F. F. Ridley (eds.), *Under the Scott-Light: British Government Seen Through the Scott Report* (Oxford: Oxford University Press, 1997). A further useful overview is I. Leigh and L. Lustgarten, 'Five Volumes in Search of Accountability: The Scott Report' (1996) 59 *Modern Law Review* 695. The *Guardian's* correspondent who covered the Scott inquiry has co-written two books on Scott: one on the inquiry and one on the report. See R. Norton-Taylor with M. Lloyd, *Truth is a Difficult Concept: Inside the Scott Inquiry* (London: 4th Estate, 1995) and R. Norton-Taylor, M. Lloyd and S. Cook, *Knee Deep in Dishonour: The Scott Report and its Aftermath* (London: Victor Gollancz, 1996). More generally, see also J. Sweeney, *Trading with the Enemy: Britain's Arming of Iraq* (London: Pan, 1993) and on the US connection, see A. Friedman, *Spider's Web: Bush, Saddam, Thatcher and the Decade of Deceit* (London: Faber, 1993). In addition, a number of the protagonists of the Scott story have published their accounts of the affair, of which the following memoirs are representative: P. Henderson, *The Unlikely Spy* (London: Bloomsbury, 1993) and G. James, *In the Public Interest* (London: Little Brown, 1995).

report itself was. Secondly, this book attempts to analyse the ongoing constitutional implications of the Scott report and its aftermath. This book does not stop where Scott stopped. Rather, it seeks to place the Scott story in the context of the shape of Britain's parliamentary government during the long Conservative hegemony and in the context of what has happened since the report was published. The publication of the Scott report did not mark the end of the story with which this book is concerned.

What was Scott all about?

All the best political scandals have two aspects: the initial affair and then the attempted cover-up. Scott was no exception. Most political scandals also arise out of quite trivial details. Here again, Scott was no exception. The initial affair which the Scott inquiry investigated related to a tension between stated government policy and actual government practice with regard to defence exports to Iraq between 1984 and 1990. Government policy, as expressed in a written answer to a parliamentary question in 1984, and known as the Howe guidelines, was that (among other things) the British government 'should not in future approve new orders for any defence equipment which in our view would significantly enhance the capability of either' Iran or Iraq to 'prolong or exacerbate' the war which they fought from 1980–8. After the end of the Iran–Iraq war, three junior ministers agreed that the guidelines should be changed. The three ministers were William Waldegrave, Alan Clark, and Lord Trefgarne. They later claimed that they were not changing policy, but merely reinterpreting the guidelines, a view which the Scott report was to describe as 'not even remotely tenable'.[3] The new guidelines stated, in place of the previous form of words, that exports should be refused only when they 'would be of direct and significant assistance to either country in the conduct of offensive operations'. This was a much less rigorous approach and allowed for significantly more defence related exports to be licensed by the government for export to Iraq than had been the case before 1988.

The three ministers decided that there should be no public announcement of the new guidelines. This made life difficult when parliamentary questions on this subject had to be answered. As we shall see in chapter one, ministers are under a constitutional 'duty to give Parliament . . . and the public as full information as possible . . . and not to deceive or mislead Parliament'.[4] How could this constitutional duty be squared with the decision to withhold from Parliament (and the public) the fact that government policy had secretly changed? The unsurprising answer in the Scott report was that it could not be.

[3] See para. D3.90.
[4] See *Questions of Procedure for Ministers*, para. 27 (1992 version). This document is discussed in ch. 1 below.

A number of answers to parliamentary questions which concerned exports to Iraq were to be described in the report as 'inaccurate and misleading' and as 'designedly uninformative'.[5] This then was the first scandal which the Scott inquiry investigated: namely, whether Conservative government ministers had lied to Parliament about the British government's involvement in the arms trade with Saddam Hussein's Iraq—a brutal regime with which Britain was itself to go to war in 1990–1.

If misleading Parliament about trade with Iraq was the initial scandal, what was it that formed the second aspect—the cover-up? In the early 1990s, customs and excise, a government prosecuting authority, brought a number of criminal prosecutions against various manufacturing companies which had been accused of having committed deception offences relating to defence exports to Iraq. Most of these prosecutions faded away without any public attention, but one did catch the media's eye because of the fantastic scale of the project which customs appeared to have uncovered. This was the so-called supergun case. It appeared that Iraq had been trying to build an enormous gun capable of firing missiles from Iraqi soil as far as Israel, and that British companies had manufactured the tubes which were to form the barrel of the gun. A prosecution was launched, but it collapsed before the case came to court.[6]

The most controversial of the customs cases concerning trade with Iraq, however, was the Matrix Churchill trial.[7] Unlike the supergun case, the trial of three directors of Matrix Churchill did come to court, but as with the supergun case, the prosecution was unsuccessful. The Matrix Churchill trial collapsed in November 1992 amid a blaze of publicity. The immediate cause of the collapse was the inconsistent evidence of a central prosecution witness, one Alan Clark MP, former Conservative minister for trade and then for defence procurement, and subsequently renowned as a diarist. The controversy of the case lay not only in Mr Clark's evidence, but also in the role that had been played throughout the case by the attorney general, Sir Nicholas Lyell MP, and the advice which he had given on a hitherto obscure area of the law of evidence known as public interest immunity, or PII. As with the Howe guidelines, the law of PII would ordinarily have been an unlikely ingredient of a major political scandal. But, like the Howe guidelines, it was not so much PII itself as the malaise it represented which was the chief cause for concern. Under the doctrine of PII, the government may legally seek to withhold from a court information which would otherwise be relevant and admissible

---

[5] See paras. D4.29 and D3.107.

[6] See section F of the report. See also Chris Cowley, *Guns, Lies and Spies: How we armed Iraq* (London: Hamish Hamilton, 1992). Cowley worked as an engineer on the supergun project, and this book is his version of the story. He argues that the supergun case was dropped on the instruction of the cabinet office and contrary to the wishes of customs once it became clear how politically damaging it would be.

[7] See generally, D. Leigh, *Betrayed: The Real Story of the Matrix Churchill Trial* (London: Bloomsbury, 1993).

evidence on the grounds that the disclosure to the court of the information would be contrary to the public interest, because, for example, it would jeopardize national security, commercial confidentiality, or the 'proper functioning of the public service'.

In the Matrix Churchill case, four ministerial PII certificates were used, signed by Kenneth Clarke, Tristan Garel-Jones, Malcolm Rifkind, and Michael Heseltine. These certificates sought to prevent the court, and therefore also the defendants and their lawyers, from having access to government papers which were to establish the defendants' innocence. The defence team wanted to run two arguments: first that the security and secret intelligence services had been informed all along as to the nature of Matrix Churchill's trade with Iraq, and secondly that the government, and in particular Alan Clark, had not only known about but had also positively encouraged Matrix Churchill's trade with Iraq. If these arguments could be established, then this would indicate that there had been no deception on the part of Matrix Churchill, and therefore that the criminal charges were unfounded. Yet the defence lawyers would only be able to establish the truth of these arguments if they could have access to crucial government documents, and it was these government papers which ministers sought to prevent the defence team from seeing in their PII certificates. In the event, the trial judge examined the evidence which was subject to the PII claims and after several days of argument allowed much of it to be disclosed, albeit with some of it heavily blacked out (or 'redacted' as it was put) for security reasons. It was during his cross-examination on the basis of these documents that Alan Clark changed his evidence, as a consequence of which the prosecution had no choice but to throw in the towel. The trial collapsed amid a media frenzy. The press portrayed the government's position at the trial as one in which they had illegally sought to use 'gagging orders' (PII certificates) to prevent the truth about their own complicity in Iraq's arms procurement network from coming out, at the risk of sending three innocent men (arms dealers) down for perhaps as long as seven years.

The government then proceeded to compound its problems by insisting that despite all the talk of unprecedented gagging orders it had done nothing wrong in claiming PII in the Matrix Churchill trial. The government was right to argue that PII was nothing new. There were, however, two new—and highly controversial—aspects of the government's use of PII in Matrix Churchill. The first was that the law of PII has developed in a series of civil law cases—cases in which the withholding of evidence may have financial implications, but not consequences for individuals' liberty as may be the case in a criminal trial. Yet in the Matrix Churchill trial the government was happy to apply PII in the quite different context of a criminal prosecution. Was this legally justifiable? The Scott report was to find that the attorney general's view of the law that PII was equally applicable in both civil and criminal cases

was 'unsound'.[8] The government also claimed that ministers could not be criticized for having claimed PII as they had had no choice in the matter: they
were under a legal duty to claim PII, whether they wanted to or not, whether
they considered it to be necessary in the public interest or not. Again, the
Scott report was to find that as a matter of law, this view was wrong. The
Scott report was to be just as critical of this part of the attorney general's
advice as it was of the first part. The report stated, for example, that Sir
Nicholas Lyell's position was 'based on a fundamental misconception of the
principles of PII law'.[9]

It was this enticing cocktail of lying to Parliament, gagging the court, and
legal controversy which generated such immense political pressure that the
prime minister John Major felt that he had no alternative but to establish a
full judicial inquiry to examine the entire matter. Accordingly, the day after
the prosecution team abandoned the Matrix Churchill case the attorney general announced to the House of Commons that Lord Justice Scott, as he then
was,[10] had agreed to chair a 'full and independent inquiry' into the affair.[11]
The following terms of reference were agreed between Scott and the government over the next few days:

Having examined the facts in relation to the export from the United Kingdom of
defence equipment and dual use goods to Iraq between December 1984 and August
1990 and the decisions reached on the export licence applications for such goods and
the basis for them, to report on whether the relevant departments, agencies, and
responsible ministers operated in accordance with the policies of her majesty's government; to examine and report on decisions taken by the prosecuting authority and
by those signing public interest immunity certificates in *R* v. *Henderson* and any other
similar cases that he considers relevant to the issues of the inquiry; and to make recommendations.[12]

These terms of reference are hardly headline grabbers, but they amounted to
an invitation to inquire into four key constitutional relationships. First, the
relationship between government ministers and Parliament: under what circumstances, if any, do government ministers have a right to mislead
Parliament, and what should the consequences be when ministers do mislead
Parliament? Secondly, the relationship between ministers and civil servants:
do the existing constitutional measures adequately protect the national interest in maintaining an impartial, politically neutral, and permanent civil
service, or are new reforms required? Thirdly, the relationship between
government and the intelligence services: are current mechanisms for ensur-

---

    [8] See para. G18.94.   [9] See para. G18.54.
    [10] When he was appointed to chair the inquiry, Lord Justice Scott was a member of the Court
of Appeal. During the course of the inquiry, and before the report was published, he was
appointed Vice-Chancellor, the head of the Chancery division of the High Court, and his proper
title became Sir Richard Scott VC.
    [11] See HC Deb., Vol. 213, col. 743, 10 Nov. 1992.   [12] See para. A2.2.

ing that all appropriate ministers see all relevant intelligence reports working and, if not, how are they best improved? Finally, the relationship between government and the courts, especially with regard to the production of government held evidence and the operation of the doctrine of PII: did government ministers behave unconstitutionally or illegally in respect of signing PII certificates in the Matrix Churchill case? These are the constitutional issues which arise out of the Scott report and which this book examines. How did Scott set about his task?

The Nature of the Inquiry

Almost immediately the form which the Scott inquiry was to take became a hotly contested issue. When governments establish public inquiries to investigate matters of political controversy the first concern of oppositions is naturally to seek to ensure that the inquiry will be wide-ranging and public. The Labour party in opposition was not initially convinced that the form of the Scott inquiry would allow for this. The opposition called for a formal statutory inquiry under the Tribunals of Inquiry (Evidence) Act 1921 which would hear evidence on oath and which would have the power to subpoena evidence.[13] The Scott inquiry was an *ad hoc* inquiry established under prerogative authority and had no legal powers either to compel testimony or to hear evidence on oath. In the light of these concerns, the prime minister announced that all ministers and civil servants had been instructed to cooperate fully with the inquiry and that all papers which the inquiry called for would be made available to it. The government also made it clear that if Scott considered that his powers were proving to be inadequate, then he was at liberty to come back to the government to ask for more. In the event, this never happened.[14]

[13] See HC Deb., Vol. 213, cols. 744 and 745, 10 Nov. 1992 (John Morris, shadow attorney general, and Menzies Campbell, Liberal Democrats' spokesman, respectively) and HC Deb., Vol. 214, cols. 654–5, 23 Nov. 1992 (Sir David Steel, former leader of the Liberal Democrats). The political disadvantage of such a statutory inquiry would have been that the *sub judice* rule would have applied, rendering impossible any parliamentary comment on the matters under investigation until the report was published. A further difficulty would have been that the attorney general has traditionally played the role of counsel to the inquiry for inquiries established under the 1921 Act. Such a role would clearly have been inappropriate where the attorney general was not only one of the protagonists in the story which the Scott inquiry was appointed to investigate but was also called to give both oral and written evidence himself. Scott initially intended to take evidence on oath but found that he was prevented from doing so by virtue of the Statutory Declarations Act 1835: see para. B2.38. Scott stated in the report that he did not believe that the inquiry was disadvantaged by the fact that it was unable to hear evidence on oath: see para. B2.41. Scott recommended that the 1835 Act should be amended so as to allow *ad hoc* non-statutory inquiries to take evidence on oath: see para. K1.8.

[14] On the roles and powers of public inquiries generally, see R. Wraith and G. Lamb, *Public Inquiries as an Instrument of Government* (London: Allen and Unwin, 1971). See also B. Winetrobe, 'Inquiries after Scott: the Return of the Tribunal of Inquiry' [1997] *Public Law* 18.

In the report, Scott stated that 'civil servants approached by the inquiry have, without exception, complied' with the government's instructions to co-operate.[15] As for ministers and departments, the report was significantly less sanguine. While Scott 'would like to believe' that the inquiry eventually succeeded in obtaining all the relevant documents,[16] he stated in the report that 'the process of extraction was sometimes difficult and often extended over a lengthy period'.[17] Scott was especially critical of various government departments and agencies which were excessively slow in delivering materials to the inquiry—to such an extent that on occasions materials requested years beforehand were not obtained by the inquiry until late 1995—just weeks before the report was to be published. The cabinet office, the ministry of defence, customs and excise and the department of trade and industry were all fingered for this failing.[18] In addition to the mountain of written evidence which the inquiry received, oral evidence from a total of eighty-one witnesses was also taken. All but eleven of those who gave oral evidence did so in public, open sessions of the inquiry.[19] There were just over eighty days of sessions of oral evidence, starting in May 1993, but with the most dramatic sessions being held in a six month period from October 1993 to March 1994.

During this extraordinary period a succession of senior cabinet ministers reluctantly followed one another into the DTI rooms near Victoria station where the inquiry was housed, resembling naughty school children summoned to see the headmaster. Never before in British constitutional history had such a spectacle been held—and although television cameras were excluded from the inquiry, this was very much a public event. Both the sitting prime minister and his immediate predecessor, John Major and Margaret Thatcher, were called to attend, as was cabinet secretary Sir Robin Butler. In addition, virtually the entire cast of senior Conservatives from the late 1980s and early 1990s were summoned, one by one, to give their versions of events. Michael Heseltine, Malcolm Rifkind, Peter Lilley, Kenneth Clarke, Sir Nicholas Lyell, William Waldegrave, Kenneth Baker, Lord Howe, Sir Patrick Mayhew, and, of course, Alan Clark all had their own days out at the inquiry. As well as dominating the news for weeks, it proved to be such good entertainment that Richard Norton-Taylor (the *Guardian's* man at the inquiry) co-wrote a play based on the inquiry which enjoyed a successful run at Kilburn's Tricycle theatre.[20] Subsequently, much of the evidence, amounting to some

---

[15] See para. A2.9.   [16] See para. B1.5.
[17] Ibid. For an indication of the scale of written materials which were submitted to the inquiry, see para. B1.15.
[18] See paras. B1.6–10.
[19] See paras. B1.20–7. Those giving oral evidence in private comprised nine members of the secret intelligence service, one member of the security service, and one member of the defence intelligence staff: see para. B1.22.
[20] The text of the play is reproduced in R. Norton-Taylor, *Truth is a Difficult Concept: Inside the Scott Inquiry* (London: 4th Estate, 1995).

20,000 printed pages, has now been published by HMSO on CD-ROM format.[21]

The bulk of the inquiry's work, however, took place on paper and in private. The oral hearings provided the drama but the most time-consuming elements of the inquiry's processes were the reading of more than 200,000 pages of written evidence and the drafting and redrafting of the report.[22] It was not until almost two years after the stream of cabinet ministers had trooped into the inquiry's rooms to give their oral evidence that the report was eventually ready for publication, on 15 February 1996.

The Publication of the Report

Even the straightforward matter of publishing a report proved to be too much for the government to manage without causing a storm. Quite outrageously, the government decided that it would grant to itself eight days when it could see the report but no one else could. The government used these eight days (surprise, surprise) to prepare its defence in the face of the criticisms the report contained and also to prepare a press-pack which would be given to the media on the day of publication, in which five government departments provided summaries of and responses to various aspects of the Scott report. Naturally, the opposition parties were disgusted that the government was going to be able to get its retaliation in first, and a strong protest was made, which was supported by the speaker of the House of Commons, Betty Boothroyd. As a result of her intervention, it was agreed that on the day of publication, one spokesman from the Labour party and one from the Liberal Democrats would be granted access to the report for three hours, in a locked and guarded room at the DTI, on condition that no photocopies were taken and that mobile phones were left outside with the guard. Thus, on the morning of 15 February, Robin Cook MP and Menzies Campbell MP were carted off and locked up with the report in a farcical test of their abilities to speed-read nearly 2,000 pages in three hours. This was a quite appalling abuse of power on the government's part and should never have been agreed to either by Parliament or by the Scott inquiry.

At 3.30 p.m. on the afternoon of 15 February, immediately after prime minister's question time, the House of Commons was suspended for ten minutes so that MPs could get their copies of the Scott report. At 3.40 p.m. Ian Lang MP, the president of the board of trade,[23] made a statement to the

[21] The CD-ROM was published in July 1996. It costs a mere £176.25.

[22] The inquiry's procedures and the controversies they generated are discussed in more detail below in the final sections of this introduction.

[23] Technically, the Scott inquiry reported to the DTI (which explains why it was Mr Lang who spoke). The prime minister decided, for reasons which have not been made public, that he would contribute to Parliament's debates on the Scott report only by maintaining a determined silence.

House on the Scott report in which he argued that the report had exonerated the government and that ministers had acted 'without any impropriety'.[24] He then went onto the offensive, arguing that the Scott report made it quite clear that the two central allegations which had been made of the government, that Britain had sold arms to Iraq and that ministers had conspired to send three innocent men to jail, were without foundation and he called on the opposition to apologize. In Mr Lang's speech, there was no contrition, no hint that the government might have something important to learn from the mistakes which Scott had spent so long investigating, and certainly no suggestion that any minister had done anything so seriously wrong that he might have to resign.

Robin Cook replied for the opposition that he did not recognize from his three hours' confinement that morning the report which Ian Lang had described. For Mr Cook the report 'fully vindicated' the two central charges which the opposition parties had made: namely, that ministers had changed the guidelines on exports to Iraq and that they had repeatedly refused to admit that they had done so, either to Parliament or to the courts.[25] And so it went on. Each side claimed that the Scott report vindicated its position. The question which dominated the political argument was whether there would be any ministerial casualties. There were two main candidates: William Waldegrave (over the issue of the changes to the guidelines and whether Parliament was misled)[26] and Sir Nicholas Lyell, the attorney general (over his advice on PII). In the event, neither resigned. Why not?

Parliamentary and Political Reaction

To force a minister to resign against his will when he has the support of his government takes immense pressure. It is sometimes possible, as David Mellor and Tim Yeo each discovered. The government managed to limit the pressure in the cases of William Waldegrave and Sir Nicholas Lyell through a combination of opportunism and good fortune. The government's line on Waldegrave was that insofar as he had misled Parliament at all he had done so only inadvertently, and ministers did not have to resign unless they had knowingly misled Parliament. The line on Lyell was simply that Scott had got the detailed and technical law of public interest immunity wrong, and Lyell's advice had all along been both legally correct and morally justified.

---

[24] See HC Deb., Vol. 271, col. 1140, 15 Feb. 1996.   [25] Ibid., col. 1145.

[26] As stated above, William Waldegrave was not the only minister responsible for the changes to the guidelines, but the other two were not MPs at the time the Scott report was published: Alan Clark did not stand in the 1992 election (although he was returned to Parliament at the 1997 election) and Lord Trefgarne was a member of the House of Lords, of course. Lord Trefgarne had left the government by the time the Scott inquiry was appointed.

The government knew that the press would have next to no time to prepare their responses to Scott. The report was not made available to them until mid-afternoon. Copy would have to be finalized within six hours, at least for the early editions. The broadcast media would have even less time. The government also knew, through its privileged access to the report prior to publication, that the report was long and complex and, crucially, contained no executive summary of conclusions. It knew that the press would find it extremely difficult to wade through the 1,806 pages of the report and comment on it and on the day's proceedings without some assistance. Hence, the government's press-pack. Five government departments (the treasury, the attorney general's chambers, the cabinet office, customs and excise, and the DTI) worked together to compile a seventy-three page pack of summaries and reaction which was deliberately designed to be media-friendly, with soundbite quotes, bullet points, and highlights. Naturally, the media relied heavily on the press-pack rather than on trying to find its own way round the four volumes of the report. Thus, the following day's papers were much stronger on the government's interpretation of the report than on the opposition's. And of course, the government's interpretation was hardly a neutral one.

It was not just a question of objectivity, however. The press-pack contained a number of serious misrepresentations. It posed the question, for example, 'Does Scott say Waldegrave misled Parliament?' and answered it 'No' whereas in fact the Scott report clearly stated that he did mislead Parliament, albeit that he did not apparently realize so at the time.[27] Further, the press-pack stated that 'answers given to parliamentary questions . . . gave an accurate description of the government's policy on exports to Iran and Iraq' when the Scott report in fact stated that 'answers to PQs in both Houses of Parliament failed to inform Parliament of the current state of government policy on non-lethal arms sales to Iraq. This failure was deliberate . . .'[28] The impact of the press-pack was enormous. It effectively killed the political effect which the Scott report should have had by deliberately pointing the media to passages of the report which were less hostile to the government. On the morning of 16 February Robin Cook and Menzies Campbell held a joint press conference to point much of this out and at which they provided their own—very different—summary of Scott, but by then it was too late. Three hours locked up with the report might have been enough to allow Robin

---

[27] See para. D4.28 where Scott described statements to Parliament by William Waldegrave as 'neither . . . adequate [nor] accurate'. Sir Robin Butler later stated that this was not a deliberate misrepresentation but a mistake. According to Sir Robin, the question should have read, 'Does Scott say Waldegrave *knowingly* misled Parliament?' but a drafting error somehow occurred, conveniently enough. See Sir Robin's evidence to the public service committee, *Ministerial Accountability and Responsibility*, HC (1995–96) 313, Vol. III, Q 789, considered further in ch. 1, below.

[28] See para. D4.42.

Cook to make Mr Lang feel a little uncomfortable in the House of Commons, but it was never going to be long enough to allow the opposition effectively to challenge the spin which the government had had eight days to prepare. The day the Scott report was published was a day when the government decided that the fate of two of its most discredited ministers was more important than any quaint notion of parliamentary democracy.

The government's opportunism was accompanied by some good fortune, however. While Messrs Lang and Cook were exchanging blows in the House of Commons Scott was giving a press conference. Indeed this was the only press conference he gave after the report was published—Scott had decided that the best thing for him to do once the report was published was to escape the mêlée that was surrounding his report and to go to Ireland for a week's hunting. At his press conference he was repeatedly asked why he had not written a summary of conclusions for ease of reference, and he stated that he had wished to avoid overly simplistic summaries of what were often complex and finely balanced conclusions. This was understandably a matter of some frustration among the media, and one tabloid journalist asked him if it would be a fair conclusion to draw that the report disclosed that there had been 'no conspiracy and no cover-up', to which Scott answered 'Yes'. Thus was born exactly the kind of soundbite which Scott had sought so strenuously to avoid. All the news bulletins that evening covered the press conference. Most covered only that one question—it became the moment people remembered. The government was off the hook. There had been no conspiracy and no cover-up, and so everything was all right. Lang, Waldegrave, and Lyell could not have wished for a better line if they had written it themselves.

The other factor which contributed to the government's good fortune and to the rescue of the two vulnerable ministers was the style of the report itself. It is hardly an easy read at the best of times. Scott certainly did the media (and Parliament) no favours by refusing to write a summary. There is a chapter of recommendations at the end of the report, and the report does come to conclusions throughout its long text, but nowhere is there a single, clear exposition of what the Scott inquiry had found on the two crucial issues—had either Waldegrave or Lyell acted wrongly, unconstitutionally or illegally? Further, even when you do manage to locate the conclusions about Waldegrave, they are hardly clear. Scott found that he had misled Parliament, and that he should have realized he was doing so at the time, but that he did not in fact realize that he was doing so at the time and so while his answers to parliamentary questions had been 'designedly uninformative', he had had no 'duplicitous intention'.[29] This is not the language the media deals in, and neither does it convert neatly into the headlines or soundbites which would have been needed if the pressure was to build up to force a resignation contrary to

---

[29] See paras. D3.107 and D3.124. See further below, ch. 1.

the prime minister's will. Scott earnestly hoped that those who were interested would make the time to read the report in full but, no matter how dedicated, the political journalists simply did not have the time—news is reported nowadays as it happens, not weeks afterwards when everybody has had the chance to digest. This is a lesson which any similar inquiry in the future should take on board. Perhaps as simple a change as bringing the publication time forward to the morning would have gone some way to reduce the extent to which the media was reliant on the government's press-pack.

Ian Lang's statement on the day the report was published was not the only occasion on which Parliament debated the Scott report. A full set piece adjournment debate in the House of Commons was set down for Monday 26 February, and the Lords would also debate the Scott report on the same day.[30] This debate would settle the argument one way or the other, and despite the government's victory in the propaganda wars of 15 February, with their wafer thin majority in the Commons it was far from certain whether they would win the debate. In the event, the government won the day by 320 votes to 319.[31] Two Conservative MPs[32] crossed the floor to vote in the opposition lobby, but with the three Democratic Unionist Party MPs deciding to abstain, it was not enough to defeat the government. It was close, however, with the Conservative MP Rupert Allason apparently deciding only minutes before the vote, during Roger Freeman's speech winding up the debate for the government, that he was not going to vote with the opposition.[33] If the government had lost the vote it would have increased the pressure on William Waldegrave and on the attorney general to resign, although this would not necessarily have followed—it was not a debate of censure, merely an adjournment debate.[34] As it was, however, the government's narrow victory effectively ended the public life of the Scott report. Less than a fortnight after its publication, the Scott report was barely mentioned again even in the broadsheet newspapers.[35] The government survived the Scott storm, and did so intact.

[30] See HC Deb., Vol. 272, cols. 589–694 and HL Deb., Vol. 569, cols. 1228–358.

[31] There was no division in the House of Lords.

[32] Quentin Davies and Richard Shepherd. The former Conservative MP Peter Thurnham who had defected the previous week also voted against the government.

[33] Mr Allason (the real name of Nigel West, the author of many spy stories) claimed that during his speech Roger Freeman had, at Mr Allason's invitation, conceded an important point on the operation of public interest immunity, and that that was why he had decided to support the government in the lobby. See HC Deb., Vol. 272, cols. 684–5, 26 Feb. 1996.

[34] Mr Waldegrave refused to participate in the debate (so much for his accountability to Parliament!) and Sir Nicholas Lyell spoke only to intervene during an opposition member's speech—see ibid., col. 634.

[35] In the two months following its publication, the Scott report was mentioned only six times in the *Financial Times* and eight times each in the *Guardian* and *Independent*, and these were the newspapers which had devoted the most extensive coverage to the inquiry: see Ralph Negrine, 'The Inquiry's Press Coverage' (1997) 50 *Parliamentary Affairs* 27, at p. 28. As for the tabloids, Scott featured there on only two days: the day after the report was published and the day after

The Failure and Hope of Parliament

The publication of the Scott report was not the end of the story, however. It was the end of the drama and of the public spectacle, but the inquiry generated considerable parliamentary work in the months following publication. In particular, the public service committee of the House of Commons (a departmental select committee) conducted a wide-ranging investigation into the constitutional position of ministers and of the civil service in the light of the Scott report.[36] Through the valuable activities of this and other parliamentary committees, an important dialogue continued between interested parties in Parliament and in the government about many of the constitutional problems which Scott identified. This was a process which Scott had hoped for, and, indeed, on which the approach of the Scott report was largely based. The substantive recommendations contained in the report were limited and specific. On the broader issues of constitutional accountability and governmental secrecy, Scott preferred not to lay down general prescriptions. Rather, he saw his principal task as one of fact-finding. He would provide an authoritative account of what had happened, but he would leave it to others to decide what should be done about it. This process of follow-up and further consideration primarily fell to Parliament.

In this way, although the Scott inquiry was established in large part because Parliament had *failed* to hold the executive effectively to account either over its policy with regard to Iraq after 1984 or as regards subsequent customs' prosecutions; and although the set piece debate in the House of Commons on 26 February was a *failure* from the point of view of forcing the government to accept responsibility for its misdeeds; despite all this, the Scott story is one of parliamentary *hope* as well as failure. That hope is exemplified by Scott's determination not to be pulled in the direction of making big recommendations about constitutional reform himself, but instead to leave these questions to Parliament. We will come across numerous examples of this throughout the book, ranging from matters such as the desirability of enacting a Freedom of Information Act (on which the Scott report was silent despite Scott's personal support for such an Act) to the need to restate and to clarify the requirements of ministerial responsibility (the Scott report identified the need but stopped

the House of Commons debate on the Scott report. Public shelf-life and ongoing importance are different matters, however. Reports such as Scott's can continue to exercise considerable influence many years after they have been forgotten by the public: witness, for example, the presence of the Crichel Down affair (of 1954—discussed in ch. 1 below) and of the Franks report (of 1957: Cmnd. 218) as late as 1966 when Harold Wilson's government introduced the Bill which was to become the Parliamentary Commissioner Act 1967: see especially the speeches during the Bill's second reading of Richard Crossman, introducing the Bill (HC Deb., Vol. 734, cols. 42–61, 18 Oct. 1966), and of Niall MacDermot, winding up the debate for the government (ibid., cols. 162–72).

[36] The work of this committee is considered in chs. 1 and 2, below.

short of providing the content). This theme—the failure and hope of Parliament—is a major theme of this book. Was Scott's faith in Parliament misplaced? Were his hopes forlorn? This book will (rather unfashionably) argue that they were not, and that we can—and should—have faith in Parliament. Some concerns persist, most notably (but not only) in the intelligence field, but Britain's parliamentary system of government came out of the post-Scott period rather well—especially in comparison with the position in the USA. Despite previous failings, we can allow ourselves to be reasonably confident that Scott's hopes that Parliament would insist that the constitutional lessons of the Scott inquiry would be learned have been justified.

Good Entertainment, but was it Fair?

Before we can move on to consider the longer term implications of the Scott inquiry, there is one further issue which needs to be considered here. At the time the Scott report was published, there were those who were deeply upset about the way in which Scott had gone about his task. Most notably—and most vociferously—Lord Howe (who as Sir Geoffrey Howe had been foreign secretary during Mrs Thatcher's premiership and who had given oral and written evidence to the Scott inquiry) was extremely critical of the procedures which the Scott inquiry had adopted.[37] Thirty years before Scott, a Royal Commission under the chairmanship of Lord Justice Salmon had been appointed to look into the fairness of procedures at public inquiries.[38] The Salmon commission had, in turn, been established in the light of concerns expressed by Lord Denning about the Profumo inquiry (which Denning had chaired in 1963)[39] and the inquiry into the espionage activities of Vassall.[40]

The Salmon commission made fifty recommendations as to procedural fairness at public inquiries which were underpinned by six 'cardinal principles', which were to be 'strictly observed'.[41] It was these cardinal principles which were to become the focus of Lord Howe's bitter argument with Scott. The Salmon principles are:

(1) No person should become involved in an inquiry until the inquiry is satisfied that that person is affected by or involved in the subject-matter of the inquiry's investigation;

[37] The following assumes that the objections raised by Lord Howe were genuine and were not merely part of some sort of scheme to undermine the inquiry or to denigrate Scott.

[38] *Report of the Royal Commission on Tribunals of Inquiry*, Cmnd. 3121 (Nov. 1966).

[39] See Cmnd. 2152 (Sept. 1963), republished as Lord Denning, *The Denning Report: The Profumo Report* (London: Pimlico, 1992). Denning stated (at para. 5) that a 'great disadvantage' of the inquiry which he conducted was that he had to be 'detective, inquisitor, advocate and judge, and it has been difficult to combine them'.

[40] Cmnd. 2009 (Apr. 1963).

[41] *Report of the Royal Commission on Tribunals of Inquiry*, op. cit., para. 32.

(2) Before witnesses are called to give evidence, they should be informed of any allegations which have been made against them and the substance of the evidence offered in support of such allegations;

(3) Witnesses should be given adequate opportunity to prepare their case and should be given legal assistance; and legal expenses should be met out of public funds;

(4) Witnesses should be given the opportunity of being examined by their own legal representatives and of stating their own case at the inquiry;

(5) Witnesses should be able to have other witnesses heard in their support, so far as is reasonably practicable;

(6) Witnesses' legal representatives should be able to cross-examine others.

The procedure adopted at the Scott inquiry differed from these principles in a number of important respects. The general pattern was that if the inquiry wished to receive evidence from a witness, the inquiry would send a detailed questionnaire which the witness would complete, with or without the assistance of lawyers, as the witness chose.[42] If after the questionnaire had been completed there remained matters which the inquiry team did not understand or which appeared to conflict with the evidence of other witnesses, then oral evidence would be called for.[43] Before such oral evidence was given the inquiry would give the witness an indication of the matters which would be raised and the reasons why the inquiry were raising them. During all of this period the witness could, if he or she so chose, make use of legal advice. Thus far there would appear to be nothing here which is at odds with the Salmon principles.

At the oral sessions themselves, however, there was no legal representation—and this was Lord Howe's first major concern. Lawyers or other lay advisers could accompany witnesses, but could not speak on their behalf: like Victorian children they could be seen but not heard. Questions were asked for the most part by Presiley Baxendale QC, counsel to the inquiry, while Scott himself would intervene from time to time. No provision was made for one witness to ask questions directly of another. Baxendale and Scott were the only question-masters. However, transcripts of the oral evidence were sent to the witness, who could then add to, modify, or clarify the evidence. Similarly, a number of witnesses were given the opportunity to respond to others' oral evidence where they had been implicated by what another witness had claimed.[44] Further, when the report came to be drafted, the inquiry team

---

[42] Some of these questionnaires were enormous. The one which was sent to Alan Moses QC (counsel for the prosecution at the Matrix Churchill trial), for example, ran to over 170 pages: see para. B2.9.

[43] A list of factors determining when oral evidence would be called for is set out at para. B1.21.

[44] For example, the former attorney general Sir Patrick Mayhew responded in a special session of the inquiry in May 1993 to the oral evidence of Sir Hal Miller about the attorney general's role in the abandoned supergun prosecution.

would send sections of the draft (under conditions of confidentiality) to witnesses who were mentioned or criticized in those sections to which witnesses could then reply. In replying, several witnesses furnished new materials and further evidence—and this part of the inquiry's processes took up a great deal of time, with drafts of the report, further evidence, new redrafts, and yet further comments being exchanged in some cases for several months. This process accounts for the length of the period between the ending of the public sessions of oral evidence in 1994 and the publication of the report in February 1996.[45]

The Role of Lawyers

In extensive correspondence, several media interventions, and published articles Lord Howe repeatedly voiced his criticisms of these procedures, arguing that they were unfair and that they improperly departed from the principles laid down by the Salmon commission.[46] In the report and in a public lecture given (and published) while the inquiry was still ongoing, Scott extensively responded to these criticisms.[47] Essentially, Howe's concerns boil down to two main criticisms: first, that witnesses were unfairly denied the opportunity to be legally represented at the inquiry and to cross-examine other witnesses; and secondly, that Scott (and Baxendale) sat alone—there were no lay assessors to assist him, leaving too much discretion in too few hands. Let us deal with each of these points in turn, taking first the issue of legal representation and cross-examination. It is clear that the Salmon principles envisage that there should be both legal representation and cross-examination. Why did Scott decide to exclude them from his inquiry[48] and how did he later seek to justify it? Both the reasons and the justifications are straightforward. The main reason was practicability. As it was, the inquiry took over three years (thirty-eight months) to complete its work. If the almost 300 witnesses (including those who gave only written evidence) had been able to

---

[45] A graph setting out the procedures adopted by the inquiry can be found at para. B2.46.

[46] Vol. V of the report, in effect an annex which was published with the text of the report in Feb. 1996, contains much of the correspondence. The *Spectator* carried one of Howe's most fiery critiques of Scott just before the report was published: see 'A Judge's Long Contest with Reality', *Spectator*, 27 Jan. 1996, pp. 6–12. A more measured attack can be found at [1996] *Public Law* 445.

[47] See ch. B2 of the report. For Scott's lecture, see 'Procedures at Inquiries: The Duty to be Fair (1995) 111 *Law Quarterly Review* 596. Christopher Muttukumaru, the secretary to the inquiry, also spoke publicly on this issue: his lecture to Jesus College Oxford is reproduced in vol. V of the report: see app. A, part D2(xvi). For an overview of the arguments between Scott and Howe, see Anthony Barker, 'The Inquiry's Procedures', (1997) 50 *Parliamentary Affairs* 9.

[48] The decision was Scott's. The government did not lay down the detailed procedures which the Scott inquiry was to adopt but left the inquiry to determine these for itself: see ch. B2 of the report, and the inquiry's early note on procedure, reproduced in vol. V of the report: app. A, part D1(i).

cross-examine each other the process would obviously have taken even longer. Further, the oral hearings, while they were the most dramatic and visible element of the inquiry's work, were not the most important either in terms of fact-finding or assessment. Lastly, there is of course the consideration of cost. Lawyers do not come cheap.

Should such considerations of effectiveness, speed, and costs be allowed to overcome Lord Howe's objections of unfairness? Questions of natural justice, procedural propriety, fairness, or whatever label is chosen, are always questions of balance and degree. Was the balance which Scott advocated an appropriate one even though it appeared significantly to differ from the Salmon principles? Scott sought to justify his departure from Salmon partly on the familiar ground that to accord fully with all six Salmon principles would be impracticable in the instance of this particular inquiry; partly on the ground that the Salmon principles were exactly that: general recommendations and principles, not hard and fast rules; and partly on the ground that he simply considered them to be ill-conceived. They might be fine procedures for a courtroom or for some other adversarial procedure, but for the inquisitorial nature of the inquiry they made less sense. The principles talk, for example, of a witness's 'case' which the inquiry should allow to be put (while other witnesses' cases can be cross-examined) and of 'allegations' made against witnesses. In Scott's view, such language has no place in the context of an inquisitorial inquiry—there are no cases, and indeed no allegations against any party. There is simply a task to find out what happened and to make recommendations accordingly.[49] Further, any departure from aspects of the Salmon principles had in Scott's view been more than adequately compensated for in the other procedural innovations which the inquiry had adopted, such as giving all those criticized in the report extensive opportunity to make comments on draft sections of the report, and so on.

Howe and Scott were clearly never going to agree on these issues. After the Scott report was published, the government announced a consultation period during which any interested parties could submit comments on the procedures which should be adopted at public inquiries. Some thirty such submissions were received, and the government decided to present them to the council on tribunals which could then consider them and draw up some conclusions. The council on tribunals is a statutory body established under the Tribunals and Inquiries Act 1958[50] which provides independent advice to the government on various matters concerning tribunals and inquiries and keeps under review the operation of a large number of such bodies. Its *Advice to the Lord Chancellor on the Procedural Issues arising in the Conduct of Public Inquiries set up by Ministers* was presented to the government in July 1996 and

---

[49] See Scott's article in the *Law Quarterly Review*, op. cit., at pp. 602–4.
[50] See now the Tribunals and Inquiries Act 1992.

was reproduced as an appendix to the council's annual report for 1995–6.[51] In its advice, the council state that, contrary to the views of Lord Howe, 'it is wholly impracticable to attempt to devise a single set of model rules or guidance' for all public inquiries.[52] Rather, the council provided a basic framework of objectives which all inquiries should seek to meet in their procedures. According to the council there are four such objectives: effectiveness, fairness, speed, and economy.[53] On the Salmon principles, the council endorsed the view which Scott had adopted: namely, that they were to be treated as recommendations rather than as strict rules of law. The council also shared Scott's view that at least some of the principles seemed to be addressed to adversarial rather than inquisitorial processes.[54]

The advice of the council on tribunals was very supportive of the flexible position as to procedural matters which the Scott inquiry had adopted, and did not echo the criticisms which Lord Howe had made. If anything, the council on tribunals was of the view that the Scott inquiry might even have gone too far in seeking to protect its witnesses. In particular, the opportunities given to witnesses to comment on draft sections of the report was an innovation which the council on tribunals argued 'should certainly not be regarded as necessary in every case'.[55] Mindful of the length of time which this procedure used up, the council stated that 'in many cases, witnesses will already have had the opportunity of dealing with the relevant points, whether evidential or judgmental, before the inquiry reaches the stage of coming to conclusions'.[56] On the specific criticism made by Lord Howe about the absence of lawyers from the oral stages of the inquiry, the council once again supported the position which Scott had adopted, stating that although it should not be assumed that cross-examination would necessarily lengthen an inquiry's procedures, among those who participated in the government's consultation exercise there appeared 'to be a consensus . . . that legal representation in this sense should not be regarded as an absolute entitlement. The inquiry must retain a discretion over the way in which evidence is given.'[57]

Scott Alone

So much for the first of Lord Howe's concerns. The second criticism which he made of the Scott inquiry's procedures was that for the most part Scott sat

---

[51] *Annual Report for the Council on Tribunals for 1995–96*, HC (1996–97) 114, pp. 67–88.

[52] Ibid., p. 67.

[53] This is strikingly similar to Scott's own analysis, in which he had stated that his procedures were designed to meet three basic criteria: fairness, efficiency, and cost: see para. B2.1. Both the council on tribunals and the Scott report indicated that where necessary the interests of speed and cost must give way to the overriding consideration of fairness: see para. B2.1 of the Scott report and para. 2.9 of the council's advice.

[54] See paras. 3.4 and 4.5 of the council's advice.

[55] Ibid., para. 7.11.

[56] Ibid.

[57] Ibid., para. 7.12.

alone. Of course he had the support of the inquiry team, most notably Presiley Baxendale QC and Christopher Muttukumaru, but he alone exercised the judgment and he alone wrote the report. In Lord Howe's view, this was an error. Lord Howe argued that in other prominent public inquiries headed by a judge the judge has been assisted by expert lay assessors, and that Scott should have followed suit.[58] The view of the Scott inquiry was that while this is a fine idea in principle, in the context of the matters which Scott was appointed to investigate, it was unclear what the issues were on which expert advice was needed, and it was equally unclear who the nominated experts should have been.[59] On this matter, the council on tribunals was less clearly supportive of the approach which had been adopted by the Scott inquiry. Without specifically mentioning Scott, the council stated in its advice to the Lord Chancellor that 'consideration should be given to appointing wing members to the inquiry. Wing members can provide a breadth of experience which can be brought to bear on the subject matter of the inquiry . . . They can afford the inquiry chairman helpful support and some protection against errors of judgment, in matters of both substance and procedure . . . if the inquiry involves considerations of broad policy issues, a spread of expertise will almost always be desirable.'[60] In addition, assessors (who would not be formal members of the inquiry) could be drafted in to provide expert advice and assistance on particular matters.[61]

The Scott inquiry might have enhanced its own position if the responsibility for and workload of the inquiry had been shared rather more than it was. Very specific matters were referred to outsiders for their opinions, but only on matters which were quite peripheral to the main thrust of the inquiry's investigations.[62] Scott the chancery lawyer would certainly have benefited from some expert assessment on such matters as interdepartmental government decision making of which Scott could have had no previous direct experience. Similarly, there are a number of passages in the report, where Scott addresses the constitutional implications of the conclusions which he has come to, where that analysis could have been improved, to say the least. As we shall see in chapter one, when Scott came to his evaluation of the Conservative

---

[58] Lord Howe pointed to the crown agents inquiry chaired by Croom-Johnson LJ and the BCCI inquiry chaired by Bingham LJ (as he then was), in both of which the chairmen were supported by experts: see 'Procedure at the Scott Inquiry' [1996] *Public Law* 445, at p. 455.

[59] In his lecture to Jesus College Oxford on the inquiry's procedures, Christopher Muttukumaru stated that the suggestion that Scott should have appointed lay expert assessors was 'wholly misconceived': see vol. V of the report, app. A, part D2(xvi), para. 38.

[60] *Annual Report for the Council on Tribunals for 1995–96*, HC (1996–97) 114, app. A: *The Council's Advice to the Lord Chancellor on the Procedural Issues arising in the Conduct of Public Inquiries set up by Ministers*, para. 5.16.

[61] Ibid., para. 5.17.

[62] Legal advice was sought from two QCs, and Arthur Andersen were retained to examine some files concerning Astra and BMARC: Arthur Andersen's report is reproduced in vol. V of the report: app. A, part C3.

government's controversial position on the constitutional doctrine of ministerial responsibility to Parliament, for example, he seemed unaware of the background to and development of the government's views and consequently failed fully to appreciate either their novelty or their danger. If Scott had employed a constitutional lawyer or other expert on constitutional matters to assist him this important section of the report would certainly have been stronger. When select committees in Parliament investigate such complex questions they generally appoint experts to assist them—as did the public service committee in 1996 when it reported on questions of ministerial responsibility in the light of the Scott report. Lord Howe was right to suggest that Scott should have done so as well.

The Structure of the Book

This book is divided into four parts. Each of the first three parts deals with one of the key constitutional relationships which were identified above as arising out of the Scott report. Part I concerns the relationship between government and Parliament. Its three chapters discuss, respectively, the constitutional position of ministers, of civil servants, and of open government and freedom of information. Part II concerns the relationship between government and the shady world of secret intelligence and examines in particular the use which government ministers make of intelligence reports and how government seeks to co-ordinate Britain's overall intelligence activity. Part III discusses the implications of the Scott story for the relationship between government and the courts, focusing on the control of evidence and use of the doctrine of public interest immunity. Finally, Part IV examines what might be dubbed the American equivalent of Scott, the little studied but revealing story of Iraqgate. First the events of Iraqgate are outlined in chapter six, and the implications of Iraqgate for the US constitution are then considered in chapter seven. Part IV sets the scene for the key questions of constitutional reform which are addressed in the conclusion. Bearing in mind that the American experience over Iraqgate suggests that a written constitution with a Bill of Rights and a Freedom of Information Act do not of themselves prevent scandals such as that which Scott investigated, the conclusion considers what reforms are now called for both to the British constitution and to British parliamentary government in practice.

PART I
Government and Parliament

1

Ministers and Parliament

A CORE concern for any constitution is to seek to regulate relations between the government, or executive, and the legislature, or Parliament. The unwritten British constitution is no exception: indeed in Britain this may be a matter of constitutional importance to an even greater extent than in many other jurisdictions as Parliament remains not only the national legislature, but also the primary environment in which the government of the day is—almost daily—held to account. The relationship between government and Parliament is a matter of profound constitutional concern in Britain. Yet, such concern has not been sufficient to preclude either uncertainty as to what the constitution provides or bitter argument as to what it should provide. The Scott report chronicled a period in recent British history when the constitution was found seriously wanting in its purported regulation of working relations between government and Parliament. In this chapter and in the two that follow it, the constitutional problems of Whitehall and Westminster as illustrated in the Scott report will be discussed in detail. We start in this chapter with the thorny issue of ministers and their responsibilities to Parliament. We then move on in chapter two to discuss the changing face and roles of the civil service, and in chapter three we examine the importance of open government and freedom of information.

Ministers and Parliament in the Scott Report

There are two main areas in the Scott report in which issues of ministers and their responsibilities to Parliament arose. The first concerned the Howe guidelines and the British government's policy with regard to the Iran–Iraq war and how government policy towards Iraq might have changed after the end of the war in 1988. The second area concerns the supergun: the Iraqi long-range gun project. In both areas the constitutional questions are the same: what was the government's true position? Did government ministers accurately relay that position to Parliament? If not, was the inaccuracy of ministers' statements to Parliament deliberate? If misleading statements were either knowingly or unintentionally given to Parliament, what should be the constitutional consequences?

The British government's policy with regard to the Iran–Iraq war was one of neutrality, impartiality and even-handedness as between the warring nations.[1] From as early as January 1981, it had been decided at cabinet level that Britain would not export any lethal arms, weapons or ammunition to either side, although, equally, even by this very early stage, the government appeared to recognize the enormous potential of Iraqi markets to British business. As the minutes of a 1981 meeting of the overseas and defence committee of the cabinet stated: 'every opportunity should be taken to exploit Iraq's potentialities as a promising market for the sale of defence equipment; and to this end "lethal items" should be interpreted in the narrowest possible sense, and the obligations of neutrality as flexibly as possible'.[2] By 1982 the value of the Iraqi market to British business was £874 million.[3] This business included a substantial amount of defence exports: in the first four years of the Iran–Iraq war, the UK exported at least £184 million worth of defence equipment to Iraq, and £13 million worth to Iran.[4]

Over the course of the first few years of the Iran–Iraq war, the government (and in particular the foreign office) became concerned about how best to present government policy on this issue to Parliament and to the public. By 1984 it was felt that the government's approach of overall yet flexible impartiality coupled with a ban on the export of lethal equipment was making it difficult to 'enable a coherent explanation to be given . . . of the basis on which defence-related equipment was being licensed for export to Iraq'.[5] Consequently, after lengthy discussion between foreign office and ministry of defence officials,[6] in November 1984 a set of guidelines was drawn up, known as the Howe guidelines. The Howe guidelines provided that:

(i) we should maintain our consistent refusal to supply any lethal equipment to either side;

(ii) subject to that overriding consideration, we should attempt to fulfil existing contracts and obligations;

(iii) we should not in future sanction[7] new orders for any defence equipment which in our view would significantly enhance the capability of either side to prolong or exacerbate the conflict;

---

[1] See para. D1.11. See, for example, the answer given in June 1984 by Paul Channon MP (then minister for trade at the DTI) in response to a parliamentary question where he stated that 'applications for licences covering the export to [Iran and Iraq] of goods . . . are carefully scrutinised to ensure that, in accordance with [the] government's policy of neutrality in the Iran-Iraq conflict, no lethal equipment is supplied'. See HC Deb., Vol. 61, col. 332 (WA), 11 June 1984. See Scott, para. D2.419.

[2] See para. D1.10.   [3] See para. D1.12.   [4] See para. D1.15.

[5] See foreign office note of Oct. 1984 cited by Scott, para. D1.37.

[6] There was also a third government department involved: the department of trade and industry, but DTI officials were less enthusiastic about the prospect of guidelines which might potentially limit trade. The Scott report described their attitude as one of 'dislike but of resigned acceptance' (para. D1.60).

[7] When the Howe guidelines were announced in Oct. 1985, the word 'sanction' was substituted by the word 'approve'. See HC Deb., Vol. 84, col. 450 (WA), 29 Oct. 1985. See note 179 on page 207 of the Scott report.

(iv) in line with this policy we should continue to scrutinise rigorously all applications for export licences for the supply of defence equipment to Iran and Iraq.'[8]

In November 1984 the decision was taken, apparently within the foreign office, that a high-profile announcement of the guidelines in Parliament would be inappropriate and that their existence and content should instead be allowed to become public[9] through answers to parliamentary questions.[10] It was also agreed between government departments that this would be an area of policy in respect of which the foreign office would take the lead and 'also take the flack and deal with complaints'.[11] Two reasons can be detected in support of the decision not to announce the new guidelines immediately: first, a fear that a formal public announcement might suggest a more fundamental change in the substance of government policy than was in fact the case and secondly, a strong desire to avoid drawing attention to the continued supply to Iran of equipment contracted to be supplied under the former Shah's regime before the 1979 Iranian revolution.[12] The guidelines were eventually published some eleven months later in October 1985 in response to a parliamentary question asked by David Steel MP.[13]

As guideline (iii) was phrased in terms of 'significantly enhanc[ing] the capability of either side to prolong or exacerbate the conflict' it was perhaps inevitable that once the conflict came to an end, some revision of the guidelines would be required. The extent to which this happened, and what the consequences of any such revision would be, are matters which were extensively discussed in the Scott report. They are also extremely controversial matters, with the government expressly disagreeing with Scott's conclusions on these issues.[14] The importance of this aspect of the Scott report can best be summed up in the report's own words: 'first, the manner in which the changes [to the guidelines] are regarded bears on the question whether the government had any obligation to make Parliament aware that changes in policy had been put in place. Second, and more important, the adequacy and accuracy of government statements that were from time to time made to Parliament . . . depends . . . on the manner in which the changes to which I have referred are regarded.'[15]

[8] See para. D1.59.   [9] Lord Howe used the phrase 'filter out'. See para. D1.145.
[10] See para. D1.65.   [11] See para. D1.71.   [12] See para. D1.88.
[13] See HC Deb., Vol. 84, col. 450 (WA), 29 Oct. 1985. See Scott, para. D1.154.
[14] See for example the exchange between Menzies Campbell MP and the president of the board of trade, Ian Lang MP, during the debate in the House of Commons on the Scott report, where Ian Lang was asked whether the government accepted Scott's conclusion 'that policy was changed and that the change was deliberately kept from Parliament'. Ian Lang's reply was 'No . . . there is a difference between the government and Sir Richard on that matter'. See HC Deb., Vol. 272, col. 590, 26 Feb. 1996. See also the government's press-pack which was published on the same day as the Scott report, in which it was insisted that 'there was *no* change of policy in 1989' (emphasis in original).
[15] See para. D3.3.

Before we can consider the effect on the guidelines of the ceasefire, we need first to understand their nature. It was the government's view that the guidelines did not themselves constitute policy, but that they constituted guidance to officials as to how the policy should be applied in individual cases.[16] The Scott report stated that 'the guidelines were not, and were never intended to be, an *exclusive* exposition of government policy'[17] but that they had, nonetheless, 'policy status'.[18] The Scott report was highly critical of the attempts of Lord Howe and others to distance the guidelines from policy, describing such an endeavour as 'really no more than a play on words' and as being 'futile and unacceptable'.[19] Thus, it would appear that to change the guidelines would be to change the policy. As to the question of whether the guidelines (and the policy) were changed after the ceasefire, the government's view was that the original 'guidelines as announced in 1985 remained in force and unchanged'.[20] This was a view which the Scott report simply did 'not accept'.[21] In the report's view, the three junior ministers concerned—William Waldegrave of the foreign office, Alan Clark of the DTI, and Lord Trefgarne of the MOD—agreed in December 1988 that the original guideline (iii) should be changed and replaced by a new and significantly different form of words.[22] The new guideline (iii) stated that exports should be denied 'which, in our view, would be of direct and significant assistance to either country in the conduct of offensive operations'.[23]

William Waldegrave persistently argued that the new guideline (iii) was not a replacement of the original guideline (iii) but was rather 'no more than an interpretation of' it.[24] After lengthy discussion, the Scott report concluded that Mr Waldegrave's view was 'not even remotely tenable'.[25] As far as the Scott report was concerned, it was quite clear that the revised guideline (iii) was to be applied by the relevant officials 'in place of the original guideline (iii)'.[26] In the report, Sir Richard further stated that Mr Waldegrave's position was 'one that does not seem to me to correspond with reality . . . To describe this revised formulation as no more than an interpretation of the old, is, in my opinion . . . so plainly inapposite as to be incapable of being sustained by serious argument.'[27]

---

[16] See the evidence of Lord Howe, cited in para. D1.80. Lord Howe described the guidelines as 'an aspect of management of the policy'. See para. D1.81.

[17] See para. D1.81, emphasis added.

[18] See para. D1.82. Sir Richard Scott made it clear in para. D1.83 that he regarded the guidelines as being an exposition of government policy (albeit not an exclusive one). For criticism of this view, see Lawrence Freedman, 'Even-handedness, Guidelines and Defence Sales to Iraq' [1996] *Public Law* 391. For treatment of this issue which is more supportive of Scott's approach, see Barry O'Toole, 'Ethics in Government' (1997) 50 *Parliamentary Affairs* 130.

[19] See paras D1.82 and D1.83.   [20] See para. D3.121.   [21] See para. D3.121.

[22] See para. D3.36.

[23] See para. D3.30. In some versions, the words 'in breach of the ceasefire' were added at the end of the new guideline (iii). See para. D3.60.

[24] See para. D3.73.   [25] See para. D3.90.   [26] See para. D3.90.

[27] See para. D3.123.

The next question was whether the change in the guidelines, described repeatedly in contemporary government documents as a 'more liberal policy',[28] should be publicly announced. Correspondence between the three ministers in January 1989 indicated that they were of the view that there should be no public announcement.[29] The changes were to be temporary, or at least on a trial basis, and accordingly neither the relevant secretaries of state nor the prime minister were informed of the newly changed, more liberal policy.[30] Why was there no public announcement? Lord Howe provided four reasons in his written evidence to the Scott inquiry, namely: the fact that there were British hostages and prisoners in Iran and Iraq, the likely reaction of Gulf states, the likely reaction of the USA, and the possible impact upon trading prospects. The Scott report, however, found that these reasons are not apparent from the contemporary government documents, which made no mention of the hostage situation.[31] In the report's view the real reason behind the decision not to announce the new guidelines was fear of hostile domestic publicity. In the light of the use by Iraq of chemical warfare against Kurds, the government was fearful that if it became known that export guidelines in respect of Iraq were being relaxed, this would provoke what the Scott report described as 'such indignation in the media and among vociferous sections of the British public as to be politically damaging'.[32]

Throughout the second half of 1989 and the first months of 1990 progress was made towards a formal review of the guidelines at a higher (i.e. cabinet) level. This culminated in an *ad hoc* meeting of relevant ministers, chaired by the then foreign secretary, Douglas Hurd, in July 1990. This meeting concluded that the Howe guidelines should be relaxed. A recommendation to this effect was put to the prime minister who granted her approval. Before this decision could be formally implemented, however, Iraq invaded Kuwait in August 1990 bringing about a UN-imposed ban on trade with Iraq and the guidelines were rendered wholly redundant (at least in respect of Iraq—a revision of the guidelines was agreed for Iran in 1991).[33]

The other aspect of the Scott story which concerned relations between ministers and Parliament involved the so-called supergun, or 'Project Babylon'.

---

[28] See paras. D3.40, D3.43, D3.47.

[29] See paras. D3.40 and D3.43. The relevant officials within the ministry of defence were informed in Feb. 1989, for example, that 'there is no intention to publish revised guidelines yet. We have been asked, however, to be more flexible and to use the revised guidelines.' See para. D3.60. Indeed, Scott listed a number of exports that were allowed under the revised guidelines which were initially refused (or would have been) under the original guidelines. See para. D3.62, for example, concerning the export of tactical radar.

[30] See para. D3.65. The prime minister was not informed at this stage despite a letter from Sir Charles Powell (Lady Thatcher's private secretary on foreign affairs) in which he had stated that 'the prime minister will wish to be kept very closely in touch at every stage and consulted on all relevant decisions'. See para. D3.14. For the Scott report's comments on the failure to keep the prime minister informed, see para. D3.102.

[31] See para. D3.108.   [32] See para. D3.109.   [33] See para. D3.165.

Dr Gerald Bull was a design engineer whose company, the Belgian based Space Research Corporation (SRC), was leading a project to design a long-range gun. Two British companies, Sheffield Forgemasters and Walter Somers, had in June 1988 agreed to manufacture and supply to SRC large diameter steel tubes measuring a total length of 52 metres and a diameter of 350mm.[34] It was known to the two British companies that these tubes were destined for Iraq. It was also known to them that SRC was a company involved in weapons. Despite the fact that the tubes were specifically designed to withstand peculiarly high pressure, the companies claimed that it was unclear to them whether they were designed for military or for petrochemical use. As a report from the secret intelligence service (SIS) of October 1989 was to put it, it should have been 'obvious that they were to be used for equipment requiring much higher performance standards of the type required for artillery pieces'.[35]

In the light of this background the two companies agreed in June 1988 that, before the exports could go ahead, the two companies would make sure that they had received approval from the DTI. Accordingly, the managing director of one of the companies contacted his local MP, the Conservative back-bencher Sir Hal Miller. On 14 June 1988 Sir Hal telephoned the private office of the minister for trade at the DTI.[36] From this point onwards the government was on notice that something was up. Further intelligence was gathered on supergun throughout 1988, with MI5 compiling intelligence notes on SRC and the two British companies in July and November 1988, the second of which clearly stated that 'weapon quality steel' was involved.[37] Yet nothing was done within government to put a stop to the manufacture of the tubes or to make it clear that they could not be exported to Iraq.

By 1989 SIS were also actively interested in the supergun affair and during the course of that year a substantial report was put together by an SIS officer known in the Scott report simply as Mr Q. Eventually, as it became clear (but only at the last minute)[38] that the tubes were to be exported to Iraq from Teesport, customs officers, accompanied by Mr Q, seized the tubes as they were being loaded on board at Middlesbrough docks in April 1990.[39] On 18 April 1990 the secretary of state for trade and industry, Nicholas Ridley MP, made a statement to the House of Commons about the seizure of the super-gun tubes in which he stated that 'until a few days ago, my department had no knowledge that the goods were designed to form part of a gun' and that the government only 'recently became aware in general terms of an Iraqi project to develop a long-range gun based on designs developed by the late Dr Gerald Bull'.[40] Sir Hal Miller MP then intervened, stating that he had

---

[34] See para. F2.18.   [35] See para. F3.37.   [36] See para. F2.19.
[37] See paras. F2.61 and F2.88.   [38] See para. F4.18.   [39] See para. F4.19.
[40] See HC Deb., Vol. 170, col. 1425, 18 Apr. 1990. See Scott, para. F4.27. Dr Bull was assassinated in Brussels on 16 Mar. 1990.

contacted the DTI about this matter 'more than two years ago',[41] which came as a bit of a shock not only to the secretary of state but to the House as a whole. Thus the question of what the government knew about supergun, and when they knew it, became a hotly contested political point and the matter was investigated by the trade and industry select committee.[42]

What did Ministers tell Parliament?

So much for the government's position. The question which now arises is what Parliament was told by government ministers about these issues. Was Parliament told the truth? The whole truth? Nothing but the truth? Should it have been? If government ministers are not under an obligation to tell Parliament the truth, the whole truth, and nothing but the truth, what is the constitutional position? Did ministers adequately fulfil their constitutional obligations to Parliament as regards the provision of information on Iraq, exports, defence sales, and the supergun? All three of the main ways in which government ministers provide information to Parliament were involved in this story: answers to parliamentary questions, letters to MPs, and formal ministerial statements. Each of these will now be examined in turn.

As far as parliamentary questions (PQs) are concerned, two sets of problems relating to the answering of PQs were identified in the Scott report. The first concerned the repeated use in answers of phrases such as 'it has been the practice of successive governments not to make public details' of the sort that are asked for in the question. For example, in June 1984 (before the Howe guidelines were drawn up) the minister for trade was asked by David Howell MP 'what equipment that could have military application is currently being exported from the UK to Iran and Iraq'. The minister (Paul Channon MP) replied: 'applications for licences covering the export to these countries of goods . . . are carefully scrutinised to ensure that, in accordance with HM government's policy of neutrality in the Iran and Iraq conflict, no lethal equipment is supplied. It has been the practice of successive governments not to make public the details of export licence applications.'[43] In analysing this answer the Scott report stated that it 'did not provide the information Mr Howell had sought'. Does this matter? According to the Scott report it matters a great deal. Erskine May provides that PQs are not in order (i.e. cannot be asked) if they fall within a class of questions which ministers have refused to answer. Among the subjects on which successive administrations have refused to answer questions are any which refer to details of arms sales to

---

[41] See HC Deb., Vol. 170, col. 1428, 18 Apr. 1990. See Scott, para. F4.30.
[42] See Trade and Industry Select Committee, *Exports to Iraq: Project Babylon and Long Range Guns*, HC (1991–92) 86.
[43] HC Deb., Vol. 61, col. 332 (WA), 11 June 1984. See Scott, para. D1.26.

particular countries.[44] The Scott report, however, was of the view that although answers such as that given by Mr Channon do seem to be in accordance with accepted parliamentary practice, such answers are in any event unjustifiable.[45]

According to the Scott report, there ought to be nothing wrong with disclosing the broad categories of military equipment being exported. Although 'the established parliamentary practice whereby ministers decline to provide "details of arms sales" is usually justified by reference to the commercial confidentiality of the information being sought [and is] easy enough to accept in relation to confidential details such as prices, delivery dates . . . and the like', where this justification is 'extended to cover a failure or refusal to give any information at all about arms sales or about exports to a particular country [it] becomes, in my opinion, spurious. Such an extension goes beyond the reasonable requirements of commercial confidentiality and beyond what would be necessary for compliance with the limitations described in Erskine May.'[46] This theme was revisited in the Scott report's chapter of recommendations in which it was suggested that the justifications for refusing to answer PQs need to be re-examined and, in particular, that Parliament and government should 'conduct a comprehensive review of the "previous practice" whereunder information . . . need not be given by ministers . . . The limitations that the public interest requires to be placed on the obligations of accountability owed by ministers need . . . to be urgently re-thought.'[47]

The second set of problems identified in the Scott report concerning answers to PQs related not to the refusal to answer questions but rather to the provision of inaccurate or misleading information. Numerous examples were cited throughout the report of incomplete, inaccurate or misleading answers. With regard first to the announcement of the Howe guidelines, questions were asked in April and in May 1985 concerning British exports to Iran and Iraq. The questions were answered by Richard Luce MP (then minister of state at the foreign office) and these were, according to the Scott report, 'inaccurate and potentially misleading'.[48] That the opportunity was not taken in response to these questions to announce the Howe guidelines but to wait instead another five months until October 1985 Scott described as unacceptable and

[44] Erskine May, *Parliamentary Practice* (London: Butterworths 21st edn., 1989) p. 292. See Scott, para. D1.28. See also the 1972 *Report from the Select Committee on Parliamentary Questions*: HC (1971–72) 393, app. 9 of which lists a number of matters about which successive administrations have refused to answer questions. This list includes many matters which are so surprising as to cast doubt on its continuing authoritativeness (see Scott, n. 21 on p. 1803). For example, agricultural workers wages, curricular matters, and trade statistics for Scotland all appear on the list!

[45] See para. D1.29.   [46] See para. D1.29. See also para. D2.432.

[47] See para. K8.13.

[48] See paras. D1.151 to D1.153. The implications of these conclusions for issues of open government and freedom of information are examined in ch. 3, below.

illogical.[49] But was the delay also unconstitutional? According to the Scott report, it certainly was. Among the important constitutional texts in this context is the cabinet office document, *Questions of Procedure for Ministers*, the 1992 version of which provided (at paragraph 27) that ministers are under 'the duty to give Parliament and the public as full information as possible about the policies, decisions and actions of the government and not to deceive or mislead Parliament or the public'.[50] Scott concluded that 'the postponement until 29 October 1985 of the announcement of the guidelines . . . cannot, in my opinion, be reconciled with these principles'.[51]

With regard to the changes to the guidelines in 1988–9, both William Waldegrave MP (minister of state at the foreign office) and Alan Clark MP (minister for trade at the DTI until July 1989; then minister for defence procurement at the MOD) gave answers to PQs which were described in the Scott report, respectively, as neither adequate nor accurate and as 'inaccurate and misleading'[52] in that they implied that in 1989 the guidelines were still being applied in their original form and that there were 'no plans to change the current restrictions'.[53] The prime minister was herself asked in April 1989 whether the government 'propose to change their current policy of prohibiting the export to Iraq of any weapon which could enhance its offensive capability'. The answer, which was drafted in the DTI, was that 'the government have not changed their policy on defence sales to Iraq'. As the Scott report concluded, this answer was 'inaccurate and misleading'.[54]

The criticism in the Scott report of the government over these (and many other similar) answers to PQs was stringent and uncompromising: 'the answers to PQs . . . failed to inform Parliament of the current state of government policy on non-lethal arms sales to Iraq. This failure was deliberate and was an inevitable result of the agreement between the three junior ministers that no publicity should be given to the decision to adopt a more liberal, or relaxed, policy . . . the overriding and determinative reason [for which] was a fear of strong public opposition.'[55] Ministers' answers and letters, according to the Scott report, were 'designedly uninformative'.[56] In his summary of this part of the report (chapter D.8) Sir Richard described the government's approach in these terms: 'Parliament and the public were designedly led to believe that a stricter policy towards non-lethal defence exports and dual-use exports to Iraq was being applied than was in fact the case.'[57]

---

[49] See para. D1.156.

[50] *Questions of Procedure for Ministers* and subsequent amendments to it are discussed further, below.

[51] See para. D1.161.   [52] See paras. D4.28 and D4.29.

[53] See HC Deb., Vol. 148, col. 124 (WA), 28 Feb. 1989 for Mr Waldegrave and HC Deb., Vol. 151, col. 260 (WA), 20 Apr. 1989 for Mr Clark. See Scott, paras. D4.26–9.

[54] See HC Deb., Vol. 151, col. 311 (WA), 21 Apr. 1989. See Scott, para. D4.30.

[55] See para. D4.42.   [56] See para. D3.107.   [57] See para. D8.16.

In addition to such criticism of answers to PQs, ministers were also heavily criticised in the Scott report in respect of inaccurate letters they had written to MPs and others. William Waldegrave MP, minister of state at the foreign office, wrote some thirty-eight letters between March and July 1989 alone which included sentences such as 'British arms supplies to both Iran and Iraq continue to be governed by the strict application of guidelines . . .' and in some cases also the sentence 'the government have not changed their policy on defence sales to Iraq or Iran'.[58] As the Scott report concluded, the reference in each of these letters to the criterion that governed the supply of non-lethal defence equipment to Iraq was 'not accurate' and, further, 'the inaccuracy should have been noticed by Mr Waldegrave'.[59] The Scott report went on to provide details of further letters signed by Mr Waldegrave dating from August 1989 which were described as 'apt to mislead'.[60] Letters sent in 1989 from Lord Trefgarne (then minister for defence procurement at the MOD) were also stringently criticized for being 'not . . . accurate' in three separate respects.[61]

Mr Waldegrave and his colleagues were, however, provided with a defence in that they were of the view that government policy had not changed (despite the fact that, as we have seen, this is a view which was described in the Scott report as being one that does not 'correspond with reality' and was 'so plainly inapposite as to be incapable of being sustained by serious argument').[62] Nonetheless, the Scott report did concede that when Mr Waldegrave signed the letters he did not, despite 'overwhelming evidence to the contrary',[63] regard the agreement he had reached with his fellow ministers as having constituted a change in policy. Sir Richard therefore declared that 'I did not receive the impression of any insincerity on [Mr Waldegrave's] part'[64] and further that 'I accept that he did not intend his letters to be misleading.'[65]

Finally, the supergun affair raised one further issue in relation to government disclosure of information to Parliament, concerning ministerial statements.[66] The statement made in April 1990 by Nicholas Ridley to the House of Commons on government knowledge of the supergun was criticized in the Scott report on two grounds. The first concerned the fact that there were clearly aspects of the affair that Mr Ridley did not refer to. This was probably because even though he was the secretary of state he had not been made aware of them by his civil servants. It appears, for example, that even though Mr Ridley's principal private secretary (Mr Stanley) knew of Sir Hal Miller's

---

[58] See paras. D4.2 and D4.3. The Scott report described this second sentence as 'untrue' and, further, that Mr Waldegrave knew this 'first hand'. See paras. D4.5 and D4.6.

[59] See para. D4.4.   [60] See paras. D4.10–12.   [61] See paras. D4.19–20.

[62] See para. D3.123.   [63] See para. D4.6.   [64] See para. D4.6.

[65] See para. D4.12.

[66] The supergun affair also raised the issue of the government's control of evidence which civil servants and retired civil servants may give to select committees, but this issue is dealt with in the next chapter.

1988 involvement, Mr Stanley had not informed Mr Ridley of this. No wonder it came as some surprise to him when Sir Hal made his intervention in the House![67] This leads to the second and constitutionally important criticism of Mr Ridley's statement: namely the declaration that the government had only 'recently' become aware of the supergun. As the Scott report put it, this 'was a far more elastic use of the word "recently" than was warranted by the known facts'.[68] Alan Clark, in evidence to the trade and industry select committee, had described it somewhat euphemistically as an 'exaggeration'.[69] The Scott report was more forthright: the use of the word recently 'is consistent with an attempt to avoid criticism of the government for not having acted sooner than it did'[70] and, further, 'it is . . . clear that the word "recently" was deliberately chosen and that its use was apt to be misleading'.[71]

Did Ministers behave Constitutionally?

The verdict of the Scott report as regards ministers' constitutional responsibilities to Parliament and their duty to provide Parliament with full information was that ministers had behaved unconstitutionally. The Scott report closely examined a number of answers to PQs and ministers' letters to MPs, as well as Mr Ridley's ministerial statement on supergun and found that ministers had been both inaccurate and misleading in what they had told Parliament. Of the ministers concerned, only one remained in office at the date of the publication of the Scott report: William Waldegrave, who had been a junior minister at the foreign office in the period examined in the Scott report, and who was by February 1996 chief secretary to the treasury in John Major's cabinet. In the aftermath of the publication of the report, there was enormous political pressure on Mr Waldegrave to resign his ministerial position. Yet the government took the view that such a move would be both constitutionally unnecessary and politically undesirable. In its press-pack, published on the same day as the report, the government went to considerable lengths to seek to defend Mr Waldegrave. The press release from the treasury, for example, posed the question, 'Does Scott say Waldegrave misled Parliament?' and answered it 'No.'[72] Yet we have seen that, on a number of occasions, the Scott report did find that Mr Waldegrave had misled

---

[67] On Mr Stanley's role, see paras. F4.31–3.   [68] See para. F4.28.
[69] TISC, *Exports to Iraq: Project Babylon and Long Range Guns*, HC (1991–92) 86, para. 110. See Scott para. F4.29.
[70] See para. F4.39.   [71] See para. F4.43.
[72] In June 1996—four months after the Scott report was published—Sir Robin Butler conceded that this had been a mistake. He stated that the question posed in the treasury press release should have included the word 'knowingly' and that its omission was a 'drafting mistake'. See Public Service Committee, *Ministerial Accountability and Responsibility*, HC (1995–96) 313, Vol. III, Q 789.

Parliament, albeit without apparently realizing so at the time. Similarly, a cabinet office paper entitled *Government Policy on the Control of Exports to Iran and Iraq 1980–1990—The Facts* claimed in paragraph 9 that 'answers given to parliamentary questions . . . gave an accurate description of the government's policy on exports to Iran and Iraq'. Again, we have seen that, according to the Scott report, this was simply not the case.

In the crucial debate on the Scott report in the House of Commons on 26 February—when the government won the division by a single vote—this line continued.[73] The government won the day by quite simply brazening it out and by openly disagreeing with the verdict that the Scott report had reached. Mr Waldegrave could not be said to have misled Parliament, as the policy on arms sales to Iraq had not been changed, but had merely been reinterpreted. In any case, the government line continued, Mr Waldegrave could not be criticized for what he had told Parliament, because, as the Scott report itself conceded, he had not *intended* to mislead Parliament: he had had no 'duplicitous intention'.[74] According to John Major's government, as we shall see, ministers are only constitutionally responsible, or personally blameworthy, if they 'knowingly' mislead Parliament.

It was far from satisfactory that, after such a lengthy (and expensive) inquiry and such a thorough report, there was left a feeling of unresolved business at the end of the debate. Why was there this apparent difference of view as to the constitutional propriety of ministers' behaviour? How did we get from the strong words ('inaccurate', 'misleading', 'designedly uninformative') of the Scott report to the position where no minister resigned? The answer is found in a combination of reasons. First, although after a careful reading of the Scott report it is clear that government ministers, including Mr Waldegrave, failed to inform Parliament fully of their true position with regard to Iraq, such a careful reading of the report takes time and the government's unique access to the report during the days immediately prior to its publication undoubtedly enabled it to publish an extremely partial (in two senses) and in places positively (i.e. knowingly and deliberately) misleading summary of and response to the report. The government press-pack inevitably coloured the media coverage of the report and meant that the opposition parties were never able to put over their interpretation of the report as convincingly or as carefully as the government was able to. The blatant unfairness and inequality of this situation has never been subjected to the outrage that it should have been—outrage that should have been directed not only at the government but also, sad to say, at the inquiry team who should never have agreed to the government's draconian conditions of publication.

---

[73] See, for example, the exchange between Menzies Campbell and Ian Lang already cited: *supra* n. 14.

[74] See para. D3.124.

This situation was arguably exacerbated by the language and style of the report itself. The report does contain conclusions. It is clear. But the conclusions are not always as immediately accessible to those who have time only to flick through the 1,806 pages—there is no overall summary of conclusions, and nor are individual conclusions or recommendations highlighted in the text of the report in bold, as is frequently done, for example, in select committee reports. As we saw in the introduction, Scott did the media (and the opposition) no favours. Even when the conclusions are reached, they are not necessarily the sharp verdicts that the media were looking for. Nowhere in the report is it unambiguously stated that the actions or statements of a government minister were unambiguously unconstitutional.[75] On Mr Waldegrave, for example, while he misled Parliament, and while he should have realized that he was doing so, he did not do so intentionally. Similarly, while government statements to Parliament were designedly uninformative, there was no duplicitous intention, and so on. These were not the absolute indictments that the opposition parties needed if they were to press successfully for a resignation.[76]

There was a good reason for this. Quite rightly, Scott did not see it as his job to secure ministerial resignations. Even when ministers have behaved unconstitutionally, they are not responsible for that misbehaviour to a judge, in whatever capacity: ministers are responsible to Parliament. Scott saw his role as exposition of fact, not dictation of consequence. He would outline, in numbing detail, what had happened, but it was for others, and in this instance for the House of Commons, to judge on what should happen as a result. That government ministers escaped resignation in the aftermath of the Scott report was in part because of the unfair advantages the government secured for itself over the publication of the report and was in small part because of the report's structure and language, but to an even greater extent, the lack of resignations was down to the inability—or political unwillingness—of the House of Commons to demand them. The Scott report may have chronicled a long and depressing period of dereliction of constitutional duty on the government's part, but Parliament, too, has played its miserable part in this ongoing saga of constitutional failure.

---

[75] Scott's own views became clearer after the report had been published. Three months after the publication of the report, Scott gave oral evidence before the public service committee during its inquiry into ministerial accountability and responsibility. During his questioning by the committee he was asked whether 'something unconstitutionally improper happened'. Scott replied 'Yes, I think it did.' When he was asked, 'Did ministers behave in ways that ministers ought constitutionally not to have behaved?' he again replied 'Yes'. See Public Service Committee, *Ministerial Accountability and Responsibility*, HC (1995–96) 313-III (July 1996), QQ 378–9.

[76] See Ralph Negrine, 'The Inquiry's Media Coverage' (1997) 50 *Parliamentary Affairs* 27.

What are Ministers Constitutionally Responsible for?

The question which this sorry story leaves is what exactly it is that ministers are now responsible for. This issue is, of course, said to be governed by the constitutional convention of ministerial responsibility, a doctrine which is among the centre-pieces of British constitutional theory.[77] As Wade and Bradley state, 'the British system has placed great weight upon the necessity of subjecting the departments of central government to control by ministers, who are the link between the executive and Parliament'.[78] Similarly, Woodhouse opens her recent study, *Ministers and Parliament*, by stating that 'a fundamental principle of the British constitution is that the government is accountable through its ministers to Parliament'.[79] Recent political practice would seem to indicate, however, that there is some distance between these grand statements of principle about the supposedly central importance of ministerial responsibility on the one hand and the crude reality of parliamentary practice on the other. In the Westland affair of 1985–6,[80] the salmonella-in-eggs scare in 1988,[81] and on the question of policy towards Iraq, ministers can be seen as having failed to account properly for what they have done. More recently, serious concerns have also been expressed on the adequacy and accuracy of information given by ministers to Parliament on issues such as the Pergau Dam affair,[82] BSE in beef and its possible transfer to humans,[83] the state of the nation's abattoirs and the ability of the ministry of agriculture, fisheries and food to enforce even minimal hygiene standards,[84] and on gulf war syndrome and what the government has known and has done about

[77] See generally, C. Turpin, 'Ministerial Responsibility' (in J. Jowell and D. Oliver (eds.), *The Changing Constitution*, Oxford: Clarendon Press, 3rd edn., 1994) pp 109–51. In his seminal article, Finer described the convention of individual responsibility to Parliament as being part of 'constitutional folklore'. This is an astute observation, made all the more so by recent events, as we shall see. See S. E. Finer, 'The Individual Responsibility of Ministers' (1956) 34 *Public Administration* 377.

[78] E. C. S. Wade and A. W. Bradley, *Constitutional and Administrative Law* (London: Longman, 11th edn. by A. W. Bradley and K. D. Ewing, 1993) pp. 111 and 125.

[79] Diana Woodhouse, *Ministers and Parliament: Accountability in Theory and Practice* (Oxford: Clarendon Press, 1994) p. 3.

[80] See generally, D. Oliver and R. Austin, 'Political and Constitutional Aspects of the Westland Affair' (1987) 40 *Parliamentary Affairs* 20 and P. Hennessy, 'Helicopter Crashes into Cabinet: Prime Minister and Constitution Hurt' (1986) 13 *Journal of Law and Society* 427.

[81] See Woodhouse, op. cit., p. 186.

[82] Here there was an allegation that ministers had linked aid (in this case to Malaysia) with arms, contrary to the government's stated policy. See House of Commons Public Accounts Committee, *The Pergau Hydro-Electric Project*, HC (1993–94) 155 and Foreign Affairs Select Committee, *Public Expenditure: The Pergau Hydro-Electric Projects, Malaysia*, HC (1993–94) 271. The report of the foreign affairs committee stated that 'ministerial replies to certain questions were literally true, though less open and less informative than the House has a right to expect'.

[83] See, for example, Tim Radford, 'Poor Cow: Beef and bad Government', *London Review of Books*, 5 Sept. 1996 and the books reviewed in that essay.

[84] See, for example, the *Observer*, 9 Mar. 1997 and the *Guardian*, 7 and 13 Mar. 1997.

it.[85] As Woodhouse has argued, 'the moral obligation of a minister to submit to the scrutiny of the House for all the decisions and actions taken in his area of responsibility . . . seems in practice to have become an obligation to submit to scrutiny only if the minister sees fit and has been unable to avoid the House securing sufficiently detailed information to pursue him'.[86]

This being so, what does the constitutional convention of individual ministerial responsibility to Parliament actually provide? Now, constitutional conventions are of course notoriously difficult to define with any accuracy, and to some extent at least 'ministerial responsibility is, at best, a matter of line-drawing, and the precise location of the line at any time owes much more to political pragmatism than to constitutional dogma'.[87] Unusually for constitutional conventions, however, in the case of ministerial responsibility we do at least have a text to which we can look to give us some clearer idea of what the convention—or at least what contemporary governmental understanding of the convention—might be. That text, first drawn up by the postwar governments of the middle of the twentieth century but not published until 1992, is called *Questions of Procedure for Ministers*, or QPM. QPM is a list of rules about ministerial conduct and procedure, dealing with a wide variety of subjects from the acceptance of gifts to attendance of meetings. It has no formal legal or constitutional status: it is a cabinet office document circulated to all ministers.[88] The first paragraph of the 1992 version stated that 'these notes detail the arrangements for the conduct of affairs by ministers. They apply to all members of the government, but not parliamentary private secretaries . . . They are intended to give guidance.' Despite this modest opening, however, QPM contains important statements about the constitutional position of ministers generally and about ministerial responsibility in particular.

Paragraph 27 of the 1992 version[89] of QPM, provided that:

---

[85] See, for example, the *Guardian*, 28 Feb. 1997. See also Defence Select Committee, *Gulf War Syndrome*, HC (1994–95) 197, Oct. 1994 and the government's response at HC (1995–96) 187, Jan. 1996 (some 15 months after the committee's report was published!). The defence committee's report described aspects of the MOD's approach to gulf war syndrome as 'less than thorough' (para. 11) and 'unacceptably slow' (para. 20). The committee stated that it was 'appalled' (para. 28) that it had taken over four years for the MOD even to contemplate compiling epidemiological data on gulf war syndrome.

[86] Woodhouse, op. cit., p. 18.

[87] G. Drewry and T. Butcher, *The Civil Service Today* (Oxford: Blackwell, 1988) pp. 153–4. While this may be most clearly demonstrated in the area of ministerial resignations (or, often, non-resignations) it is not confined to this aspect of responsibility. On questions of resignation, see generally Woodhouse, op. cit., and R. Brazier, 'It *is* a Constitutional Issue: Fitness for Ministerial Office in the 1990s' [1994] *Public Law* 431.

[88] It is published through the cabinet office but is drawn up by the prime minister. It is binding on all ministers. Tony Blair's revised edition, given the new title *Code of Conduct and Guidance on Procedures for Ministers* was published in July 1997.

[89] More recent amendments to QPM are considered below. The Scott report assumed that previous versions of QPM which would have been in force during the period considered by the inquiry were identical to the 1992 version as far as its treatment of ministerial responsibility was concerned. Nothing which the government has stated about this issue since the publication of the

Ministers are accountable to Parliament, in the sense that they have a duty to explain in Parliament the exercise of their powers and duties and to give an account to Parliament of what is done by them in their capacity as ministers or by their departments. This includes the duty to give Parliament, including its select committees, and the public as full information as possible about the policies, decisions and actions of the government, and not to deceive or mislead Parliament and the public.

The absolutely central democratic importance of this obligation is obvious. As the Scott report put it: 'a failure by ministers to meet the obligations of ministerial accountability by providing information about the activities of their departments undermines . . . the democratic process'.[90] The provision of full and accurate information is a central aspect of ministers' constitutional responsibilities to Parliament. If an account given by a minister to Parliament (whether in answering a PQ, whether in a statement or in a debate, or whether in evidence to a select committee) withholds information on the matter under review, 'it is not a full account and the obligation of ministerial accountability has, *prima facie*, not been discharged'.[91] As the defence select committee argued in its report on the Westland affair, it is unacceptable and unconstitutional for a minister to accept responsibility for a matter but to refuse to explain what had happened.[92] Paragraph 27 of the 1992 QPM echoed this view, but in addition to this centrally produced document, some government departments have their own (often stricter) guidelines. Ministry of defence guidelines, for example, state that 'answers [to PQs] must be meticulously accurate and worded in clear and unambiguous terms. An error of fact or an answer that misleads the House can be dreadfully embarrassing for the minister.'[93] Further, as Erskine May's *Parliamentary Practice*[94] states, Parliament may treat the making of a deliberately misleading statement as a contempt.

If only it were so simple. These may be the basics, but they have been subject to considerable debate and amendment, partly as a result of the Scott report, and partly as a consequence of other factors. There are three areas where the Conservative government sought to refine the doctrine of individual ministerial responsibility to Parliament: each of these will now be considered in turn. The first relates to the issue at the heart of Scott's concerns

report has challenged this assumption. On the history and development of QPM, see Peter Hennessy, *The Hidden Wiring: Unearthing the British Constitution* (London: Indigo, 1996).

[90] See para. K8.3.   [91] See para. K8.3.

[92] *Westland: The Government's Decision-Making*, HC (1985–86) 519, para. 235. See Woodhouse, op. cit., p. 30.

[93] The *Guardian*, 9 Mar. 1994.

[94] Erskine May, *Parliamentary Practice*, op. cit., pp. 142 and 681: 'witnesses who give false evidence, prevaricate, present forged or falsified documents . . . with intent to deceive' may be found in contempt. However, contempt proceedings based on a refusal to answer are 'extremely rare'. Instead, the House has 'acquiesced' in a number of conventions which effectively permit ministers to decline to provide details. See Public Service Committee, *Ministerial Accountability and Responsibility*, HC (1995–96) 313, para. 61, quoting the evidence of the clerk of the House of Commons. This issue is discussed further in ch. 3, below.

about ministerial responsibility: namely the obligation not to mislead Parliament and the qualification of that obligation by the new inclusion of the adverb 'knowingly'. The second refinement is the distinction favoured by the Major government between operations and policy. This refinement was most controversially employed by Michael Howard when, as home secretary in October 1995, he avoided resignation, over a series of high profile escapes from prison, by sacking Derek Lewis, the civil servant in charge of the prison service within the home office. The third refinement, which is related to the second, is another distinction favoured by the Conservative government. This is the distinction between the constitutional accountability of ministers on the one hand and their personal responsibility on the other. These are developments with enormous constitutional implications and consequences, and deserve to be examined in some detail. Behind all these distinctions and refinements to the basic doctrine lies the shadow of Crichel Down, the 'most famous farm in British constitutional history' as John Griffith put it.[95] That unhappy precedent—much cited but little understood—will also have to be re-examined if we are fully to appreciate the gravity of the Major government's attempts at constitutional reform by stealth.

Knowingly Mislead

The first sign that the Conservative government was intending to change the wording of paragraph 27 came in 1994 when John Major himself wrote a letter to the treasury and civil service committee which was at that time conducting an important investigation into the role of the civil service. In his letter, Mr Major stated that 'it is clearly of paramount importance that ministers give accurate and truthful information to the House. If they *knowingly* fail to do this, then they should relinquish their positions except in the quite exceptional circumstances of which a devaluation or time of war or other danger to national security have been quoted as examples.'[96] Later in 1994 the prime minister appointed the Nolan committee to review and to report on standards in public life. In its first report, published in May 1995, the Nolan committee addressed the issue of relations between ministers and Parliament (among other things).[97] Its report argued that 'there is a need for greater

[95] J. A. G. Griffith, 'Crichel Down: the Most Famous Farm in British Constitutional History' (1987) 1 *Contemporary Record* 35.

[96] Letter dated 5 Apr. 1994, emphasis added. Cited in the government's response to the recommendation in para. 134 of the treasury and civil service committee's report on the role of the civil service: *The Civil Service: Taking Forward Continuity and Change* (Cm. 2748, Jan. 1995).

[97] *Standards in Public Life* (first report of the committee on standards in public life, chairman Lord Nolan, Cm. 2850). The Nolan committee was established in Oct. 1994 to 'examine current concerns about standards of conduct of all holders of public office . . . and make recommendations'. The committee's first report focuses on three groups: MPs, ministers and civil servants, and quangos.

clarity about the standards of conduct expected of ministers'.[98] At the most general level the committee set out a list of seven 'principles of public life': selflessness, integrity, objectivity, accountability, openness, honesty, and leadership, of which two (openness and honesty) may be seen as directly relevant here. Quite what the value of such elementary preaching against sin is seems rather unclear. At a more specific level (and more usefully perhaps) the committee also stated that it is possible to distil (from QPM and elsewhere) general principles of conduct which are applicable to ministers. In the committee's view, these should be more clearly set out, because, while this would not stop misconduct, it would 'do much to counter present public uncertainty about what is and is not acceptable'.[99] To this end, the committee recommended that the prime minister should produce a document drawing out the 'ethical principles and rules which [QPM] contains' which would then form a free-standing code of conduct for ministers.[100] While the eventual wording of such a code of conduct would be a matter for the prime minister, the committee made some suggestions, namely: 'ministers of the crown are expected to behave according to the highest standards of constitutional and personal conduct. In particular they must observe the following principles of ministerial conduct: . . . (ii) ministers must not mislead Parliament. They must be as open as possible with Parliament and the public; (iii) ministers are accountable to Parliament for the policies and operations of their departments and agencies . . .'[101]

In the government's response to the Nolan committee's report, the principle contained in QPM was redrafted. The government stated that 'ministers are accountable to Parliament for the policies, decisions and actions of their departments and agencies' and that 'ministers must not *knowingly* mislead Parliament and the public and should correct any inadvertent errors at the earliest possible opportunity. They must be as open as possible with Parliament and the public, *withholding information only when disclosure would not be in the public interest*.'[102] Do these textual refinements affect the essence

---

[98] Nolan, ibid., principal conclusion to chapter 3: 'The Executive, Ministers and Civil Servants' page 46.

[99] Nolan, ibid., para. 3.14.   [100] Nolan, ibid., para. 3.15.

[101] Nolan, ibid., para. 3.16. This rather bland wording was very disappointing. Perhaps it was necessary in order to achieve unanimity among the ten members of the committee but, nonetheless, not to have grappled with the important (if difficult) matters of detail which it should properly have considered left at least this aspect of the Nolan report looking very thin and anodyne indeed.

[102] *The Government's Response to the First Report from the Committee on Standards in Public Life*, Cm. 2931, July 1995, annex A. Emphasis added. See Scott, para. K8.4. See generally D. Oliver [1995] *Public Law* 497. In a House of Commons debate on the Nolan report, Peter Shore MP (an opposition member of the Nolan Committee) argued that refusals to disclose should be limited to 'exceptional circumstances' but the government has refused to go this far: see HC Deb., Vol. 265, col. 455, 2 Nov. 1995. The cabinet minister responsible for this area of policy (Roger Freeman, chancellor of the Duchy of Lancaster) stated in the debate, however, that the government would add to their new formulation of QPM the statement that the public interest 'should

of ministers' constitutional obligations to Parliament? According to the Scott report, they do not. On the inclusion of 'knowingly' the Scott report stated that this should not 'make any material difference to the substance of the obligation . . . It must, I believe, always have been the case that misleading statements made in ignorance of the true facts were not regarded as a breach of a minister's obligation to be honest' although questions might of course arise as to why the minister was ignorant.[103] Similarly, according to the Scott report, on the second change: 'the withholding of information by an accountable minister should never be based on reasons of convenience or for the avoidance of political embarrassment, but should always require special and carefully considered justification'.[104]

However, there is room for considerable doubt as to whether these changes are really as innocuous and innocent as the Scott report made out. Even if William Waldegrave did not mean to lie to Parliament, he should have realized that what he was telling Parliament was untrue, as the Scott report stated.[105] Constitutionally, should William Waldegrave have been allowed to have continued in office simply because he wrongly failed to realize that his answers and letters were misleading? As Lord Callaghan put it in the House of Lords' debate on the Scott report, if Mr Waldegrave 'was not a knave what was he, a simpleton?'[106] What happened to the days when ministers were constitutionally responsible to Parliament for their incompetence as well as for their dishonesty? Of course, ministers must not knowingly mislead Parliament—they must not tell outright lies, and should they do so, they must resign. The two (and only two) exceptions to this basic position appear to be in cases of devaluation and in times of war or other emergency threatening national security.[107] But limiting ministers' culpability to situations where they have knowingly and deliberately lied to Parliament is confining their

be decided in accordance with established parliamentary convention, the law, and any relevant government code of practice'. See HC Deb., Vol. 265, col. 456, 2 Nov. 1995. See further below, n. 142 and accompanying text.

[103] See para. K8.5.   [104] See para. K8.5.   [105] See para. D4.4.

[106] See HL Deb., Vol. 569, col. 1254, 26 Feb. 1996. Lord Hailsham interrupted Lord Callaghan with the words 'Neither. He is a fellow of All Souls College Oxford' to which Lord Callaghan responded, 'Perhaps then . . . he was a clever silly. That is it.'

[107] In his evidence to the treasury and civil service committee in Mar. 1994 William Waldegrave argued that 'in exceptional cases [such as] devaluation . . . it is necessary to say something that is untrue to the House of Commons. The House of Commons understands that and has always accepted it.' Treasury and Civil Service Committee, *The Role of the Civil Service*, Minutes of Evidence, 8 Mar. 1994: HC (1993–94) 27(vi). Mr Waldegrave cited Lord Callaghan and the devaluation of Nov. 1967 as an example. Lord Callaghan responded to the committee that 'Mr Waldegrave is indisputably wrong in asserting that I told the House of Commons a lie.' He then added that devaluation does not justify 'a minister in lying to Parliament and Mr Waldegrave's false analogy must not be allowed to become a precedent to justify doing so', see the letter from Lord Callaghan to the treasury and civil service committee, 19 Apr. 1994, printed at HC (1993–94) 27-III, app. 41, p. 141. After the devaluation of 1967 Mr Callaghan resigned his position as chancellor of the exchequer, although the prime minister Harold Wilson immediately restored Callaghan to the cabinet, as home secretary.

responsibilities too narrowly, and the Scott report erred in not saying so. As Ann Taylor put it when she was shadow leader of the House, 'it sends out the wrong signals'.[108] If ministers are only constitutionally responsible when they know that Parliament is being misled, who is constitutionally responsible when ministers do not know? Should culpable civil servants be directly accountable and responsible to Parliament? To move down this path would lead to a radical reworking of the existing constitutional regulation of the relationship between ministers, civil servants, and Parliament which would certainly require a move away from the Conservative government's view that civil servants are primarily servants of their minister and give evidence to Parliament's select committees, for example, 'on behalf of their ministers'.[109]

What of the situation, for example, where Parliament has been misled, and the minister does not realize this, but it turns out that the minister has been given inaccurate information by his department which he has then relayed to Parliament and that in giving the inaccurate information to the minister the official was merely following the department's usual routines for relaying information, as laid down by the minister's own instructions. Do ministers not have a constitutional responsibility to organize and issue instructions to their departments in such a way as to ensure that such a situation does not occur? Of course they do. Certainly this was the view of Reginald Maudling when he was home secretary in the early 1970s. In a debate on the Vehicle and General affair Maudling stated that 'ministers are responsible not only for their personal decisions but also for seeing that there is a system in their departments by which they are informed of important matters which arise. They are also responsible for minimizing the dangers of errors and mistakes as far as possible, and, clearly, they are responsible for the general efficiency of their departments.'[110] Confining ministers' responsibilities as regards information as narrowly as John Major's government sought to do misses this essential element of ministerial responsibility because, as Vernon Bogdanor has argued, 'the formula "knowingly mislead" . . . does not provide for a situation in which a minister has been negligent or incompetent, in which he failed to apprise himself of things that he ought to have known'.[111]

It should go without saying that ministers must not lie to Parliament, that they should not knowingly mislead, but it should also go without saying that this is but the first aspect, and not the entirety, of ministers' obligations. Under no circumstances should ministers mislead Parliament—either designedly or inadvertently—but if they do, Parliament should be informed

---

[108] See Public Service Committee, *Ministerial Accountability and Responsibility*, HC (1995–96) 313, Vol. III, Q 1055.

[109] This is an issue which we will examine in more detail in the next chapter.

[110] See HC Deb., Vol. 836, col. 159, 1 May 1972. See also R. J. S. Baker, 'The Vehicle and General Affair and Ministerial Responsibility' (1972) 43 *Political Quarterly* 340.

[111] Vernon Bogdanor, 'Ministerial Accountability' (1997) 50 *Parliamentary Affairs* 71, at p. 74.

immediately the minister realizes what has happened. The minister should then explain to Parliament why it was misled, and irrespective of the reason and irrespective of the minister's intent, if Parliament is dissatisfied with the minister's apology and explanation, then Parliament can enforce sanctions (which include the ultimate sanction of forcing the minister's resignation) against that minister. In that sense ministers are constitutionally and personally responsible to Parliament for all the information they give to Parliament, whether or not that information is knowingly misleading. While ministers will not necessarily be asked or expected to resign every time Parliament is inadvertently misled, ministers are constitutionally and personally responsible for ensuring that under no circumstances do they or their departments mislead Parliament. Parliament must be more wary than the Scott report appeared to be of any attempt to dilute that essential obligation by the insertion into the relevant constitutional texts of unwelcome adverbs.

Policy and Operational Matters

In September 1994 six armed IRA prisoners attempted to escape from Whitemoor maximum-security prison in Cambridgeshire. The prisoners had obtained guns and semtex explosive and had tried to shoot their way out of jail. The home secretary, Michael Howard, described the situation at Whitemoor as a 'dreadful state of affairs'.[112] On 3 January 1995 three very high-risk prisoners escaped from Parkhurst high-security prison on the Isle of Wight. Michael Howard, still home secretary at that stage, appointed Sir John Learmont, a retired army general, to inquire into prison security in England and Wales in the light of these high-profile events and to report. Learmont's report was published in October 1995.[113] The report was highly critical of the prison service (a next steps agency within the home office)[114] and of the entire system of prison management, from the level of prison governors and more junior staff all the way up to the chief executive of the prisons agency and to the home office and its ministerial team itself. In his covering letter to Mr Howard, Learmont indicated that one cause of the malaise in the prison service which he outlined in his report was the poor 'liaison between the prison service and the home office' which, he said, needed 'to improve'.[115] Chapter 3 of the report was replete with examples of how the problems in the prison service were not self-contained, but implicated the

[112] See Anthony Barker, 'Political Responsibility for UK Prison Security: Ministers Escape Again', *Essex Papers in Politics and Government*, no. 106 (Apr. 1996), p. 7.
[113] *Review of Prison Service Security in England and Wales and the Escape from Parkhurst Prison*, Cm. 3020, Oct. 1995.
[114] Next steps agencies are discussed further in the next chapter.
[115] Learmont report, op. cit. n. 113, p. i.

home office and, indeed, the home secretary. Learmont stated, for example, that the structure of the senior management of the prison service was 'unfortunate'—something for which ministers, not civil servants, were responsible.[116] Further, Learmont indicated that this structure resulted in there being too much management in the prison service and not enough leadership (i.e. too much planning and control and insufficient vision and inspiration).[117] But the framework document, outlining the role of the service and its senior management team, was not chosen by Mr Lewis: it was imposed by ministers. If Mr Lewis could not provide enough of the vision thing, it was because Mr Howard got in the way, as Learmont indicated: 'the current management style of the prison service appears to owe much to an historically close involvement of the home office, *particularly in major operational matters*'.[118] The closeness of this relationship, even after the prison service achieved agency status in 1993, is illustrated by the incredible volume of correspondence between the headquarters of the prison service and the home office. In the eighty-three working days between October 1994 and January 1995 alone Learmont found that over 1,000 letters were sent. As Learmont stated in his report, this was in part because of the high profile of the problems of the prison service during that period (with the number of riots, escapes, and so on) but 'it is at just such times that top management attention needs to be firmly fixed on solving the problem, not merely explaining it. Such a level of upwards-focused activity needs to be carefully managed if it is not to interefere' with headquarters' proper role.[119] It was as a direct result of this priority of always having to spend time communicating with home office ministers (with headquarters having to submit almost daily defensive briefings to ministers on 'every press story' relating to prisons, for example)[120] that the prison service developed its ethos of responding to ministers rather than leading the staff employed in the service, which the Learmont report was so critical of and which was the ultimate cause of Mr Lewis's dismissal: a cause which was, in turn, entirely caused by ministers!

When the Learmont report was published, a huge political storm broke out, and the opposition called for the home secretary's resignation. Mr Howard refused to resign, however, and instead called for the resignation of Derek Lewis, the chief executive of the prison service. When Mr Lewis refused to resign, Mr Howard dismissed him.[121] Why was it Mr Lewis who was held to be responsible in this way, and not the minister? Michael Howard claimed in Parliament that he as secretary of state was responsible only for

---

[116] Learmont report, op. cit. para. 3.18.   [117] Ibid., para. 3.19.
[118] Ibid., para. 3.77. Emphasis added.   [119] Ibid., para. 3.83.
[120] Ibid., para. 3.85.
[121] Mr Lewis issued a writ for wrongful dismissal, but the action was settled before it came to court. For newspaper coverage of the story, see the *Guardian*, 18–20 Oct. 1995. See also Derek Lewis, *Hidden Agendas: Politics, Law and Order* (London: Hamish Hamilton, 1997).

policy matters, and the problems which had been identified in the Learmont report were operational concerns, not matters of policy. The person responsible for operational matters both in principle and under the terms of the framework document of the prisons agency was the chief executive, not the secretary of state, and therefore Derek Lewis was responsible, not Michael Howard. The secretary of state would naturally have to come to the House of Commons and explain—or give an account of—what had happened (he was in that sense constitutionally accountable to Parliament) but he was neither personally nor constitutionally responsible.[122]

Thus, here we have the clearest and most famous example of the Major government's second attempted refinement of the basic doctrine of individual ministerial responsibility: namely the notion that ministers are responsible to Parliament only for matters of policy, and not for operational concerns. Operational matters are the responsibility of civil servants, and that responsibility is owed not to Parliament but to ministers—it is not constitutional responsibility, but internal, executive or management responsibility. Relations between civil servants and ministers and between civil servants and Parliament are the subject of the next chapter, but insofar as developments in this field relate to ministerial responsibility we do also have to consider aspects of this issue here. On the one hand it is nothing new for government ministers to refuse to resign over escapes from prisons. After the 1983 Maze break-out the then secretary of state for Northern Ireland and his minister (James Prior and Nicholas Scott) continued in office, although the assistant governor of the prison was transferred and the governor retired.[123] Similarly, after two suspected IRA remand prisoners escaped from Brixton prison, the then home secretary Kenneth Baker refused to resign although, again, officials within the home office and at the prison were transferred or retired.[124]

On the other hand, the purported distinction between policy and operations is controversial and very difficult: Anthony Barker has described it as 'superficial and self-serving'.[125] There are two levels of criticism: the first relates specifically to Michael Howard and his relationship with Derek Lewis, and the second is more general. As to the first, Mr Howard claimed that as a

---

[122] After the Conservatives lost the 1997 general election it emerged that Ann Widdecombe, the minister of state for prisons at the home office at the time of Mr Lewis's dismissal, disagreed with and strongly disapproved of Mr Howard's behaviour in firing Mr Lewis, behaviour which she described as 'brutal', 'dubious' and 'not sustainable', implying that during the course of the episode Mr Howard had misled the House of Commons. She also said that she regretted not having resigned over the matter. She indicated that she had considered resigning at the time (Oct. 1995) but had decided against it on the ground that such a course of action would be contrary to the interests of the Conservative party. See the *Independent*, 12 May 1997 and the *Guardian*, 14 May 1997.

[123] See Anthony Barker, 'Political Responsibility for UK Prison Security: Ministers Escape Again', *Essex Papers in Politics and Government*, no. 106 (Apr. 1996), p. 4.

[124] See ibid., p. 6.   [125] Ibid., p. 20.

matter of fact he was not involved in operational matters concerning the prisons agency. This was a hotly disputed point, and one which, as we have seen, is not entirely supported by the Learmont report. After his dismissal Derek Lewis launched what has been described as a 'media blitz'[126] against Mr Howard, stating that the agency's daily work had been frequently and repeatedly interrupted by the secretary of state, sometimes many times in the same day, and often this ministerial involvement (or interference) would relate to very specific operational matters, such as whether an individual prisoner should be searched, and so on. In his evidence to the public service committee in 1996, Mr Lewis stated that Michael Howard's involvement 'grew to a level where I believe it was acting to the detriment of the performance of the prison service. For two reasons. One, it was proving to be a distraction for me . . . and secondly, it was a level which caused those within the service to be uncertain about who was actually calling the shots.'[127]

More significantly, however, there is a broader, more general problem with the policy/operation distinction. It is extremely difficult to know how to classify something as either policy or operational: is a decision to reduce prisoners' visiting time a policy or an operational decision? What about overcrowding, or the reintroduction of slopping out, or staff shortages, or deciding to keep a set of prisoners confined in their cells for twenty-three hours per day—are these policy matters or operational matters, and how can we tell? The first division association (FDA), the trade union for senior civil servants, of which Derek Lewis was a member, stated in its written evidence to the public service committee that a rigid distinction between policy and operations 'would be exceptionally difficult to define in principle, and indeed there is no agreed statement as to how such a distinction should be applied in practice'.[128] In its (unanimous) report, the public service committee broadly agreed with this view, stating that while ministers cannot be personally blamed for individual operational failures, they could be blamed for 'a broader pattern of incompetence' and further, that if even an individual operational failure was serious enough and was closely connected to the minister's

---

[126] See ibid., p. 18.

[127] See Public Service Committee, *Ministerial Accountability and Responsibility*, HC (1995–96) 313, Vol. III, Q 637. It is not only where relations are poor between ministers and senior civil servants that there will be significant ministerial involvement in matters of operations as well as in policy. The evidence of Lawrie Haynes (chief executive of the highways agency in the department of transport) neatly illustrates how intertwined ministers and chief executives will normally be in decision-making on both policy and operational matters. See ibid., QQ 514–17 and 549. Mr Haynes agreed that decision making 'in practice is actually a mixture of policy, adjusted to practical operations and considerations'. Ibid., Q 550.

[128] See ibid., HC (1995–96) 313, Vol. III, p. 3 (para. 23 of the FDA's memorandum of evidence). The FDA gave its own example of a decision relating to prisoners which could be classified as being either policy or operational or both: namely a decision to allow dangerous inmates to keep up blinds which exclude visual access to their hobbies room, rather than run the risk of riot if such blinds are removed. See para. 25 of the FDA's memorandum of evidence.

responsibility for the overall organization of his department, it might be appropriate for the minister to resign.[129] The committee's report went on to state that 'what ministers must never do is to put the blame onto civil servants for the effects of unworkable policies and their setting of unrealistic targets'.[130] The committee was quite clear that, contrary to the position which Mr Howard had adopted, there is no clear-cut constitutional distinction between ministerial responsibilities for policy on the one hand and operational matters on the other.

Responsibility and Accountability

In 1994 William Waldegrave and Sir Robin Butler presented the Major government's views on ministers' parliamentary responsibilities in evidence to the treasury and civil service committee.[131] They argued that a distinction ought to be drawn between ministerial accountability and ministerial responsibility. Ministerial *accountability* to Parliament, they argued, consisted of a minister's ultimate duty to account to Parliament for the work of his department. This would mean that in the last resort ministers could be challenged about any action of the civil service, since civil servants act on behalf of and are accountable to government ministers, and ministers alone are accountable to Parliament. Ministerial *responsibility* arises only where a minister is directly and personally involved in an action or decision and implies that the minister carries personal credit or blame for that action or decision. The treasury and civil service committee criticized the Waldegrave/Butler position, describing it as 'unconvincing',[132] and 'more novel than its advocates are prepared to admit'.[133] The government argued that its position was not an original one, but was based on the constitutional precedent of the Crichel Down affair of

[129] See Public Service Committee, *Ministerial Accountability and Responsibility*, HC (1995–96) 313, para. 19. For a more severe view, see the comments of Enoch Powell (then a Unionist MP) reacting angrily to James Prior's refusal to resign over the Maze break-out. Powell argued that the distinction between policy and operations was 'invalid' and represented a 'fallacious' view of the constitution. In his view ministers are constitutionally responsible for the entirety of their departments. The public service committee described Mr Powell as making an 'extreme case': see ibid., para. 19. For Mr Powell's views, see HC Deb., Vol. 53, cols. 1060–1, 9 Feb. 1984.

[130] Ibid., para. 20.

[131] See, for example, Treasury and Civil Service Committee, *The Role of the Civil Service*, HC (1993–94) 27, para. 120. William Waldegrave was at that time the chancellor of the Duchy of Lancaster, the cabinet minister with responsibility for open government and the citizen's charter, among other things.

[132] HC (1993–94) 27, para. 132.

[133] Ibid., para. 122. Even academics who have supported the distinction between responsibility and accountability have conceded, contrary to the Conservative government's view, that it is 'fairly new'. See the evidence of Rodney Brazier, Public Service Committee, *Ministerial Accountability and Responsibility*, HC (1995–96) 313, Vol. II, p. 3.

1954.[134] The government clarified its views in its response to the select committee's report[135] in which it was argued that (1) a minister is accountable for everything that happens in his or her department in the sense that Parliament can call the minister to account for it; (2) a minister is responsible for the policies of his or her department, for the framework through which policies are delivered, and for the resources which are allocated; and (3) a minister is not responsible for everything in his or her department in the sense of having personal knowledge and control of every action taken and being personally blameworthy when delegated tasks are carried out incompetently or when mistakes or errors of judgement are made at operational level.

The essence of the point behind making this distinction is that the conduct of government has grown so complex and the need for ministerial delegation has become so great as 'to render unreal the attaching of blame to a minister simply because something has gone wrong' in his department.[136] In his report, Sir Richard Scott appeared to accept this approach, stating that 'for my part, I find it difficult to disagree'.[137] However, importantly, the Scott report went on to state that if the government's views as to this matter are accepted, this would have significant implications as to the obligation of ministers to provide information to Parliament: 'if ministers are to be excused blame and personal criticism on the basis of the absence of personal knowledge or involvement, the corollary ought to be an acceptance of the obligation to be forthcoming with information about the incident in question'.[138] Otherwise Parliament (and the public) will be unable to assess whether a minister's claim of lack of personal involvement has been fairly and properly made. Despite Sir Richard Scott's views, however, this remains a controversial issue, with heavyweight opinion being lined up on both sides. The Conservative government, Sir Richard Scott, and Sir Robin Butler have received academic support from Rodney Brazier and from senior civil servants such as Michael Bichard and Richard Mottram,[139] but on the other hand their position has been strongly criticized by the Council of Civil Service Unions (CCSU) and by seasoned constitutional observers such as Graham

---

[134] In its response to the treasury and civil service committee's report, the government insisted that the distinction between ministerial responsibility and accountability 'is not a new doctrine' and specifically cited the speech of the then home secretary Sir David Maxwell-Fyfe in the 1954 Crichel Down debate. See *The Civil Service: Taking Forward Continuity and Change*, Cm. 2748, Jan. 1995, pp. 27–9. The Maxwell-Fyfe speech and the Crichel Down affair are discussed further below.

[135] Cm 2748, *ibid.*   [136] See para. K8.15.

[137] Ibid. Sir Richard Scott further endorsed the distinction between responsibility and accountability in his evidence to the public service committee, when he seemed to take the view that accountability was a constitutional matter (of explaining) and responsibility was a personal matter (of being blameworthy). See Public Service Committee, *Ministerial Accountability and Responsibility*, HC (1995–96) 313, Vol. III, Q 394.

[138] See para. K8.16.

[139] For the former, see n. 132 above, and for the latter, see Public Service Committee, *Ministerial Accountability and Responsibility*, HC (1995–96) 313, Vol. III, QQ 912 and 954.

Mather MEP, among others.[140] Nonetheless, after the publication of the Scott report, the Conservative government continued to make the distinction between what by 1996 they called ministerial responsibility and constitutional accountability, most notably in its evidence to the public service committee. Moreover, Crichel Down remained at the heart of the argument, with Sir Robin Butler stating in his evidence to that committee (in June 1996), for example, that the government's position 'only repeats what has been in existence since Crichel Down'.[141]

In November 1995 Roger Freeman announced that, as a result of the Nolan committee's recommendations, and no doubt with half an eye on the (at that stage still forthcoming) Scott report, the government had redrafted the opening paragraph of *Questions of Procedure for Ministers* in order to bring together the various developments which we have discussed here. It is a useful summary of all the changes which the Major adminstration saw fit to make, and is worth quoting in full:[142]

Ministers of the crown are expected to behave according the highest standards of constitutional and personal conduct in the performance of their duties. In particular they must observe the following principles of ministerial conduct:

(i) Ministers must uphold the principle of collective responsibility;
(ii) Ministers are accountable to Parliament for the policies, decisions and actions of their departments and agencies;
(iii) Ministers must not knowingly mislead Parliament and the public and should correct any inadvertent errors at the earliest opportunity. They must be as open as possible with Parliament and the public, withholding information only when disclosure would not be in the public interest, which should be decided in accordance with established parliamentary convention, the law, and any relevant government code of practice;
(iv) Ministers must ensure that no conflict arises, or appears to arise, between their public duties and the private interests;
(v) Ministers should avoid accepting any gift or hospitality which might, or might reasonably appear to, compromise their judgement or place them under an improper obligation;
(vi) Ministers in the House of Commons must keep separate their roles as ministers and constituency members;
(vii) Ministers must not use public resources for party political purposes. They must uphold the political impartiality of the civil service and not ask civil servants to act in any other way which would conflict with the civil service code.

---

[140] Ibid., Vol. II, p. 13 (CCSU) and Vol. III, pp. 121–2 (Mather).
[141] Ibid., Vol. III, Q 872.
[142] The old para. 27 remained in this 1995 version, but Mr Freeman indicated that the new opening paragraph was to be read in preference to it: see Scott report, para. K8.4. For Mr Freeman's statement, see HC Deb., Vol. 265, col. 456, 2 Nov. 1995. A slightly reworded version of this opening paragraph appears in Tony Blair's revised edition of the Code, published in July 1997. The old para 27 has now been removed.

The paragraph concludes by stating that the substance of QPM 'should be read against the background of the[se] general obligations, and in the context of protecting the integrity of public life. It will be for individual ministers to judge how best to act in order to uphold the highest standards. They are responsible for justifying their conduct to Parliament, and they can only remain in office for as long as they retain the prime minister's confidence.'

What now remains is how these attempted refinements should be assessed. As we have seen, John Major's ministers were anxious to stress that their views on ministerial responsibility, and particularly on the purported distinction between responsibility and accountability, were not new, and were firmly based on constitutional history, most notably the precedent of Crichel Down. We will therefore begin our assessment of the recent refinements to ministerial responsibility with an examination of what happened in the Crichel Down affair and what was said both at the time and subsequently about how Crichel Down affected the doctrine of ministerial responsibility. This is important, because most people, the government included, have made serious errors in their selective recollection of Crichel Down, as we shall see. After we have set the record straight, we can then move on to examine how the debate was further developed in the 1996 report of the public service committee.

The Unhappy Precedent of Crichel Down

In 1938 the government purchased 725 acres of chalk downland in north Dorset for military use. The land was bought from three separate owners, all of whom were paid for the land, and two of whom were also paid compensation for what was termed 'injurious affection' arising out of the severance of part of their lands.[143] In 1950 the land was transferred to the ministry of agriculture and the Labour minister, Thomas Williams, placed it under the management of the agricultural land commission (ALC), an independent statutory body. The ALC decided to maintain the land as a single farming block and not to split it up into smaller units. Commander Marten, whose family had owned one part of the land until 1938, challenged this decision—Commander Marten wanted to purchase the land. Accordingly, in 1952 Sir Thomas Dugdale, the Conservative minister of agriculture in Churchill's government, looked into the ALC's decision but he concluded that it was satisfactory. Sir Thomas Dugdale decided that the land should not be sold back to Commander Marten as there continued to be in 1952 a serious national food shortage. Dugdale therefore preferred to keep the land in state control, and it was accordingly sold on to the commissioners of crown lands. The difficulty with this was that, in the process, previous promises which had been made by officials at the ALC

---

[143] The phrase was used by Sir Thomas Dugdale in his resignation speech: see HC Deb., Vol. 530, col. 1178, 20 July 1954.

and elsewhere to potential purchasers of the land (such as Commander Marten) were ignored, causing a serious political controversy, with repeated allegations of wrongdoing and double standards (to say the least) in the ministry of agriculture and at the ALC. Sir Thomas Dugdale appointed Andrew Clark QC to look into the controversy and to report back to him. Much to Dugdale's relief, Clark's report concluded that 'there was no trace . . . of anything in the nature of bribery, corruption or personal dishonesty'[144] in the sale or management of Crichel Down, and Dugdale went to the House of Commons and claimed that the affair was all over and although 'errors of judgment' were made, 'no further action' was necessary.[145]

This attitude was treated with some shock, not to say anger, especially among back-bench Conservative MPs from farming constituencies. *Hansard* records cries of 'robbery' while Dugdale was asserting his view that 'the land cannot be sold back' to Commander Marten, for example.[146] There was no time, however, to press matters, and the House of Commons had to wait a further month before a full debate on Crichel Down and on Clark's report could be held. It is this debate—like the Scott debate on 26 February 1996, an adjournment debate—to which Sir Thomas Dugdale and Sir David Maxwell-Fyfe contributed, making important statements about the nature of ministerial responsibility.

Sir Thomas Dugdale opened the debate. During his long speech (which lasted for fifty minutes) he reviewed the events of the Crichel Down saga and right at the end of his speech he announced that he had offered his resignation to the prime minister. During his speech Dugdale gave no indication that he was about to announce his resignation, and there is therefore little in his speech to which we can turn to elucidate quite why he resigned. During the course of his speech he stated that 'I, as minister, must accept full responsibility to Parliament for any mistakes and inefficiency of officials in my department, just as, when my officials bring off any successes, I take full credit for them.' He continued, 'any departure from this long-established rule is bound to bring the civil service right into the political arena, and that we should all, on both sides of the House, deprecate most vigorously'.[147] He also noted that he had been widely criticized for his statement to the House the previous month, in which, it had been said, he had appeared complacent. He stated that this had not been his intention. He concluded his speech by stating that the government's policy had now changed and, as food supplies were now growing, agricultural lands would be sold off wherever practicable.[148] He then announced his resignation.

---

[144] *Report of the Public Inquiry ordered by the Minister of Agriculture into the Disposal of Land at Crichel Down*, Cmd. 9176 (June 1954), cited by Sir Thomas Dugdale at HC Deb., Vol. 528, col. 1745, 15 June 1954.

[145] Statement of Sir Thomas Dugdale, HC Deb., Vol. 528, col. 1745, 15 June 1954.

[146] Ibid., col. 1747.   [147] HC Deb., Vol. 530, col. 1186, 20 July 1954.

[148] Ibid., cols. 1190–3.

For the opposition, the Labour MP George Brown expressed his sympathy for Dugdale, although his speech was not without its criticisms of him. He stated that 'government backbenchers . . . have given [Dugdale] the minimum of support when he has been in trouble, which has arisen very largely because of the demands which have been made on him and not by his own will. They have hunted and harassed him . . .'[149] This was borne out in a number of speeches from the Conservative backbenches. In the contributions from Conservatives such as Anthony Hurd (MP for Newbury), Robert Crouch (MP for Dorset North), and Viscount Lambton (MP for Berwick-upon-Tweed) it was evident that among Tory MPs from the country there was widespread dislike of bureaucrats in general and of officials from the ministry of agriculture in particular, and that this was coupled by a distinct lack of sympathy for Dugdale himself.[150]

This is important for our purposes because it illustrates that MPs' concerns about accountability were not the same in the mid-1950s as they were forty years later in the debates about the Scott report. In the 1990s the concern has been that ministers are not as constitutionally responsible as they once were, and that in particular they do not resign as they once did. Peter Hennessy has stated, for example, that 'there has been a distinct absence of walking since 1982'.[151] Similarly, when she was shadow leader of the House, Ann Taylor MP stated with regard to the criticisms of ministers in the Scott report that 'if you go back, 12, 15, 20 years, I think we would all have expected ministers to go'.[152] In the 1950s, however, the concerns were not about ministers: they were about civil servants. The fear was that the civil service had grown enormously during the first half of the twentieth century, spurred on by two world wars and by the advent of larger, more interventionist socialist government, and had become a force unto itself, and certainly one which Parliament could not hope to hold to account. As it was put during the Crichel Down debate, 'there has been criticism that the principle [of ministerial responsibility] operates so as to oblige ministers to extend total protection to their officials and to endorse their acts, and to cause the position that civil servants cannot be called to account and are effectively responsible to no-one'.[153] Crichel Down represented the focal point for the expression of these fears—here was a situation where faceless bureaucratic officials were threatening dearly-held Tory values of private land-ownership, and who was accountable? It is the

---

[149] HC Deb., Vol. 530, col. 1195. George Brown also stated that Crichel Down was not as much a story of civil servants' failures as it was of the collective failure of Conservative ministers to stick to a single agriculture policy and 'to know what they wanted to do'. See ibid., cols. 1198 and 1212.

[150] See, among many examples, ibid., cols. 1214, 1230, 1234–5, and 1272.

[151] Public Service Committee, *Ministerial Accountability and Responsibility*, HC (1995–96) 313, Vol. III, Q 68.

[152] Ibid., Q 1038.

[153] Per Sir David Maxwell-Fyfe, HC Deb., Vol. 530, col. 1285, 20 July 1954.

background of this fear as to the *civil service* that explains Dugdale's comments in his speech to the effect that he as minister must accept responsibility for officials' mistakes and inefficiency. This background must also be borne in mind when rereading the speeches which summed up the debate, from Labour's Herbert Morrison and from the home secretary Sir David Maxwell-Fyfe. These speakers were not seeking to define or to limit *ministerial* responsibility in the way that John Major's ministers were in the 1990s: rather they were aiming to satisfy Parliament that *civil servants* were not unaccountable faceless bureaucrats, but were fully accountable to their ministers who in turn were fully accountable to Parliament. It may help us not to misinterpret Morrison's and Maxwell-Fyfe's speeches if we bear this essential context in mind.

Herbert Morrison stated that ministers are responsible to Parliament for all acts (and for all failures to act) of civil servants in their department. When civil servants make errors, Parliament has a right to be assured that such errors and such civil servants have been properly dealt with. This does not mean that ministers must always defend their civil servants irrespective of what has occurred, but ministers must satisfy Parliament that they are dealing with matters adequately.[154] On the specific instance of Sir Thomas Dugdale's resignation, Morrison stated that in his view Dugdale should have remained loyal to his initial policy and resigned on grounds of collective responsibility, rather than change the policy to one in which he did not personally believe and then resign on the pretext that he was taking constitutional responsibility for his officials.[155]

The debate was wound up by the home secretary, Sir David Maxwell-Fyfe, who also addressed himself to issues of ministers' responsibilities to Parliament. Famously, Maxwell-Fyfe distinguished between four different situations. First, 'in the case where there is an explicit order by a minister, the minister must protect the civil servant who has carried out his order'. Secondly, 'equally, where the civil servant acts properly in accordance with policy laid down by the minister, the minister must protect and defend him'. Thirdly, 'where an official makes a mistake or causes some delay, but not on an important issue of policy and not where a claim to individual rights is seriously involved, the minister acknowledges the mistake and he accepts the responsibility, although he is not personally involved. He states that he will take corrective action in the department . . . [but] he would not . . . expose the official to public criticism.' Finally, 'where action has been taken by a civil servant of which the minister disapproves and has no prior knowledge, and the conduct of the official is reprehensible, then there is no obligation on the part of the minister to endorse what he believes to be wrong or to defend what are clearly shown to be errors of his officers', but even in this situation,

---

[154] Ibid., col. 1274.   [155] Ibid., col. 1282.

Maxwell-Fyfe continued, the minister will 'of course' remain 'constitutionally responsible to Parliament for the fact that something has gone wrong, and he alone can tell Parliament what had occurred and render an account of his stewardship'.[156] As for the idea that government had grown so large that ministers could not properly keep track of their departments, Maxwell-Fyfe dismissed this notion, stating that this could be dealt with by ministers laying down adequate instructions for their department's operations.

This is an extremely weak precedent for the position adopted by John Major's government. The purpose of Maxwell-Fyfe's speech was to indicate that contrary to popular fears at the time, ministers were fully responsible to Parliament for the actions and failures of civil servants. This purpose is entirely at odds with the more recent government contributions to the development of the doctrine of ministerial responsibility, which are more concerned with limiting ministers' responsibilities, rather than laying them out as fully as possible. Further, nowhere in Maxwell-Fyfe's speech is there any indication that there might be a constitutionally recognized distinction between responsibility and accountability. On the contrary, the essence of his speech is that ministers are both responsible and accountable to Parliament in all four of his situations. In all four examples, a minister has to 'render an account of his stewardship' and at all times ministers remain 'of course . . . constitutionally responsible'.

For thirty years constitutional commentators misunderstood the reasons for Dugdale's resignation. From D. N. Chester (writing in *Public Administration* in 1954) onwards, such figures as Bernard Levin, Anthony Sampson, H. W. R. Wade, and John Mackintosh all—wrongly—asserted that Dugdale resigned because he felt constitutionally bound to resign for the failures of his civil servants even though such failings were not his personal fault.[157] Only since the government's records of the Crichel Down affair became available in the mid-1980s (under the thirty year rule of the Public Records Act) has this myth been exploded.[158] Dugdale did not sacrifice himself on the altar of constitutional convention: he resigned because his inherited (socialist) policy of keeping farms under state control was hated by Tory back-benchers[159] to such an extent that eventually he lost support in cabinet (which is why he had to announce the change in policy just before he resigned in July 1954). Dugdale's resignation was the first aspect of Crichel Down that suffered from years of misunderstanding. It is imperative that Maxwell-Fyfe's

---

[156] Ibid., cols. 1285–7.

[157] See J. A. G. Griffith, 'Crichel Down: The Most Famous Farm in British Constitutional History' (1987) 1 *Contemporary Record* 35, at p. 36.

[158] See especially I. F. Nicolson, *The Mystery of Crichel Down* (Oxford: Clarendon Press, 1986).

[159] Especially those from the shires who were supported by the national farmers' union and the country landowners' association.

speech does not now suffer the same fate. A rereading of the debates from 1954 shows that the refinements which more recent Conservative government ministers have sought to make to the doctrine of ministerial responsibility are a good deal more novel than those ministers would like to imagine. Crichel Down cannot be used as a crutch to support the crippled version of what is a central tenet of the British constitution and a vital reinforcement of parliamentary democracy.

The Aftermath of Scott: the Public Service Committee

In the light of the Scott report, these matters were extensively examined during 1996 by the public service committee. The public service committee is a departmental select committee of the House of Commons, made up of eleven MPs. In 1996 it had a Conservative majority of one. Its chairman was Giles Radice MP, a Labour MP. It was established in December 1995 as the departmental select committee in respect of the office of public service (OPS) which was reorganized in July of that year.[160] OPS comprised the public service functions and responsibilities of the former office of public service and science,[161] together with the deregulation and competitiveness responsibilities formerly discharged by the DTI. In John Major's last cabinet, the minister in charge of the OPS was a cabinet minister, the chancellor of the Duchy of Lancaster. At the time of the committee's investigation of ministerial responsibility this was Roger Freeman.[162]

By the time the Scott report was published the public service committee had already decided to commence an investigation into ministerial responsibility and next steps agencies, in part in response to the Michael Howard/Derek Lewis episode, and in part as a follow-up to the 1994 report of the committee's predecessor, the treasury and civil service committee.[163] After the publication of the Scott report, it became clear that the House of Commons would need to look more generally at questions of ministerial responsibility, and the committee accordingly broadened its inquiry, although its initial focus on next steps agencies remained a part of the investigation. The committee took

[160] OPS was reorganized in the reshuffle which followed John Major's resignation and subsequent re-election as leader of the Conservative party. It was in this reshuffle that Michael Heseltine became deputy prime minister and first secretary of state. OPS became one of the government departments which reported to Mr Heseltine. See Public Service Committee, *Work of the OPS*, HC (1995–96) 147, Jan. 1996.

[161] The science responsibilities of the former OPSS were transferred to the DTI in July 1995.

[162] Previous holders of this post in John Major's cabinet (William Waldegrave and David Hunt) had also had responsibility for overseeing the citizen's charter and open government. Interestingly, David Hunt became one of the Conservative members of the select committee after he left the government in 1995.

[163] Treasury and Civil Service Committee, *The Role of the Civil Service*, HC (1993–94) 27.

evidence—oral and written[164]—throughout the spring and summer of 1996 and issued its unanimous report in late July of that year.[165]

The work of the committee and its report are extremely important and represent a valuable contribution to the issues addressed in this chapter (and indeed throughout this book). While not all of the committee's recommendations had been put into effect by the time of the general election of May 1997, significant changes had been made. The first substantive chapter of the committee's report (paragraphs 8–33) deals in detail with the overall framework of ministerial responsibility and with the purported distinction between responsibility and accountability. Like its predecessor committee (the treasury and civil service committee) the public service committee declared itself to be uncertain that the distinction is a useful one.[166] In a strong statement, the committee rejected the notion that the doctrine of ministerial responsibility could be segregated into two separate components: the committee stated that 'it is not possible absolutely to distinguish an area in which a minister is personally responsible, and liable to take blame, from one in which he is constitutionally accountable'.[167] However, although the doctrine could not be divided into two wholly separate parts, the committee did recognize that it consisted of two complementary aspects, which it characterized as the 'obligation to give an account' and the 'liability to be held to account'.[168] The former obliges 'the executive . . . to provide full information about and explain its actions in Parliament so that [it is] subject to proper democratic scrutiny'.[169] The latter requires ministers 'to respond to concerns and criticism raised in Parliament' about the actions and failures to act of their departments and agencies. The committee stated that 'a minister has to conduct himself, and direct the work of his department in a manner likely to ensure that he retains the confidence both of his own party and of the House'.[170]

The government's response to the committee's recommendations on ministerial responsibility was largely positive. The government agreed that no 'absolute distinction between constitutional accountability and personal responsibility' could be drawn[171] although it did continue to press the point that even if the distinction is not absolute, it is nonetheless a useful one in

---

[164] Oral evidence was taken from a variety of academics, civil servants, and MPs and also from Sir Richard Scott and other members of the Scott inquiry team. The minutes of the oral evidence are published as vol. III of the report. Memoranda of written evidence are published as vol. II.

[165] Public Service Committee, *Ministerial Accountability and Responsibility*, HC (1995–96) 313.

[166] Ibid., para. 18.

[167] Ibid., para. 21. In the subsequent debate in the House of Commons on the committee's report, the committee's chairman, Giles Radice MP, stated that 'the committee rejected the distinction that Sir Robin Butler attempted to draw . . . between accountability and responsibility'. See HC Deb., Vol. 290, col. 273, 12 Feb. 1997.

[168] Ibid., para. 32.   [169] Ibid.   [170] Ibid.

[171] *Government Response to the Report of the Public Service Committee on Ministerial Accountability and Responsibility*, HC (1996–97) 67, p. vi (Nov. 1996).

certain circumstances. Importantly, the government also agreed with the committee that ministers must 'fully discharge their obligations to account to Parliament for their [own and for] their department's policies, decisions and actions and . . . [must] respond to criticism made in Parliament. It is for Parliament to determine whether it is satisfied with the account it receives and what sanctions, if any, should follow.'[172] This last sentence is crucial and welcome, as it indicates that by late 1996 the government had accepted the essential proposition which it had earlier seemed to deny that sanctions, including forcing a ministerial resignation, could be imposed by Parliament if it was unhappy with a minister even if that minister had not knowingly misled Parliament. In a welcome change of tone, far less belligerent than had been adopted in the heat of the debate on the Scott report the previous February, the government in November 1996 conceded that 'where a failure has occurred it is important for the government to demonstrate to Parliament that the appropriate action has been taken to put right what went wrong, and to prevent any recurrence. This is why one of the areas for which a minister takes direct personal responsibility is responding to major failure or expressions of parliamentary or public concern.'[173]

This may be welcome, but it is also late. The government should have taken this line in February, although if it had done so it would of course have been considerably more difficult for William Waldegrave (and for that matter for Sir Nicholas Lyell, the attorney general)[174] to cling onto office. As we saw, Waldegrave simply did not take responsibility in the way the Conservative government later conceded he should have done for the major failures identified in the Scott report and neither did he fully respond to the parliamentary concerns which were expressed at the time. It is one thing for the government quietly to state in a little-noticed response to a select committee report that all is well with ministerial responsibility at a time when ministers' necks are not on the block: it is another thing for the government to keep to its word when the going gets a little tougher. The Major government was not so quick to remind Parliament that it had agreed that ministers were responsible for responding to major failures and to parliamentary concerns when Douglas Hogg (minister for agriculture) denied that he had anything to do with his department's failure adequately to distribute a key report into meat hygiene[175] or when Nicholas Soames (minister for the armed forces) denied that he had anything to do with the MOD's knowledge of a likely connection between the use of pesticides and gulf war syndrome.[176] While the government's response to the public service committee's approach to ministerial

---

[172] Ibid.   [173] Ibid.
[174] The position of Sir Nicholas Lyell and his role in the Scott report and in the parliamentary debates which followed it are considered further in ch. 5.
[175] See the *Times*, 6 Mar. 1997 and the *Guardian*, 7 Mar. 1997.
[176] See the *Guardian*, 28 Feb. 1997.

responsibility was largely positive, even at this late stage some distance remained between the Major government's words and the actions of its ministers.

The public service committee argued, as the Scott report had done, that the primary constitutional importance of ministerial responsibility lies not in the occasional drama of forcing resignations but in the quality of the daily account of their policies, decisions, and actions that ministers provide to Parliament. In this vein the committee stated that 'proper and rigorous scrutiny and accountability may be more important to Parliament's ability to correct error than forcing resignations'.[177] However, because of the central constitutional importance of such ministerial responsibilities to Parliament, the committee also took the view that it should not be ministers alone who set the terms of the debate about their obligations to Parliament. As we have seen, it has been a feature of the purported refinements to the constitutional doctrine of ministerial responsibility that they have been introduced by the government and, in terms of making amendments to QPM, also in certain aspects put into effect by the government. What sort of constitution is it that allows the government—the very creature that the constitution purports to regulate—to set the terms of its own constitutional regulation? As the committee put it, 'it seems extraordinary to us that the only explicit statement of how ministers are expected to discharge their obligations to Parliament appears not in a parliamentary document, but in a document issued by the prime minister which deals (among other things) with the travelling expenses of their spouses and the acceptance of decorations from foreign governments'.[178]

In an important recommendation the public service committee accordingly proposed that the House of Commons should do more to make it clear that ministers owe their responsibilities to Parliament not because the government says so (in QPM and elsewhere) but because the British parliamentary constitution ordains it. Ministerial responsibility is an obligation which ministers owe to Parliament because Parliament requires it, not because the government has voluntarily submitted to it. The committee recommended that the House of Commons should pass a resolution along the following lines:

All members of this House and all witnesses who come before it are obliged not to obstruct or impede it in the performance of its functions . . . This applies to ministers and to civil servants giving evidence in Parliament, just as it applies to any other person; and because ministers have a duty to account to Parliament for the policies, decisions and actions of their departments and agencies, the House will regard breaches by them of the obligation described above as particularly serious. Ministers must take special care, therefore, to provide information that is full and accurate to Parliament,

---

[177] Public Service Committee, *Ministerial Accountability and Responsibility*, HC (1995–96) 313, para. 27.
[178] Ibid., para. 53.

and must, in their dealings with Parliament, conduct themselves frankly and with candour . . .[179]

In its response to the committee's report, the government stated that it shared the committee's view that there could be value in the House making it explicit how it expects ministers to discharge their responsibilities to Parliament, but that to have full authority any resolution would have to have cross-party support. The Conservative government was unable to support the entirety of the committee's wording on the ground that it felt that the resolution as drafted would have the effect of weakening civil servants' responsibility to ministers by making them more directly responsible to Parliament.[180] However, Roger Freeman consulted with the major opposition parties in both Houses of Parliament to establish whether cross-party support might be attainable for some form of resolution before the pending dissolution of Parliament. For a while, it appeared that this would not be possible, as the Liberal Democrat party was strongly of the view that any resolution should declare that chief executives of next steps agencies should be directly and independently accountable and responsible to select committees (and not give evidence to them on behalf of ministers). As this idea has always been resisted by the Conservatives, it seemed that no such resolution would be agreed. The House of Commons debated the issue on 12 February 1997[181] and while spokesmen for all the main parties expressed their hopes that a resolution could be passed before dissolution, it is evident that at this stage there remained significant differences between the parties.

However, on 20 March 1997, the day before the House of Commons was controversially prorogued,[182] a (very) short debate took place in the House of Lords during which a resolution was introduced and passed, apparently with all-party consent.[183] The resolution provides that:

In the opinion of this House, the following principles should govern the conduct of ministers of the crown in relation to Parliament:

---

[179] Ibid., para. 60.

[180] See *Government Response to the Report of the Public Service Committee on Ministerial Accountability and Responsibility*, HC (1996–97) 67, p. ix. This issue is considered in more detail in the next chapter.

[181] See HC Deb., Vol. 290, cols. 273–93, 12 Feb. 1997. The debate usefully sets out the positions of the leading players: see in particular the speeches of Giles Radice (the chairman of the public service committee), Robert Maclennan (for the Liberal Democrats), Derek Foster (for the Labour party), and Roger Freeman (for the government).

[182] The controversy surrounded the unusually long period between prorogation (21 March) and dissolution (8 April) and speculation on the opposition benches that Parliament was being prorogued early on the insistence of the prime minister in order to delay the publication of the full report by Sir Gordon Downey on the so-called 'cash-for-questions' affair.

[183] See HL Deb., Vol. 579, col. 1055. Lord Richard (for the Labour party) stated that the resolution represented a 'sensible statement on ministerial responsibility'. Lord Harris of Greenwich stated that Lord Jenkins of Hillhead (for the Liberal Democrats) had been consulted and that 'he is content, as are the rest of us on these benches'. See ibid., col. 1057 for both statements.

(1) Ministers have a duty to Parliament to account, and be held to account, for the policies, decisions and actions of their departments and next steps agencies;

(2) It is of paramount importance that ministers should give accurate and truthful information to Parliament, correcting any inadvertent error at the earliest opportunity. Ministers who knowingly mislead Parliament will be expected to offer their resignation to the prime minister;

(3) Ministers should be as open as possible with Parliament, refusing to provide information only when disclosure would not be in the public interest;

(4) Ministers should require civil servants who give evidence before parliamentary committees on their behalf and under their directions to be as helpful as possible in providing accurate, truthful and full information;

(5) The interpretation of 'public interest' in paragraph (3) shall be decided in accordance with statute and the Government's Code of Practice on Access to Government Information . . .; and compliance with the duty in paragraph (4) shall be in accordance with the duties and responsibilities of civil servants set out in the Civil Service Code . . .

At 2 o'clock in the morning of 20 March the House of Commons passed a similar resolution, without bothering either to hold a debate or to have a division.[184]

These resolutions mark an important constitutional breakthrough. No longer is ministerial responsibility merely an unwritten constitutional convention. No longer is it even a doctrine of political practice formally written down only in the government's own documents. It is now a clear parliamentary rule, set down in resolutions by both Houses of Parliament, although of course future Parliaments are (legally) at liberty to rescind or modify previous resolutions at a later date.[185] The point is, the government acting on its own cannot now change the terms of ministers' responsibilities to Parliament in the way that the Conservative government did throughout its period in office. How happy should we be, however, with the contents of the resolutions? Does their detail represent a victory for the government, for the Butler doctrine, for the other refinements which the Conservatives made to ministerial responsibility?

---

[184] See HC Deb., Vol. 292, cols. 1046–7, 19 Mar. 1997 (it was still 19 Mar. according to the parliamentary clock, and therefore according to *Hansard*, even though in the real world it was 20 Mar.). On the resolutions generally, see Diana Woodhouse, 'Ministerial Responsibility: Something Old, Something New' [1997] *Public Law* 262. The words of the House of Commons' resolution are the same as those of the House of Lords' resolution, but the two are differently structured. In the Commons version para. 5 of the Lords resolution is interwoven with paras. 3 and 4.

[185] In the debate in the House of Commons on ministerial responsibility in February 1997 Roger Freeman stated that the government had been advised that a resolution of the House of Commons will 'remain through sessions and Parliaments until the House wishes to return to it. Indeed, the House can return to a motion that we pass at any time, and amend it at any time.' See HC Deb., Vol. 290, col. 293, 12 Feb. 1997. Erskine May has little to say about resolutions in the House of Lords (see 21st edn., 1989, p. 425 but states that resolutions in the House of Commons can be rescinded or modified by subsequent Parliaments, but only once notice has been given (see pp. 360–3).

Or has Parliament effectively put an end to all these changes and reasserted its historic constitutional role of holding ministers fully responsible and account-able for everything which they and their departments do?

The answer is that the resolutions are a compromise. On the one hand, as the government would have wanted, the resolutions talk of a duty to 'account' and a liability to be held to 'account', rather than focusing on min-isterial 'responsibilities'. Similarly, that word 'knowingly' keeps its place in the context of misleading information, and finally, civil servants are still to give evidence to select committees only on behalf of ministers. All of these aspects of the resolutions accord with the Conservative government's views. On the other hand, however, the interests of Parliament and the general thrust of the recommendations of the public service committee have been accom-modated by insisting that ministers' responsibilities are not limited merely to giving an account but also extend to being liable for what they and their departments do. Similarly, even though the word 'knowingly' has not been scrubbed out, the resolutions make it quite clear that ministers' obligations extend beyond merely trying to ensure that they do not deliberately lie to Parliament: the resolutions state that ministers have a responsibility 'of para-mount importance' always to give accurate and truthful information to Parliament. Finally, although ministers will still have some degree of overall control as to what civil servants may tell select committees, ministers are now under a clear obligation to assist Parliament in its efforts to acquire helpful and full information from civil servants. This is a compromise, but from a constitutional point of view it is a very good one. The fact of the resolutions means that governments will no longer be able to seek to dictate the terms of the debate about the extent of ministers' obligations and responsibilities to Parliament, while the content of the resolutions should mean that, as long as Parliament has the political will to enforce them properly, ministers will find it considerably harder to escape parliamentary censure, whether it is directed at them or at their departments.

Conclusion

How then should we view the contribution which the Scott report and subse-quent developments have made to the debates on ministerial responsibility? In terms of what it stated on the subject of ministers and Parliament, the Scott report is best seen as but one of a number of exchanges between the govern-ment and others on the meaning and future development of ministers' respon-sibilities to Parliament. That Scott himself did not see the report in this light, and that his comments on ministerial responsibility were not expressed in the context of a continuing conversation in Westminster and Whitehall about the nature of ministers' responsibilities, is a weakness of the report, stemming in part from Scott's refusal to appoint constitutional experts (or lay assessors) to aid him in navigating what was after all his first foray into this particular constitutional quagmire. The report's lack of appreciation as to the scale of the debate that had already been conducted on the committee corridor since at least the Westland affair in 1985–6 led to the report's rather flat and unreflective acceptance of the Conservative government's quite radical stance on ministerial responsibility. The Scott report simply did not appreciate the degree to which the government's positions on these matters were contested and novel, not to say also dubious and self-serving.

However, read in the light of the 1994 report from the treasury and civil service committee which preceded it and in the light of the subsequent work of the public service committee, the Scott report has helped to contribute to a welcome, timely, and unusually thorough reappraisal of the doctrine of ministerial responsibility. Certainly the doctrine is in a healthier condition now than it was at the beginning of the 1990s, not least because of the attention that has been given to the government's attempts to refine (some might say redefine) the meaning of responsibility. There are those who argue that we should simply abandon the pretence of ministerial responsibility, which, it is argued, is nothing more than a 'conspiracy against openness'[186] and does nothing other than 'obscur[e] real responsibility for decisions'.[187] No doubt, if the Conservative government had won the debate, there would have been much in this. The Conservative position clearly left an accountability gap, as exposed by Graham Mather MEP in his evidence to the public service committee: under what he called the Butler doctrine, a minister is responsible only when some personal responsibility can be pinned on him. Ministerial accountability is discharged simply by giving information to Parliament. Even if this information is misleading, the minister will not be responsible unless it has been given in bad faith. Officials, meanwhile, remain accountable only to their departmental heads (ultimately ministers) and not to Parliament.[188] As we have seen, however, this narrow version of ministerial responsibility enjoys no constitutional precedent (the government's reliance on Crichel Down having been persistent but mistaken) and has been so thoroughly attacked by the two select committee reports (of 1994 and 1996) that even the architects of the Butler version were forced to concede that 'the government agrees that it is not always possible to make an absolute distinction between constitutional accountability and personal responsibility'.[189]

[186] Oral evidence of Norman Lewis, Public Service Committee, *Ministerial Accountability and Responsibility*, HC (1995–96) 313, Vol. III, Q 729.

[187] Norman Lewis and Diane Longley, 'Ministerial Responsibility: The Next Steps' [1996] *Public Law* 490, at p. 495.

[188] See Public Service Committee, *Ministerial Accountability and Responsibility*, HC (1995–96) 313, Vol. III, p. 121.

[189] See *Government Response to the Report of the Public Service Committee on Ministerial Accountability and Responsibility*, HC (1996–97) 67, p. vi.

So where are we now? Clearly, it is no longer sufficient simply to proclaim that ministers are constitutionally responsible to Parliament for everything that they do and for everything that is done in their name by their civil servants, and hope that everyone will agree on what this doctrine will mean in practice. But, if before the Scott report it was unclear what the doctrine would mean in practice, after the report it should no longer be. Before the report, the focus was on ministerial resignations. When would they resign? Was resignation always a constitutional issue? Did the practice of resignations indicate that ministers were really responsible not to Parliament, but to the prime minister, or to the minister's own party or back-benchers? And so on. These were the questions which constitutional scholars from S. E. Finer to Diana Woodhouse to Rodney Brazier have focused on for some time.[190] Now, the focus has shifted away from the occasional drama of resignation towards a more mundane but far more important concern: namely, the quality of the account of their (and their departments') policies, decisions, and actions that ministers must give to Parliament on a day-to-day basis.[191] That is the first important step forwards that been made as a result of the Scott report.

However, in its understandable enthusiasm for a move away from focusing on matters of resignation, the Conservative government put forward a radical version of ministerial responsibility which undoubtedly went too far in limiting the responsibilities of ministers, as the two select committee reports made plain. Just because greater attention is now being paid to the daily account that ministers give to Parliament of their activities this does not mean that questions of responsibility are to be diluted. To move the focus away from resignations is not to trivialize them, and it is certainly not to suggest that ministers should be afforded greater protection against being forced to resign or that ministers should be regarded as being responsible for less, as the Butler doctrine would seem to indicate. At the heart of the Conservative refinements—all three of them—lies a serious confusion. In attempting to explain away previous confusions about the terms responsibility and accountability, the government created a new confusion. That is to say, the Butler doctrine seems to equate responsibility with resignation. Under the Butler doctrine ministerial responsibility becomes a *personal* matter—ministers' *constitutional* obligations lie in the field of giving an account, of being accountable. This is wrong. Clearly, resignation will be a personal matter, in the sense that everybody now accepts that ministers do not resign and will not be expected to resign over matters for which they are not personally at fault.

---

[190] See S. E. Finer, 'The Individual Responsibility of Ministers' (1956) 34 *Public Administration* 377; Diana Woodhouse, *Ministers and Parliament: Accountability in Theory and Practice* (Oxford: Clarendon Press, 1994); and Rodney Brazier, 'It *is* a Constitutional Issue: Fitness for Ministerial Office in the 1990s' [1994] *Public Law* 431.

[191] This is not to say, however, that it would be right to reduce ministerial responsibility solely to questions of information and accountability, any more than it would be to reduce it to issues of resignation.

That old myth of Crichel Down was laid to rest more than ten years ago. However, ministerial responsibility should not be reduced to a personal matter: ministerial responsibility is a constitutional obligation which ministers owe to Parliament. It is an obligation which includes—but which is emphatically not limited to—explaining what has happened. Giving an account is clearly one part of being responsible, but it is not the whole story. Responsibility of ministers to Parliament requires not only that ministers should explain their (and their departments') conduct to Parliament, but also that ministers can be ordered to stop or reverse what they (or their departments) are doing.[192] Responsibility implies that there are sanctions. Forcing a resignation is merely the ultimate sanction of last resort—that is why it is only to be used when a minister is personally at fault.

In 1994 the treasury and civil service committee stated that ministerial responsibility 'depends upon two vital elements: clarity about who can be held to account and held responsible when things go wrong; [and] confidence that Parliament is able to gain the accurate information required to hold the executive to account and to ascertain where responsibility lies'.[193] While the committee was 'not convinced' that the Butler doctrine met these requirements, the interpretation of ministerial responsibility advocated by the (unanimous) report of the public service committee and the text of the subsequent resolutions surely do. Ministers are constitutionally responsible to Parliament for their (and for their departments') policies, decisions, and actions. That responsibility includes an obligation to account, but it also means that ministers must respond to and act on Parliament's concerns and criticisms.

In the introduction it was suggested that the Scott report demonstrated the failure, but also the hope, of Parliament. Both failure and hope are amply illustrated here. Parliament failed to be sufficiently critical of and concerned by the constitutionally improper antics of ministers such as William Waldegrave and Michael Howard. But Parliament has also subsequently agreed that the government's self-serving refinements to the doctrine of ministerial responsibility (which allowed the likes of Waldegrave and Howard to avoid more severe parliamentary censure) are unacceptable. While there have been calls for disputed cases of ministerial responsibility to be resolved not by Parliament but by the courts or by some kind of Parliamentary Commissioner for Accountability,[194] the hope is that Parliament has learnt its lesson. Ministers are all drawn from Parliament, they exercise governmen-

---

[192] See Geoffrey Marshall's written evidence, Public Service Committee, *Ministerial Accountability and Responsibility*, HC (1995–96) 313, Vol. II, p. 33.

[193] Treasury and Civil Service Committee, *The Role of the Civil Service*, HC (1993–94) 27, para. 132.

[194] See, for example, Sir Richard Scott, 'Ministerial Accountability' [1996] *Public Law* 410. These possible reforms were considered by the public service committee, but formed no part of its recommendations.

tal power and authority for only as long as Parliament allows, and it is there-fore preferable that it should if possible remain Parliament (rather than courts or bureaucrats) to which ministers should owe their obligations and responsibilities. Now that the public service committee's rejection of the Butler doctrine and of the other refinements which John Major's government sought to make has been endorsed in the resolutions passed by both Houses of Parliament, after the failures of the 1990s, the path is once again clear for ministers to accept their constitutional responsibilities to Parliament, and, equally, for Parliament to enforce its constitutional authority over the government. The changes which Parliament has made in the aftermath of the failures illustrated by the Scott story rejuvenate the hope that ministerial responsibility can return to its proper status as an effective weapon in Parliament's armoury by which ministers are held fully to account and are made truly, and constitutionally, responsible.

2

The Civil Service

THE civil service played a prominent role in the Scott story, yet escaped any mention in the report's recommendations and hardly figured in the subsequent parliamentary debates. Ever present but rarely noticed, central yet ignored: such has been the habitual fate of the British civil service in considerations by constitutional lawyers, and the Scott report was no exception. Yet the civil service was subject to the most wide-ranging constitutional reforms of the long Conservative period in office. Although during the 1997 general election campaign John Major frequently raised constitutional reform as an area where Labour could not be trusted and was a threat to the future of this United Kingdom, his government was the most constitutionally reform-minded since Wilson's first administration in the 1960s. Nowhere was this more evident than with the civil service. The massive changes that the Conservatives imposed on the civil service started under Lady Thatcher but only accelerated once John Major took over in 1990. Given a more public platform and a more coherent direction under the auspices of his much maligned Citizen's Charter in 1991, the reforms affected all aspects of life in the civil service, including overall numbers, recruitment, contracts and conditions of employment, as well as issues of constitutional governance and regulation.

The Scott report did not consider many of these issues overtly, but the report did contain a number of passages in which civil servants figured prominently and were subjected to considerable criticism. From these passages we can build up a picture of the civil service at work: how civil servants relate to ministers; how they act towards Parliament; where they come from; and how they conceive of their responsibilities. The picture is a revealing one, and gives rise to some serious questions about the constitutional role of the civil service, both in theory and in practice. As with questions of ministerial responsibility, these questions were not just left hanging in the air after the publication of the Scott report. The public service committee which examined ministerial accountability and responsibility in the light of Scott also considered issues concerning the civil service. The work of that committee, and the broader context of the changes which the civil service has undergone since the 1980s, are the subject of the later part of this chapter. First, however, let us turn to how the civil service fared in the Scott report.

Civil Servants and Ministers: Evidence from the Scott Report

Export licensing for defence equipment to be sold to countries such as Iraq was not a matter for only one government department. Although there was a government-wide policy on exports to Iran and Iraq (as represented in the Howe guidelines, considered in the previous chapter) this was a policy which had to be implemented not by one government department but by three: the department of trade and industry, the foreign office, and the ministry of defence. As is usually the case in government, the policy, while it was made (and changed) by ministers, was implemented on a day-to-day basis by civil servants. Although junior ministers were from time to time involved in making particularly difficult or important decisions as to how the guidelines should be interpreted or applied in any particular case, this was more normally a matter for officials to determine, rather than ministers. In doing so, how closely did departmental officials stick to the stated government policy? While it is only natural for each of the three departments to have slightly different concerns in mind when applying the guidelines (it is only to be expected that the DTI should be more concerned about facilitating British trade, that the MOD should be more worried about the defence of the realm, and that the FCO should be preoccupied with the foreign relations implications) the Scott report was replete with examples indicating that the differences between the three departments went much further. It appears that officials in each department, but especially in the DTI, developed their own strong attitude towards defence exports to Iraq, attitudes which were often seemingly independent of the Howe guidelines and which were allowed to develop into departmental policies of their own. The Scott report was very critical of this tendency and expressed disquiet about the distance which was evident between the 'prohibitory language' of the Howe guidelines and the much more pro-trade attitude prevalent in the export licensing bureau of the DTI which resulted in export licence applications not being subjected to the 'rigorous scrutiny' which ministers had claimed.[1]

This alternative policy or independent culture which grew in the DTI (and also to a lesser extent in the FCO and in the defence export services secretariat in the MOD[2]) was a significant factor in determining how 'official' government policy was interpreted both during and after the Iran–Iraq war. While ministers were not routinely involved in the daily administration of the Howe

---

[1] See para. D2.428.

[2] Civil servants in the MOD and the FCO were criticized in the Scott report for making important decisions independently of ministers over the matter of defence exports to Jordan, widely known to have been a conduit to Iraq. See, for example, paras. E2.19 and E2.62. Similarly, unnamed civil servants in the MOD were criticized in the report for failing to keep ministers properly informed on big projects such as Astra and Project Babylon, or supergun, on which see para. F3.88.

guidelines, when difficult or new issues arose, they would be referred up to ministers to be resolved. From time to time, therefore, the three ministers (Alan Clark, William Waldegrave, and Lord Trefgarne) would meet to discuss whether a particular set of export licence applications should be granted or not. Many of these meetings (and the decisions which the ministers took during them) proved to be controversial, and they received quite lengthy consideration in the Scott report.[3]

The quality of the decision making at these interdepartmental ministerial meetings would obviously be directly affected by the quality of the information which the ministers could take to the meetings, and for that information, of course, ministers were wholly dependent on the officials in their departments who dealt with the detail of export licensing on a daily basis. How did such officials perform? On a number of occasions, civil servants were found to be seriously wanting in the advice they offered to ministers. In 1989, for example, the three ministers met several times to consider various export licence applications which had been submitted by Matrix Churchill. The DTI briefing for one such meeting stated that intelligence reports disclosed 'no evidence' that previous Matrix Churchill shipments had been used in Iraq for the manufacture of munitions. In fact there was extensive intelligence that clearly indicated exactly that: i.e. that previous Matrix Churchill exports were being used by Iraq to make weapons, as the DTI officials knew.[4] Why did the DTI's civil servants not draw this to their minister's attention? According to the Scott report, 'the main reason for the deficiencies was a lack of concern on the part of [the officials] about the possible, or even probable, use of the machine tools for the manufacture of . . . weapons'.[5] Although end-use and military purpose were clearly relevant as far as official government policy was concerned, they were of little apparent concern in the DTI. The Scott report took a dim view of the stance adopted by the DTI's officials, describing their work as 'highly unsatisfactory' and their advice to the minister as 'positively misleading'.[6] At one point the Scott report went even further in its trenchant criticism of the DTI civil servants' attitude towards defence exports to Iraq, describing their inaction over this matter as 'unacceptable negligence'.[7]

---

[3] The ministers' decisions and the intelligence information on which they were based are outlined in greater detail below in ch. 4.

[4] See further ch. 4, below.

[5] See para. D6.135. The two civil servants responsible for the briefing were named in the Scott report. They were Tony Steadman, the head of the export licensing bureau, and Eric Beston, Steadman's boss in the DTI.

[6] See paras. D6.133 and D6.135. Further criticisms of the same officials were made at para. D6.144.

[7] See para. D6.70. It will not always be so easy to pin the blame on any one individual. In the previous chapter the statement on supergun made to Parliament by the late Nicholas Ridley MP was considered. Mr Ridley did not apparently know that his colleague Sir Hal Miller MP had expressed his concern about British involvement in supergun some two years previously. Officials in the DTI knew this. Why was the secretary of state not informed? This information was contained in a submission to Mr Ridley, but he did not apparently read it. Instead, his principal

The Scott report was also critical of briefings drawn up for these meetings by civil servants in the MOD. Instead of writing their own briefing papers using sources from within the MOD, the MOD officials borrowed from the FCO's briefings, with the consequence that they failed to take into account the views of the defence intelligence staff.[8] In the words of the Scott report, the MOD officials 'failed to put before the minister a balanced recommendation'. The MOD ministers were 'ill served' by their officials.[9] These criticisms relate to the working relationship between relatively senior civil servants (not permanent secretaries, but officials of grade five and above) and junior ministers outside the cabinet. But the failures in effective communication between officials and ministers identified in the Scott report were not limited to this level of government. At the end of the Iran–Iraq war, the prime minister Lady Thatcher had made it clear to her government colleagues that she wished to be 'kept very closely in touch at every stage and consulted on all relevant decisions' regarding defence sales to Iran or Iraq.[10] Yet she was neither informed of nor consulted about the changes in government policy which junior ministers agreed in 1988 and 1989. Quite whose fault this was is unclear in the report: did junior ministers and their officials fail to keep No. 10 informed, or did Sir Charles Powell, Lady Thatcher's foreign policy adviser and personal secretary on foreign policy matters, fail to pass on to her the correspondence which the three departments had copied to him?[11] Lady Thatcher's line was that she was not involved and should not have been involved (even though she had stated that she wanted to be) with such matters of detail, with matters of what she saw as the implementation of the guidelines rather than the overall direction of government policy.[12]

Civil Servants beyond Government: More from the Scott Report

If the first constitutional problem concerning the civil service which was illustrated by the Scott report was the poor state of many officials' working

private secretary (Mr Stanley) read it, and failed to pass on to the secretary of state the details of Sir Hal's prior involvement. Whose fault is that: Mr Ridley's for not reading his briefing, or Mr Stanley's for summarizing the 'wrong' bits of the submission when he briefed the secretary of state? See paras. F4.31–3.

[8] DIS is the part of the intelligence community which operates within the MOD. DIS and its role and relations with other parts of the intelligence community are discussed in ch. 4, below.

[9] See para. D6.102. The official who was most closely responsible for this failure was named as Mr Barrett, of the defence export services secretariat in the MOD. See also paras. D6.128 and D6.148.

[10] See para. D3.102.

[11] It remains unclear exactly why the Scott inquiry did not get to the bottom of this matter. While Lady Thatcher did give oral evidence, Sir Charles Powell, rather surprisingly, was not called to give oral evidence.

[12] The *Guardian* parodied this evidence brilliantly with the comment, 'her performance was part Nixon, who took the responsibility but not the blame, part Reagan, who remembered nothing, and part Ceausescu, who regretted nothing and how dare they?' See Matthew Engel, 'It's no good asking me, I was only prime minister', the *Guardian*, 9 Dec. 1993.

relations with ministers, the second area of constitutional concern relates to civil servants' relations with the outside world beyond Whitehall. The Scott report contained telling criticisms of civil servants in their involvement in criminal courts, in the inquiry, and in Parliament. What all of these concerns have in common is an underlying worry that the civil service (or individuals within it) serve not the public interest which is their constitutional role, but some other more private or individual interest which may conflict with the public interest. These are problematic terms, and may not be easy to pin down, but before we consider them more carefully, let us look at the ways in which they arose in the Scott report.

The first and most obvious way in which the public interest and a private (or a commercial) interest collided in the Scott report concerns the membership of the civil service. One of the Conservative government's main aims in its extensive reforms of the civil service—and indeed of the public service more generally, in local as well as central government—was to make the public sector more like the private sector. The goal was to force the public sector to become more overtly concerned with questions of efficiency and good value for money than it had previously been.[13] One of the many mechanisms through which the government sought to realize this goal was through the greater recruitment of individuals into the civil service from industry and business, often on short-term contracts. One such individual was Sir Colin Chandler, who from 1985–9 was the head of defence sales in the MOD. Prior to his appointment Sir Colin had been a marketing director at British Aerospace (BAe), a company which was, among other things, trying to sell its Hawk aircraft to a number of countries around the world, including Iraq. One of the people Sir Colin had recruited to BAe was David Hastie, who was heavily involved in the Hawk project. In 1988 Mr Hastie was also, in turn, recruited to the MOD to work for one year as business development adviser to Sir Colin Chandler.[14] After his secondment to the MOD Mr Hastie, astonishingly, continued to play a significant part in the Hawk project, but now, apparently, on behalf of the government, not BAe. As the Scott report made clear, Mr Hastie was 'placed in a position of potential conflict between interest and duty'[15] which could easily and should certainly have been avoided. In a strong statement, the Scott report argued that the MOD was wrong not to

---

[13] See further below. There is now an extensive literature on 'new public management', as this process is often referred to. See for example C. D. Foster and F. J. Plowden, *The State Under Stress* (Buckingham: Open University Press, 1996) ch. 3; P. Barberis (ed.), *The Whitehall Reader* (Buckingham: Open University Press, 1996) ch. 5; N. Lewis, 'The Citizen's Charter and Next Steps: A New Way of Governing' (1993) 64 *Political Quarterly* 316; J. Stewart and K. Walsh, 'Change in the Management of Public Services' (1992) 70 *Public Administration* 499; and R. Rhodes, 'The Hollowing Out of the State: The Changing Nature of the Public Service in Britain' (1994) 65 *Political Quarterly* 138.

[14] See para. D6.29.

[15] See para. D6.34. The Scott report stated that this was not Mr Hastie's fault.

have ring-fenced Mr Hastie (whose salary during his secondment to the MOD continued to be paid by BAe) from involvement in Hawk or any other BAe project: 'the principle that people should not be placed in a position in which their interest and duty may conflict is not simply an ancient principle of equity . . . but also ought, in my opinion, to be regarded as a necessary principle to be applied to all secondment into government service from industry'.[16]

This episode represents an obvious, pecuniary, form of conflict of interest which is relatively easy to identify and to remedy. But there are other, more insidious, ways in which these questions can arise as well. As is well known, the immediate impetus behind the establishment of the Scott inquiry was the collapse of the Matrix Churchill trial. A key witness for the prosecution at that trial was Eric Beston, a senior official at the DTI with overall responsibility for the export licensing bureau. He was one of the civil servants in the DTI responsible for the much criticized ministerial briefings considered above. The Scott report reviewed the evidence which Mr Beston gave in court during the Matrix Churchill trial and found that it was 'not consistent' with intelligence reports on Matrix Churchill which Mr Beston had seen. According to the Scott report, Mr Beston's evidence 'was designed to avoid giving what he may have thought would be a damaging admission' (i.e. that the government knew that licensed exports shipped by Matrix Churchill had been used in Iraq for the manufacture of weapons and that the government knew this before subsequent export licences were granted for further shipments to Iraq).[17] In contrast to the evidence which he had given at the trial, before the Scott inquiry Mr Beston did concede that the government had indeed known more of the destiny of Matrix Churchill's exports than he had admitted in court. When asked why there was this apparent inconsistency between his evidence in court and before the inquiry, Mr Beston merely replied, 'I quite simply misled myself.'[18]

Mr Beston's colleague in the DTI, Tony Steadman, was also heavily criticized in the Scott report for his evidence. But whereas Mr Beston was criticized for his evidence in court, Mr Steadman was reprimanded for the evidence he gave to the inquiry. When giving oral evidence to the inquiry, Mr Steadman had sought to defend his attitude to at least some of Matrix Churchill's exports to Iraq by stating that he considered that the goods Matrix Churchill exported to Iraq for trade fairs would be returned to the UK once the trade fairs were finished, and that this justified the granting of the

---

[16] Ibid. In his evidence to the public service committee, Sir Michael Quinlan, the permanent secretary at the MOD, admitted that Mr Hastie's position had made him feel 'uneasy' and had been 'artificial and uncomfortable'. See *Ministerial Accountability and Responsibility*, HC (1995–96) 313, Vol. III, Q 178.

[17] See para. G17.13. In Scott's view, Mr Beston's evidence 'was overly conditioned by a desire to avoid answers that might prove embarrassing to senior officials and ministers': see para. G17.16.

[18] See para. G17.14.

export licences even when the government knew that previous Matrix Churchill goods had been used in arms manufacture. According to the Scott report this defence was a complete fabrication. Sir Richard wrote in the report that 'I do not accept this evidence . . . I do not accept for one moment that it was ever supposed by Matrix Churchill or by Mr Steadman that the machines would be returned to the UK. And they never were.'[19]

David Gore-Booth, former head of the Middle East desk (MED) at the FCO[20] was also criticized for the evidence he had given to the Scott inquiry. Although he had been in a position of some authority within the FCO and could (and in Scott's view should) have exercised his authority to ensure that ministers were better briefed, when this was pointed out to him during his oral evidence to the inquiry, he appeared wholly 'unconcerned' about the 'misleading nature' of his department's briefings to ministers.[21] In his report, Sir Richard complained that 'I found it a matter of regret that the impatience with the inquiry evinced by Mr Gore-Booth throughout his oral evidence seemed to prevent him from facing up to the possibility that deficiencies in MED procedures or errors by MED personnel might have contributed to the lamentable fact that a misleading submission had been placed before' the minister.[22]

It is not only the courts and the the Scott inquiry which suffered from civil servants' uncooperative attitudes or misleading evidence: Parliament too was a victim of this. In the light of Parliament's central constitutional role of holding the government to account, this is a matter of particular constitutional concern. It is well illustrated by the government's response to a letter sent in January 1987 to the prime minister from the former leader of the Liberal party, David Steel MP (as he then was). In his letter Mr Steel had requested that the government place in the library of the House of Commons a list of the defence equipment which UK firms had sold to Iran or to Iraq since 1980 so that MPs could judge for themselves whether the government's public claims that all such equipment was non-lethal were true or not. Sir Charles Powell suggested to the FCO that at the least, a list of the equipment sold to Iran in the previous two years could be placed in the library, but an official at the FCO's Middle East desk decided to recommend that no list at all could be issued. In his submission to the deputy under secretary of state at the FCO, the official (named in the Scott report as Mr Young) gave three reasons for his recommendation: that to place the information in the library would not be in conformity with previous government practice in this area; that to publish a list would expose the government to further pressure, at home and abroad; and that the list could be misleading if it did not make clear that there was in

---

[19] See para. D6.205.
[20] After he left the foreign office in London, Gore-Booth continued to develop a glittering career as a diplomat, as British ambassador first to Saudi Arabia, and then to India.
[21] See para. D6.159.   [22] Ibid.

some cases a difference between granting an export licence on the one hand and the goods in question actually being exported on the other. Mr Young's recommendation not to place any such list in the library of the House was accepted and the prime minister's curt reply to Mr Steel stated simply that it is not the 'normal practice of government to give details of individual export licences or applications'.[23]

Unsurprisingly, this episode was heavily criticized in the Scott report. The first and third of Mr Young's reasons were described in the report as being 'insubstantial'. Of the other reason, the Scott report stated, 'the avoidance of domestic criticism is, in my opinion, an unacceptable reason for withholding from Parliament information about the activities of government'.[24] Overall, the Scott report concluded that 'it is a striking feature of Mr Young's sub-mission that no specific reference was made to the public interest in Parliament being fully informed'.[25] Why is it that (at least some) civil servants appear to be more interested in assisting the government in withholding infor-mation from Parliament than in serving what the Scott report described as the public interest? This story—as with all the issues concerning civil servants raised in the Scott report—highlights the question of what civil servants are for. Are they the servants of the state, of the public, of parliamentary democ-racy, or of the political party which happens to form the government of the day?

The Constitutional Position of the Civil Service

As with the constitutional position of ministers, discussed in the previous chapter, the status and role of the civil service are matters which are some-what shrouded in constitutional convention, royal prerogative, unwritten assumption, and outmoded precedent. At law, civil servants are servants of the crown, employed under the royal prerogative. While there is no single legal definition of civil servants, they are generally seen as 'servants of the crown, other than holders of political or judicial offices, who are employed in a civil [i.e. non-military] capacity and whose remuneration is paid wholly and directly out of moneys voted by Parliament'.[26] Day to day matters of

[23] See paras. D2.432–3.
[24] See para. D2.434. The issue of government information and Parliament is considered in the next chapter. As we will see in that chapter, for the government to refuse to disclose information on the ground that it wished to avoid domestic criticism would (since 1994) be contrary to the government's Code of Practice on Access to Government Information.   [25] Ibid.
[26] This model definition is taken from the Fulton report: *Report of the Committee on the Civil Service*, Cmnd. 3638, 1968. See H. W. R. Wade and C. F. Forsyth, *Administrative Law* (Oxford: Clarendon Press, 7th edn, 1994) p. 57. Finding an accurate definition of the civil service is fraught with difficulty, as the Expenditure Committee of the House of Commons found in 1977: see the appendix to its report (HC (1976–77) 535) quoted in K. Dowding, *The Civil Service* (London: Routledge, 1995) pp. 17–19.

management and employment are governed by the Civil Service Order in Council 1995[27] (the Order) and by the Civil Service Management Code (the CSMC) issued under it. In addition to these well-established authorities, there has since January 1996 been a Civil Service Code (the Code) concerning questions of ethics and political propriety.[28] While it remains the case that the civil service is largely regulated by extra-statutory measures, there are some statutory provisions which affect the civil service, most notably the Civil Service (Management Functions) Act 1992.[29]

The Order establishes the principles of appointment on merit and of recruitment based on fair and open competition.[30] These principles are maintained by the civil service commissioners, appointed under the Order by her majesty in council. The commissioners hold office during pleasure. The commissioners are also responsible for hearing and determining appeals.[31] Overall responsibility, however, remains with the minister for the civil service, who is technically the prime minister, although in John Major's last administration the machinery of government for dealing with civil service matters was contained within the office of public service, for which the minister was Roger Freeman MP.[32] Under the Order ministers retain overall responsibility for deciding on numbers and grades of civil service posts, for remuneration, expenses and allowances, for holidays and hours of work, for retirement, and for redundancy and redeployment.[33]

The CSMC puts a little more flesh on the bare skeleton of the Order, and covers a broad range of issues affecting the terms and conditions of employment in the civil service, but on the constitutional questions concerning civil servants and their relations between ministers and Parliament, the CSMC is largely silent. To the extent that the CSMC addresses these issues at all, it does so only in the most general terms, stating broad principles but not providing a great deal of assistance as to how the principles should be interpreted in practice. Section 4 of the CSMC, for example, states (the rather obvious point) that 'civil servants are servants of the crown and owe a duty of loyal service to the crown as their employer' and that 'since constitutionally the crown acts on the advice of ministers who are answerable for their depart-

[27] As amended by the Civil Service (Amendment) Order 1995 and the Civil Service (Amendment) Order 1996.

[28] The Code and the background underlying its introduction are considered in more detail below. The Order, the CSMC, and the Code have all been made available on the government's web site on the world wide web: see www.open.gov.uk/.

[29] In addition to which, of course, civil servants fall within the provisions of a number of Acts dealing with disclosure of official information, most notoriously the Official Secrets Act 1989.

[30] Civil Service Order in Council 1995, art. 2.

[31] Ibid., art. 4.

[32] For a detailed description (and diagram) outlining the structure of the office of public service, see Public Service Committee, *Work of the Office of Public Service*, HC (1995–96) 147, p. 7.

[33] Civil Service Order in Council 1995, art. 10.

ments and agencies in Parliament, that duty is . . . owed to the duly constituted government' of the day. This raises more questions than it answers. Is
the constitutional obligation of the civil service limited to serving the government of the day, irrespective of what that government is proposing to do?
What if the government is divided: does a civil servant follow the wishes as she
sees them of the government as a whole or of her own minister, even if that
minister is a known dissentient from the view of a majority in government?
What if a minister asks a civil servant to act in such a way as would undermine parliamentary democracy, such as by drafting a false answer to a parliamentary question. In that situation, is the only duty of the civil service to
the lying government?[34]

The CSMC does little to answer these central questions. Only the most general principles are laid down in the CSMC. Paragraph 4.1.3 of the CSMC
states the four principles which should ensure that civil servants are 'honest
and impartial'. These principles, as might be expected in a document drawn
up by the government, place considerable duties on civil servants to follow the
lead of their ministers apparently no matter what that lead is. First, civil servants must not misuse official information or disclose it without authority
and 'they must not seek to frustrate the policies, decisions or actions of government either by declining to take, or abstaining from, action which flows
from ministerial decisions'. Secondly, 'civil servants must not take part in any
political or public activity which compromises . . . their impartial service to
the government of the day or any future government'. Thirdly, 'civil servants
must not misuse their official position or information acquired in the course
of their official duties to further their private interests . . . where a conflict of
interest arises, civil servants must declare their interest to senior management
so that senior management can determine how best to proceed'. Finally, 'civil
servants must not receive gifts, hospitality or benefits . . . from a third party
which might be seen to compromise their personal judgement'.

In terms of resolving the constitutional problems concerning the civil service raised in the first sections of this chapter, these official sources do not
take us very far. More revealing are the doctrines or conventions which have
developed to articulate more clearly the political position of the civil service.
Traditionally, there are three such doctrines: namely that civil servants are
anonymous, permanent, and politically neutral and independent. At least two
of these three traditional doctrines are now without doubt wrong, in the sense
that they do not accurately describe the modern British civil service, which is
neither anonymous nor permanent. And the third doctrine has also been seriously questioned, although hard evidence of political partiality within the

---

[34] For empirical research into senior civil servants' attitudes to these issues, see A. Barker and
G. Wilson, 'Whitehall's Disobedient Servants? Senior Officials' Potential Resistance to Ministers
in British Government Departments' (1997) 27 *British Journal of Political Science* 223.

civil service is still difficult for the outsider to find. The issue of anonymity can be quickly dealt with. We need look no further than the Scott report to find numerous civil servants being publicly criticized and named. The Scott story is replete with them, as we have already seen in this and the previous chapters. Nor is the Scott report unusual in this respect: the Crichel Down and the Westland sagas both involved the public naming of civil servants, dragged reluctantly into the public arena by an embarrassed government.[35]

As for the notion of permanence, let us consider the following episodes. In 1965 Barbara Castle MP, the then secretary of state for transport, attempted to remove her permanent secretary (Sir Thomas Padmore) but she found that she could not. In her subsequently published diaries she complained of this, asking why it was that she could have no powers of hire and fire when she as minister was responsible for her department's work. The answer, presumably, is that the civil service is employed by the crown and not by an individual minister—and is permanent and independent. Or at least, this presumably would have been the answer in the 1960s. By the 1990s, however, things appear rather alarmingly to have changed. In 1981, for example, Mrs Thatcher managed to bring about the premature retirement of the then head of the civil service and his deputy, Sir Ian Bancroft and Sir John Herbecq.[36] In 1992, William Waldegrave brought about the removal of Sir Peter Kemp when, as the manager of the next steps project, he did not become permanent secretary of the new office of public service and science. In 1993 Kenneth Clarke as home secretary managed to ensure that the key post of chief executive of the prison service did not go to the front runner (Joe Pilling) but to Derek Lewis, an outsider from Granada television known to be a keen supporter of Conservative party policy on opening up the prison service to outside competition and private contractors. Similarly, in 1993 John Patten, the then secretary of state for education, reportedly brought about the resignation of his permanent secretary, Sir Geoffrey Holland.[37]

For our purposes, however, it is the last of the three traditional doctrines which, as well as being the most difficult one, is also the most important. That civil servants are supposed to be politically neutral and impartial has many ramifications. Most obviously this rule affects civil servants' personal party political activities, but it also closely relates to one of the key questions surrounding the civil service which was raised in the Scott report: namely, relations between ministers and civil servants. What if a minister asks a civil servant to act in a political manner, or to do something which the civil servant

---

[35] Crichel Down was considered in ch. 1, above; Westland is outlined in ch. 3, below.

[36] Further politically motivated personnel changes made in Mrs Thatcher's first term as prime minister are outlined in H. Young, *One of Us* (London: Macmillan, 1991) pp. 336–40.

[37] The government denied that Sir Geoffrey Holland's resignation was attributable to any breakdown in his relationship with the secretary of state: see HC (1993–94) 27, para. 83. For further details, see W. Plowden, *Ministers and Mandarins*, (London: Institute for Public Policy Research, 1994) pp. 88–98.

finds to be politically unacceptable, or ethically improper? What can the official do, if anything? What constitutional or other regulation governs these situations?

The Armstrong Memorandum

Until the mid-1980s, the constitution was very quiet on these issues, but the Ponting and Westland affairs prompted the government to act. In 1985 Sir Robert Armstrong, the then head of the civil service and cabinet secretary, drew up a memorandum entitled *Note of Guidance on the Duties and Responsibilities of Civil Servants in Relation to Ministers.*[38] This memorandum (generally known as the Armstrong memorandum) was a broad restatement of orthodox constitutional theory. In echoing the Civil Service Management Code, it stated that 'civil servants are servants of the crown. For all practical purposes the crown in this context means and is represented by the government of the day', but it went on to state that the 'civil service as such has no constitutional personality or responsibility separate from that of the government of the day' and that while 'the civil service serves the government of the day as a whole, that is to say Her Majesty's ministers collectively . . . the duty of the individual civil servant is first and foremost to the minister of the crown who is in charge of the department in which he or she is serving'.

The Armstrong memorandum was roundly criticized as an 'impeccable statement of constitutional theory, but a parody of political practice'.[39] As the first division association (the trade union for senior civil servants) observed, it was 'a narrow statement of existing conventions with heavy emphasis on a civil servant's duty'. It contained only rather offhand treatment of ministers' reciprocal obligations, although these are dealt with a little more fully in *Questions of Procedure for Ministers*, which provides that: 'ministers have a duty to give fair consideration and due weight to informed and impartial advice from civil servants, as well as to other considerations and advice, in reaching policy decisions; a duty to refrain from asking or instructing civil servants to do things which they should not do . . . Civil servants should not be asked to engage in activities likely to call in question

---

[38] HC Deb., Vol. 74, cols. 128–30 (WA), 26 Feb. 1985; revised HC Deb. Vol. 123, cols. 572–5 (WA), 2 Dec. 1987. See R. Brazier, *Constitutional Texts* (Oxford: Clarendon Press, 1990) pp. 488–92.

[39] W. Plowden, *Ministers and Mandarins*, (London: Institute for Public Policy Research, 1994) p. 112. See also Sir Geoffrey Chipperfield, 'The Civil Servant's Duty' (in P. Barberis (ed.), *The Whitehall Reader* (Buckingham: Open University Press, 1996) pp. 132–6). At p. 134 Chipperfield described the Armstrong memorandum as 'minatory and exhortatory' in its approach and as 'lapidary' in its phraseology. The focus on civil servants' duties he found 'unhelpful' and the emphasis placed on duties to individual ministers (rather than to the government as a whole) he described as 'out of kilter with my experience of how the system works'.

their political impartiality, or to give rise to the criticism that people paid from public funds are being used for party political purposes.'[40] The FDA has also criticized this—arguing that 'there remains doubt as to how far ministers owe duties to their civil servants'.[41] William Plowden described this part of *Questions of Procedure for Ministers* as inadequate in that it provides no 'standard against which to test ministerial actions (or inaction)'.[42] Certainly, it is odd that these important limitations on what ministers may ask civil servants to do for them are not incorporated into the CSMC (which is circulated to civil servants) but appear only in QPM (which is circulated to ministers).

Further, and more importantly, the Armstrong memorandum strongly asserted that civil servants are servants of the crown, and that the crown means the government of the day. We have already seen how this rather rigid view of the constitutional status of the civil service might cause significant problems. In 1994 the government issued a statement clarifying this aspect of the Armstrong memorandum. In written evidence to the Scott inquiry, the cabinet office argued that:

the Armstrong memorandum cannot be given the interpretation that a civil servant has no duties except to the government of the day. As well as having the normal obligation of any employee to give honest and faithful service, to obey the lawful orders of his employer and to act in a manner consistent with the bond of trust and confidence between employer and employee, civil servants have a number of other duties, including, like any other citizen, a general duty to obey the law and to deal honestly. They may also have specific professional duties . . . equally they may have dictates of conscience which are individual to them. The Armstrong memorandum fully recognizes that all these exist and is indeed designed to give guidance on what to do if civil servants feel that they are being given instructions which conflict with them. None of this is inconsistent with saying that civil servants are subservient to ministers as the representatives of the crown in Parliament.[43]

A final criticism of the Armstrong memorandum is that it has not really worked. Aspects of the Armstrong memorandum were revised and amended in 1986–7[44] when limited internal appeal procedures were introduced where civil servants believed that they were being asked to do something unethical or improper, or where their conscience prevented them from doing something which they had been asked to do. These appeal procedures, however, were used only once in eight years,[45] which, according to the FDA, illustrated civil

---

[40] *Questions of Procedure for Ministers*, para. 55 (1992 version).

[41] Cited by the treasury and civil service committee: HC (1993–94) 27, para. 93. [42] Ibid.

[43] Cabinet office memorandum to the Scott inquiry, placed in the House of Commons library at the request of the treasury and civil service committee, and reproduced in the committee's report on the *Role of the Civil Service*, HC (1993–94) 27, para. 90.

[44] See the government's response (Cmnd. 9841, 1986) to the report of the treasury and civil service committee: HC (1985–86) 92. The revised version can be found at HC Deb., Vol. 123, cols. 572–5 (WA), 2 Dec. 1987.

[45] HC (1993–94) 27, para. 97. See also the first report of the Nolan committee, *Standards in Public Life* (Cm. 2850, May 1995) para. 3.53.

servants' overwhelming reluctance to use them for fear of adverse effects and because the procedures are entirely internal and require the civil servant to use the same chain of command from where the initial instruction came.[46] The Armstrong memorandum was designed to clarify the relationship between ministers and senior civil servants, yet even a decade after it was first introduced, that relationship remained blurred and unsatisfactory.

Towards the Civil Service Code

In the early 1990s both the FDA and William Plowden, writing for the centre-left think tank, the institute of public policy research (IPPR), proposed as a solution to these problems that a code on ministers and civil servants should be introduced, and both bodies produced (very similar) drafts. Plowden's draft code included, for example, a provision that 'no minister shall at any time or under any circumstance request or require civil servants to act contrary to law or to the provisions of this code, and no civil servant shall suffer any detriment, penalty or punishment for refusing to carry out any such request or instructions' and that 'ministers shall not act in such a manner as to compromise the political neutrality of the civil service'. The draft code provided for the establishment of a civil service ethics tribunal, to be composed of three privy councillors, to be appointed by the prime minister from a list of candidates nominated by the treasury and civil service committee. Under the provisions of the code, if a civil servant is requested to undertake work which he or she believes to be incompatible with his or her political neutrality, then he or she would be able to seek advice from his or her department's permanent head. If the request is not withdrawn, then the civil servant would be able to refer the matter to the civil service ethics tribunal. Similarly, if a civil servant believed that a minister has misled or intended to mislead Parliament, he or she may refer the matter directly to the civil service ethics tribunal.

In its extensive report in 1994 on the future of the civil service, the treasury and civil service committee (as it then was) made similar recommendations. While the Conservative government initially argued that the existing documents (the Armstrong memorandum and *Questions of Procedure for Ministers*) 'provide[d] a satisfactory framework for maintaining the essential values of the civil service' and that 'the standards and ethics essential to the operation of the civil service described in these documents are well founded and well understood', the committee took a different view, stating that it did 'not agree with this sanguine verdict. None of the documents examined states the essential values of the civil service with sufficient clarity.'[47] In order to remedy this the committee made three main recommendations: first, that a

---

[46] HC (1993–94) 27, para. 98.   [47] Ibid., para. 101.

new civil service code should be drawn up; secondly, that this code should incorporate a new appeals procedure, not to an ethics tribunal as recommended by Plowden and the FDA, but to newly strengthened and independent civil service commissioners; and thirdly, that this should be done by statute and that a new Civil Service Act should accordingly be introduced.[48]

The government's response to the committee's recommendations was largely positive.[49] The government accepted that there was a need for a civil service code which would include a right of appeal to independent civil service commissioners. As the Nolan committee put it, this represented an important step forward, towards both a more realistic recognition and more appropriate regulation of the dilemmas faced by civil servants who find themselves troubled by the things which ministers ask them to do. The Nolan committee did, however, recommend that a small number of changes should be made to the government's draft code. The draft envisaged an appeal being made by a civil servant who had been asked 'to act in a way which is illegal, improper, unethical or in breach of constitutional convention'. The Nolan committee recommended that this should be broadened to include also civil servants who are not necessarily personally involved, but who are aware of wrongdoing or maladministration.[50] The committee also recommended that, because the official appeal procedures are used so infrequently, there should additionally be a 'parallel system allowing staff to raise their concerns in confidence without necessarily having to take them through the management structure in the first instance . . . departments and agencies should nominate one or more officials entrusted with the duty of investigating staff concerns raised confidentially'. Such person(s) must operate outside of the line management structure for the complainant.[51] Such arrangements are common in the private sector and would be welcome also in the civil service.[52]

Following on from these recommendations, and in an atmosphere of continuing disquiet over the one-sided nature of the Armstrong memorandum, the government finally introduced a Civil Service Code, which came into effect in January 1996. This short Code, while it incorporates some sections from the Armstrong memorandum, also improves on it by adding important

---

[48] HC (1993–94) 27, paras. 105–17.

[49] See *The Civil Service: Taking Forward Continuity and Change* (Cm. 2748, Jan. 1995).

[50] See the first report of the Nolan committee, *Standards in Public Life* (Cm. 2850, May 1995) para. 3.51.

[51] Nolan, ibid., para. 3.53.

[52] The Nolan committee suggested that this reform 'represents something of a novelty' (para. 3.54) but there is a (sort of) precedent within the civil service: namely the security and intelligence services staff counsellor: see L. Lustgarten and I. Leigh, *In From The Cold: National Security and Parliamentary Democracy* (Oxford: Clarendon Press, 1994) p. 430. The Nolan committee's recommendations are strengthened by further suggestions, first that 'the cabinet office should continue to survey and disseminate best practice on maintaining standards of conduct' and secondly that 'there should be regular surveys in departments and agencies of the knowledge and understanding staff have of ethical standards which apply to them' (paras. 3.59 and 3.61 respectively).

passages which may go a little way towards answering some of the concerns about the civil service raised by the Scott report. The Code repeats the familiar position that civil servants are servants of the crown, which in effect means servants of the government of the day, and that it is to the ministers of that duly constituted government to whom civil servants owe their duties. But for the first time, this traditional view is placed in the context of a broader duty on civil servants to act with 'integrity, honesty, impartiality and objectivity'.[53] Further, unlike the Armstrong memorandum, the Code echoes the duties contained in QPM which ministers owe to civil servants as well as those which civil servants owe to ministers, making the Code much less one-sided than was its predecessor.

Although it is clear that even under the Code the government has not shifted from its basic position that civil servants are accountable primarily to their ministers and that it is ministers (not some abstract notion of the public interest and certainly not Parliament) which civil servants are to serve, on the other hand the Code does go further than previous documents have done in providing for a broader, albeit constitutionally secondary, set of obligations and responsibilities. On openness, for example, the Code provides that 'civil servants should conduct themselves with . . . honesty' and 'should not deceive or knowingly mislead ministers, Parliament or the public'.[54] However, despite this welcome addition, the Code maintains the position that civil servants 'should not seek to frustrate or influence the policies, decisions or actions of government by the unauthorized, improper or premature disclosure outside government of any information to which they have had access as civil servants'.[55] Quite how these two principles are to be reconciled if a civil servant is asked to draft an answer to a PQ which he or she knows to be inaccurate is difficult to tell.[56] Similarly, on the revolving door syndrome the Code states that 'civil servants should not misuse their official position or information acquired in the course of their duties to further their private interests or those of others',[57] although how someone put in the position in which Mr Hastie found himself could possibly avoid breaching this principle is hard to see.

The final paragraphs of the Code deal with complaints which civil servants may have of their ministers. Paragraph 11 provides that 'where a civil servant believes he or she is being required to act in a way which: is illegal, improper or unethical; is in breach of constitutional convention or a professional code; may involve possible maladministration; or is otherwise inconsistent with this Code' he or she may (indeed 'should') report the matter in accordance with that civil servant's internal departmental procedures, i.e., back up the chain

---

[53] Civil Service Code, Jan. 1996, para. 1.   [54] Ibid., para. 5.   [55] Ibid., para. 10.
[56] Presumably the only option would be for the civil servant to make a complaint under the Code, on which see further below.
[57] Civil Service Code, para. 8.

of command. Significantly, civil servants may also report breaches of the Code which are being perpetrated by others. If a civil servant is unhappy with the response from within his or her own department once a complaint has been made, he or she may then report the matter to the civil service commissioners, who will investigate and who will have the last word. If, after the civil service commissioners have looked into the matter, the civil servant is still unhappy, tough: he or she will have to carry out the minister's instructions or resign from the civil service. Of course, after resignation, civil servants 'should continue to observe their duties of confidentiality'.[58] The Code is not as far-reaching as those which had been advocated by the IPPR and others, but is nonetheless a limited step in the right general direction. Whether the complaints procedure, based as it is on the departmental chain of command, will prove to be any more widely used than it was under the Armstrong memorandum, remains to be seen. But at least there is now some degree of formal recognition that civil servants may have broader responsibilities than merely to their immediate ministerial bosses.

The Constitution and the Civil Service: The Next Steps?

By the time the Scott report was published the public service committee had already started work on an investigation into the Michael Howard/Derek Lewis affair of October 1995, which was considered in part in the previous chapter. Although, in the light of the Scott report, the committee eventually considered quite broad questions of ministerial responsibility, much of the focus of its work remained on the civil service and, especially, on matters of civil service accountability—both to ministers and to Parliament. In the committee's eyes, the biggest single issue of contention as regards the accountability of civil servants was the advent of next steps agencies, and much of the committee's work was focused on the relationship between agencies, ministers, and Parliament. Next steps agencies did not feature in the Scott report. However, despite the focus on agencies, which was not shared by the Scott report, the consideration by the public service committee of questions of civil service accountability is nonetheless very helpful in evaluating the problems outlined in the report.

   Before we consider the work of the committee, a word should be added about the evolution and importance of next steps agencies. As is well known, the Thatcher and Major administrations imposed more far-reaching reforms on the civil service than any other peace-time government since the mid-nineteenth century. These reforms started well before the next steps project commenced in 1988, but saw their peak with the next steps report of that year

---

[58] Civil Service Code, para. 13.

and with its subsequent implementation. In brief, a next steps (or executive) agency, named after a report drawn up by the prime minister's efficiency unit entitled *Improving Management in Government: The Next Steps*, is a self-contained unit within a government department which, instead of merely being but one part of a bigger government department, is hived off and given a budget, a framework document, a designated staff headed by a chief executive, and a set of performance targets of its own. Next steps agencies were designed to further the government's aim of achieving greater economy, efficiency, and effectiveness across government by establishing a greater division between policy advice (the core civil service) and implementation or service delivery (which could be hived off from the core). By the end of 1996 some 67 per cent of civil servants were employed in the 110 agencies which had by then been created, which varied in size and public profile from the enormous social security benefits agency (employing some 67,000 people) to the tiny defence animal centre.[59]

When Mrs Thatcher first came to power she 'appeared to have no idea of what to do about the civil service . . . other than to distrust it'[60] and to cut its numbers. During the early 1980s various initiatives were put into effect, largely with a view to cutting down the overall size of the civil service[61] and to reducing costs. In the early 1980s Sir Derek Rayner was brought in from the private sector to oversee a succession of limited 'scrutinies'. These were followed by the Financial Management Initiative which, the government claimed, had resulted in over £950 million of savings by 1986.[62] This was followed by the next steps project, and when John Major became prime minister in 1990 the reshaping of government and the reforms to the civil service became one part of his overarching Citizen's Charter programme. The Citizen's Charter gave what had by 1991 become a crusade in some parts of government a degree of intellectual coherence which had previously been lacking. In the earlier part of the long Conservative period in office there had been no set dogma as to how the civil service must be changed: rather, there had merely been a view that it should be reduced and that economies should be found where possible. By 1991, however, the pace of reform had accelerated and had been packaged around a number of ideas which can be helpfully grouped together under the heading new public management (NPM). NPM,

[59] See Public Service Committee, *Ministerial Accountability and Responsibility*, HC (1995–96) 313, Vol. II, pp. 54–5 for a complete list of the agencies which had been created by the end of 1995. By 1997 a further 57 candidates were due to become next steps agencies, bringing the proportion of the civil service employed in agencies to around 75%.

[60] K. Dowding, *The Civil Service* (London: Routledge, 1995) p. 63.

[61] Overall numbers of civil servants fell during the Thatcher years from 735,000 in 1979 to 567,000 in 1990. Numbers continued to fall under John Major and by Oct. 1995 had fallen by 31% from the 1979 level. In 1995 numbers were forecast to fall still further, to 483,000 by 1997–8. The machinery of government division (within the cabinet office) publishes the figures periodically. They are available on the government's web site (www.open.gov.uk).

[62] Dowding, op. cit., p. 66.

which had been experimented with in the US,[63] incorporated a number of ideals of bureaucratic efficiency which were informed both by modern organization theory in general and elements of the political philosophy of the new right in particular, as endorsed by the Conservative governments of Thatcher and Major. Under NPM, the citizen is seen primarily as a customer, buying services from the state. Naturally, the citizen-customer wants those services to be of good quality, but NPM redefines what 'good quality' means. For adherents of NPM, public services are of good quality when they are cheap, efficient, effective, privatized or contracted out where possible, or otherwise subjected to the disciplines of the market. Large parts of the Conservative programme of government were inspired by NPM. The Citizen's Charter programme with its league tables of schools and railway lines (so that we might identify and choose the 'best' school or train); the internal market within the NHS; compulsory competitive tendering in local government; and, of course, next steps agencies in the civil service were all introduced under this ideological umbrella.

This is important for present purposes because it makes it clear that next steps agencies are not simply a value-neutral mechanism for changing the formal structure of government departments. On the contrary, they are part of what became a political drive to percolate a new set of values, borrowed from private enterprise, industry and business, through the public sector and the civil service. Why is this important? It matters because if new, private sector values are introduced into the public sector, that may bring about sweeping changes in the ways in which the public sector is made accountable. If 'good quality' advice and decision making before NPM was that which was rational and reasonable or fair and equitable, after NPM it has become that which is cheap and efficient or market-driven and privatized.

These changes have introduced a paradox into the heart of the civil service. There are now two sets of values against which the civil service is judged—two sets of values which are not always complementary. On the one hand there are the relatively new values of NPM, while on the other hand there remain what might be called the constitutional values found in the Civil Service Code and in the other sources examined above. The values of NPM may have been filtered through the civil service and may have affected its behaviour, but they do not appear to have reached as far as the formal constitutional structures which purport to regulate the civil service. Such regulation, as we have seen, clings even after the advent of NPM to the more traditional Weberian view that civil servants are merely the value-neutral cogs in the machine which indifferently implements the will of the minister. According to this model,

---

[63] See especially D. Osborne and T. Gaebler, *Reinventing Government* (Reading MA: Addison-Wesley, 1992). For an overview, see C. Foster and F. Plowden, *The State under Stress* (Buckingham: Open University Press, 1996) ch. 3. See also C. Campbell and G. Wilson, *The End of Whitehall: Death of a Paradigm?* (Oxford: Blackwell, 1995) chs. 4–5.

civil servants are to have no individual personality or interests; they will have no creative input into the machinery of government; and, therefore, the only level of accountability which is required is the individual civil servant's accountability to his or her departmental minister.[64] It is because the constitution clings to this outmoded ideal-type of what it is to be a civil servant that explains the under-regulation of the civil service by the constitutional documents such as the Civil Service Code. That is why there is no constitutional obligation on civil servants to operate in the public interest, but only in the interest of their ministers. That is why Parliament may not hold individual civil servants responsible and why Parliament's select committees may hear evidence from civil servants only on terms laid down by ministers.[65]

Yet the changes which have been imposed on the civil service in the last decade or more have shown, should there have been any doubt, that this model of the civil service was deeply flawed. It had already been seriously challenged in the 1960s and 1970s when Labour ministers, especially those from the left of the party, complained that senior civil servants were institutionally and personally opposed to much of what the government was trying to do.[66] After NPM the traditional constitutional model has been shown to be both unrealistic and inadequate. As both the Scott report and the débâcle between Michael Howard and Derek Lewis showed, civil servants are far more than the tail that is wagged by the ministerial dog. Civil servants, both individually and within units in departments (such as the export licensing bureau at the DTI or the defence export services secretariat at the MOD) and in agencies (such as the prison service), do develop attitudes, approaches, and policies of their own, sometimes because of ministerial support or indifference (as in the cases examined in the Scott report) and sometimes despite ministerial opposition (as in the case of the prison service). Yet, because the relevant constitutional documents do not appear to recognize these phenomena, they go unregulated and the problems of unaccountability and secrecy in the civil service continue.

The Public Service Committee: Accountability and Secrecy in the Civil Service

The issues might be constitutionally under-regulated, but they have not passed entirely unnoticed. The public service committee spent the first half of 1996 looking carefully into many of these problems, and the evidence which

---

[64] On the Weberian model of bureaucracy, see K. Dowding, op. cit., pp. 7–16 and D. Beetham, *Bureaucracy* (Milton Keynes: Open University Press, 1987) pp. 11–23.

[65] This issue and the Osmotherly rules which govern it are considered in more detail in the next chapter.

[66] See for example (among many examples in his diaries) Tony Benn, *Against the Tide: Diaries 1973–76* (London: Arrow, 1989) pp. 210–11. See also the various memoirs and diaries cited by Dowding, op. cit., p. 52.

was presented to the committee, and the committee's findings, repay some consideration. To start with the issue which was the immediate influence behind the committee's work: the dismissal of Derek Lewis by Michael Howard in October 1995. The background of the notorious prison escapes and the subsequent highly critical Learmont report was outlined in the previous chapter, but what does that story tell us about the problems of accountability and secrecy in the civil service? Is it not in many ways a 'good' story, in that it reveals that any problems which there might be have been greatly exaggerated? After all, here we have the public dismissal of the man who was responsible for the system which allowed the escapes to occur, following on from a published report which sets out the facts of the matter[67] in some detail—where is the lack of accountability? Where is the secrecy in that? Such a spin on the events of October 1995 would, however, be highly misleading.

We saw in the previous chapter how Michael Howard wrongly presented the failures over which he sacked Derek Lewis as operational, thus avoiding the prospect of taking responsibility himself, as ministers, in his view, are responsible only for policy matters. Yet it is quite clear from his oral and written evidence to the public service committee that Mr Lewis did not consider that all the problems outlined in the Learmont report related only to operational matters. This is not simply a disagreement between two egotistic and angry men who were both attempting to rescue their careers and who had clearly fallen out with each other long before October 1995. The problem is that until after he was dismissed, Mr Lewis was unable to present to Parliament his version of what was going wrong within the prison service, because of the Osmotherly rules and the constitutional position that civil servants (including those who work in executive agencies) are servants of their minister. Only Mr Howard's version could be relayed to Parliament—even when it was Mr Lewis who was relaying it, he was in no position to inform Parliament of his own analysis where it differed from that of the home secretary. The Howard/Lewis fiasco was not therefore a 'good' story whereby the right man was publicly held responsible and dismissed. It was a cynical manipulation of the constitutionally weak position of vulnerable civil servants by a powerful politician who firstly prevented Parliament from having access to the professional views of the chief executive of the prison service knowing that Parliament would thereby be disabled from learning of the serious disagreements as to prisons policy and management that existed between the two protagonists, and who secondly got away with sacking the chief executive rather than resigning himself only because Parliament was not at that point properly informed of anybody's views on the matter other than those of the home secretary himself. Michael Howard might have dressed the episode up as one which demonstrated both the accountability and the openness of

---

[67] Learmont's account of the 'facts' was contested, in particular by Derek Lewis: see *Hidden Agendas: Politics, Law and Order* (London: Hamish Hamilton, 1997).

the new civil service, but in fact, this dressing was nothing more than a self-serving façade. The home secretary was able to sack Mr Lewis only because of the unaccountability of the civil service to Parliament and the consequent ministerial bias which pollutes the information which reaches Parliament.

What then should be done? In his evidence to the public service committee Lord Armstrong, the former cabinet secretary and author of the Armstrong memorandum, stated that in his view, although he was generally supportive of the next steps project, the prison service was an agency too far and should not have been made into a next steps agency. In his view, the model of the next steps agency was designed for relatively small and politically uncontroversial areas of government, exemplified perhaps by the driver and vehicle licensing authority (which was one of the first next steps agencies). The structure of next steps agencies was not designed for politically sensitive fields where there was likely to be controversy and a high level of parliamentary interest. It was therefore inevitable in his view that a row along the lines of that between Messrs Howard and Lewis would develop, if not in the prison service then in one of the other big agencies such as the benefits agency or the employment service.[68] Lord Armstrong's successor as cabinet secretary, Sir Robin Butler, disagreed with his predecessor's views and saw no inherent flaw in making the prison service a next steps agency.[69]

Derek Lewis probably gave the most interesting evidence. In his view a distinction should be drawn between the big, politically sensitive agencies and the smaller, relatively uncontroversial ones. The former, including the prison service, the benefits agency, the employment service, and the child support agency should be reformed, taken out of government departments altogether and made under statute into non-departmental public bodies (NDPBs) modelled perhaps on the police. They would then have an independent board responsible for management, with ministers setting policy through delegated legislation (much as home office ministers already do under the Prison Rules). Under this system, ministers would continue to be responsible to Parliament for policy, but chief executives of the new NDPBs would become directly accountable to the relevant select committee and would give evidence to the committee on their own behalf, not on behalf of their ministers.[70] In Mr Lewis's view this would give chief executives 'greater freedom to account for their performance . . . [and] to explain the impact of policy decisions on their services'[71] thus enabling Parliament to be better informed of the consequences on service delivery of the policy decisions of ministers, something

---

[68] See Public Service Committee, *Ministerial Accountability and Responsibility*, HC (1995–96) 313, Vol. III, QQ 109–18.

[69] Ibid., Q 848. In his conservative and rather defensive evidence, Sir Robin Butler offered no solution to the issues of unaccountability and secrecy in next steps agencies and elsewhere in the civil service largely on the ground that he appeared not to consider these issues to be problems in need of attention.

[70] Ibid., Vol. III, pp. 91–2 and Q 643.   [71] Ibid., Q 643.

about which Parliament was painfully ignorant during the Howard/Lewis episode.

The gist of Derek Lewis's suggestions was supported by a number of other witnesses who gave evidence to the public service committee, including Sir Richard Scott. Sir Richard did not comment on the transforming of the bigger next steps agencies into NDPBs but he did advocate that civil servants (and retired civil servants) should, where appropriate, give evidence to select committees on their own behalf and not on behalf of their ministers. Sir Richard did not see this as exposing or as politicizing civil servants, but as liberating them: he stated that civil servants should be 'free to give first-hand information to select committees'.[72] Professors Peter Hennessy and Norman Lewis also supported the idea that at least some civil servants (such as chief executives of next steps agencies) should be directly accountable to select committees and that this would not mean that such civil servants would become any more politicized than they already are.[73] In a slightly different vein, but to the same basic end, Peter Kemp, one of the architects of the next steps project, suggested another way in which select committees could enjoy greater powers of scrutiny of next steps agencies. He argued that the framework documents which establish the goals and targets of the agencies as laid down by the minister and the department should be examined by the appropriate select committee.[74] At present, framework documents are placed in Parliament's libraries, but there is no *a priori* scrutiny of them in draft and consequently no parliamentary input as to what they should provide. This would be a useful development, and was supported even by Sir Robin Butler.[75]

The 1994 report of the then treasury and civil service committee recommended that agency chief executives should be 'directly and personally accountable to select committees in relation to their annual performance agreements' but the government rejected this recommendation on the spurious ground that it would somehow lead to a dilution of ministerial responsibility.[76] Why ministers could not continue to be held responsible just because select committees were able to glean more information from chief executives is hard to determine. In turn the public service committee in its 1996 report recommended both that the Osmotherly rules (governing the evidence which civil servants may give to select committees)[77] should be amended to allow chief executives to give evidence on matters falling within their responsibility

---

[72] See Public Service Committee, *Ministerial Accountability and Responsibility*, HC (1995–96) 313, Vol. III, Q 428.

[73] Ibid., QQ 92 and 735, respectively. [74] Ibid., Vol. III, pp. 108–10 and Q 715.

[75] Ibid., Q 866.

[76] See Treasury and Civil Service Committee, *The Role of the Civil Service*, HC (1993–94) 27 (Nov. 1994) and the government response, *The Civil Service: Taking Forward Continuity and Change*, Cm. 2748 (Jan. 1995).

[77] The Osmotherly rules are considered in more detail in the next chapter.

under their framework documents without prior ministerial approval and that the government should invite select committees to review and comment on framework documents before they are published.[78] The government broadly accepted the tenor of these recommendations.[79]

These might be steps in the right direction in that they begin to enhance the accountability of the civil service to Parliament and to reduce the secrecy of the senior civil service, but they are only modest developments. Even after the committee's extensive investigation and even after the Scott report, civil servants other than chief executives of next steps agencies remain in an extraordinarily weak position *vis-à-vis* Parliament. They cannot do or say anything without prior ministerial approval, and while they may report evidence of wrongdoing to their immediate superiors (under the Civil Service Code) and ultimately to the civil service commissioners, civil servants most certainly may not inform Parliament of any such wrongdoing. Should there be greater provision for whistle-blowing and protection for whistle-blowers? Under the Civil Service Code, civil servants are able to report wrong-doing, but there is no clear duty on them to do so. This contrasts with the position of accounting officers who are under a duty to report financial mismanagement to the comptroller and auditor general.[80] The public service committee, although it considered the issue of whistle-blowing, did not make any recommendations as to whether the provisions of the Civil Service Code should be strengthened. This is disappointing. There is no reason why Britain should not follow the US model whereby those who 'disclose government illegality, waste and corruption' are protected against dismissal under the Whistleblower Protection Act 1989. In the US, in addition to this statutory protection, each government department employs a special counsel who has the responsibility to protect government employees from 'prohibited personnel practices'. The role of the special counsel is similar to that of the staff counsellor as recommended by the Nolan committee in its first report.[81] It is a shame that the public service committee did not take the opportunity to repeat and reinforce Nolan's sensible suggestion.

---

[78] Public Service Committee, *Ministerial Accountability and Responsibility*, HC (1995–96) 313, paras. 114 and 123.

[79] See the government response to the committee's report, HC (1996–97) 67, pp. xii–xiii.

[80] Each department will have an accounting officer, who is usually the permanent secretary. Most chief executives are mini accounting officers for their agencies, but the permanent secretary retains overall responsibility. The most important episode to highlight the role of accounting officers in recent times was the Pergau Dam scandal, on which see HC (1992–93) 908 (the report of the national audit office); HC (1993–94) 155 (the report of the public accounts committee); and HC (1993–94) 271 (the report of the foreign affairs committee). See also, F. White, I. Harden and K. Donnelly, 'Audit, Accounting Officers and Accountability: the Pergau Dam Affair' [1994] *Public Law* 526.

[81] See above, n. 52 and accompanying text.

Conclusion: Still Hazy after all these Years

Despite the fact that the constitutional position of the civil service has been examined and re-examined in a succession of parliamentary and government reports during the past decade, many problems remain. This chapter has outlined those problems, as evidenced in the Scott report and elsewhere. At the heart of the matter lies one key issue which acts as a brake on everything the civil service does: namely, the repeated insistence that civil servants owe their duties to their individual ministers (as emanations of the crown). Civil servants have no obligations to any broader notion of the public interest, as only individual ministers can determine what the public interest is at any given moment. Even after the endless official reconsiderations of the functions and values of the civil service, we are apparently no nearer to erasing this basic mistake. The fear among government ministers has been that if the civil service is allowed to develop its own constitutional personality independent of ministers and if the civil service is entrusted with the obligation of upholding some notion of the public interest which is separate from the short-term political interests of the government of the day, then the civil service will become an unelected independent political force which rivals rather than complements that of ministers.

This fear is grossly exaggerated. No one is suggesting that the civil service should entirely detach itself from the ministerial hook on which it currently depends. On the contrary, all that is being suggested is that the ministerial view of the public interest will not always be the only one, and will sometimes be one that is not in the public interest at all. As civil servants are in a unique position to be able to identify when the ministerial interpretation of the public interest has collapsed into a self-interested political bias, civil servants should be given the responsibility of reporting such occurrences to Parliament so that Parliament may act accordingly and hold the relevant ministers more effectively to account than it is currently able to do. Nothing illustrates this more clearly than the Scott report, which revealed how a number of ministers had secretly agreed to tilt government policy, without apparently informing the prime minister and certainly without informing Parliament. Those ministers may have felt that they were acting in the public interest in that their decision would enhance British trading opportunities in Iraq, but it was in their own interests (to avoid domestic criticism and political embarrassment) and not in the public interest that they decided to keep Parliament in the dark. Why should a civil servant who is aware of the impropriety of misleading Parliament on a matter such as this not be able to inform Parliament that its ministers are acting in this way? How would such a step be contrary to the public interest? The Conservative government took the view that to move down this road would be to undermine the constitutional doctrine of ministerial responsibility, but surely it is the ministers conspiring to mislead Parliament which is the abnegation of responsibility. Is it not the case that giving civil servants who know of improper ministerial decisions the opportunity of informing Parliament would enhance, not undermine, Parliament's central task of holding the executive to account?

The sorts of situations in which this might apply do not extend to the inevitable occasions when a civil servant simply disagrees with a decision that a minister has made or is proposing to make,[82] but relate to the more serious circumstances (as illustrated in the Scott report) when ministers' actions or proposals breach the government's own codes, such as *Questions of Procedure for Ministers* or the Civil Service Code. There are a number of different ways in which this aim could be realized. Parliament could establish a select committee modelled perhaps on the privileges and standards committee, to hear evidence or complaints from civil servants. Alternatively, departments could establish officers to whom these matters could be referred, officers who are not in the normal chain of departmental command, as Nolan suggested. More modestly, Sir Douglas Wass has suggested that departments could establish a parliamentary branch responsible for ensuring that 'the department met with the spirit and the letter of its duty to be accurate and informative in its dealings with Parliament'.[83] At the very least the Civil Service Code and QPM should be amended to make it crystal clear that civil servants owe an obligation of honesty and a duty to report all impropriety known to them which transcends their basic obligation of loyal service to (honest) ministers. Civil servants might be accountable to their ministers, but their responsibilities should extend much further. There is an urgent need to create some body outside the usual chain of command to which a civil servant can turn in such situations. The establishment of such a body would reinforce, not undermine, the proper constitutional relations between ministers, civil servants, and Parliament. Honest ministers have nothing to fear.

In the previous chapter we discussed the benefits of Parliament taking the lead in defining the scope of ministerial responsibility. Parliament should do the same with regard to the civil service. The civil service is not the plaything of the government of the day. Yet the past decade has seen tremendous changes being imposed on the civil service by Conservative governments, for the most part without legislation, and, aside from the attentions of two select

---

[82] Except that it may be the case that had senior civil servants shown more good sense and less blind loyalty to ministers some recent policy disasters might have been avoided—most notably the poll tax. This may be the fault of the Thatcher government which notoriously preferred to surround itself with 'can-do yes-men' who were 'one of us'. See D. Butler, A. Adonis and T. Travers, *Failure in British Government: the Politics of the Poll Tax* (Oxford: Oxford University Press, 1994).

[83] See Sir Douglas Wass, 'Scott and Whitehall' [1996] *Public Law* 461, at p. 470. On contemporary views within the senior civil service on 'going outside the department' see A. Barker and G. Wilson, op. cit., n. 34.

committees, without parliamentary debate, let alone authorization. As it has done with ministerial responsibility, Parliament should assert its primary authority on the regulation of the civil service. Parliament should legislate to demarcate a new, clearer constitutional function for the civil service. The cloak of the crown, so convenient to the government, should be stripped away, and the civil service should be reclothed in a new parliamentary garb. The lesson of the Scott report, and the lesson of the Howard/Lewis débâcle, is that Parliament must act to reformulate the role of the civil service not as a body which exists solely for the benefit of ministers, however dishonest or disingenuous they are, but as a body which serves the public in the public interest. The public interest is not a matter only for ministers, but should be enshrined in statute to include what might be called basic constitutional values or, as the Nolan committee put it, the standards of public life, such as openness, honesty, integrity, objectivity, and accountability.

Civil servants have already been handed one relatively new set of priorities in the changes which the Conservatives introduced during the second half of their long period in office. As the treasury and civil service committee and then the public service committee have recognized, these reforms have valuably enhanced the efficiency and effectiveness of much of what the civil service delivers. However, the privileging of the values of new public management and value for money has meant that other values such as the basic constitutional values or Nolan standards listed above have been sidelined and placed in the shadow of the overriding ideological aim of economy. Parliament must now work hard to ensure that honesty, openness, and accountability come out from the shadows and are placed at the heart of a revitalized and truly public service.

3

Freedom of Information

ISSUES of open government and of freedom of information have already been encountered in the previous two chapters. While there is a close relationship between the subjects of ministerial responsibility, the civil service, and freedom of information, in this chapter we will not repeat what we have already noticed about freedom of information as it relates to ministers' responsibilities not (knowingly) to mislead Parliament or as regards the evidence which civil servants give to select committees. Rather, the purpose of this chapter is, having drawn these threads together, to examine what the Scott story has to teach us about government information and Parliament more generally. While the two chief concerns illuminated in the Scott report as to freedom of information were the two which have already been discussed in the previous chapters (ministers' answers to PQs and evidence to select committees from civil servants) the topic of open government is not limited to these two specific problems. In concluding the section of this book which examines issues of government and Parliament, this chapter begins to move away from the detail of Scott and examines the experiences of open government evidenced by the Scott report in the light of recent developments in the field of parliamentary access to information more broadly, especially as regards the important Code of Practice on Access to Government Information, first introduced in 1994.

Underlying the entire activity of the Scott inquiry lay a perennial problem: namely that Parliament could not be relied upon adequately or accurately to discover what the government was doing. This was just as true of the period between 1984–9 (What was the policy on exports to Iraq? What did the policy amount to in practice? How was the policy interpreted and implemented? Who had responsibility for the implementation of the policy/ies?) as it was of the period of the criminal proceedings, from 1990–2 (What was the relationship between Matrix Churchill and the government? What was the position of the secret intelligence community? Why was the government using public interest immunity certificates to cover up important details?). If Parliament had itself been able to answer these questions to its own satisfaction, there would have been no need for the government to ask a judge to answer them on Parliament's behalf. If Parliament had been more effective or more assertive of its powers over the executive there would have been no delegation of parliamentary responsibility to a judicial inquiry. This raises the question, why was it necessary? Why could Parliament not do its own work properly? Does Parliament lack power, or does it lack the willingness to use its powers with sufficient boldness or independence, or both? This chapter will explore these questions, both as regards the chambers of the Houses and as regards their committees, especially in the House of Commons. After examining contemporary parliamentary practice we will move on to discuss the implications of more recent developments such as the 1994 Code and the responses of both Parliament and the government to the criticisms voiced in the Scott report.

Parliamentary Questions

Parliamentary questions (PQs) are not the only mechanism by which Parliament attempts to acquire information about or held by the government, but they are certainly one of the most important and dramatic. Nothing is more representative of the fundamental obligation of the government to account to Parliament than the spectacle of ministers sweating at the dispatch box, standing up to respond to questions thrown at them from all sides of the chamber. Every minister must undergo this ordeal once every four weeks or so during parliamentary session, and of course the prime minister must endure a thirty minute session of oral questions every week.[1] In addition to the television-friendly slots of oral questions, however, *Hansard* is full every day of columns and columns of written answers to questions from MPs, answers which are often of some length and which can contain considerable detail.[2] The processes of PQs are not limited to the rough and tumble of question time.

Their dramatic value may be high, and their column inches may be considerable, but are PQs an effective mechanism for enabling Parliament to acquire accurate governmental information? Opinions vary greatly on the merits of PQs: at one extreme they are regarded as 'the jewel in the parliamentary crown'[3] and at the other as 'hardly more useful than a punch and judy show'.[4] While there is little doubt that parliamentary questions and in particular 'question time can be a very effective means of keeping check on the govern-

---

[1] Within ten days of having become prime minister Tony Blair changed prime minister's question time from two weekly sessions of 15 minutes each to one weekly session of half an hour. See D. McKie, 'Democratic Institution that can look more like a Blood Sport', the *Guardian*, 10 May 1997.

[2] In the session 1994–5, 4,903 oral questions and 44,924 written questions appeared on the order paper. They were answered at an approximate cost of £6 million. Twenty years earlier there were 9,215 oral and 27,843 written questions. See the written evidence of the office of public service to the public service committee, *Ministerial Accountability and Responsibility*, HC (1995–96) 313, Vol. III, p. 196.

[3] See R. L. Borthwick, 'On the Floor of the House', in M. Franklin and P. Norton (eds.), *Parliamentary Questions* (Oxford: Clarendon Press, 1993) p. 73.

[4] Woodrow (now Lord) Wyatt, *Turn Again, Westminster* (London: Andre Deutsch, 1973) p. 31, cited by R. L. Borthwick, ibid.

ment, . . . all too frequently it develops into a parliamentary game more impressive in the appearance than in the substance'.[5] But despite this cynicism, PQs clearly remain a central aspect of day to day parliamentary life, especially in the House of Commons.[6] As Frank Dobson MP has put it, questions are a 'crucial part of the mechanism by which the freely elected members of the legislature attempt to carry out their function of holding the executive to account'.[7]

The content of parliamentary questions is not regulated in the House's standing orders but by speaker's rulings, which are enforced by the speaker and by the table office. The rulings generally relate to the asking of questions, rather than the provision of (accurate or full) answers, but in essence they provide that: the question must be addressed to the minister responsible; it must ask for information or press for action; and it must not ask for answers which ministers have already refused,[8] although a question is not usually ruled out of order simply because a government department has said that it should be. Questions to ministers should relate to the public affairs with which they are officially connected, to proceedings pending in Parliament, or to matters of administration for which they are responsible. With regard to answers, Erskine May states simply that 'an answer should be confined to the points contained in the questions, with such explanation only as renders the answer intelligible'.[9] An answer to a question cannot be insisted upon if the answer is refused by a minister; the speaker has refused to allow supplementary questions in these circumstances. The refusal of a minister to answer a question on a ground of public interest cannot be challenged as a matter of parliamentary privilege.[10]

---

[5] M. Rush, *Parliamentary Government in Britain* (London: Pitman, 1981) p. 207, cited by R. L. Borthwick, ibid. In *British Government and its Discontents* (London: Pitman, 1981) p. 126, G. Smith and N. Polsby argue that question time is 'an occasion not for the serious examination of the issues or for eliciting information in any depth from ministers, but displaying one's opponents to the greatest possible disadvantage'.

[6] On parliamentary questions in the House of Lords, see D. Shell, 'Questions in the House of Lords', in M. Franklin and P. Norton (eds.), *Parliamentary Questions* (Oxford: Clarendon Press, 1993) ch. 6.

[7] See Procedure Committee, *Parliamentary Questions*, HC (1990–91) 178, para. 63.

[8] An example of a ruling made in relation to this requirement is the one speaker Betty Boothroyd made in Feb. 1994 banning one Labour MP, Llew Smith, from asking ministers any further questions on the Scott inquiry and related matters. See the *Observer*, 17 Feb. 1994.

[9] Erskine May, *Parliamentary Practice* (London: Butterworths, 21st edn., 1989) p. 295.

[10] There appears to be a relatively low rate of ministers flatly refusing to answer questions: as an example of what they say is a typical parliamentary day, Griffith and Ryle take 20 Apr. 1988, on which day only 9 out of 298 questions asked were not answered 'because the information was not readily available'. However, Griffith and Ryle do conclude that 'it is impossible to compel a minister to tell everything he knows on every topic. However . . . it is difficult for a minister to avoid giving even politically embarrassing information unless he is willing specifically to refuse it . . . This is rare.' See J. A. G. Griffith and M. Ryle, *Parliament: Functions, Practice and Procedure* (London: Sweet and Maxwell, 1989) p. 374.

The regulation of parliamentary questions was reviewed by the House of Commons select committee on procedure in 1990.[11] While a small number of minor recommendations were made,[12] the committee took the view that present practices with regard both to oral and written questions were generally satisfactory. The committee concluded that despite the fact that theirs was the first major review of the operation of parliamentary questions since the early 1970s[13] 'the very small number of responses we have received to submit evidence suggests that, with a few isolated exceptions, there is no dissatisfaction with the way in which parliamentary questions currently operate'.[14] This broad satisfaction with parliamentary questions echoes the findings of a survey carried out in 1989 by Franklin and Norton for the study of Parliament group[15] in which 72 per cent of MPs who participated in the survey said that they thought that parliamentary questions were a satisfactory way of getting information on government policy and on the work of government and in which 97 per cent of MPs who responded said that written questions were a useful way of discovering information that might be hard to obtain elsewhere.[16] It was an early promise of Tony Blair's incoming government in 1997 that many aspects of parliamentary practice, including PQs, should be extensively reviewed by the House.

Answers to PQs: The incomplete meets the inaccurate?

The Scott report provided numerous examples indicating that the rather complacent approach of the procedure committee's 1990 report was somewhat misplaced. One difficulty is that the regulation of parliamentary questions overwhelmingly concerns the asking of questions, rather than the giving of (accurate or truthful) answers. The procedure committee recognized this in its report, and stated in its conclusions that:

the content of answers is entirely the responsibility of ministers . . . No changes to rules governing admissibility of questions . . . will ever guarantee answers of model clarity, nor banish completely the occasional lapse into replies containing obfuscation, delib-

---

[11] *Parliamentary Questions*, HC (1990–91) 178.

[12] For example, with regard to 'blocks': see paras. 110–14 of the committee's report (ibid.). Some reforms to the previous 'blocking' system were introduced in 1993. It is now the position that a PQ can only be ruled out by the table office if a minister has previously refused to answer it *in the current session*. According to the table office, 'in practice this has led to a marked lifting of the restrictions on questions. Not only must each block be re-established each session, but also the block is applied only to the terms of the question and not to the subject matter more generally.' Quoted in the public service committee's report, *Ministerial Accountability and Responsibility*, HC (1995–96) 313, para. 39.

[13] See HC (1971–72) 39.   [14] HC (1990–91) 178, para. 135.

[15] See M. Franklin and P. Norton, 'Questions and Members', in M. Franklin and P. Norton (eds.), *Parliamentary Questions* (Oxford: Clarendon Press, 1993) ch. 4.

[16] Ibid., pp. 107–9.

erate ambiguity, and evasion . . . It remains a truism that failure to answer a question directly, or a refusal to reply at all, can, in their own way, shed just as much light on government policy (or the lack of it) in a particular area as a full and detailed response, which in practice may conceal more than it reveals.[17]

This may or may not be the case as far as the refusal to answer is concerned, but what of the trickier situation in which some sort of answer to a PQ is given, but the answer is only a very partial answer?

The Scott report is replete with instances where the government preferred to give an answer which was 'presentationally convenient' rather than 'factually accurate'.[18] Some government ministers went as far as to seek to defend this position when challenged on it during the Scott inquiry's hearings. In his evidence to the Scott inquiry, for example, Lord Howe asserted that there was 'nothing necessarily open to criticism in incompatibility between policy and presentation of policy'.[19] Senior officials supported this ministerial line, with both David Gore-Booth[20] and Sir Robin Butler advocating the view that the government was as forthcoming as possible, and, although there were sometimes foreign policy reasons for giving only half the picture rather than the whole picture, 'half the picture can be true'.[21] The problem with this 'half the picture' approach is, however, that, as the Scott report put it, 'those to whom the incomplete statement is addressed do not know . . . that an undisclosed half is being withheld from them. They are almost bound, therefore, to be misled' by it.[22]

While Sir Richard Scott and Sir Robin Butler entertained themselves during the inquiry with a nice philosophical argument as to the nature of 'true' answers and the differences between incomplete and inaccurate answers,[23] the proper constitutional question is not so much whether half the picture can in any given example be said to be true or untrue, but instead whether incomplete ministerial responses to PQs are, in the circumstances, justified. In cases of details concerning the operations of the security and secret intelligence services, or in the context of information about imminent proposed changes in interest or exchange rates[24] it might be justifiable to withhold information from Parliament, but these were not the reasons cited in respect of informa-

---

[17] HC (1990–91) 178, para. 136.

[18] See, for example, para. D6.27. The more significant examples were given above in ch. 1.

[19] Oral evidence of Lord Howe, 12 Jan. 1994, see paras. D3.19 and D4.52. In response to this and other comments, Lord Howe was asked by the inquiry whether his was 'a sort of "government knows best" approach' to which his answer was 'Yes'. See para. D4.54.

[20] Formerly at the Middle East department in the foreign office and subsequently British ambassador to Saudi Arabia and then to India.

[21] See paras. D4.53–4.   [22] See para. D4.55.

[23] See also, Public Service Committee, *Ministerial Accountability and Responsibility*, HC (1995–96) 313, para. 43.

[24] It may be that neither of these examples applies any longer: since May 1997 interest rates have been set by the monetary committee of the Bank of England, not by the chancellor, and exchange rate policy now seems to be a relic from the past.

tion connected with the Howe guidelines and changes to them (which were, in the main, reasons relating either to foreign relations or to domestic political fallout). So was the government's presentation of only half the picture justified in this case? On this point the Scott report was quite clear that it was not: the report stated that it was not 'in the least obvious that the . . . reasons identified by Lord Howe were sufficient to justify the repeated provision to Parliament . . . of information about government policy that was by design incomplete and in certain respects misleading'.[25]

Did this trenchant criticism stem from a misunderstanding of the nature of parliamentary questions? Did the Scott report take parliamentary questions too seriously as a means of acquiring useful information and consequently did it underplay their sometimes rather mischievous or political point-scoring purposes? An argument along these lines was put to the Scott inquiry in an interesting paper by Sir Michael Quinlan, permanent under-secretary at the MOD from 1988–92. Sir Michael suggested that parliamentary questions should be understood as being 'analogous to a game'. Although the form of the activity might be to bring information into the public domain, 'as between the government and the opposition that is not normally its key purpose. The prime purpose for opposition members . . . is to give the government a hard time; and the reactive purpose of the government is to avoid having a hard time.'[26] Given this, it is, in Sir Michael's view, unrealistic to suppose that information will be provided or used in the same manner and spirit as if the actors were participants in a seminar or witnesses in a court of law. Moreover, he continued, the game has 'been played in essentially the current way by every government and opposition in living memory, irrespective of party', although interestingly Sir Michael did concede that 'a long period with one party in power may accentuate its features'.[27]

The Scott report accepted much of the tenor of this argument, but emphasized also that game-playing is not the only aspect of parliamentary questions. Sir Michael's points aside, parliamentary questions remain a central medium by which information about government and its activities is made available to Parliament and to the public, and, as such, government statements about policy on defence exports to Iraq 'consistently failed' to comply with constitutional standards of openness and accountability.[28] This level of criticism encouraged the public service committee to consider questions of open government and freedom of information in its broad post-Scott inquiry, and the government, in turn, announced new guidelines on answering PQs

---

[25] See para. D4.60.   [26] See para. D4.61.   [27] Ibid.
[28] See paras. D4.62–3. It might be added that if PQs and especially oral questions are taken rather less than seriously in some quarters, this should serve to render the work of select committees all the more serious and important.

which should, if properly implemented in practice, meet most of the criticisms Scott identified.[29]

Evidence was given to the public service committee, just as it had been to the Scott inquiry, that practices commonly adopted by ministers and civil servants 'hardly implie[d] a strong presumption of disclosure to Parliament'.[30] The FDA told the committee, for example, that 'there is a commonly accepted culture that the function of the answer to a PQ is to give no more information than the minister thinks will be helpful to him or her, the minister, in the process of political debate in the House. Individual officials are aware of that assumption and in preparing a draft answer will act accordingly.'[31] The FDA rather cynically explained to the committee that in the light of the Scott report and the government's immediate response to it, three draft answers to PQs might now be put to ministers: first, the complete answer which fully accords with QPM; secondly, the answer which 'deliberately withholds information, but does not knowingly mislead'; and thirdly, the answer which 'designedly leads Parliament to believe one policy is in place where overwhelming evidence is to the contrary, but does so unintentionally'.[32] As with all good cynicism, this view contains a measure of truth, and it is a view with some heritage. H. E. Dale wrote over fifty years ago that 'the perfect reply to an embarrassing question in the House of Commons is one that is brief, appears to answer the question completely, if challenged can be proved to be accurate in every word, gives no opening for awkward supplementaries, and discloses really nothing'.[33] The political problem is, as Philip Giddings has pointed out, that the means which are used in Parliament to secure accountability are also used to 'wage party warfare'—and any distinction between legislative oversight and constitutional scrutiny of the government on the one hand, and scoring cheap political points and trying merely to discredit the government for the sake of it on the other, becomes blurred.[34] Even Sir Robin Butler agreed that this was 'a difficulty'.[35] However, in their evidence to the public service committee, government ministers did not agree with the Quinlan view on PQs, especially when it came to written answers.[36]

[29] See Public Service Committee, *Ministerial Accountability and Responsibility*, HC (1995–96) 313 (July 1996) and the government's response, HC (1996–97) 67 (Nov. 1996). The new guidance, which is discussed below, can be found at HC (1996–97) 67, p. xxiv.

[30] Public Service Committee, *Ministerial Accountability and Responsibility*, HC (1995–96) 313, para. 34.

[31] See ibid., Vol. III, Q 21.

[32] See ibid., Vol. III, p. 4, at para. 41 of the FDA's written memorandum of evidence.

[33] H. E. Dale, *The Higher Civil Service of Great Britain* (Oxford University Press, 1941) pp. 104–5, quoted by Philip Giddings, 'Parliament and the Executive' (1997) 50 *Parliamentary Affairs* 84, at p. 87.

[34] See Giddings, ibid., p. 87.

[35] Public Service Committee, *Ministerial Accountability and Responsibility*, HC (1995–96) 313, Vol. III, Q 828.

[36] See ibid., Vol. III, Q 1146 (evidence of Roger Freeman and Tony Newton).

In its report, the public service committee stated that 'ministers who approve the answers to PQs, and civil servants who draft them, should be prepared to be more open and clear in their answers than they have hitherto been prepared to be'.[37] In terms of ministerial refusals to answer, the committee recommended that the table office should each session publish a memorandum listing answers to PQs in which ministers had refused to give information.[38] The committee further recommended that the government should make it a standard practice when withholding information in an answer to a PQ to explain the grounds on which the information is being withheld.[39] The government's *Guidance to Officials on Drafting Answers to Parliamentary Questions*, announced in November 1996, now incorporates this recommendation.[40] The guidance provides that answers to PQs must always be formulated in the context of ministers' constitutional obligations to Parliament, as set out in QPM. It then provides, in what might be dubbed its 'political realism' paragraph, that ministers have the right to decide how their obligations under QPM are to be fulfilled, and this includes the right to 'explain and present government policy and actions in a positive light'. Ministers therefore have the right to 'expect a draft answer that does full justice to the government's position'. More positively, the guidance instructs civil servants to 'approach every question predisposed to give relevant information fully, as concisely as possible and in accordance with guidance on disproportionate cost'. Apparent conflicts between openness and any requirement to protect information from disclosure should be resolved in accordance with statute and then under the government's Code of Practice on Access to Government Information. In a clear echo of the Scott report, officials are specifically instructed not to 'omit information sought merely because disclosure could lead to political embarrassment or administrative inconvenience'. Borderline cases must be drawn to ministers' attention, as should any decision to give an answer which discloses information which is not normally revealed. Finally, if it is concluded that material information must be withheld and if as a result the PQ cannot be fully answered, the answer must make this clear and must explain the reasons why information is being withheld, using the terms of the Code of Practice on Access to Government Information.

If it is properly followed, this guidance should prevent any recurrence of the worst excesses of half-truth and obfuscation found by the Scott inquiry, but that 'if' is a big one. The system still depends on political goodwill among ministers and senior civil servants with few opportunities either for scrutiny or effective sanction. If it is found not to work, then Parliament will have no

---

[37] Public Service Committee, *Ministerial Accountability and Responsibility*, HC (1995–96) 313, Vol. III, para. 50.

[38] Ibid., para. 68. In its response to the committee's report, the government stated that this was a matter for the table office, not for the government, but that the government had no objection in principle: see HC (1996–97) 67, p. x.

[39] Ibid., para. 70.   [40] HC (1996–97) 67, p. xxiv.

option but to go one step further and create an official body (perhaps by extending the brief of the parliamentary commissioner for standards) to police answers to PQs, to report on abuses, and positively to enforce the standards which the guidance now lays down. Let us hope that the Labour government, with its manifesto 'pledge . . . to more open government'[41] renders any such move unnecessary by acting fully within the letter and spirit of the guidance.

Select Committees

In addition to PQs the second mechanism which Parliament employs in order to discover more in the way of detail of the government's policies, decisions, and actions and to hold the government to account is the system of select committees. Select committees are important in both Houses, but since 1979 the departmental select committees of the House of Commons have been particularly influential. To what extent, however, have select committees contributed to the flow from Whitehall to Parliament of governmental information? How powerful are select committees, and how effectively have they used their powers to acquire and make use of government information? In the House of Commons, standing order 130 provides that the role of the departmental select committees is 'to examine the expenditure, administration and policy of the principal government departments'.[42] In order to carry out these tasks select committees have the power to send for persons, papers, and records; they have their own small staff and may appoint specialist advisers; once appointed they may decide for themselves which aspects of departmental administration and policy they should investigate. Hearings of witnesses by select committees are held in public, although deliberations on draft reports are generally conducted in private.[43]

But what do these powers actually amount to in practice? Taking first the power to send for persons, while this appears to be an unqualified power, in practice it is limited by the constitutional doctrines of parliamentary privilege and royal prerogative. The basic position is that a select committee may summon those witnesses it requires to hear who are not MPs and who are not peers. If such a 'stranger' refuses a summons, they may be reported to the House in contempt and may be ordered to attend the bar of the House. If they

[41] Labour party manifesto for the 1997 general election, *Because Britain Deserves Better*, p. 33.

[42] Erskine May, op. cit., p. 1019.

[43] An exception, however, is the privileges committee, which usually sits in private, even when taking oral evidence. When Tony Benn, a member of the privileges committee, stated in Nov. 1994 that he would issue his personal report of the committee's proceedings in the face of the committee's failure to conduct its business in public, he was expelled from the committee: for a (very brief) report on this episode, see Committee of Privileges, *Special Report*, HC (1994–95) 27.

do not obey this order, they may be ordered to be sent for in custody of the serjeant-at-arms.[44] MPs and peers (whether ministers or not) are invited, rather than summoned, to appear.[45] While MPs (again, whether ministers or not) may be required to attend if an initial invitation is refused, peers cannot be compelled by the House of Commons to attend—the attendance of peers is subject to their personal agreement and to the consent of the House of Lords.[46] Although the House of Commons may order an MP to attend a select committee, this has not happened this century. Never has a minister been ordered to attend.[47]

While these powers appear to be quite broad in terms of getting hold of witnesses, is there any power to control what witnesses will say once they appear? Do select committee have powers, for example, to force witnesses to tell the truth, not to mislead Parliament, or to be as forthcoming as possible? Although the government has given a commitment that, where there is evidence of widespread general concern in the House on this point, it would seek to provide time for the House to express its view,[48] there are cases which illustrate that on occasion ministers still have the political ability to avoid detailed scrutiny, such as, most famously, the Westland saga of 1985–6, the salmonella-in-eggs affair of 1988–9, and the supergun investigation of 1992.[49] We shall now examine each of these in turn.

Select Committees and Information from Ministers

The Westland affair concerned a government rescue package for the Westland helicopter company. There was a choice between two rival packages: a European one favoured by Michael Heseltine at the ministry of defence, and an American one favoured by Leon Brittan at the department of

---

[44] This is the technical position. In practice these powers are generally kept in reserve with select committees preferring more informally to invite witnesses wherever possible.

[45] In its report on BMARC and export licensing, the trade and industry committee suggested that departmental select committees should be given the power to order the attendance of MPs: see HC (1995–96) 87, para. 166. This would reflect the position *vis-à-vis* the committee on standards and privileges. In its end of session report on *The Work of the Select Committees* the liaison committee endorsed this suggestion: see HC (1996–97) 323, para. 12.

[46] Standing order 22 (HL) provides that any peer requested by a Commons committee to attend shall have the leave of the House (of Lords) to attend if he thinks fit.

[47] See Diana Woodhouse, *Ministers and Parliament: Accountability in Theory and Practice* (Oxford: Clarendon Press, 1994) pp. 180–3. See also Griffith and Ryle, op. cit., pp. 280 ff and Erskine May, op. cit., ch. 25.

[48] HC Deb., Vol. 996, col. 1312, 16 Jan. 1981. In such circumstances it would be for members of the committee to argue why the House should exercise its powers to require the production of papers, and for ministers to explain the reasons of public policy for withholding them. No such formal confrontation has yet arisen.

[49] To which might be added the refusal of former prime minister Lady Thatcher to appear before the foreign affairs committee during its inquiry into the Pergau Dam affair: see HC (1993–94) 271.

trade and industry. When it appeared that the American deal would win the day, Mr Heseltine made his dissent public, saying that he was not bound by collective ministerial responsibility as the issue had not been discussed at cabinet. Mr Brittan responded to Mr Heseltine's public campaigning, but in a rather more discreet way (so discreet, in fact, that his actions were described as 'underhand and unworthy').[50] Mr Brittan employed such methods as using his civil servants at the DTI to lobby MPs, including members of the defence select committee. Then the bombshell came: Mr Heseltine had written a letter to the European consortium to the effect that if the US package was chosen, Westland might no longer be a welcome participant in European collaborations. This letter was leaked. The solicitor general, Sir Patrick Mayhew, responded in a letter to Mr Heseltine in which he advised that Mr Heseltine's letter had contained 'material inaccuracies'. The solicitor general's letter was also leaked—within hours of its being sent—and the leaking of selective parts of the letter, apparently by the DTI, seemed 'calculated to do the maximum damage to Mr Heseltine's case and his personal credibility'.[51] Three days later, in January 1986, Mr Heseltine famously, and rather dramatically, stormed out of Mrs Thatcher's cabinet and resigned.

There was an immediate inquiry into the leaking of the solicitor general's letter, headed by the cabinet secretary, Sir Robert Armstrong. He reported to the prime minister in late January 1986, and although the report has never been made public, when the prime minister reported the outline of Sir Robert's findings to Parliament, Mr Brittan resigned from the government. Significantly for our purposes, the defence select committee decided to launch an investigation into the affair—an investigation which proved almost as controversial as the initial saga had been. The committee wanted to question a number of named civil servants from the DTI (Colette Bowe, John Mitchell, and John Mogg, Mr Brittan's personal private secretary) and two named members of Mrs Thatcher's staff at No. 10 (Charles Powell and Bernard Ingham) but the government refused permission for any of these individuals to appear. The committee expressed its displeasure at the government's action, but decided not to bring the matter before the full House. Instead, the cabinet secretary, Sir Robert Armstrong, and Leon Brittan appeared before the committee, although when Mr Brittan attended he refused to answer questions concerning the leaking of the solicitor general's letter, saying he was 'not in a position' to answer such questions. In response to this, the defence select committee angrily stated in its report that 'accountability involves *accounting* in detail for actions as a minister'.[52]

In the parliamentary debate which followed Westland, John Biffen, then leader of the House, assured the Commons that there was no intention on the

---

[50] Woodhouse, op. cit., p. 107.
[51] According to the defence select committee in its report: HC (1985–86) 519, para. 162.
[52] HC (1985–86) 519.

part of the government to reduce the effectiveness of select committees: 'a select committee will be free to seek an account from the minister concerned ... we do not seek to prevent select committees from pursuing their inquiries into the expenditure, administration or policies of departments'.[53] What, however, is a select committee to do if a minister simply refuses to explain? Mr Biffen's rather bland reassurances provide no answer to this.

A further episode which illustrates the limitations of select committees' powers to force information out of the government is the affair in 1988–9 concerning salmonella and eggs. In December 1988 Edwina Currie, a junior minister at the Department of Health, stated in a television interview that 'we do warn people now that most of the egg production of this country, sadly, is now infected with salmonella'.[54] This statement led immediately to two weeks of political and media controversy, and eventually to Mrs Currie's resignation from the government. The agriculture select committee conducted an investigation into egg production and invited Mrs Currie to attend the committee—an invitation which she refused. When a second invitation was also refused, the committee resolved to put down a motion ordering that she should attend, and at this point Mrs Currie did agree to appear. When she attended the committee, however, she refused in her answers to the committee's questioning to add to her earlier statements, and, under pressure from its chairman, the committee did not press her. In its report the agriculture select committee was deeply critical of the ministers involved, and stated that 'we believe MPs have a clear duty to assist select committees' inquiries'.[55] As Woodhouse has argued, both the Westland and the salmonella-scare cases serve to illustrate the important point that 'the emphasis is on the select committee's ability to ask questions, not on the obligation of the minister to answer them' or to answer them truthfully or completely.[56]

Select Committees and Information from Civil Servants

If the Westland and salmonella-in-eggs cases illustrate the difficulties select committees have experienced in terms of freedom of information and ministers, the next case is indicative of the problems select committees face more generally as regards open government and civil servants. Before the Scott inquiry was established the trade and industry select committee (TISC) had already examined some aspects of the supergun part of the story which Scott was to investigate. The TISC report was weak and problematic, for at least three reasons: it split along party lines; it came only weeks before the 1992 general election and the issues it raised were therefore even more politically controversial than they would otherwise have been; and most significantly for

---

53 HC Deb., Vol. 103, col. 415, 29 Oct. 1986.   54 HC (1988–89) 108.
55 HC (1988–89) 108. See Woodhouse, op. cit., p. 186.   56 Woodhouse, op. cit., p. 211.

our purposes the committee was denied access to evidence from four key sources that did appear before the Scott inquiry.[57] These sources were Sir Hal Miller MP, two retired MOD officials, source materials from customs and excise, and evidence from the security and secret intelligence services as well as from the defence intelligence staff.[58]

The refusal of Sir Hal Miller to appear before TISC was (presumably) not the fault of the government. At the time of the TISC investigation he was still a Conservative back-bencher, although he retired at the 1992 general election. Quite why he refused to appear before TISC yet did offer evidence to the Scott inquiry is rather unclear, although it has been reported that he was upset at the treatment he received after his intervention in the House in April 1990 and consequently simply retreated into his shell.[59] Similarly the limited access granted to TISC of customs and excise source materials may in part have been explained by the *sub judice* rule (although only in part: by the time TISC was conducting its inquiry into the supergun, customs' prosecution in that case had been dropped even though other related prosecutions had not been). Again, select committees' extremely limited access to security and secret intelligence sources is nothing new: many previous investigations by select committees have been hampered in this respect.[60]

The government's refusal to allow two retired civil servants from the MOD to appear before TISC, however, is another matter altogether, as the Scott report pointed out. In February 1992 TISC wrote to the MOD stating that it wished to take evidence from the two retired officials. The MOD refused on the ground that as civil servants give evidence on behalf of their ministers, it was inappropriate for retired officials to appear before select committees.[61] In the view of the Scott report, while the MOD's approach to this matter (which was adopted in consultation with Sir Robin Butler, the cabinet secretary)[62] was not inconsistent with existing convention governing civil servants' evidence to select committees,[63] there was another approach which the government could (and should) have adopted. According to Scott, the government should seek to facilitate the provision of relevant evidence to a select

---

[57] Trade and Industry Committee, *Exports to Iraq: Project Babylon and Long Range Guns*, HC (1991–92) 86. For the government's response, see Cm. 2019 (1992). See Phythian and Little, 'Parliament and Arms Sales: Lessons of the Matrix Churchill Affair' (1993) 46 *Parliamentary Affairs* 293.

[58] See para. F1.2. Interestingly, although he thought that his inquiry was better positioned in these respects than was the TISC inquiry, Sir Richard Scott nonetheless felt that 'even the full inquiry which I have carried out into the state of government knowledge [on supergun] has left some unanswered questions'. See para. F1.4.

[59] See ch. 1 above. See Paul Foot, *Not the Scott Report: A Private Eye Arms to Iraq Special* (London: Pressdram, 1994) p. 4.

[60] See, for example, Home Affairs Select Committee, *Special Branch*, HC (1984–85) 71; Home Affairs Select Committee, *The Accountability of the Security Service*, HC (1993–94) 265.

[61] See para. F4.54.   [62] See paras. F4.55–63.

[63] See *Departmental Evidence and Response to Select Committees* (formally known as the Osmotherly rules) (Cabinet Office, 1997). This important document is discussed below.

committee where it lies in its power to do so, in order that the select committee may be better able to establish the relevant facts. As the Scott report put it: 'the provision of evidence to establish the relevant facts ought not to have been regarded as a matter on which the officials with first hand knowledge of those facts would have been giving evidence "on behalf of ministers" '.[64] A minister's duty to account to Parliament for what his department has done must surely be recognized as extending to an obligation to assist a select committee's investigation at least in terms of enabling it to obtain the best first-hand information available. As the Scott report stated: 'the refusal to facilitate the giving of evidence to TISC by [the two retired officials] may be regarded as a failure to comply fully with the obligations of accountability owed to Parliament'.[65]

As we saw in chapter one, the resolutions on ministerial responsibility passed by both Houses of Parliament in March 1997 have, to some extent, addressed these criticisms. The resolution states that 'ministers should require civil servants who give evidence before parliamentary committees on their behalf and under their directions to be as helpful as possible in providing accurate, truthful and full information'. This only partly addresses the criticisms voiced in the Scott report, however, as only serving civil servants (and not retired civil servants) are specifically covered under the terms of the resolutions. Even after the work of the public service committee and the new resolutions, select committees still have no sure way of being able to hear evidence from retired civil servants unless, exceptionally, ministers give their permission. It may be that select committees would want or need to hear evidence from retired civil servants only very rarely but, as the experience of TISC and of the Scott inquiry demonstrated, there will be some occasions when such evidence is nothing less than essential.

When a select committee wishes to hear evidence from a civil servant, the usual practice is for the committee to notify the relevant government department that it is looking for an official to give evidence on a particular topic, and the department will then nominate the appropriate civil servant(s). Erskine May states that 'successive governments have taken the view that officials giving evidence before select committees do so on behalf of their ministers and it is therefore customary for ministers to decide which official should represent them for that purpose'.[66] What constitutional instruments exist to ensure that civil servants are as forthcoming as possible in their evidence to select committees? The cabinet office has drawn up a memorandum of guidance for officials appearing before select committees. Formerly known

---

[64] See para. D4.64.

[65] See para. F4.66. In its end of session report the liaison committee added its voice to these criticisms, stating that 'it is unacceptable that committees should be denied access to civil servants whose knowledge of and involvement in government activity is essential to a committee inquiry' (see HC (1996–97) 323, para. 13).

[66] Erskine May, op. cit., p. 629.

as the Osmotherly rules, and now (since its 1994 redraft) entitled *Departmental Evidence and Response to Select Committees*,[67] specifically in terms of government information and Parliament, this memorandum states that 'the central principle to be followed is that it is the duty of officials to be as helpful as possible to select committees . . . [and that] any withholding of information should be limited to reservations that are necessary in the public interest'.[68] This general stance is supported by the principles of the white paper on *Open Government*[69] and the subsequent Code of Practice on Access to Government Information which were incorporated into the 1997 draft, which states that information should be handled in a way which 'promotes informed policy making and debate'; the citizen should be entitled to the provision of 'timely and accessible information' to explain government policies, actions, and decisions; and access to information should only be restricted 'when there are good reasons for doing so'.[70]

Formerly, after this initially promising tone the bulk of the memorandum was concerned with detailing the many restrictions which are placed on civil servants' evidence to select committees. In the 1994 edition,[71] for example, civil servants were barred from giving evidence relating to national security, private affairs, confidential information, ministers' quasi-judicial functions, matters subject to sensitive negotiation or legislative proposals.[72] Further, 'it has generally been accepted that the internal discussion and advice which has preceded ministerial decisions should not be disclosed'[73] and that while 'witnesses may answer questions on whether or not particular decisions were referred to and approved by ministers, [they] should not disclose: internal advice given to ministers . . .; inter-departmental exchanges on policy issues; the specific level at which particular decisions were taken; which particular minister or official took the decision; or the manner in which a minister consulted colleagues'.[74] In 1990 the select committee on procedure criticized the Osmotherly rules as being too restrictive: 'we doubt whether the fabric of constitutional government would suffer fatal injury if witnesses were more forthcoming'.[75] As Peter Hennessy has argued, 'MPs [are] denied any real knowledge of the inside workings of the Whitehall machine and any chance

---

[67] The Osmotherly rules were first issued in Sept. 1976 and were published by the procedure committee: HC (1977–78) 588, app. D. The most recent version was published in 1997 and is available from the machinery of government division of the cabinet office.

[68] *Departmental Evidence and Response to Select Committees* (Cabinet Office, 1997) para. 46.

[69] Cm. 2290 (1993).

[70] *Departmental Evidence and Response to Select Committees* (Cabinet Office, 1997) para. 62.

[71] The 1994 edition was the immediate predecessor of the 1997 edition.

[72] *Departmental Evidence and Response to Select Committees* (Cabinet Office, 1994) para. 61.

[73] Ibid., para. 66.   [74] Ibid., para. 67.

[75] HC (1989–90) 19. In 1994 Peter Hennessy told the treasury and civil service committee that in his view these rules were an affront to Parliament and that all they do is provide civil servants with sixty ways of saying no to select committees: see HC (1993–94) 27, para. 130.

of making bureaucratic brokers of concealed power accountable.'[76] A former civil servant told the treasury and civil service committee in 1994 that 'when I last had to give evidence to a Commons select committee I re-read the rules and considered then that for any civil servant to follow them would make his or her evidence at best anodyne and at worst positively misleading'.[77]

The 1997 edition removed many of these restrictions from the text of the memorandum and replaced them with the restrictions on the provision of information contained in the Code of Practice of Access to Government Information, which apply to the disclosure of government information in a number of situations, including that of officials' evidence to select committees. These limitations are hardly any less extensive than previous editions of the Osmotherly rules were.

All of this concerns select committees' powers to send for persons. What of their powers to send for records and papers? Select committees may order papers from government departments headed by a minister, but most are technically headed by a secretary of state. Parliament may only compel the production of documents from such departments or from the privy council through an address to the crown.[78] As Woodhouse has argued, these are 'historical restrictions of little relevance today'.[79] In its 1997 end of session report on the work of select committees, the liaison committee stated that 'there have been a significant number of cases where committees have been refused specific documents but the government has not provided time for the subject to be debated' on the floor of the House.[80] The committee recommended that to alleviate this position, 'the onus should be shifted onto the government to defend in the House its refusal to disclose information to a select committee' and further that if the chairman of a committee 'tables a motion on behalf of the committee that a specific document be laid before the committee the motion should be debated on the floor of the House within ten sitting days'.[81] These are important recommendations and should surely be implemented without delay.

The 1997 edition of *Departmental Evidence and Response to Select Committees* contains important guidelines with regard to select committees' rights of access to governmental papers. It provides, for example, that 'the government's commitment to provide as much information as possible to select committees is met largely through the provision of memoranda . . . it does not amount to a commitment to provide access to internal files, private correspondence, . . . advice given on a confidential basis or working papers'.[82]

---

[76] P. Hennessy, *Whitehall* (London: Fontana, 1990) pp. 362–3.

[77] HC (1993–94) 27, para. 130.

[78] See Erskine May, op. cit., p. 630. In 1985 the leader of the House stated that the government did not intend to take advantage of a select committee's inability to order papers from a secretary of state.

[79] Woodhouse, op. cit., p. 189.   [80] See HC (1996–97) 323, para. 16.   [81] Ibid.

[82] *Departmental Evidence and Response to Select Committees* (Cabinet Office, 1997) para. 50.

Further, even in those areas where the national audit office or the parliamentary commissioner for administration has direct access to departmental papers, this does not itself confer a similar right of access on the committees which they serve.[83]

In his evidence to the public service committee in 1996, Sir Richard Scott (among others) was deeply critical of the Osmotherly rules, arguing that they constituted a 'denial of an important part of the obligations of ministerial accountability' which, he stated, 'require ministers to facilitate select committees obtaining first-hand evidence from those with first-hand knowledge of the matter in question'.[84] It should be noted, as Philip Norton has pointed out, that the Osmotherly rules are not rules of the House: they have been laid down by the government, not by Parliament.[85] If the rules are so objectionable, why does Parliament not draw up its own rules? Just as Parliament has (at last) realized that ministerial responsibility is a constitutional obligation which ministers owe to Parliament and in respect of which Parliament (not the government of the day) should set the terms of the debate, so too should Parliament take more of an initiative in regulating the quality and the sources of the information which its committees receive from the government.

To this end the public service committee recommended that the liaison committee should reconsider the role of the national audit office *vis-à-vis* the departmental select committees. If one of the main problems for the select committees is the length of time spent on acquiring factual information, it might be possible for them to enlist the assistance of specialist bodies whose role this is (such as the NAO) without duplicating the work already carried out by the public accounts committee.[86] In its end of session report the liaison committee gave some thought to these matters and concluded that there was no demand across select committees to formalize the present *ad hoc* working relations between the NAO and the departmental select committees, but that the procedure committee in the next Parliament (i.e. after the 1997 election) should examine the related question of whether parliamentary commissions should be established. These would be akin to royal commissions or other public inquiries, but set up under the auspices of (and reporting to) Parliament, not government.[87] This is a valuable idea and should be taken further.

While it could be argued that select committees do lack some important powers (especially in terms of resources and in securing independent research, information gathering, and advice), is the more significant problem that select

---

[83] Ibid., para. 51.

[84] See Public Service Committee, *Ministerial Accountability and Responsibility*, HC (1995–96) 313, Vol. III, Q 397. See also Q 458.

[85] See ibid., Vol. II, p. 77. Despite the criticisms the government was not unhappy with the contents or the operation of the Osmotherly rules: see, e.g., the evidence of Roger Freeman, ibid., vol. III, p. 186 and Q 1113.

[86] See HC (1995–96) 313, para. 140.   [87] See HC (1996–97) 323, paras. 25–7.

committees have not exercised their existing powers with sufficient determination? Certainly this is the view of such seasoned observers as Peter Hennessy ('the problem with select committees . . . is the poverty of their aspirations')[88] and such prominent Whitehall insiders as Kate Jenkins ('Parliament itself may need to re-think its role and may need to adopt a much more professional approach in dealing with' matters of accountability and information).[89] This was also the view of Sir Richard Scott, who argued that 'select committees should be prepared to insist on answers being given or witnesses being produced, and . . . in the last resort should be prepared to use contempt proceedings, as courts do, in the event of refusals'.[90] While select committees in the House of Commons have since 1979 successfully operated across the party divide in many instances, there remains a considerable way to go in rejuvenating Parliament's independent identity, free (or at least freer) from governmental interest and close party control.[91]

Griffith and Ryle conclude that overall on the question of select committees and governmental information, 'the real power of select committees to secure evidence they want from ministers and civil servants lies in publicity. Ministers do not wish to be seen to be refusing to comply with requests. So committees almost always get what they want. But the Westland inquiries show that some information may be refused, even when the reason for the refusal seems to be to save ministers from embarrassment.'[92] On the whole, the reformed select committees may have increased the amount of government information made publicly available and may have ensured that there is now more routine departmental accountability as a result, but where the government considers it politically expedient to withhold information, even where to do so may mislead a committee, select committees' powers are, it seems, of little consequence.

Open Government and the Code of Practice

John Major's governments did more than any other in recent times to advance the causes of freedom of information and open government. Although the many legislative restrictions on open government remain unre-

---

[88] See ibid., Vol. III, Q 90. Hennessy was paraphrasing Ernest Bevin who used the phrase in the context of the working class.

[89] See ibid., Vol. III, Q 692. Kate Jenkins was one of the principal architects, along with Sir Peter Kemp and others, of the executive agency model adopted by the Conservative governments in their civil service reforms of the late 1980s and 1990s.

[90] Public Service Committee, *Ministerial Accountability and Responsibility*, HC (1995–96) 313, Vol. III, Q 419.

[91] A good overview is provided by G. Drewry (ed.), *The New Select Committees* (Oxford: Clarendon Press, 2nd edn. 1989).

[92] Griffith and Ryle, op. cit., p. 451.

pealed,[93] and although new statutory rights to access to information have not been enacted,[94] significant changes have nonetheless been put into effect. The central constitutional code of conduct for ministers, *Questions of Procedure for Ministers*, for example, even though it was first drawn up by Attlee's and Churchill's postwar governments, was not published until John Major decided that it should be, in 1992. In 1993 the government published a white paper on *Open Government*[95] and in April the following year the Code of Practice on Access to Government Information came into effect.[96]

This Code is extremely important. It applies to all bodies which are subject to the jurisdiction of the parliamentary commissioner for administration (PCA or ombudsman) under the Parliamentary Commissioner Act 1967. Under the Code, such bodies have an obligation, subject to a number of exemptions which are discussed below, (1) to publish the facts and the analysis of facts which form the backdrop to government policy; (2) to publish explanatory material on departments' dealings with the public; (3) to give reasons for administrative decisions to those affected; (4) to publish full information about how services are run, how much they cost, who is in charge, what complaints and redress procedures are available, what targets are set, and what standards are achieved; and (5) to release in response to specific requests information relating to government policies, actions, and decisions. The commitment is to release information, not original documents. Charges can be (and are) made by departments and other public bodies. Complaints under the Code are investigated first by the department concerned and then, where appropriate, by the ombudsman (via an MP in the usual way). The Code stipulates that 'the approach to the release of information should in all cases be based on the assumption that information should be released'[97] unless disclosure would 'not be in the public interest' as specified in the exemptions listed in part II of the Code. This is a major breakthrough in British government, reversing the traditional position of presumed secrecy. For the first time, the starting point is now that information should be released. Further, even where the Code provides for information to be

[93] The 1993 white paper on *Open Government* (Cm. 2290, July 1993) listed over 200 statutory restrictions on openness, and in many instances breaches are prohibited under the criminal law.

[94] The white paper (ibid.) stated that two new rights would be enacted covering greater rights of access to personal records held by government and by other public sector authorities, and public rights of access to information concerning human health and safety held by public authorities. The first of these would be necessary to meet the requirements of the draft EU general directive on data protection, due to come into force at the beginning of 1998. As of 1996 neither right had been enacted: a long delay which was roundly criticized by the select committee on the PCA in its report on *Open Government*, HC (1995–96) 84, paras. 91–5.

[95] Cm. 2290.

[96] A second, slightly revised, edition of the Code was introduced and came into effect on 1 Feb. 1997.

[97] Para. 1 of the Code. This passage was added in 1997 to the second edition of the Code on the recommendation of the select committee on the PCA: see HC (1995–96) 84, para. 25.

withheld under one of the harm-based exemptions the Code makes it clear
that 'the presumption remains that information should be disclosed unless the
harm likely to arise from disclosure would outweigh the public interest in
making the information available'.[98]

Part II of the Code lists fifteen exemptions to the basic principle in favour
of disclosure. Some of the exemptions are no more than one would expect and
merely mirror provisions of the Official Secrets Act 1989, but others go well
beyond. The exemptions are: (1) defence, security, and international relations; (2) internal discussion and advice; (3) communications with the royal
household; (4) law enforcement and legal proceedings; (5) immigration and
nationality; (6) effective management of the economy and collection of tax;
(7) effective management and operations of the public service; (8) public
employment, public appointments, and honours; (9) voluminous or vexatious
requests; (10) information which already is, or is about to be, published; (11)
research, statistics, and analysis; (12) privacy of an individual; (13) third
parties' commercial confidences; (14) information given in confidence; and
(15) information whose disclosure is prohibited under statute.[99]

The Code does not, of course, repeal any of the Acts of Parliament which,
in addition to the Official Secrets Acts, provide for limitations as to government openness and publication of information. However, the Code does represent a positive, if limited, step towards more open government. The
exemptions may be more broadly defined than one would ideally like; the
powers of the ombudsman as to enforcement and publicity may be limited;
and levels of public awareness (and use) of the Code may be disappointing,[100]
but the picture is not an entirely bleak one. The government has (at last)
accepted and acted on the basic principle of the importance of openness and
freedom of information and has strengthened Parliament's capabilities as
regards holding the executive to account.

Parliament, in the form of the select committee on the parliamentary commissioner for administration, has welcomed the government's Code. In an
important report published in March 1996 the committee outlined how the
Code had been implemented and how it had operated in its first two years.[101]
While the committee was not without its criticisms and reservations (as to the
lack of resources the government had committed to publicizing the Code, and
as to some of the overly broad exemptions in part II of the Code, for example) the unanimous report of the all-party committee was largely positive,

---

[98] Preamble to part II of the Code, 2nd edn., 1997. Again, this point of clarification was
added on the recommendation of the PCA select committee: HC (1995–96) 84, paras. 26–7.

[99] According to the government's analysis, the five exemptions most commonly relied on by
departments are numbers 2, 4, 7, 13, and 14: see OPS, *1996 Monitoring Report on the Code*, Mar.
1997, para. 29.

[100] This is discussed further below.

[101] This report was debated in the chamber of the House of Commons on 10 Dec. 1996 (see
Hansard, cols. 145 ff).

about both the need for open government and the contribution that the Code ought to make. In the committee's view, the Code is 'an important step forward which is already resulting in greater openness from government'.[102] In his evidence to the committee, the then ombudsman, William Reid, agreed that the Code represented 'a pretty immense attitude change within the public service'.[103] Underlining the more positive, modern executive attitude to open government, Roger Freeman MP, the cabinet minister in John Major's government with responsibility for open government, stated that 'it is very important [that] in government there should be a culture, a spirit of openness, because that makes for better decision-making amongst civil servants and ministers',[104] and further, that 'when you start saying, "well, we must only reveal the minimum amount of information possible to the public", and the presumption is that the public and Parliament do not have the right to know, you lead towards totalitarianism and political dictatorship'.[105]

Evaluating the Code

So much for the political rhetoric. How can we assess the Code in the light of the dismal failures of the government to be as open as it has now promised to be as illustrated throughout the Scott report? The Code came into force after the Scott inquiry had been established and well after the events which the inquiry investigated had occurred. If it had been in force at the time, would it have made any difference? Does the Code do enough to enhance Parliament's ability to hold the government to account? Is its contribution to the mechanisms which Parliament can employ to secure information from the government adequate? There are two levels at which these questions can be addressed: first, in terms of the Code itself, and secondly, in terms of the adjudications on complaints made under the Code which have been published by the ombudsman. Before we can examine these issues, however, it is important that we first understand why they are important. Freedom of information and open government are not simply ends in themselves: rather, they should be seen as contributing to broader goals. Three such goals were identified by the select committee on the PCA in its report on *Open Government* in March 1996: namely, greater accuracy and objectivity of personal files; improved decision making by ministers and civil servants; and more fully informed parliamentary and public debate on the issues of the day.[106] It is the second and third of these aims which are of most obvious importance in the context of the Scott report. To these three, however, we should also add the constitutional goal of holding the executive to account for its policies, decisions, and

---

[102] Select Committee on the PCA, *Open Government*, HC (1995–96) 84, para. 127.
[103] Ibid., para. 23.   [104] Ibid., para. 12.   [105] Ibid., para. 11.
[106] See HC (1995–96) 84, para. 20.

actions. It is not simply that the more information Parliament as a whole or one of its committees has, the easier it should be to hold the government fully to account, although that is part of the battle. Genuine open government relates not only to the quantity of information which is made available: it should also be concerned with the quality of that information. How quickly and effectively is Parliament able to turn raw information into valuable knowledge about the details of government policy or behaviour? Clearly, a number of factors combined to obstruct Parliament in this task when it came to defence exports to Iraq and the subsequent criminal prosecutions. Would the Code help to prevent these failures from recurring?

The terms of the Code suffer from a number of drawbacks. The Code applies only to those departments and agencies which fall within the jurisdiction of the ombudsman under the 1967 Act.[107] A number of bodies are excluded from the jurisdiction of the ombudsman, including the cabinet office. No doubt this is because it was envisaged in 1967 that the cabinet office would have so little direct contact with individual citizens that it would be difficult to conceive how individuals could sustain 'injustice in consequence of [its] maladministration' under the terms of section 5 of the Act.[108] However, the cabinet office is responsible for co-ordinating large amounts of government machinery, duties which include significant responsibilities as regards open government and freedom of information. While there may be a sensible reason for excluding the cabinet office from the jurisdiction of the ombudsman in terms of his usual role in investigating complaints of injustice and maladministration, this reason simply evaporates in the context of open government. Further, a number of important non-departmental public bodies (NDPBs, or quangos) are excluded from the ombudsman's jurisdiction, including the atomic energy agency, the monopolies and mergers commission, the civil aviation authority, the crown prosecution service, the Bank of England, the national curriculum council, and the broadcasting standards council, among many others.[109] The security and secret intelligence services are also expressly excluded from the Code, as is 'information obtained from or relating to them'.[110] As the campaign for freedom of information put it, 'it is unlikely that anyone devising an open government scheme from first principles would exclude [all these bodies] from its scope'.[111]

Further, even among those bodies which the ombudsman may investigate, there are limitations galore in terms of what may be investigated. Schedule 3

---

[107] The Code does apply in Northern Ireland, where the Northern Ireland parliamentary ombudsman has jurisdiction: see HC (1995–96) 185. There is a separate Code in respect of the NHS: see HC (1995–96) 84, para. 8.

[108] Individual complainants do not have to show that they have suffered personal injustice for the ombudsman to accept their complaints under the Code: see the ombudsman's report, *Access to Official Information: The First Eight Months*, HC (1994–95) 91, para. 3.

[109] See HC (1995–96) 84, para. 112.   [110] Para 6 of the Code (2nd edn., 1997).

[111] See HC (1995–96) 84, para. 112.

to the 1967 Act lists a number of such excluded matters, including international relations, consular matters, extradition, criminal investigations, criminal or civil proceedings, the prerogative of mercy, the detention of the mentally ill, contractual or commercial transactions, appointments, pay and other personnel matters, and the grant of honours. In addition, although the ombudsman enjoys considerable powers of access to information (under section 8 of the Act) there is one important limitation even here: section 8(4) prevents the ombudsman from having access to cabinet papers or papers of cabinet committees. This has seriously hampered the ombudsman in at least one investigation under the Code which had to be aborted as a result. This investigation concerned a request for access to the report of an interdepartmental working group which had considered the implications of the House of Lords' ruling in *Pepper* v. *Hart*. This gives rise to a serious anomaly: although cabinet papers are not as such exempted from disclosure under the terms of the Code, the ombudsman, in investigating complaints made to him under the Code, has no right of access to such papers! As the select committee on the PCA put it (echoing a recommendation the committee had made as long ago as 1978), this provision of the 1967 Act should be repealed immediately.[112]

If these are the main weaknesses of the Code as far as the position of the ombudsman is concerned, the Code is also limited in that it requires the disclosure of information, but not of documents themselves. Both the select committee on the PCA and the public service committee have called for this limitation to be lifted, but the government has refused. The Conservative government's position was that while original documents would in some cases be an important source of information, in many instances releasing original documents would be undesirable. Not only would it be practically easier to use modern information technology to respond to Code requests rather than to use paper records which would in many cases need time-consuming and careful editing, but further, automatic release of documents rather than information 'would lead to too great an emphasis on the form of the material rather than its substance . . . it could also lead to authors of documents being identified and associated with a particular policy stance'. Moreover, the government pointed out that the Code did not prohibit the release of original documents where that would be appropriate.[113]

---

[112] According to the 1978 and 1996 recommendations, 'no harm would be done by allowing the commissioner access to cabinet or cabinet committee papers in the very rare cases where he considered it necessary, except where the attorney general certified that such access would itself be prejudicial to the safety of the state or otherwise contrary to the public interest'. See HC (1995–96) 84, para. 113. In its response to the committee's report, the government rejected this recommendation, asserting (rather spuriously) that as far as cabinet papers are concerned, there is a 'presumption that disclosure would be harmful to the public interest'. See HC (1996–97) 75, p. vii.

[113] See HC (1996–97) 75, p. vi. For the respective committees' recommendations, see HC (1995–96) 84, para. 83 and HC (1995–96) 313, para. 160.

A final concern relates to the low publicity which the Code has attracted. The select committee on the PCA was critical of the very low levels of funding which the government granted to publicizing the Code, which the committee described as 'meagre'. In the committee's words, 'the vigour with which the government publicizes the Code is a key test of the sincerity of its concern for openness. Is open government regarded as an enthusiastic initiative or a grudging concession? The facts to date suggest a government machine suspicious of its own Code and unwilling to encourage its use.'[114] The poor publicity is reflected in the low use of the Code: in its first year, only forty-one complaints were referred to the ombudsman. Of course, this may be because initial requests under the Code to departments are being responded to so quickly and fully that those seeking information have nothing to complain about. Sadly, however, this is difficult to determine. Government statistics on departmental use of the Code are poor. The government was slow to agree any criteria across departments as to how a 'Code request' is to be defined for the purpose of collating data on the Code, and there has accordingly been little effective monitoring by the office of public service on the implementation of the Code. Needless to say the select committee on the PCA was extremely critical of this failure.[115] The ombudsman himself has complained that 'there remains a wholly insufficient level of awareness of the opportunities afforded by the Code to the citizen'.[116] By 1996 the OPS had begun to put this right and had agreed on a government-wide definition of 'Code request' which it could then monitor. According to government figures there were 1,353 requests for information under the Code in 1995 and 2,033 in 1996.[117] This indicates that the Code is now beginning to attain a higher profile, as a practical result perhaps of the government's belated advertising campaign which during 1996 led to almost 5,000 responses asking for information about the Code.[118] However, although there is some evidence that the increased public awareness of the Code is having an effect in terms of the numbers of Code requests being received by departments, this effect is limited and has not yet manifested itself in terms of complaints being referred to the ombudsman.

So the Code is not perfect. Even the second edition of the Code, published in February 1997, which incorporates modest changes in response to some of the criticisms rehearsed above, has not satisfied all of the recommendations of the PCA committee.[119] However, despite its weaknesses, the Code is nonetheless the single most significant development towards open government which

---

[114] HC (1995–96) 84, para. 59.   [115] See ibid., para. 51.   [116] See ibid., para. 56.
[117] OPS, *1996 Monitoring Report for the Code*, Mar. 1997, paras. 16–20.
[118] Ibid., para. 44.
[119] The Code still focuses on information rather than documents, for example, and exemption 5 (immigration and nationality) remains, albeit in an amended form, despite the committee's recommendation that it should be written out.

the British constitution has seen. There are aspects of the Code which are very welcome. Most significantly, both the select committee on the PCA and the public service committee were strongly enthusiastic about the role of the ombudsman under the Code. Even the campaign for freedom of information stated that the Code 'is capable of eliciting information which would previously not have been disclosed. The prospect of an investigation by the ombudsman does appear to make departments whose objections to disclosure are not well-founded think again.'[120] The fact that the Code is enforced by the ombudsman (and not by the courts) should be seen as one of its main strengths and as a positive reminder and reinforcement of Parliament's constitutional role of holding the government to account. The ombudsman is, of course, not an independent or isolated figure, but an officer of the House of Commons—a part of the parliamentary constitution. There are numerous advantages in having the ombudsman as the adjudicator in cases of open government. The most obvious and important one is that the courts have repeatedly and convincingly demonstrated that they would be wholly inappropriate arbiters of freedom of information disputes, as the long history of public interest immunity which is fully examined in chapter five below illustrates. Relying on the ombudsman means that we do not have to rely on the courts.

But there are also more positive arguments in favour of the ombudsman's role: for example, there are no costs to the complainant; the investigation is quick or, at least, quicker than legal processes tend to be; the ombudsman avoids the courts' more confrontational and adversarial approach; the ombudsman enjoys greater flexibility of approach than courts do; the ombudsman is already an important and influential part of British parliamentary government, enjoying hard-earned and widespread respect across government; and the ombudsman is able to make valuable longer-term broad recommendations in ways which courts are unable to.[121] These considerable advantages are borne out by Australian experience of open government initiatives. The ombudsman in Queensland, for example, has argued that 'the ombudsman, because of his experience, currently existing powers, cheapness, flexibility, informality and non-confrontational approach [is] ideally placed to serve as the external review mechanism' for freedom of information.[122] The British ombudsman in post at the time the Code was introduced, William Reid, agreed with this view, stating that because of the way the ombudsman regularly works with government departments, he is far better placed than courts would be not only to provide the individual with redress but also to affect the philosophy of departments and the procedure they adopt in relation to open government.[123]

---

[120] See HC (1995–96) 84, para. 34.   [121] See ibid., para. 104.   [122] See ibid., para. 103.
[123] See ibid., para. 105.

The select committee on the PCA was persuaded by these arguments and recommended that in the future, even if there are further changes in the regime of open government in Britain, the central role of the ombudsman should be preserved: 'more recent FOI regimes established abroad have followed the ombudsman model . . . [and] we have an ombudsman institution which . . . has achieved an influential, respected and highly effective place in our administrative life. We recommend that the ombudsman . . . model remain the external review mechanism for consideration of FOI complaints'.[124] Whether the Labour government will accept this view remains to be seen. Although it was a manifesto commitment to enact statutory rights to freedom of information, no such bill was outlined in the Blair government's first queen's speech in May 1997, although a (further) white paper was promised for later in 1997 with a bill to follow in early 1998.

The Work of the Ombudsman under the Code

While the ombudsman and his committee are happy with the role played by the ombudsman under the Code, the question remains: how has this role been carried out in practice? Has the work of the ombudsman actually pushed forward the causes of open government and freedom of information? Statistically the workload of the ombudsman has been quite low: only seventy-two complaints under the Code were received by the ombudsman in the first twenty months of the Code's operation (April 1994–December 1995) of which twenty-eight were received in 1994 and forty-four in 1995. The ombudsman has stated that this number was much lower than he had expected based on initial experience in other countries. In the ombudsman's view this is in part because of the lack of public awareness of the Code but also partly due to the number of obstacles which must be overcome before a complaint may be made. The procedure is rather clumsy: first, a written request must be made to the relevant department for information; then (supposing the department has decided not to release the information) a request for an internal review must be made; this must in turn be followed by an approach to an MP; and then finally the MP can refer the matter to the ombudsman. In the ombudsman's words, this obstacle course is 'quite daunting'.[125] Of the forty-four complaints received in 1995 the ombudsman agreed to investigate sixteen. Nine investigations were reported in 1995, the average length of investigation being thirty-three weeks—significantly longer than the ombudsman's target of thirteen weeks.[126] Two reasons are given for the

---

[124] Ibid., para. 109. The (Conservative) government welcomed this endorsement of the ombudsman's role: HC (1996–97) 75, p. xiv.

[125] See *Access to Official Information: The First Eight Months*, HC (1994–95) 91, para. 12.

[126] See HC (1995–96) 84, para. 110. In contrast, government departments are generally meeting their targets in responding to Code requests: in 1996 departments met their 20-day target in 93% of cases. See OPS, *1996 Monitoring Report on the Code*, Mar. 1997, para. 31.

lengthy investigations: first, some of the cases are extremely complex 'test' cases; and secondly, some departments have tended to use every argument that can conceivably be employed to resist disclosure, and the ombudsman has found it time consuming to consider all the defences which such departments have raised.[127] On the other hand, it would be wrong to assume that the overall picture of the Code's operations can be fully appreciated solely from examining the work of the ombudsman. Extensive lists of information which has been voluntarily released by government departments and agencies without the involvement of the ombudsman are published in the OPS's annual monitoring reports on the implementation of the Code. These lists give a strong impression of a government genuinely if steadily coming to terms with the new, higher, standards of openness laid down by the Code.

However, despite their small numbers, it is the cases which have reached the ombudsman which deserve the closest scrutiny, as it is these cases, in which the government has initially refused disclosure, which demonstrate just how powerful an instrument the Code is in securing the release of information which the government does not really want to publish. A number of collections of the ombudsman's adjudications made under the Code have been published.[128] These reports give a very positive impression, and indicate that the ombudsman takes his responsibilities under the Code seriously. He has ruled, for example, that he has the right to interpret the Code independently of (and more broadly than) the government's interpretation of it in its official guidance for departments on the implementation of the Code.[129] Similarly, the ombudsman has shown that although in strictly legal terms his enforcement of the Code lacks binding sanctions, his office is capable (and willing) to exert considerable pressure on departments to persuade them to comply with his rulings. The select committee on the PCA—habitually a keen observer of these matters—has stated that it is satisfied that the ombudsman's adjudications under the Code are *de facto* binding.[130] This is borne out by the campaign for freedom of information, which told the committee that its initial experience of the Code had been good and that it had encountered 'no

[127] HC (1995–96) 84, para. 110.

[128] The first four collections are published at HC (1994–95) 14; HC (1994–95) 606; HC (1994–95) 758; and HC (1995–96) 86. The decisions reported in these collections are considered, below.

[129] See Case A.11/95, reported at HC (1994–95) 758, pp. 13–14. Although the guidance states that it is 'advisory only', the ombudsman was told by the permanent secretary involved in that case (which concerned the home office and records held by the security service) that the guidance was 'a firm and authoritative statement' as to the meaning of the Code. The ombudsman flatly—and rightly—rejected this view, and, although the complaint in question was unsuccessful, in deciding the case the ombudsman took a different view of the Code from that which was expressed in the government's guidance. Although the complainant lost, this adjudication sends out a strong message to government departments that the ombudsman cannot be manipulated by the government in his enforcement of the Code.

[130] See HC (1994–95) 84, para. 118.

evidence of departmental reluctance' to implement decisions taken by the ombudsman under the Code.[131]

Of the fifteen cases reported in the first four collections of the ombudsman's decisions under the Code, information was released which the government was not initially going to release in ten cases, sometimes as a direct result of a ruling by the ombudsman, and in other cases simply because of a complaint being referred to the ombudsman. Something of the breadth of the Code can be gleaned from a brief survey of these fifteen cases. Let us take first the five cases in which the government was not compelled to disclose further information. In these cases the ombudsman ruled that the inland revenue commissioners were right not to disclose to a complainant the name of a third party who had bought a property in Wales (applying exemption 12: privacy);[132] that the department of health was justified in not disclosing the details of those involved in discussions about drafting a code of practice for the pharmaceuticals industry (exemption 7: effective operations of the public service);[133] that the driver and vehicle licensing agency was right not to disclose the name of an individual who had (wrongly) informed it that the complainant was medically unfit to drive (exemption 14: information given in confidence);[134] that the ombudsman has no jurisdiction to investigate records held by the security service which directly concerned the protection of the security of the state (under schedule 3 to the Parliamentary Commissioner Act 1967);[135] and that the ministry of agriculture, fisheries and food was justified in refusing to disclose the identity of an importer who had sold to the complainant a cow which was suffering from foot and mouth disease where MAFF had offered the complainant *ex gratia* compensation after the cow had been slaughtered (exemption 13: third party's commercial confidences).[136]

On the other side of the equation, however, are the ten cases which did result in further disclosure. Among these cases are the ombudsman's decision that the report of a planning inspector concerning Birmingham's northern relief road should be disclosed;[137] that information given by the highways agency to the European commission concerning the environmental impact assessment of a motorway widening scheme should be released;[138] that details of a government contract for an airborne radiometric survey on Scotland should be disclosed;[139] that complainants were entitled to see their national insurance report and other reports which had been presented to or compiled by the department of social security;[140] that information concerning the

---

[131] See HC (1994–95) 84, para. 115.   [132] Case A.7/94, reported at HC (1994–95) 14.
[133] Case A.5/94, ibid.   [134] Case A.21/95, reported at HC (1994–95) 606.
[135] Case A.11/95, reported at HC (1994–95) 758. See sch. 3, para. 5, and s. 5(3).
[136] Case A.22/94, reported at HC (1995–96) 86.
[137] Case A.4/94, reported at HC (1994–95) 14.
[138] Case A.3/94, reported at HC (1994–95) 606.   [139] Case A.6/94, ibid.
[140] Cases A.17/94 and A.24/95, reported at HC (1994–95) 606 and HC (1994–95) 758, respectively.

review of the former broadcasting ban on Sinn Fein and others should be released by the department of national heritage;[141] that details about a pension fund operated under the auspices of the department of transport should not be withheld;[142] that treasury information concerning financial malpractice in Whitehall should be revealed;[143] that the charity commissioners should disclose information concerning a certain charity;[144] and that details of a working group sponsored by the department of the environment looking into questions of air pollution should be disclosed.[145]

What do these cases tell us? Clearly, fifteen adjudications is not a great deal to go on, but initial experience under the Code as illustrated by these decisions is overwhelmingly positive. In several of the cases in which information has been forthcoming as a result of the ombudsman's intervention, that information has been disclosed without the ombudsman having to resort to making a full investigation and formal finding that the Code has been breached: often, the department or agency concerned has simply handed over the information to the complainant as soon as it has heard that a complaint has been made (the case involving the charity commissioners and one of the cases concerning the DSS come within this category). In these cases the ombudsman's report is accompanied by a note that the relevant agency or department has apologized for its tardiness in disclosing the information and has now reformed its procedures. This last point is an important aspect of the ombudsman's role. As was noted above, the ombudsman is not solely concerned with redress of individual grievances: he is also concerned with improving public administration for the future. In the context of open government, the decision on the Birmingham relief road is a good example of this. After the ombudsman's ruling that the inspector's report on the scheme should be disclosed (incidentally, the decision was that the document itself should be disclosed, so here we have a case of the Code being used to secure the release of original documents, not merely of information) the department of transport decided that other reports withheld in similar circumstances would also in the future be released, a response which the ombudsman welcomed in his report.[146]

The Code has not changed the world—and nor has it entirely changed the face of British government—but despite its weaknesses, it has done more than any other single initiative to begin to render British central government more open. All those who have examined or worked with the Code have acknowledged this, including the campaign for freedom of information. While the exemptions are too broadly drawn, and while there are limitations in the jurisdiction of the ombudsman and in the scope of the Code, the central thrust of the Code is nonetheless a welcome and valuable reinforcement of

---

[141] Case A.12/95, reported at HC (1994–95) 758.   [142] Case A.8/94, ibid.
[143] Case A.20/95, ibid.   [144] Case A.4/95, reported at HC (1995–96) 86.
[145] Case A.9/95, ibid.
[146] Case A.4/94, reported at HC (1994–95) 14. See esp. pp. 1 and 4.

Parliament's constitutional functions in holding the government to account. Whether the desperate stories recounted in the Scott report of obsessive government secrecy and extensive, almost habitual, uncooperativeness would have been prevented by the Code we cannot know.[147] Initial experience has been positive, but it is still too soon to tell whether the Code will fulfil its promise and grow into a high-profile, binding contract between Whitehall and the people it serves, or whether in the longer term it will wither away, suffering the same rather pathetic fate as the Croham directive of the late 1970s.[148]

Do we need a Freedom of Information Act?

In the present political climate, however, the debate rages on as to whether Britain should have a Freedom of Information Act (FOIA). The two select committees which considered this question in 1996 came to different conclusions, with the PCA committee recommending that there should be an Act, albeit one which preserved the functions of the ombudsman and did not transfer his role to the court, and the public service committee recommending that amendments to the Code should suffice and that an amended Code would obviate the need for any Act.[149] In its evidence to these committees the Conservative government outlined its opposition to enacting a FOIA, arguing that the system of having a Code accompanied by a series of Acts affecting information is preferable because it is 'more flexible' as the Code could be quickly amended or extended. In the Conservatives' view, the Code is also 'cheaper and quicker' to use than an Act would be, although this argument assumes that an Act would place any enforcement functions onto the courts rather than with the ombudsman. Quite why the government made this assumption is rather unclear.[150]

The select committee on the PCA, however, found three reasons for supporting the enactment of a FOIA which, in its view, overrode the government's objections. First, a far greater degree of publicity would attach to the passing of an Act than the Code has managed to attract. Secondly, an Act, with the full parliamentary and public debate which would accompany it, would be more influential in changing the culture of government than a Code could be. Finally,

---

[147] Even the most ardent advocates of a Freedom of Information Act have had to admit that 'quite simply, we shall never know whether a Freedom of Information Act would have prevented the Matrix Churchill episode' and that 'by itself, it probably would not have done so'. See P. Birkinshaw, 'Freedom of Information' (1997) 50 *Parliamentary Affairs* at p. 166.

[148] On which, see R. Austin, 'Freedom of Information: The Constitutional Impact', in J. Jowell and D. Oliver (eds.), *The Changing Constitution* (Oxford: Clarendon Press, 3rd edn, 1994) at p. 419. The select committee on the PCA was optimistic that, because of the 'changing climate' and the external role of the ombudsman, the Code was a significant improvement on the Croham Directive: see HC (1995–96) 84, para. 121.

[149] See, respectively, HC (1995–96) 84, para. 126 and HC (1995–96) 313, paras. 155 and 160.

[150] See HC (1995–96) 84, para. 122.

and for the committee most significantly, under EU initiatives the government will have to make changes in this direction in any event: statutory rights of access to personal information and to health and safety information (rights which would be enforced not by the ombudsman but by the data protection registrar and by a new tribunal) are intended. In the committee's view, it would be preferable, rather than adding new bits and pieces to an already crowded picture, simply to incorporate all these various developments, including the Code, in a single Act, keeping the ombudsman at the heart of the matter.[151]

This is surely a sensible recommendation. That it was not supported by the public service committee is surprising, for there is a more compelling, constitutional argument in favour of enshrining these matters in a FOIA which appears to have been missed by both the committees. As we saw in chapter one, the public service committee was concerned that questions of ministerial responsibility had been manipulated by the government, which had sought to redefine the meaning of the doctrine by amending the various constitutional texts which dealt with it. These texts, such as *Questions of Procedure for Ministers*, were government documents, not statutory materials. Accordingly, the committee recommended that the issue of ministerial responsibility should no longer be outlined only in government papers but should be the subject of parliamentary concern, a recommendation which led to the resolutions on ministerial responsibility in March 1997. Surely the same argument should be made about freedom of information. Open government is too important an issue to leave to the government. Roger Freeman stated that flexibility was one of the main strengths of the Code, but why should the government be able to change the rules regulating the extent to which it is open? This should be a matter for Parliament, not for Whitehall, to determine. The main advantage of a FOIA is that the government would no longer be bound by its own rules but by those laid down by those superior to it: namely, Parliament. Thus, as has resulted from the changes in the area of ministerial responsibility, the government would become accountable to the constitution, and not the other way round.

The Scott report did not recommend the enactment of a FOIA, to many people's disappointment and surprise. However, after the report had been published, Sir Richard Scott did advocate in public that in his view there should be an Act. In his evidence to the public service committee, for example, he stated that although he 'used not to think that there would be any great value in a statutory FOIA', he had changed his mind. He gave two reasons: first, because it would lead to a change of culture across government, and secondly, because it would enhance the role of the courts.[152] This being the

---

[151] Ibid., paras. 124–6.
[152] See HC (1995–96) 313, Vol. III, Q 421. Scott obviously assumed that any FOIA would be judicially enforced, not policed by the ombudsman. From his evidence to the committee, this seems to have been a bald assumption rather than a reasoned argument on his part.

case, why did Scott not say so at the one point where the government might have listened to him, i.e. in the report? The answer is that Scott did not think that such a recommendation would be appropriate. He saw his job as simply to report on what had happened as regards defence exports to Iraq. What had happened was that the government had not given a true or complete picture to Parliament or to the public as to its policy in this field. That was what the Scott inquiry found, and that was what the report stated. In Scott's view, it was then for others (i.e. Parliament) to determine what the broader constitutional consequences of his findings might be, and not for him to lay down what he thought they ought to be. Whether it was modesty, exhaustion or a commitment to democratic principle which primarily informed Scott's self-denying ordinance is hard to tell, but whatever its cause, it inevitably lessened the immediate impact of the report.

A strong recommendation in the report that Britain urgently needed a modern Freedom of Information Act would have been difficult for the government to reject. No doubt such an Act would not of itself have prevented the scandals which the Scott inquiry was appointed to investigate, but it would have made it easier to identify and expose the failures of the government's policy towards Iraq and it would have allowed Parliament and the public to hold the government more firmly to account for their uninformative answers and their misleading statements. The Code of Practice on Access to Government Information and the subsequent strengthening of the regulation of answers to PQs constitute an improvement on the position as the Scott report found it to be, but the continuing effect of the appalling Osmotherly rules and the lack of a good Freedom of Information Act mean that the constitutional control of official information is still too much in the hands of the government of the day, rather than with Parliament and the public.

PART II
Government and Secret Intelligence

4

Governing Without Intelligence

THE Scott inquiry was the longest and most public investigation into Britain's security and secret intelligence communities that we have ever seen. Yet little has been said of this aspect of the Scott inquiry either in the parliamentary debates which followed the publication of the report or in the subsequent literature.[1] On one level this is not surprising. There is no chapter of the Scott report headed 'intelligence' to which one can turn to find with ease what Scott has to say about the successes and failures of the intelligence services in the story which the inquiry uncovered. Instead, one has to pick through the report's more obscure passages such as the detailed lists of specific cases of the application of the Howe guidelines on exports to Iran and Iraq in chapter D2 (a mere 435 paragraphs) and again in chapter D6 (a further 485 paragraphs) piecing together coded references about export licence 3G/53234/88 and a telegram sent by Mr O of the secret intelligence service to Mr P of the security service in December 1988.[2] This detective work reveals a hitherto private world of government decision making and secret intelligence. This is exactly the constitutional value of Scott: despite its lack of political bite the Scott story remains one of not only high but unprecedented constitutional importance. Although public lawyers and political observers may long have suspected that all was not well in the murky world of intelligence and government, now we know. Never before has a public inquiry uncovered so much information so close to the heart of British central government on such a sensitive issue.

There are three separate parts of the Scott story which involve security and secret intelligence. The first concerns the export licensing process. Companies such as Matrix Churchill were prosecuted for breaches of export licensing law—in the Matrix Churchill case three company directors were charged with deception offences relating to their export licences. The question which concerns us is what the intelligence community and the government ministers and officials knew, at the time the export licences were applied for and processed, about the true nature of Matrix Churchill's business with Iraq. The second aspect of the Scott story with an intelligence link is the supergun case. Why did it take the intelligence agencies so long to uncover and then to act on this gigantic project? Why was this case, which customs regarded as their biggest

---

[1] Although for a brief summary, see Davina Miller, 'Intelligence and Proliferation: Lessons from the Matrix Churchill Affair' (1996) 11 *Intelligence and National Security* 193.

[2] Among many examples: see paras. D6.73 and D6.78.

ever, a prosecution failure? Thirdly, there is also an important connection (more accurately disconnection) between relevant intelligence and the prosecution teams from customs and excise: why, for example, did leading counsel for the prosecution in the Matrix Churchill case not see one ultimately crucial intelligence report until after the beginning of the trial? If the prosecution teams had seen the relevant intelligence earlier, would the trial have gone ahead at all? The first parts of this chapter will outline what the Scott report told us about each of these episodes, and then the later parts of the chapter will seek to move towards an evaluation of what it is we have to learn from the appalling chronicle of intelligence failure which Scott revealed.

Intelligence and Government Decision Making

Before we can examine Matrix Churchill's export licences in detail, a little needs to be said as to the nature of government decision making in the field of export licensing. Three government departments were directly involved in the control of export licensing: the FCO, the MOD, and the DTI. Of these, the DTI was the department which was responsible for most of the administrative work. The export licensing bureau (ELB) was located within the DTI; export licences were granted by the ELB, in consultation with the other two departments (the FCO and MOD). These departments and their ministers were assisted by a number of advisory groups and committees, most notably the restricted enforcement unit (REU), the working group on Iraqi procurement (WGIP), and the MOD working group (MODWG). The precise composition and functions of each of these committees will be outlined as they come to be mentioned in the text, below. This network of government decision makers was supported by the intelligence community. For our purposes, the intelligence community is constituted by five separate organizations. First there are the three agencies: colloquially known as MI5, SIS (or MI6), and GCHQ. The security service (or MI5) is responsible for protecting national security, in particular, against 'threats from espionage, terrorism and sabotage'.[3] It was established in 1909 but not given statutory authority until the Security Service Act 1989.[4] It has close links with the home office. The secret intelligence service (SIS) is responsible for obtaining and providing 'information relating to the actions or intentions of persons outside the British islands'.[5] SIS performs these tasks in the 'interests of national security', in the 'interests of the economic well-being of the UK' or 'in support of the prevention or detection of serious crime'.[6] SIS was put on the statute book along

---

[3] Security Service Act 1989, s. 1(2).
[4] See now also the Security Service Act 1996, which formally extends MI5's responsibilities with regard to supporting the police in the 'prevention and detection of serious crime' (s.1(1)).
[5] Intelligence Services Act 1994, s. 1(1)(a).   [6] Ibid., s. 1(2).

with GCHQ by the Intelligence Services Act 1994. SIS has close links with the foreign office. Government communications headquarters (GCHQ) is responsible for signals intelligence (SIGINT).[7] In addition to these three agencies, two other intelligence organizations played an important role in the Scott story: the defence intelligence staff (DIS) and the joint intelligence committee (JIC). DIS was formally established in an MOD restructuring in 1964. It has no specific statutory authority but is thought to be responsible for providing and analysing intelligence on military matters and defence policy to the MOD. SIS also has a branch located within the MOD, 'whose existence is not normally acknowledged'.[8] What the relationship is between DIS and the MOD branch of SIS is unknown. Finally, the JIC, which is located in the cabinet office, is responsible for co-ordinating intelligence across government. Its roles are considered in detail towards the end of this chapter.

A thorough examination of the export licensing process and the role(s) of secret intelligence in that process as it applied to Iran and Iraq during the entire period covered by the Scott report would take several hundred pages. To make matters more comprehensible the focus here will be on the characters that became the protagonists of the drama: Matrix Churchill. It is important that the reasons for this are not misunderstood. The Scott report concerned matters far broader and deeper than merely what happened to one Iraqi owned Coventry based company in the late 1980s and early 1990s. Their sad story of another 600 unemployed in the West Midlands does not need a multimillion pound public inquiry in order for it to be told. But the collapse of the Matrix Churchill trial in November 1992 was the immediate reason behind the establishment of the Scott inquiry; the Matrix Churchill case (*R* v. *Henderson and others*) was the only one to be expressly mentioned in the terms of reference of the Scott inquiry; and as the Matrix Churchill case has become the one about which we know most, due to the focus on it in the Scott report itself, it is the one about which most can be said with certainty and accuracy. Moreover, the fact that what happened to Matrix Churchill also happened elsewhere heightens rather than reduces the importance of their particular story. As a close reading of the Scott report will disclose, other branches of the Iraqi arms procurement network, other companies, other failed prosecutions, could quite easily have become the household names instead of Matrix Churchill: BSA, Wickman Bennett, and so on. Matrix Churchill is thus a story in and of itself, but it is also a representative story, revealing a malaise at the centre of British government which was to affect not only that one company, but which spread well beyond.

---

[7] The Intelligence Services Act 1994, s. 3(1)(a) provides that GCHQ shall 'monitor or interfere with electromagnetic, acoustic and other emissions'. The expenditure for the three agencies in 1995–6 was £782 million, £70 million less than in 1994–5. Figures for each agency separately are not published: the available figure derives from the single intelligence vote: see Intelligence and Security Committee, *Annual Report 1996* (Cm. 3574, Feb. 1997) para. 21.

[8] See para. F2.36.

The first Matrix Churchill Export Licence Applications

So much for the background. Three sets of Matrix Churchill export licence applications (ELAs) fall to be examined. The first dates from 1987. In August 1987 Matrix Churchill applied for export licences to export machine tools to Hutteen in Iraq. The ELA stated that the nature of Hutteen's business was 'general engineering' and that the precise purpose of the goods to be exported was the 'manufacturing of general engineering products'.[9] No further details were provided. As the Scott report commented, such a brief statement is the very 'antithesis of a "precise" purpose' which the ELA called for, yet this degree of imprecision was apparently routinely accepted by the DTI.[10] Perhaps if a more rigorous approach to the information provided on ELAs had been taken from the beginning, the Scott story could have been avoided altogether. With regard to the Matrix Churchill ELAs, there was some concern initially within the MOD that the goods might be destined ultimately for the USSR but, after seeking further specifications, this fear was allayed and in October 1987 it was agreed that the machine tools could be exported to Iraq, as they would not constitute a 'significant enhancement' of Iraq's military capability.[11]

An intelligence report on Hutteen was drawn up by SIS in late 1987. It was dated 30 November 1987. The report stated in clear terms that Iraq had been signing contracts with British based companies 'for the purchase of general purpose heavy machinery and for the production of armaments in Iraq'. Five British companies were named in the report, including Matrix Churchill, BSA, and Wickman Bennett. Existing contracts between Iraq and these companies were valued at £44 million. The intelligence report also stated that 'Iraq intends to use the machinery purchased to manufacture its own munitions'.[12] This was not the first intelligence on Hutteen. DIS had known 'for some years' that Hutteen was an armaments factory. The 30 November report was, however, the first intelligence regarding Hutteen that was passed on to the export licensing departments of the FCO, MOD, and DTI.[13] The source for this intelligence was Mark Gutteridge, a senior executive and exports manager at Matrix Churchill. Throughout the late 1980s Gutteridge had been in regular contact with MI5 and from at least May 1987 he had been meeting an MI5 officer, known to him as Michael Ford and to the Scott report as Mr P. In May 1987 Mr P drew up a contact note in which he wrote that Iraq was 'buying up milling machines specifically tooled up for arms

---

⁹ See para. D2.271.   ¹⁰ Ibid. See also para. D2.279.
¹¹ See para. D2.272. This is a reference to guideline (iii) of the Howe guidelines as they stood in 1987. Guideline (iii) provided that 'we should not in future sanction new orders for any defence equipment which in our view would significantly enhance the capability of either side [i.e. Iran or Iraq] to prolong or exacerbate the conflict'. (See para. D1.59, and ch. 1, above.)
¹² See paras. D2.265–6.   ¹³ See para. D2.267.

production'.[14] The note also recorded the concern (which was to become important in early 1988, as we shall see) that this business should not be interfered with since 'it is of high value and will be taken up by the West Germans' if Matrix Churchill are forced to withdraw.[15] It was MI5's contact with Gutteridge and Mr P's contact note that was to form the basis of the 30 November 1987 intelligence report.

By the date of this intelligence report the Matrix Churchill ELAs of 1987 had already been approved. Could they now be revoked? According to the Scott report, it was generally agreed among relevant witnesses to the inquiry that if the contents of the 30 November intelligence report had been known by the officials in the export licensing departments of the FCO, MOD, and DTI at the time the Matrix Churchill ELAs had been dealt with, the 'export licences would not have been granted'.[16] Despite this, the possibility of revoking the licences was not even discussed until January 1988. The Scott report was very critical of this inordinate delay. Why did the government departments concerned not act on the intelligence more quickly?

As far as the MOD is concerned, the Scott report stated that 'the failure of anyone in the MOD to take prompt action on the report as soon as it was received within the department was . . . a failure of system within DIS rather than a failure on the part of any individual. There was, at the time, no clearly understood system within DIS under which intelligence with implications for export sales policy would be brought to the attention' of the relevant people. Scott described the MOD/DIS system as having been 'unsatisfactorily haphazard'. Scott was, however, happy that institutional reforms within the MOD had resolved this problem by the end of 1994.[17] As regards the FCO, Scott singled out an official in the Middle East desk (MED), a Mr Patey, who was described as 'plainly unsatisfactory . . . his failure to react to [the intelligence report] until early January 1988 was, in my opinion, a failure for which no adequate explanation has been offered'. As regards the DTI, the official most directly concerned—Mr Tony Steadman, the head of the export licensing bureau—did not receive the security clearance necessary to permit him to see such intelligence until January 1988, some eight months after he had taken up that post.[18] His superior, Mr Eric Beston, may have read the intelligence

---

[14] See para. D2.265. See also D. Leigh, *Betrayed: The Real Story of the Matrix Churchill Trial* (London: Bloomsbury, 1993) p. 102.

[15] See para. D2.265.

[16] See para. D2.282. This was so despite the fact that even before 30 November 'the licences had been granted in the knowledge that the machine tools were capable of use in making components for munitions'. See para. D2.279.

[17] See para. D2.287. We are not told the nature of such reforms—we are merely assured that they have happened and that all is now well.

[18] Scott described this as 'plainly unacceptable' (see para. D2.293). Scott was told by Mr Steadman's superior, Mr Eric Beston, that the procedure for security clearance was 'very long, very slow and quite costly'. No indication was given in the Scott report as to whether this has changed.

report, but if so not until January 1988. Scott described the system in the DTI as rather hit and miss (and this was a miss) but is less critical of the DTI than of the MOD and FCO, on the ground that the issue of probable munitions manufacture was one which should have been primarily of their (i.e. MOD and FCO) concern.[19]

As it turned out, even by the middle of January 1988, only thirteen of the 141 machine tools for which Matrix Churchill had received export licences had actually been shipped. It was therefore still not too late effectively to revoke the licences. But this did not happen. The licences were allowed to stand, despite the intelligence of 30 November. Why? The ELB contacted Matrix Churchill in January 1988 explaining that the licences were being reconsidered due to concerns about their suspected munitions use. Matrix Churchill's directors were highly concerned about the significant loss of trade that this would entail, and a meeting was arranged for 20 January 1988 between the minister for trade, Alan Clark MP, and the machine tools trade association (MTTA) of which Matrix Churchill was a member. Paul Henderson, the managing director of Matrix Churchill, was to attend the meeting. Tony Steadman and Eric Beston were the officials who briefed Alan Clark for this meeting.[20] Their briefing referred to the 30 November 1987 intelligence report and stated that the MTTA companies should be advised to 'maintain a low profile . . . press or public attention would make it more difficult to permit fulfilment of the contracts'.[21] Significantly, the briefing went on to state that 'the providers of the intelligence are most anxious that their source [Gutteridge] should not inadvertently be put at risk . . . For this reason, they, like DTI and other officials, would favour allowing the present contracts to be completed and export licences refused only for any future suspect business.'[22]

Although it was only a DTI minister who was directly involved in the 20 January 1988 meeting, ministers in the MOD and FCO also received submissions on this issue. The MOD submission to Lord Trefgarne stated that 'the intelligence community recommends against revoking the licences as they fear for the safety of their source and they also believe that far more important information could cease to become available as a result'.[23] As the Scott report made clear, this was misleading. The intelligence community did not fear for Gutteridge's life or limb: they merely felt that if his identity were to become known, his value as a source would be at an end.[24] A source's value and his safety are surely somewhat different concerns.

---

[19] See para. D2.292. As with the MOD, we are told that the DTI's system was improved in 1989, but we are not told how.
[20] This was the meeting that was later relied on by the defendants in the Matrix Churchill trial and in respect of which Alan Clark was famously cross-examined as the trial collapsed around him. For details of Alan Clark's evidence, see para. G17.29.
[21] See para. D2.302.   [22] See para. D2.304.
[23] See para. D2.311(iv).   [24] Ibid. See also para. D2.322.

By this time, the 30 November 1987 intelligence report was not the only intelligence which was available. An anonymous employee of Matrix Churchill wrote to the foreign secretary, Sir Geoffrey Howe, on 22 January 1988, stating that her employers were 'working on a £30 million order for CNC lathes to be used for munitions production in Iraq'.[25] This letter was copied by the FCO to the MOD and to SIS, yet although, in Scott's words, it 'should have been recognized as highly significant',[26] no action was taken on it.[27]

The Scott report viewed this episode with an understandable lack of sympathy. The report stated that the Matrix Churchill ELAs were 'attended by muddle and confusion'[28] and that key officials demonstrated 'unacceptable carelessness'.[29] Scott's concerns, however, focused on the handling of ELAs and on the rather gung-ho pro-trade attitude of DTI officials rather than on matters of intelligence. Yet serious questions need to be raised in respect of the role played by the intelligence report and its authors in this episode. Here was a story that could and should have been an intelligence success. The intelligence services had worked together to glean, analyse, and distribute information which directly related to government policy on defence sales to Iraq, and moreover they had done so in time. The government, through the intelligence services, had ascertained that British based companies such as Matrix Churchill were being used by the Iraqis as sources of arms procurement and manufacture. This was contrary to the government's clearly stated policy as articulated in the Howe guidelines, and, thankfully, the government was in a position to put a stop to this illegal arms procurement by denying export licences to the relevant companies.

Instead, the intelligence services put pressure on the government departments concerned not to revoke the licences and thereby to protect their source. Thus, this was not a case of the intelligence services discovering something undesirable and illegal and the government putting a stop to it. Rather, it was a case of the intelligence services discovering something undesirable and illegal and then persuading the government not to put a stop to it in order that the intelligence services could carry on discovering that this undesirable and illegal thing was happening. As Alan Clark described it in his evidence to the Scott inquiry, this was 'an absurd paradox. Intelligence was telling you what [the exports] were being used for. But the machines had to be provided [to Iraq] in order to protect the source telling you how they were being used. It was a total circularity.'[30]

---

[25] See para. D2.318. CNC lathes are high speed computer numerically controlled lathes.

[26] See para. D2.320.

[27] Further intelligence became available in Apr. 1988 when the defence attaché at the British embassy in Baghdad sent a telex to the effect that he 'could not see any reason for granting export licences for anything connected with' Hutteen. See para. D2.326.

[28] See para. D2.336.   [29] See para. D2.342.

[30] See R. Norton-Taylor, *Truth is a Difficult Concept: Inside the Scott Inquiry* (London: 4th Estate, 1995) p. 107.

Further Matrix Churchill Export Licence Applications

In October 1988 Matrix Churchill lodged a new ELA with the DTI, known as ELA 53234. This was one of the ELAs in respect of which Matrix Churchill directors were later charged and prosecuted by customs and excise. ELA 53234 related to twelve vertical spindle machining centres and two high speed lathes. The goods were to be exported to Nassr in Iraq.[31] As with Hutteen, DIS had long suspected that Nassr had an arms production facility.[32] The intelligence report of 30 November 1987 confirmed this—it had referred to Nassr as well as to Hutteen. ELA 53234 related to the so-called ABA Project which was being orchestrated by Cardoen, a renowned Chilean arms dealer. The ELA was as imprecise in its information as the 1987 ones had been. The nature of Nassr's business was stated to be 'mechanical engineering' and the precise (*sic*) purpose for which the goods were to be used was stated to be 'production of metal components'.[33] As Scott observed, considering the fact that by October 1988 it was known that Nassr was a munitions factory, the absence of any precision in the statement was glaring. No attempt was made by the DTI to obtain further details.[34]

The MOD's working group on export licence applications, which made recommendations to the MOD as to how ELAs should be dealt with (their recommendations were based on a military assessment of the goods in question), initially recommended that ELA 53234 should be refused, on the ground that it would constitute a 'significant enhancement'.[35] But the MOD was not the only interested party. The security and secret intelligence services were also concerned about the way in which this new Matrix Churchill ELA would be handled. Mr O of SIS sent a telegram to Mr P of MI5 in December 1988. It stated that 'the problem of source protection again raises its ugly head . . . we are saying that the applications should be considered . . . on the merits of export guidelines. There is of course a fine dividing line between lathes and tools for industrial use and those for military use.'[36] The reference in this telegram to source protection was ambiguous, but in the view of the Scott report it was intended to mean that source protection was not a factor as far as SIS were concerned.[37] MI5 were not so sure. In his response to Mr O, Mr P wrote that 'it is important to maintain source protection. There seem to be so many uncertainties that granting this particular set of export licences will at least give time for [the intelligence agencies] to discover more about Iraqi intentions.'[38] DIS took a completely different view, arguing that ELA 53234 offered Iraq a 'significant enhancement which is contrary to the current ministerial guidelines . . . DIS will oppose most vigorously any shipment of machine tools to [Nassr] . . .'[39]

[31] See para. D6.73.   [32] See para. D2.267.   [33] See para. D6.73.
[34] See para. D6.75.   [35] See n 11 above.   [36] See para. D6.78.
[37] See para. D6.80.   [38] See para. D6.81.   [39] See para. D6.84.

Thus the three intelligence agencies most directly concerned each took quite different lines: SIS appeared neutral—their Iraqi concerns really lay elsewhere and were primarily focused on Iraqi nuclear capacity.[40] SIS were not so bothered about the conventional exports such as those that Matrix Churchill proposed. MI5 wanted to protect (i.e. keep) their source (Gutteridge) and were prepared to allow the goods to be exported despite knowledge about Nassr in order to prevent Gutteridge's devaluation as a source. DIS were concerned with more broadly based matters than either MI5 or SIS. They were interested in all Iraqi military enhancement and procurement, whether nuclear or not, and were also, interestingly, the only one of the three intelligence agencies to present their concerns in the light of (official) government policy, as articulated and published in the Howe guidelines.

Ministers from the FCO, MOD, and DTI were to decide the fate of ELA 53234 in February 1989. Much of January was therefore taken up with the preparation of ministerial briefings. From the intelligence point of view, the most interesting of these submissions is that prepared by the FCO for William Waldegrave. This stated that 'we have reason to believe that the refusal of these export licences could force Matrix Churchill to close down. If this happened, we would lose our intelligence access to [Iraq's] procurement network.'[41] The FCO official responsible for this submission (Mr Lillie) stated in his evidence to the Scott inquiry that the submission had been cleared with SIS. SIS officers, however, disagreed. They argued that both the tone and the content of the submission was misleading. With regard to the passage just quoted, Mr C3 of SIS told the Scott inquiry that he did not consider that 'the submission accurately reflect[ed] our knowledge at the time on Iraqi military procurement and production, nor of Matrix Churchill's part in it . . . I consider it to have been misleading to say that forcing Matrix Churchill to close down would lose our intelligence access . . . I consider too much weight was given, in the submission, to retaining Gutteridge.'[42]

The MOD submission incorporated the FCO briefing. Astonishingly, the MOD submission did not draw the minister's attention to the concerns which had been strongly expressed by DIS. This appears to have been because the relevant MOD officials took the view that 'it was far more important to protect the intelligence source and more particularly the flow of information than it was to uphold the guidelines'.[43] In the view of the Scott report, the MOD minister (Lord Trefgarne) was 'ill served' by his officials, who 'failed to put before [him] a balanced recommendation'.[44] On the basis of these submissions, the ministers agreed to grant ELA 53234. One MOD adviser,

---

[40] See paras. D6.82 and D6.87.   [41] See para. D6.94.

[42] See para. D6.96. The question of communication breakdown between SIS and the FCO is discussed further below.

[43] Comments of Mr Barrett, MOD official, in evidence to the Scott inquiry. See para. D6.103.

[44] See para. D6.103.

Lieut.-Colonel Glazebrook, had described the machine tools that were to be sent to Nassr as being 'sufficient to equip a factory designed to produce 500,000 × 155mm shells per annum'. In the event, not all of the goods had been exported by the time the licence expired. A renewal was applied for and in July 1990 approved. But in August 1990 Iraq invaded Kuwait and the consequent UN embargo intervened before the remaining goods (the machining centres) could be exported.[45]

The final set of Matrix Churchill ELAs which need to be examined are those which were considered by the relevant government departments in late 1989. There are three pairs of ELAs to be discussed here:[46]

(i) ELAs 52039 and 0440 which concerned the export of high speed lathes and machining centres to Nassr in relation to a scheme known as project 1728.[47]

(ii) ELAs 22351 and 23006 which related to eleven high speed lathes and to twenty-four machining centres destined for Nassr and which the Chilean arms dealer Cardoen was involved with.[48] Customs and excise later charged Matrix Churchill directors with offences relating to these two ELAs.

(iii) ELAs 27311 and 27315 which were destined for Nassr's so-called central tool room project.[49]

Again, as before, the MOD working group recommended that these ELAs should be refused. So too, this time, did William Waldegrave at the FCO.[50] But the views of officials and ministers in the MOD and the DTI were significantly less cautious. There had been an imporant change between these two ministries: in July 1989 Alan Clark and Lord Trefgarne swapped ministerial positions. Mr Clark became the minister for defence procurement at the MOD and Lord Trefgarne became the minister for trade at the DTI. This was significant because as minister for trade Alan Clark had been largely much more supportive of British trade with Iraq than either Lord Trefgarne or William Waldegrave, who outnumbered him. Mr Clark took this enthusiasm for trade with him to the MOD, which had traditionally had slightly different concerns from those of the DTI and had accordingly been more cautious. Lord Trefgarne, on the other hand, began to change his position once he arrived at the DTI—he took to the DTI line (in favour of trade) much more keenly than Mr Clark took to what had traditionally been the MOD line. Thus, as a direct consequence of the July 1989 exchange of ministries, a significant tilt towards favouring trade with Iraq developed and it became Mr Waldegrave who was to a greater extent left in the minority.[51]

---

45 See para. D6.106 and also para. D6.246.
47 See paras. D2.336 and D6.58.
49 See para. D6.115.   50 See para. D6.123.

46 See para. D6.116.
48 See para. D6.112.
51 See paras. D3.132–9.

In late 1989 both Mr Clark and Lord Trefgarne accordingly expressed their disagreement with Mr Waldegrave's view that the remaining Matrix Churchill ELAs should be refused. In this they were supported by submissions from their officials. The Scott report was very critical of these controversial submissions, primarily on the ground that they wrongly failed to take into account recent relevant intelligence information. In September 1989 three pertinent intelligence reports were issued. The first two were SIS reports both dated 5 September 1989. These reports identified project 1728 at Nassr (with which two of the Matrix Churchill ELAs were concerned) as a 'large Iraqi missile project'.[52] The reports stated that Iraq had negotiated with British based companies for the export to Nassr of 'specially manufactured components, machinery, production tools, production lines' for the manufacture of missiles. Copies of this report were sent to the FCO and to DIS, but not to other MOD desks and not to the DTI. The third intelligence report, also from September 1989, concerned the central tool room plant at Nassr (with which another two of the Matrix Churchill ELAs were connected) which was identified as being for the design and manufacture of shells, cartridges, and mortars. The intelligence stated, however, that there were insufficient machines in the establishment to make large quantities of these armaments, apart from missiles, 'where there might be sufficient resources for a production run'.[53] The distribution of this report was, for our purposes, the same as that for the other two intelligence reports.

Why did the relevant officials fail to draw this intelligence to the attention of their ministers? The submission to Alan Clark (at the MOD) was prepared by Mr Barrett. Mr Barrett was the number two at DESS, the defence export services secretariat. The intelligence reports were not circulated to DESS, but Mr Barrett should nonetheless have known about them on the grounds that both he and the relevant SIS officers regularly met in their capacity as members of a group called the working group on Iraqi procurement (WGIP). This was a group of government officials and intelligence officers 'set up in order to provide a venue in which to discuss Iraqi procurement . . . The idea behind the meetings was to discuss all the latest snippets of information that SIS and other Whitehall departments had obtained on the Iraqi network.'[54] In evidence to the Scott inquiry Mr Barrett accepted that he had failed to mention intelligence imparted at WGIP meetings in his submission to Alan Clark. This was put down to a lapse in memory.[55] In the event of such memory failure, there was no fall-back in the system: the intelligence would simply be forgotten. Of course, had it been DESS practice to clear relevant ministerial submissions with DIS (who had been sent copies of the September 1989

---

[52] See para. D5.25(xviii).　　　　　　　　　　[53] See para. D5.25(xx).

[54] The words of Mr C2, an SIS officer who attended WGIP meetings, in evidence to the Scott inquiry. See para. C2.73.

[55] See para. D6.128.

intelligence reports) then this error might have been detected and corrected in time, but this was not DESS's practice.

The submission to Lord Trefgarne at the DTI was prepared by Mr Steadman, head of the export licensing bureau, and his superior within the DTI, Mr Beston. The submission stated that 'there was no evidence that British made machine tools would be used other than for the purpose originally stated' (i.e. general metalworking or engineering). As the Scott report concluded, this was 'a positively misleading' statement.[56] The Scott report described the DTI submissions to Lord Trefgarne as 'highly unsatisfactory',[57] 'unbalanced'[58] and 'seriously inaccurate'.[59] What was the cause of this state of affairs? The Scott report put it down to a fundamental lack of concern on Mr Steadman's and Mr Bestons's part as to the possibility or even the probability that the machine tools would be used for munitions manufacture.[60]

The effect of the inadequate submissions to Alan Clark and Lord Trefgarne was compounded by a quite different problem concerning the FCO briefing to Mr Waldegrave. The FCO submission was prepared by Mr Sherrington. Mr Sherrington was new to his job: he had joined the Middle East desk at the FCO only in late September 1989. No one in MED referred the intelligence reports to Mr Sherrington, despite the fact that they had been circulated to MED. This may have been in part because Mr Sherrington was not cleared to see relevant intelligence until early in October 1989. This could only be part of the answer, however: Mr Sherrington's submission was not finished until 31 October. His submission stated that 'our friends [i.e. SIS] have . . . said that they believe that the lathes may not, at any rate initially, be used for the direct manufacture of munitions'.[61] As we have seen, and as Mr O, an SIS officer told the Scott inquiry, 'all the evidence' from SIS in fact showed something quite different.[62] How had this evident misunderstanding between the FCO and SIS come about? While Mr Sherrington was at MED, he was frequently visited by Mr O, from SIS. He quite naturally thought, therefore, that he should use Mr O to obtain SIS clearance for his ministerial briefings which might concern SIS. Mr O was the only SIS officer he had regular contact with. This view, although understandable, was unfortunately a misconception of Mr O's role. There were in fact quite different channels for SIS approval—to give such approval was not a part of Mr O's job. Mr O knew this and never considered that his conversations with Mr Sherrington were being taken by Mr Sherrington as constituting formal SIS approval for

---

[56] See para. D6.133. [57] See para. D6.135. [58] See para. D6.144. [59] Ibid.

[60] As the Scott report put it, these submissions represented one 'step in the process whereby it became, by the time of the Matrix Churchill prosecution, part of the DTI credo that government had had no knowledge of the intended use of Matrix Churchill machine tools for production of military goods'. See para. D6.133. Problems with the DTI's use of intelligence are also addressed at para. D6.242. The problem of officials developing their own policy approaches within different departments was discussed in ch. 2, above.

[61] See para. D6.150. [62] See para. D6.151.

his submission to Mr Waldegrave. Nobody realized that this mistake had been made.[63] While the making of this mistake was, in the view of the Scott report, an unfortunate accident for which no individual was to blame, the report was critical of those involved for not detecting the mistake more quickly and for not acting more rapidly to rectify it. When they did realize what had happened, the SIS officers involved (Mr O and Mr C3) made no written note to correct the erroneous representation of SIS's position in the submission to Mr Waldegrave. This failure was described in the Scott report as 'a serious error of judgment'.[64]

The unsurprising consequence of this depressing catalogue of forgetfulness, laziness, complacency, and error was that on 1 November 1989 the three ministers concerned met and agreed to grant the Matrix Churchill ELAs. In the view of the Scott report, they did so on an entirely false footing brought about by a 'failure to take into account the abundance of current and previous intelligence'.[65] Scott attributed most of the blame for this not to ministers but to their officials. Also criticized, however, was the distribution of the intelligence reports. Why, for example, were they sent to DIS but not to DESS? SIS claimed that this was largely because when DESS, as a Whitehall intelligence customer, explained (in September 1986) to SIS what intelligence would be relevant to them, they failed to mention that they had any connection with export licensing: DESS's requirements appeared to SIS to be more of the nature of strategic intelligence on supplier countries rather than recipients.[66] This aside, Scott nonetheless concluded that the poor distribution of intelligence within the MOD was 'clearly an unacceptable state of affairs and indicate[d] shortcomings in the system operating within the MOD'[67] although the report did state that the DIS system of distribution has been reformed with a view to the prevention of any recurrence. We are not told in the report what these reforms are; nor are we given any indication as to whether they might be working.

There is one final episode of this story. In an intelligence report (which has not thus far been mentioned) dated 13 October 1989 it was reported that the Chilean arms firm, Cardoen, was under contract with various Iraqi organizations to build a large munitions factory. Two of the 1989 Matrix Churchill ELAs, it will be remembered, were connected with Cardoen. The 13 October intelligence report further stated that a 'UK firm' was to supply twenty-four machining centres for various types of fuses as well as eighteen high speed lathes for this project. This 'UK firm' was identified as Matrix Churchill at a meeting of officials on 8 December 1989—a mere five weeks after the Matrix Churchill ELAs had been approved. Despite this, the ministers who had granted the licences were not told of the identification of the UK firm as being Matrix Churchill; they were not told that this ended any plausible doubt

---

[63] See paras. D6.149–54.   [64] See para. D6.154.   [65] See para. D6.169.
[66] See para. D6.178.   [67] See para. D6.182.

about the military use of the Matrix Churchill exports; they were not told that the basis on which they had granted the ELAs five weeks earlier had turned out to be unfounded; and consideration of the ELAs was not reopened, although, in the opinion of the Scott report, it should have been.[68]

Postscript on Intelligence and Decision Making: The Malaise Reaches Higher

As we saw above in chapter one, a major controversy of the Scott story was whether government policy on export sales to Iran and Iraq secretly changed after the cease-fire in the Iran–Iraq war in 1988. By the summer of 1990, Nicholas Ridley, the secretary of state at the DTI, had become anxious about the content and presentation of government policy in this area and expressed his concern in a letter to the prime minister, Mrs Thatcher, dated 21 June 1990. Mrs Thatcher's response was to establish an *ad hoc* committee, chaired by the foreign secretary, Douglas Hurd, to examine the government's position with regard to defence sales to Iraq and to report back to her. This was to be a high-powered meeting and it brought about considerable preparatory paperwork. It was decided that the best way to proceed was for the committee to consider a paper, which became known as the Iraq note. All the relevant government departments (FCO, MOD, and DTI) would contribute to the preparation of the Iraq note, which was to be co-ordinated by the cabinet office.

One part of the Iraq note concerned the role that had been played in the export licensing process by secret intelligence. It stated that 'ministers have allowed the supply of some Matrix Churchill machine tools for *ad hoc* reasons of an intelligence nature'.[69] No draft of the Iraq note was passed to the intelligence services, but after the final draft had been agreed, it was sent to SIS. Mr T2, a senior officer in SIS, took exception to the statement about intelligence reasons for allowing Matrix Churchill exports. He stated in a letter to the cabinet office that:

our understanding of the situation is somewhat different. At an early stage of our coverage of Iraqi procurement activities in the UK, we did indeed express some reservations about a proposal to take action against Matrix Churchill . . . on the grounds that it might compromise our operational interest in the matter. However, we later withdrew our reservations, and made it clear to those concerned in other departments that . . . we had no objection to departments taking whatever actions they might think fit on any applications for export licences by Matrix Churchill. These discussions took place some 18 months to 2 years ago [i.e. mid-1988—early 1989].[70]

The Iraq note was not amended in the light of these observations, because by the time they had been received in the cabinet office in August 1990 Iraq had

[68] See para. D6.188. For details of the intelligence report, see para. D5.25(xxiii).
[69] See para. D3.155(iv).   [70] Ibid.

invaded Kuwait and rather different considerations had come into play. After August 1990 there was no suggestion that British policy on defence exports to Iraq should be further liberalized! The correspondence from SIS to the cabinet office is nonetheless interesting as it confirms and reinforces the sense that we have already identified that there was a considerable, substantive, and long-lasting misunderstanding between SIS and government departments as to the position with regard to Matrix Churchill that SIS had adopted. We have already seen how this misunderstanding infected official submissions to ministers throughout 1989. It appears from the Iraq note that it was to continue to infect government decision making, even at the highest level, right up to the point of the Iraqi invasion of Kuwait.

To conclude on the export licensing process, it appears that although there was throughout the period under consideration an abundance of relevant intelligence, this was either (a) overridden for reasons of source protection, notwithstanding knowledge of intended military use, or (b) ignored, overlooked or forgotten.[71] This 'failure of the licensing departments to make effective use of available intelligence was compounded by the failure of . . . SIS officers to draw attention to inaccurate statements about current intelligence' contained in ministerial submissions.[72] One final point needs to be made here: this concerns the role of the JIC. SIS's failure to amend misleading submissions was caused at least in part by the fact that they were primarily concerned with Iraqi acquisition or development of weapons of mass destruction such as nuclear weapons: they were much less concerned with conventional weapons. This priority attached within SIS to nuclear-related intelligence was not one which SIS had invented for themselves: SIS were merely following instructions issued to them by the JIC.[73] The question of whether the JIC's imposition of such an intelligence priority was wise or appropriate will be discussed below. As regards export licensing, the JIC also bore further responsibilities for the abject lack of intelligence co-ordination which peppered this story. Despite the considerable volume of available intelligence 'no one person was familiar with all the accumulated intelligence'[74] until the Iraq note was drawn up in July 1990. The evident lack of co-ordination or central monitoring of intelligence relating to British involvement in Iraqi arms procurement from 1987 onwards represents a colossal JIC failure. This is a matter which will be returned to below.

Intelligence and Supergun

Before we can turn to an evaluation of the broader implications of this story, however, we must first consider the remaining aspects of the Scott report

---

[71] See para. D8.10.   [72] See para. D8.12.   [73] See para. D8.14.
[74] See para. D8.11.

which raise concerns about intelligence. The supergun story amplifies and further illustrates many of the issues encountered above and serves to confirm many of the problems we have already identified.[75] A number of intelligence reports on supergun were drawn up by MI5 and SIS during 1988 and 1989. Yet as we saw in chapter one above nothing was done within government to put an end to the project (even after the intervention of Sir Hal Miller MP) until it eventually became clear that the supergun tubes were about to be exported to Iraq from Teesport. Customs officers, accompanied by an SIS officer, seized the tubes as they were being loaded on board at Middlesbrough docks in April 1990.[76] On 18 April 1990 the secretary of state for trade and industry, Nicholas Ridley MP, made the statement to the House of Commons about the seizure of the supergun tubes in which he stated that 'until a few days ago, my department had no knowledge that the goods were designed to form part of a gun' and that the government only 'recently became aware in general terms of an Iraqi project to develop a long-range gun based on designs developed by the late Dr Gerald Bull'.[77] We saw in chapter one that the Scott report strongly criticized this statement as being 'misleading'[78] but in addition to the questions of ministerial responsibility which the supergun story raises, difficult issues of secret intelligence also emerge from this episode.

What intelligence was there on supergun before April 1990 and who saw it? It appears that although the intelligence agencies were not slow to acquire intelligence on supergun, they were slow to realize its importance and the government was consequently extraordinarily lethargic in acting on it. From as early as July 1988 there was intelligence from MI5 on supergun. A note dated 5 July 1988 stated that the likely uses of the tubes being manufactured for SRC 'would be (a) as pressure vessels, or (b) in the nuclear industry (but this was unlikely) or (c) as gun barrels'. The following comment was added: 'while there is little precedent for the use of guns of such a large calibre, the Germans did build an 80cm (31.5″) gun and some 60cm (23.6″) howitzers during World War II'.[79] The author of the note was Mr F. A further MI5 note was made on 4 November 1988. This clearly stated that 'Sheffield Forgemasters . . . are supplying weapon quality steel billets to the machine works of Walter Somers . . . [who] have been approached by Space Research of Brussels to machine lengths of gun steel tubing of 50″ and 80″ in diameter'.[80] The 4 November note also stated that it had become clear that the tubing 'would eventually be sent to Iraq'. The author of this note was Mr I; it was circulated within MI5 to Mr F and to Miss H.

---

[75] The background to and leading characters in the supergun story were introduced in ch. 1, above.
[76] See para. F4.19.
[77] See HC Deb., Vol. 170, col. 1425, 18 Apr. 1990. See Scott, para. F4.27.
[78] See para. F4.43.   [79] See para. F2.61.   [80] See para. F2.88.

Neither the July nor the November notes, nor the information contained in them, were passed on to relevant Whitehall departments. This was both odd and extremely unfortunate. There is no reason whatsoever, despite the limited internal circulation of these notes, why they could not have been brought to the attention of the relevant government departmental officials. Both Mr F and Miss H were members of a committee known as the restricted enforcement unit (REU).[81] The REU was an *ad hoc* interdepartmental committee that was established in 1987 for the purpose of providing a 'forum for identification and discussion of information on actual or suspected breaches of UK export controls . . . and to facilitate timely, considered, and, as necessary, concerted action in appropriate cases'.[82] The REU met monthly and its membership had high level security clearance. It had no executive functions. It was rather a conduit for the passing of information between government departments and the intelligence community. Its meetings were attended by representatives from the DTI, FCO, MOD, customs and excise, MI5, SIS, and GCHQ.[83] As the Scott report put it, MI5 'should have assumed a degree of responsibility'[84] in terms of passing on its information to the REU, yet in this case at least, this did not happen. The REU was not informed of the July or November MI5 notes on supergun.

SIS became actively concerned about the supergun affair in 1989. They had received information on SRC via a metropolitan police special branch source. An SIS briefing note dated 6 October 1989 on SRC was prepared by Mr C2. This note stated that 'although we initially thought [that . . .] information on the SRC project to develop a 600km range artillery gun to be beyond belief, following discussions with MOD . . . we have learnt that although no such gun exists it is indeed technically feasible for one to be produced'. With regard to government knowledge about SRC and supergun, the note stated that 'in June 1988 the SRC was involved in an attempt to acquire high pressure vessels . . . which were probably intended for use as artillery gun barrels . . . Walter Somers through its dealings with SRC were given the impression that the company intended to evade export controls, and the DTI was informed.'[85]

This last passage of the 6 October 1989 briefing note caused some controversy at the Scott inquiry. Clearly the note is of considerable significance in determining the state of government knowledge of the supergun project in 1988. If we know that someone within the government knew about the supergun project, and if we know that no one in the government appeared to do a great deal about it until the last minute in April 1990, the question becomes which government officials knew but failed to act. Which government official(s) were the sources behind the last quoted passage of the SIS note?

---

[81] See para. F2. 94.
[82] These were the stated objectives of the REU, as recorded by the DTI. See para. C2.68.
[83] See para. C2.69.   [84] Ibid.   [85] See para. F3.37.

The author of the note, Mr C2, thought that a Mr Bill Weir was the source. Weir, however, strenuously denied this.[86] Weir was a metallurgist employed by the MOD as a principal scientific officer. His duties included the assessment and analysis of technical information and to provide advice on the military significance of the production and use of metallic materials in foreign countries.[87] Scott concluded that we do not know what the answer to this dilemma is. The report stated that quite clearly there were government officials who knew or who had strong suspicions about supergun as early as June 1988, although they cannot be positively identified.[88]

In the aftermath of the seizure of the supergun tubes in April 1990 and the government's subsequent embarrassment, which was only worsened by the decision in November 1990 to abandon the supergun prosecution, 'a great deal of work was being done within Whitehall to try to establish the history of the state of government knowledge of the supergun project'.[89] In this attempt, the SIS briefing note of 6 October 1989 played an important role. One SIS officer—Mr Q, of whom more below—wrote in November 1990 to the head of SIS, Sir Colin McColl, that 'clearly, this [briefing note] indicates that we (SIS) could have made th[e] connection earlier . . .'.[90] Later the same month, Sir Colin wrote to Sir Percy Cradock, then the prime minister's foreign policy adviser, stating, even in the light of the October 1989 briefing note, that 'I believe that ministers remain on safe ground in continuing to state that in June 1988, [the government] had no knowledge of the existence of an Iraqi supergun project and therefore no grounds to refuse the export of any high pressure tubes on those grounds'.[91] The Scott report described this letter as 'incorrect in a number of respects . . . the 6 October briefing note suggested . . . that a branch of government had had knowledge of the project since June 1988 . . . Ministers and the cabinet office could reasonably have expected a response which was consistent with the information available to SIS, whereas the response [in Sir Colin's letter] was not consistent with what was known.'[92] The Scott report continued by stating that the letter from Sir Colin had the strong appearance of being 'a defensive operation to seek to distance SIS from responsibility for the failure to act on such information as had become available by October 1989'.[93]

There is one remaining piece of the supergun/intelligence jigsaw to put into place. As well as Mr C2's briefing note on SRC, another SIS officer also started working on supergun in 1989. This is the Mr Q referred to above. By the end of 1989 Mr Q had become the principal SIS 'hound' (as he was described in the Scott report)[94] in the hunt to uncover the details of the supergun affair. Mr Q, however, was not shown either of the MI5 notes referred to

[86] See paras. F3.39–55 for the views on this matter of Mr C2 and Mr Weir.
[87] See para. F2.11.   [88] See para. F3.55.   [89] See para. F3.57.
[90] See para. F3.58.   [91] See para. F3.60.   [92] See para. F3.61.   [93] Ibid.
[94] See para. F3.5.

above—indeed, he stated in evidence to the Scott inquiry that he believed that 'no other officer in SIS saw the [November 1988] note . . . we believe that it was only given internal circulation within MI5'.[95] Neither was he shown the 6 October 1989 SIS briefing note until well after it had been finalized.[96] Despite being seriously hampered in this way, Mr Q produced an intelligence report on supergun dated 30 November 1989.[97] Reaction to Mr Q's report, however, was oddly muted. The Scott report states that the evidence suggested that, generally, officials were far less interested in Mr Q's work than might have been expected. In his evidence to the inquiry, Mr Q described the Whitehall reaction to his report as being 'rather like throwing a brick into a puddle of treacle, a loud plop and nobody took any interest, so the barrel [i.e. the supergun parts] became an issue to me because I was suffering a credibility problem with the people to whom I was addressing my reports'.[98] Mr Q issued a supplementary report in December 1989 in which he stated that project Babylon was intended to develop 'an ultra long range gun as an alternative to ballistic missiles in the strategic bombardment role [and] requires the acquisition of technology from European manufacturers'.[99]

Despite widespread disbelief of and consequent disinterest in supergun, Mr Q continued his investigations into 1990. He was helped when Mr David James became chairman of Eagle Trust, which owned Walter Somers. When Mr James became aware of outstanding Iraqi orders involving Walter Somers, he visited Walter Somers's shop floor in Halesowen, where the supergun tubes were located. He saw the tubes, which he knew to be destined for Iraq, but was reassured by Walter Somers that they were for petrochemical use.[100] Mr James remained unhappy, however, and during the first months of 1990 he started doing some investigating himself. Eventually, as his suspicions grew, he contacted an SIS officer, who in turn contacted Mr Q.[101] In late March Mr Q and Mr James met. The final parts of the story were at last coming together. Over the following weekend SIS received information from a foreign intelligence organization to the effect that the tubes were due to be shipped out from Teesport within the next 24–48 hours.[102] Mr Q travelled to Teesport, accompanied by officers from customs and excise. The gun parts were loaded on board the MV *Gur Mariner* at Middlesbrough docks and the consignment had been entered for export to Iraq. On Mr Q's advice, the tubes were seized, 'it all went rather public',[103] and Mr Q 'got out of the scene as fast as possible'.[104] A few days later Nicholas Ridley made his statement to the House of Commons.

With the exception of Mr Q, who comes out of the Scott report very well, the supergun saga is a dreadfully embarrassing one for British intelligence.

[95] Ibid.   [96] See para. F3.46.   [97] See paras. F3.17 and F3.79.
[98] See para. F3.80.   [99] See para. F3.81.   [100] See para. F4.3.
[101] See para. F4.9.   [102] See para. F4.18.
[103] Words of Mr Q, in evidence to the Scott inquiry. See para. F4.19.   [104] Ibid.

Disbelief coupled with incompetence, secrecy, and appalling judgement meant that not only were government departments deprived of intelligence which should have been readily available to them, but even the intelligence agencies appeared to deprive themselves (and each other) of crucial intelligence. As a cabinet office note submitted by Sir Robin Butler to Peter Lilley (Nicholas Ridley's replacement as secretary of state for trade and industry) in December 1990 stated, 'at the beginning of June 1988 knowledge of Dr Bull, his company the SRC and his involvement with long-range guns was in the public domain, but was not collated by any government department or agency'.[105] What an indictment of Britain's security and secret intelligence services—and coming not from a critical journalist or an academic, but from the head of the civil service.

Intelligence and the Matrix Churchill Prosecution

The final intelligence related aspect of the Scott story concerns customs' investigation and prosecution of the Matrix Churchill case. The matters which arise here do not reveal any significantly new issues, but further reflect many of the trends of amateurishness, incompetence, and lack of adequate communication already identified in the preceding sections. Briefly, customs and excise commenced their investigation into Matrix Churchill and the other related machine tools cases (BSA, Wickman Bennett) in March 1990 after they had received information from West German customs that these British based companies had been involved in the Iraqi arms procurement network.[106] Quite why the investigations did not commence earlier is unknown—customs officers had been members of the REU and had therefore seen intelligence (by 1989 at the latest) that linked Matrix Churchill with Iraqi defence exports.[107] The October 1989 SIS intelligence report linking Matrix Churchill with Cardoen arms deals had been circulated to customs, who retained it until May 1990 when it was returned to its originators for destruction. Despite this, however, it played no part at all in customs' investigation into Matrix Churchill and the existence of this intelligence report was never disclosed to the defendants in the trial.[108] One possible explanation for this somewhat odd state of affairs might be that the number of customs officers with security clearance to see 'top secret' classified material, was, as a matter of policy, kept to an absolute minimum and that the investigators within the investigation division of customs and excise did not come within

---

[105] See para. F3.44.   [106] See para. G2.1.
[107] See para. G2.2. The REU and the identification of Matrix Churchill as the 'UK firm' at an REU meeting in Dec. 1989 are discussed above.
[108] See para. G2.8.

this small ring-fenced security group.[109] But whatever the immediate reason, the problem was exacerbated by the fact that within the investigation division of customs and excise there was no formal system for cross-referring the subject matter of an investigation with earlier relevant reporting to customs from the intelligence services. The system was over-reliant on the memory of a limited number of officers.[110]

Paul Henderson and his co-defendants were arrested by Customs officers on 16 October 1990. At this time, customs knew that Mr Henderson had in the past been a SIS informant, but only realized some nine days later that he had passed information on to SIS about Matrix Churchill's recent trade with Iraq.[111] It was only at this point (some seven months after the customs investigation had begun) that the prosecution started to realize the nature of Matrix Churchill's probable defences—that the intelligence services knew of the nature of Matrix Churchill's trade and that the government had indeed encouraged it. In November 1990 customs investigators met with lawyers and officers from SIS to discuss the case against Mr Henderson.[112]

More significant, perhaps, was the importance attached to intelligence in the preparation of prosecution witnesses' statements. Alan Clark's statement, for example, claimed that at his meeting with Matrix Churchill's employers' association, the MTTA, at which Mr Henderson had been present, he had been assured by the MTTA that 'the machine tools were intended for general engineering purposes'[113] yet this is not so, and furthermore Mr Clark knew from the intelligence report of 30 November 1987 that the exports were intended for munitions production.[114] When cross examined on this point, Mr Clark claimed that by 'general engineering purposes' he meant both civil and military purposes, thus rendering his witness statement 'singularly meaningless' as the Scott report put it.[115] Such ambiguity and deliberate vagueness could and should have been avoided if due weight had been attached in the preparation of the prosecution's case to relevant intelligence reports. The same problem manifested itself again in the preparation of Tony Steadman's witness statement. It will be recalled that Mr Steadman, a key official, was head of the export licensing bureau in the DTI. His witness statement claimed that there was 'no evidence' that the intended use of the machine tools to be exported by Matrix Churchill was for military production. This was simply untrue, as the intelligence report of 30 November 1987 again makes clear.[116]

---

[109] See para. G2.4. As we have already seen, this is evidently a problem which is reflected throughout central government: just because the security and secret intelligence services distribute an intelligence report to a department is clearly no guarantee that the 'right' people in that department will eventually see the intelligence. Distribution within departments, as well as between departments, seems to be a perennial difficulty with regard to intelligence throughout Whitehall.

[110] See para. G3.6.   [111] See paras. G4.2 and G4.5.   [112] See para. G5.27.
[113] See para. G6.19.   [114] Ibid.   [115] Ibid.
[116] See para. G6.24.

The mysterious absence of intelligence information was not just a feature of the witness statements. Prosecution counsel, led by Alan Moses QC, did not see a number of vital intelligence reports—eight critical intelligence reports were listed by the Scott report as having never been brought to the attention of Mr Moses,[117] including all of those discussed at length in the first sections of this chapter: the 30 November 1987 report, the two reports from 5 September 1989, and the 13 October 1989 report. Mr Moses stated in his evidence to the inquiry that had he seen the 30 November 1987 report earlier, he 'would not have gone on with the prosecution' in which case we would probably never have had a Scott inquiry at all.[118]

In terms of the intelligence customs saw, and in terms of the intelligence customs used (or rather did not use) in the prosecution, the Matrix Churchill case can be seen as a very public intelligence failure. As Alan Moses made clear, it was a failure which more appropriate use of intelligence would have prevented. As with the export licences which should never have been granted and the supergun tubes which should never have been manufactured, the Matrix Churchill trial is one which should simply never have happened.

Evaluation

Having outlined the various roles played by secret intelligence in the Scott story, we can now turn to a more general assessment and evaluation of how well the government machine operated and, in particular, of how effectively the work of the intelligence services was incorporated into the government decision making process. We have seen that there were clearly some significant problems in the intelligence story which Scott uncovered, but how are we to assess the lessons which must now be learned? This is very difficult. Writing on matters of secret intelligence is always fraught with difficulty for the obvious reason that much of the detailed material is secret. Much of what is written about contemporary matters in the specialist journals, whilst useful to some degree, is generally very limited. Even when former diplomats, civil servants, and intelligence officers write in such journals, there is a persistent absence of detailed supporting material and much of what is written has to be taken on trust. That said, the Scott report does offer glimpses into what is normally a closed off world—the view may still be clouded, but it is nonetheless a clearer picture than we are usually privileged to see. The question remains, what are we to make of the intelligence story Scott has revealed? Scott himself was reluctant to draw stark conclusions or make broad recommendations for change. He stated in the report that the inquiry 'has disclosed a failure on a number of occasions for proper use to be made of available

---

[117] See para. G9.2(i)–(viii). See also para. G12.28.   [118] Ibid.

intelligence. I do not feel qualified to make recommendations as to how the systems in place in the respective agencies and departments might be improved. I propose, therefore, simply to identify the respects in which there evidently are, or were, problems.'[119] Scott identified a number of matters which we have already mentioned, including distribution,[120] over-reliance on memory,[121] the slowness of getting security clearance,[122] and misrepresentations of SIS views in submissions to ministers.[123]

Three main concerns can be distilled from this. The first relates to what the proper constitutional relationship is and ought to be between ministers and intelligence agencies. Who controls whom? Who sets whose agenda? What happens when the agendas are so different from each other? The second concerns intelligence distribution (who gets to see what?) and intelligence quality (what do those who get to see the intelligence actually think of it?). Why did officials who did see relevant intelligence not pass that intelligence information on in their submissions to ministers? Finally, the overall lack of intelligence co-ordination revealed throughout these episodes also raises questions about the functioning of Britain's central intelligence machinery (which is supposed to perform this task), especially of the joint intelligence committee. All of these questions call for further review in the light of the Scott report. Each of these will now be examined in turn, and in the final sections of this chapter we will assess the prospects for the future. With the bleak intelligence picture which Scott painted in our minds, what is the likelihood that those who are in a position to oversee the sleepy British intelligence community might be moved to act on the damning indictment which Scott laid at its door?

Ministers and Intelligence Agencies: The Constitutional Relationship

The first area which calls for further examination is the question of how ministers and the intelligence services are supposed to relate to one another. Quite what the proper constitutional relationship between ministers and intelligence agencies should be is unclear from both a formal, legal point of view and from a practical point of view.[124] Oddly, it seems that there can be both

---

[119] Para. K7.1.   [120] Paras. K7.2–4.   [121] Para. K7.5.   [122] Ibid.
[123] Para. K7.7.

[124] This problem is frequently compounded by the issue of whether the intelligence agencies (but especially MI5 and SIS) prefer to co-operate, to interfere with or to ignore each other. This, too, is a perennial one which features throughout the literature on intelligence. As with questions of distribution and quality, it is also a problem with a long history. In *The Secret State*, Richard Thurlow argues that even when the security and secret intelligence services were first established in 1909 there were 'continuing tensions' and even 'rivalry between the home and foreign offices' and that because of 'institutional rivalries there was little co-ordination or exchange of information between MI5 and SIS before 1940'. (See R. Thurlow, *The Secret State: British Internal Security in the Twentieth Century*, (Oxford: Blackwell, 1994) p. 6.) Thurlow states that between

too much, and too little ministerial control. That there can be too much min-isterial control is shown in the story broken by Cathy Massiter that MI5 were 'breaking their own rules' in their surveillance of CND in the early to mid 1980s. The role of the MOD in using MI5 for partisan purposes has never adequately been investigated or debated.[125] That there can be too little min-isterial control is illustrated in the series of events related by Peter Wright in *Spycatcher*.[126] If true, these revelations depict a security agency which had become an independent power centre, uncontrolled by ministers, and deter-mining its own targets, priorities, and mandate.

The formal legal position with regard to MI5 under the Security Service Act 1989 is that the director-general (appointed by the secretary of state) is placed in 'control' of the 'operations' of the service.[127] The director-general has direct access to the prime minister, but the Act also provides that the ser-vice is under the 'authority' of the secretary of state,[128] which 'at the very least could provide a basis for leadership in matters of policy'.[129] The director-general is under a statutory duty to deliver an annual report to the secretary of state and to the prime minister. This report remains secret.[130] Apart from this general framework, the legislation is almost completely silent on what relations should be between government departments and the security and secret intelligence services. The only other legislative references to ministers concern the issuing and duration of warrants.[131] The MI5 publication, *The Security Service*, states on relations between MI5 and the home office that 'the home secretary receives advice from the director-general on the threats to national security. He also discusses with the director-general matters of pol-icy affecting the service, for example, to do with resources, or legislation . . . The security service is [however] not part of the home office. It is a separate entity, with a distinct statutory basis under which the director-general is per-sonally responsible to the secretary of state.'[132] Thus the official sources are

the two world wars, 'institutional rivalry, frictional hostility, ambition and pride delayed the emergence of a co-ordinated security service until 1931. Even then, over-lapping areas of counter-espionage and counter-intelligence with SIS caused continuing organizational problems' (p. 51).

[125] L. Lustgarten and I. Leigh, *In From the Cold: National Security and Parliamentary Democracy* (Oxford: Clarendon Press, 1994) p. 364.

[126] See K. D. Ewing and C. A. Gearty, *Freedom Under Thatcher: Civil Liberties in Modern Britain* (Oxford: Clarendon Press, 1990) pp. 152–3.

[127] Security Service Act 1989, s. 2(1).   [128] Ibid., s. 1(1).

[129] Lustgarten and Leigh, p. 425. Interestingly, however, when the home affairs select com-mittee invited the then director-general of MI5, Stella Rimington, to appear before the commit-tee, the incumbent home secretary, Kenneth Clarke, refused to allow her to do so and he himself appeared instead: see *The Accountability of the Security Service*, HC (1993–94) 265.

[130] Exactly the same formulation was adopted in the Intelligence Services Act 1994 in respect of SIS (ss. 1–2) and GCHQ (ss. 3–4). The secretary of state in respect of MI5 is the home secre-tary; that in respect of SIS and GCHQ is the foreign secretary.

[131] Intelligence Services Act 1994, ss. 5–7.

[132] *The Security Service* (London: HMSO, 2nd edn. 1996) p. 6.

hardly precise and take no account of the kind of difficulties evidenced in the Scott report which Alan Clark described as 'absurd'.[133] Existing academic work, too, provides little more than a snapshot of working relations between government departments and the intelligence services.

According to empirical research conducted by Laurence Lustgarten and Ian Leigh, there is some degree of formalized contact between home office officials and MI5. They 'talk in general terms about priorities and the "operational landscape" but no attempt is made to exercise day-to-day supervision, let alone control, over the service'.[134] There is an evident 'presumption of regularity'. MI5 is not seen as a 'wild tiger' needing to be caged, but as an organization 'disposed to carry out its functions in a legal and honest way'. Home office officials also feel restricted by the 'need to know' principle: 'our own natural curiosity might lead us further in than is necessary . . . There is greater reluctance on our part to ask questions, than of the service to answer them.' Thus, as Lustgarten and Leigh conclude, 'the relationship between the home office and the security service is a matter of trust. To an outsider it seems more akin to a religious faith than empirically based judgment.'[135] The views of the home office with regard to the information that ought to be presented before ministers are also illuminating. In their view there cannot be an 'automatic duty to inform ministers of everything, given their numerous other responsibilities and the fact that many matters, seemingly vital at the time, later prove false or of exaggerated consequence. Only matters of "intrinsic importance" should be raised with ministers.'[136] But what does this mean, in practice? According to Lustgarten and Leigh, 'what seemed to be the paramount element in this amorphous concept was the potential to embarrass the government'.[137]

The connected question of relations between the FCO and SIS is, as we have seen, alluded to in a number of places in the Scott report. One revealing instance concerned British relations with Jordan, a country which is normally looked upon as one of Britain's closest allies in the Middle East. During the late 1980s and early 1990s there was considerable concern in the foreign office that Jordan was acting as a conduit for arms sales to Iraq. The FCO felt that it had to make strong representations to Jordan over this matter, but this was a question which had to be dealt with very carefully, as it was not perceived to be in Britain's interests in any way to offend Jordan. Thus, it appears that the FCO decided that an appropriate way to proceed would be to make the necessary representations through intelligence channels. The FCO asked SIS to pass a message on to Jordan concerning its links with Iraq. This apparently caused considerable anxiety within SIS who were highly reluctant to carry out this delicate policy matter. In the event, by the time the matter could be resolved, Iraq invaded Kuwait and the picture completely changed. It is,

---

[133] See above, n. 30.   [134] Lustgarten and Leigh, op. cit., p. 427.   [135] Ibid., p. 427.
[136] Ibid., p. 428.   [137] Ibid.

nonetheless, a rare (if frustratingly incomplete) insight into the political tensions that can arise between an intelligence agency and its parent government department.[138] What is now needed is a thorough examination of the proper constitutional relationship between ministers and the intelligence services which manages to go beyond the mere snatches and glimpses which we have thus far been allowed to see.

Distribution, Quantity, and Quality of Intelligence

On the second issue, concerning the distribution, quality, and quantity of intelligence information, William Waldegrave stated in his evidence to the Scott inquiry that ministers and officials 'who took . . . decisions did not actually have' the right information. While the information had 'gone into the government machinery [it] did not come out in the right place'.[139] Alan Clark echoed this view in his evidence to the inquiry. He complained that he had 'no personal knowledge' as a minister. He was 'a spectator'. He referred to the 'obsessional possessiveness' of the intelligence agencies.[140] These views are apparently shared across government: according to Lord Howe, for example, one of the most difficult tasks in Whitehall is to ensure the prompt availability of intelligence 'everywhere it should have been available while at the same time ensuring that it was not available anywhere else'. It is like trying to 'design and operate a high-speed, multi-directional, leak-proof sieve'.[141] The problem of distribution is compounded by that of quantity. In his evidence to the Scott inquiry, John Major explained that the FCO alone receives in the region of 40,000 intelligence reports every year: 'they would be of varying grades. Some . . . would be extremely valuable, others not so. Quite a strong filtering process is needed. It is clearly absurd that ministers should read 40,000 pieces of intelligence, but it would be filtered through the appropriate machinery and, where intelligence was thought to be relevant, validated and reliable—reliable being a key point—the officials would endeavour to put that before ministers.'[142]

Once intelligence has been properly distributed, there remains the problem of the quality of the intelligence that ministers get to see. Too frequently, it appears, ministers simply did not take the intelligence they saw sufficiently seriously. David Mellor, former minister at the home office and at the FCO, for example, stated in evidence to the Scott inquiry that intelligence reports did not contain 'shattering information about who was doing what to whom . . . they didn't tell you all you wanted to know about life'.[143] Similarly, David

---

[138] See para. E2.26.

[139] See R. Norton-Taylor, *Truth is a Difficult Concept: Inside the Scott Inquiry* (London: 4th Estate, 1995) p. 106.

[140] Ibid., p. 107.   [141] Ibid., p. 100.   [142] Ibid.   [143] Ibid., p. 99.

Gore-Booth, former head of the Middle East desk at the FCO, stated in evidence to the Scott inquiry that 'intelligence is a very imprecise art'.[144] Lord Howe stated in his evidence to the inquiry that 'in my early days I was naive enough to get excited about intelligence reports. Many look at first sight to be important and interesting and significant, and then when we check them, they are not even straws in the wind. They are cornflakes in the wind.'[145] Gore-Booth argued in his evidence to the Scott inquiry that intelligence would have needed to have been 'incontrovertible' for it to have prevented exports to Iraq. This is problematic, as we know from Gore-Booth and from Howe that intelligence is a very imprecise art—so how could it ever be incontrovertible?[146] Herein lies the second issue which calls for thorough review: namely, how to render Lord Howe's leak-proof sieve and his cornflakes in the wind more effective; how to find systems which are less reliant on memory and which might better serve their stated purposes.

Central Intelligence Machinery

At the heart of the intelligence failures outlined in the Scott report, as has already been indicated, lies the JIC and the British government's central intelligence machinery. The roles of this machinery have been enhanced in recent decades with the growing importance within the cabinet office of the joint intelligence secretariat, the intelligence co-ordinator, and the joint intelligence committee. In 1993, as part of the Conservative government's policy towards (slightly) greater open government, the cabinet office published a short document entitled *Central Intelligence Machinery*, in which John Major wrote that 'it is a strength of the British system that ministers do not receive conflicting or piecemeal intelligence assessments on situations or issues of concern. Through the JIC they are provided with assessments agreed between departments which provide an objective background to the discussion of policy.'[147] Clearly, this system did not quite work in the Matrix Churchill case, but what is the JIC supposed to do? The JIC was established in 1936 as a joint services subcommittee reporting to the chiefs of staff of the armed services.

---

[144] Ibid.

[145] Ibid., p. 100. This apparently widely shared view was also evident in the DTI: Tony Steadman stated in a letter in 1991 that 'intelligence information could not be regarded as evidence or firm evidence' (see para. G6.52).

[146] As with the previous issue, this too is a problem with a long history. As Thurlow argues in *The Secret State*, 'inability to distinguish between relevant intelligence, rumour and innuendo [is] a persistent weakness of British intelligence administration' (p. 87). Thurlow cites many examples, including the intelligence failures surrounding the Easter uprising in Dublin in 1916 in respect of which he states that 'it was difficult to distinguish between hard intelligence and background noise' (p. 86).

[147] A second edition was published in 1996. This document is available on the government's web site: see www.open.gov.uk.

During the second world war the home defence (security) executive (HD(S)E) was established to iron out duplication between the various intelligence agencies and to prevent overlap with regard to domestic surveillance. After the war this role was taken over by the JIC and the HD(S)E was abolished.[148] In 1957 the JIC was brought within the cabinet office. In 1968 the post of intelligence co-ordinator was established and an assessments staff was created to co-ordinate and prepare papers for JIC discussion.[149]

The JIC is responsible, subject to ministerial approval, both for setting the UK's national intelligence requirements and for producing a weekly survey on intelligence, colloquially known as the red book. This contains assessments for ministers and officials on situations of current concern.[150] The JIC meets weekly. Its members include representatives from the FCO, the MOD, and the treasury as well as the heads of the three intelligence agencies (MI5, SIS, and GCHQ), the intelligence co-ordinator, and the chief of assessments staff. The chairman of the JIC is specifically responsible for ensuring that the committee's warning and monitoring roles are adequately discharged. He has a right of direct access to the prime minister. After the Falklands war, the chairmanship of the JIC passed from the FCO to the cabinet office.[151]

The published terms of reference for the JIC are as follows:

The committee is charged with the following responsibilities:
- to give direction to, and to keep under review, the organization and working of British intelligence activity as a whole at home and overseas in order to ensure efficiency, economy and prompt adaptation to changing requirements;
- to submit, at agreed intervals, for approval by ministers, statements of the requirements and priorities for intelligence gathering and other tasks to be conducted by the intelligence agencies;
- to co-ordinate, as necessary, inter-departmental plans for intelligence activity;
- to monitor and give early warning of the development of direct or indirect foreign threats to British interests, whether political, military or ecomonic;
- on the basis of available information, to assess events and situations relating to external affairs, defence, terrorism, major international criminal activity, scientific, technical and economic matters . . .

The last major review of the JIC and the central intelligence machinery occurred in the aftermath of the Falklands war when a committee of privy counsellors under the chairmanship of Lord Franks was appointed to review the circumstances which led to the Argentinian invasion of the Falkland

---

[148] R. Thurlow, *The Secret State,* pp. 243 and 288.

[149] The intelligence co-ordinator is responsible for advising the cabinet secretary on the co-ordination of the intelligence machinery and its resources and programmes.

[150] JIC assessments are prepared by geographically-based current intelligence groups (CIGs) made up of those in the relevant departments with special knowledge of the area: see M. Herman, 'Assessment Machinery: British and American Models' (1995) 10 *Intelligence and National Security* (special issue) 13–33, at p. 15.

[151] This has subsequently reverted to the FCO, however. See Herman, ibid., p. 18.

Islands in 1982.[152] The terms of reference for the Franks Committee were 'to review the way in which the responsibilities of government in relation to the Falkland Islands . . . were discharged in the period leading up to the Argentine invasion . . .'.[153] This clearly included significant consideration of the government's access to and assessment of relevant intelligence in the months immediately prior to the invasion. While the Franks report was not critical of the 'reliability of the intelligence that was regularly received from a variety of sources' the committee was 'surprised that the events in the first three months of 1982 . . . did not prompt the joint intelligence organization to assess the situation afresh'.[154] The Franks committee continued that 'we remain doubtful about . . . aspects of the work of the joint intelligence organization . . . We do not seek to attach blame to the individuals involved [but there is a] need for a clearer understanding of the relative roles of the assessment staff, the FCO and the MOD, and for closer liaison between them.'[155]

While in theory monitoring and assessment are matters for the JIC, in practice it appears that DIS have a considerable role to play here as well. As Michael Herman has written, while DIS's official remit focuses on defence intelligence, 'in practice DIS has always been landed with urgent non-defence analysis tasks, from support for Rhodesian sanctions in the 1960s onwards, simply because there is no other body to take them on. The result smacks of analysis reacting to events instead of trying to anticipate them. If there was a British intelligence failure before the invasion of Kuwait in August 1990 it may have been because it was no-one's job to study the parlous state of the Iraqi economy in detail and draw on the results in assessing Saddam Hussein's intentions.'[156] Herman is clearly critical of the methods of intelligence assessment employed by the JIC and DIS. Of the JIC he states: 'it incorporates the principle of the search for truth through the medium of the seminar'.[157] This, he argues, leads to a propensity to blandness, to the establishment of a lowest common denominator of agreement, and to the search for the drafting solution which papers over the cracks and consequently softens meaning. This is compounded by the fact that the JIC is composed of essentially departmental interests. It works by stitching departmental

---

[152] *Falkland Islands Review: Report of a Committee of Privy Counsellors* (Cmnd. 8787, Jan. 1983). See W. Wallace, 'How frank was Franks?' (1983) 59 *International Affairs* 453–8 and L. Freedman, 'Intelligence Operations in the Falklands' (1986) 1 *Intelligence and National Security* 309–35.

[153] See A. Danchev, 'The Franks Report: A Chronicle of Unripe Time' in A. Danchev (ed.) *International Perspectives on the Falklands Conflict* (London: St Martin's Press, 1992) pp. 127–52, at p. 128.

[154] *Falkland Islands Review*, paras. 314–31.

[155] *Falkland Islands Review*, paras. 316–17.

[156] M. Herman, 'Assessment Machinery: British and American Models' (1995) 10 *Intelligence and National Security* (special issue) 13–33, at p. 21. Herman was a British civil servant for 35 years.

[157] Ibid., p. 23.

segments together rather than by looking at subjects as a whole.[158] This brings with it a sort of institutional pecking order which in turn reinforces institutional mind-sets. Herman concludes that while the Franks report stated that the JIC was 'too passive in operations to respond quickly and critically to a rapidly changing situation which demanded urgent attention'[159] this may well have been because those concerned were too busy handling the Falklands crisis departmentally to make an adequate overall intelligence assessment.[160]

This theme of the over-departmentalization of British intelligence assessment is echoed by Davies, who, in his recent examination of what he terms the 'producer/consumer interface', argues that the primarily departmental concerns of MI5 and SIS significantly weakens the position of the JIC.[161] In the case of SIS and GCHQ this is in large part because although their tasks are set by the JIC, their customers are individual government departments, primarily the foreign office. Customers have requirements: indeed, SIS and GCHQ regularly receive detailed lists of their customers' requirements. As the 1995 report of the intelligence and security committee put it, 'agencies meet regularly with customer departments to ensure that they are meeting their needs . . . customers put forward proposals for new or amended requirements . . . at any time'.[162] This system predates and effectively bypasses the JIC. This leads to a very important conclusion. The notion that the intelligence agencies exist to provide intelligence for some common good appears to be a false assumption: in practice, they serve more diverse, and more private aims. The benefits of intelligence accrue to departments.[163]

In the light of this, quite clearly the roles, composition, and working practices of the JIC need urgently to be thoroughly reviewed—in the light of experience since the Falklands conflict and in the light of the utter failure, demonstrated in the Scott report, of the JIC effectively to co-ordinate intelligence on Iraqi arms procurement in the late 1980s. Thus far, only one minor reform has been made to the UK's central intelligence machinery in the light

---

[158] M. Herman, 'Assessment Machinery: British and American Models' (1995) 10 *Intelligence and National Security* (special issue) 13–33, at p. 23.

[159] *Falkland Islands Review*, para. 318.

[160] Herman, p. 23. For a contrary view, see D. King, 'Intelligence Failures and the Falklands War: A Reassessment' (1987) 2 *Intelligence and National Security* 336–40. King, a retired lieut.-colonel in the British army, argues that the Falklands conflict should not be seen as an intelligence failure just because the JIC did not predict the Argentinian invasion. Surprise is, according to King, a major feature of the start of wars: 'even with perfect intelligence collection, rapid assessment and briefing, and highly attuned officials and ministers, reliance on intelligence alone predestined an indefensible Falklands' (p. 336). He further argues that 'intelligence experts deal with ambiguous evidence open to multiple interpretations. Certainty of assessment is almost always misplaced, and the alternative explanation should always be sought' (pp. 338–9).

[161] See P. Davies, 'Organizational Politics and the Development of Britain's Intelligence Producer/Consumer Interface' (1995) 10 *Intelligence and National Security* (special issue) 113–32.

[162] Intelligence and Security Committee, *Annual Report 1995*, Cm. 3198, para. 14.

[163] See Davies, pp. 115–16.

of the Scott report. In 1996 it was announced that a new subcommittee of the cabinet office committee on security (known as the subcommittee on security service priorities and performance, or SO(SSPP)) had been established. Its published terms of reference are to 'review the performance of the security service [MI5] against plans and objectives, to examine future service priorities and to advise the cabinet secretary and PSIS [the permanent secretaries' committee on the intelligence services] as appropriate'.[164] While this modest reform may do more to bring the security service within the ambit of the JIC and the cabinet office's responsibilities as to overall security and intelligence co-ordination, it affects only one part of the intelligence community—MI5— and can therefore not be regarded as the wholesale reform which the Scott report called for. Surely what is required is not one small secret committee dealing with but one part of the intelligence community, but rather a powerful overarching committee to oversee the work of all the intelligence agencies and services. This would require reform of the JIC as a whole, not the tacking on of yet another subcommittee to the already incoherent cabinet office structure.

The Intelligence and Security Committee

What is needed is a thorough examination of all three of these major issues: the proper constitutional relationship between ministers and the intelligence services; the organizational concerns as to distribution and use of intelligence; and the crucially important central direction which is given to the intelligence community through the JIC and the cabinet office. It is quite remarkable that even in the light of the unprecedented opportunity afforded by the publication of the Scott report, there has been no serious review of the role of intelligence in government decision making. Yet there is a body which is well placed to conduct just such a review. The Intelligence Services Act 1994 provided for the establishment of an intelligence and security committee, composed of nine parliamentarians (drawn from both Houses) 'to examine the expenditure, administration and policy' of MI5, SIS, and GCHQ.[165] The first chairman of the committee was Tom King MP, a former Conservative defence secretary. It has published several reports, including an introductory, interim report,[166] a special report on MI5's expanding roles in the field of organized crime,[167]

---

[164] See Cabinet Office, *Central Intelligence Machinery*, (2nd edn., 1996) annex D.

[165] Intelligence Services Act 1994, s. 10(1). The committee operates within the so-called 'ring of secrecy' as all of its members have been formally notified under the Official Secrets Act. It meets every week during parliamentary session (it meets in Whitehall, not in Westminster). See generally, Peter Gill, 'Reasserting Control: Changes in the Oversight of the UK Intelligence Community' (1996) 11 *Intelligence and National Security* 313.

[166] *Interim Report of the Intelligence and Security Committee* (Cm. 2873, May 1995).

[167] *Report on Security Service Work Against Organised Crime* (Cm. 3065, Dec. 1995).

as well as its annual reports.[168] In addition to these published reports, the committee has made a number of further reports to the prime minister on specific matters relating to security and intelligence which remain unpublished. We do not know what the subject matters of all these reports are, but at least one of them concerned the work of the security and secret intelligence services in the field of the 'interests of the economic well-being of the UK'.[169] The decision as to whether (and if so how much of) these reports should be published is one for the prime minister. It is still too early to know whether or not this will prove to be an area where Tony Blair encourages a greater degree of open government than his predecessor did.

The intelligence and security committee has made it plain that it will be concerned with some big questions. It is set to examine, among other things, overall government/intelligence structure, especially the government's assessment of intelligence.[170] The committee has stated that 'our first major inquiry shall address how the agencies have adapted in general to the new situations post-cold war and, in particular, how tasks and the priorities attached to them have altered, and whether the resources now provided are appropriate to those tasks and used in a cost effective way'.[171] More pertinent to the issues raised in this chapter, the committee has also made it clear that it intends to examine 'the dissemination and uses made of the agencies' product by government customers, in particular the briefing of intelligence and security information and procedures to ministers and senior officials and the suitability of the present ministerial structures for dealing with these matters'.[172] However, the committee's treatment of these issues to date has been thoroughly disappointing, although there is perhaps little surprise in this, given that the committee's make-up has been dominated by former foreign office and MOD ministers (including the likes of Lord Howe, Sir Archie Hamilton, former armed forces minister, Michael Mates, former Northern Ireland minister, as well as Tom King).[173] In its very thin response to the serious intelligence 'deficiencies'[174] illustrated with care and at considerable length in the Scott report, the intelligence and security committee disgracefully made no substantive findings and only a small number of minor, almost trivial,

---

[168] See *Annual Report 1995* (Cm. 3198, Mar. 1996) and *Annual Report 1996* (Cm. 3574, Feb. 1997).

[169] See *Annual Report 1996*, para. 2.　　　　　　　　　　　[170] *Interim Report,* para. 4.

[171] *Interim Report,* para. 11. The *Annual Report 1996* stated that this inquiry was still in progress: see para. 7.

[172] *Annual Report 1995*, para. 40.

[173] In addition to which its secretariat is composed of officials from the cabinet office, i.e. the very department which houses the JIC and the government's intelligence assessment staff: hardly an inspiring choice for a supposedly independent scrutineer! See P. Gill, op. cit., n. 165, p. 324.

[174] Even the former prime minister John Major described the performance of the government *vis-à-vis* the intelligence services as evidenced in the Scott report as one which identified a number of 'deficiencies'. See Intelligence and Security Committee, *Annual Report 1996*, Cm. 3574, p. 3, letter from John Major to Tom King.

recommendations. It is as if the members of the committee were somehow happy with the appalling state of British intelligence which the Scott report revealed. One can only assume that this was because the committee thought that what Scott had to say was nothing new, undisturbing, and perfectly ordinary—which only makes it all the more damning, of course.

The committee blithely observed that 'getting intelligence to those government customers who need to see it, in a timely and secure fashion, will present a continuing challenge' in respect of which there can be 'no guaranteed solutions'.[175] In its superficially reassuring manner, the committee continued, 'better links between producer and consumer . . . are being introduced and these should be vigorously pursued, as should improvements to electronic and other distribution systems'.[176] Is this really the tough, independent parliamentary regulation to which Sir Richard Scott was happy to delegate the responsibility of enforcing a more rigorous and reliable system of intelligence? While the committee stated that the intelligence agencies 'should be proactive with customers to ensure that intelligence needs . . . are fully understood' there is no detail as to how this aim should be achieved and nor is there any indication as to whether it is being achieved. No target is set against which performance might be measured. No evaluation is made as to whether the abominable breakdown in communications between major departments of state and the intelligence services which so concerned Scott could too easily recur.

Instead, the committee seems happy almost to ignore Scott and to satisfy itself that even before the Scott report was published it was already out of date. The committee cited the (unpublished) work of a 1993 cabinet office review of protective security and a 1994 review of intelligence requirements conducted by Sir Michael Quinlan, former permanent secretary at the MOD. Without providing details or substance, the committee asserted that the former 'made it easier to disseminate intelligence more widely and removed anomalies relating to staff security clearance' and that the latter 'brought about a number of changes to the national requirements-setting processes'[177] and that the criticisms of these matters in the Scott report had accordingly been superseded by events. Although these reviews came after the events chronicled in the Scott report, they came before the report was published. If Scott believed that these changes genuinely did ameliorate the appalling catalogue of error and laziness which he revealed, why did he not say so in his report? Why did he leave the strong impression that his report illustrated a series of mammoth intelligence failures which were yet to be remedied and which required urgent consideration by others? That such a professional and rigorous consideration has not arisen in the subsequent work of the intelligence and security committee is a damning indictment of the continuing

---

[175] Ibid., para. 45.   [176] Ibid., para. 46.   [177] Ibid., para. 41.

weakness of British intelligence oversight—an indictment which Parliament
(and the Labour government) should act on without delay. Something more
than a mere change in the personnel of the intelligence and security committee is required. A genuinely independent, parliamentary committee is needed
to replace the Whitehall-based insiders who have thus far dominated and
effectively crippled the work of the intelligence and security committee.

Conclusion: Towards Standards in Intelligence?

As things stand, the intelligence field is without doubt the area in which the
Scott report has had least impact. Whereas the public service committee
enthusiastically took up the challenge and valuably reviewed questions of
civil service accountability and ministerial responsibility in the light of the
Scott report, the intelligence and security committee failed to follow suit in
the context of intelligence. Responsibility for this must lie in part with the
structure of the committee (with its base in Whitehall rather than
Westminster), in part with the lack of political realization in February 1996
that the Scott report was as concerned in its detail with matters of intelligence
as this chapter has suggested, and in part with those who staffed the committee, dominated as they were with insiders with little evident desire for independent political scrutiny of intelligence failures. Quite what the prospects are
for improvements in this most sensitive area of constitutional accountability
are unclear. While it might be unwise to assess Tony Blair's administration by
drawing on earlier experience of Labour governments, it has to be said that
Labour governments do not exactly have any more glowing a record than do
their Conservative rivals when it comes to encouraging rigorous parliamentary scrutiny of the UK's security and secret intelligence services.

Some of the issues identified in this chapter are obviously going to be quite
difficult to resolve. It is hard to say, for example, from a position outside of
the intelligence world, what can be done to reduce unnecessary intelligence
information going to ministers and to focus ministerial minds more closely on
(what turns out to be) the relevant information. Similarly, we know so little
of the detail of the daily operations of the JIC that from this distance it is
impossible to make sensible suggestions as to how best the cabinet office
should reform itself in response to the Scott report. But the intelligence and
security committee should not suffer from these problems—indeed, it has
considerable powers to call for persons, papers, and records (on the lines of
those discussed in relation to select committees in the previous chapter) and
in none of its reports has the committee complained that it is unable to see the
information it requires.

On the other hand, however, the task of clarifying the proper constitutional
relationship between government ministers and the intelligence services

should not be such a difficult one. The general constitutional framework of ministerial responsibility has already been extensively reviewed by Parliament and by government, as we have already seen. Why can that framework not form a basis for examining precisely how the rather vague outline of the Security Service and Intelligence Services Acts should operate in practice in the form of a published document which could then be used as a point of reference to seek to avoid future repetitions of the breakdowns which Scott illustrated? Such a document could even be usefully amplified by reference to the 'standards in public life' laid down by the Nolan committee.[178] The Nolan committee outlined seven principles of public life, which, according to the committee, should 'apply to all aspects of public life'.[179] These could be taken on board and applied to the field of secret intelligence. The seven principles are selflessness, integrity, objectivity, accountability, openness, honesty, and leadership. Two of these seven are especially pertinent here: accountability and openness. The Nolan committee stated that by accountability it had in mind the notion that 'holders of public office [should be] accountable for their decisions and actions to the public and must submit themselves to whatever scrutiny is appropriate to their office'. On openness, the Nolan committee stated that 'holders of public office should be as open as possible about all the decisions and actions that they take. They should give reasons for their decisions and restrict information only when the wider public interest clearly demands.'[180] The Nolan committee recommended that 'all public bodies should draw up codes of conduct incorporating' these principles of public life.[181] If these basic standards were to be adopted in a new framework document for the security and secret intelligence services, perhaps the intelligence failures identified in the Scott report might be more successfully avoided in the future.

All it takes is for somebody to take the lead (another one of those Nolan principles—leadership). It may be that this is nothing more than idle wishful thinking—another example of Lord Howe's academic 'cornflakes in the wind' perhaps. But in a genuinely mature and modern democracy even the most traditionally secretive parts of constitutional governance should be opened up, reviewed, reformed, and improved. That the British constitution under the Conservatives manifestly failed to provide ways to facilitate any such review in the field of secret intelligence after the Scott report demonstrates that the constitution still has some way to travel before those lofty ideals of mature and modern democracy can truly be applied to it. As we enter a period (so we are promised) of further constitutional renewal it remains a key question of Tony Blair's new politics as to whether the spirit of change and openness will be permitted to permeate thoroughly enough to illuminate

---

[178] See *First Report of the Committee on Standards in Public Life*, Chairman Lord Nolan, Cm. 2850, May 1995.
[179] Nolan, ibid., p. 14.   [180] Ibid.   [181] Ibid., p. 3.

the murky depths of secret intelligence and national security. Let us hope that the Labour administration has the courage and foresight to ask the difficult questions and confront the awkward issues of intelligence and government which its Conservative predecessor characteristically refused even to acknowledge. In this, more than any other area touched by the Scott report, much remains to be done.

PART III

Government and Courts

5

Public Interest Immunity

PUBLIC interest immunity (PII) was the first aspect of the Matrix Churchill story to attract the attention of public lawyers, and this small part of the law of evidence retained its high-profile position in the Scott report and in subsequent parliamentary debates and academic literature. This is not because PII is all that interesting. Rather, it has more to do with the fact that, as with all major political scandals, it is the cover-up as much as it is the initial cock-up which attracts such controversy. PII played the role of cover-up in the Scott story. The Conservative government used the doctrine of PII to seek to prevent the court in the Matrix Churchill trial (and hence also the public) from finding out about the scale of the government's involvement throughout the late 1980s in Iraq's arms procurement network. One commentator recently wrote that, as a non-lawyer, he found the argument concerning the PII aspects of the Scott story to be a 'case of the obtuse discussing the absurd, believing it abstruse'.[1] There is much to agree with in this sentiment. In terms of its technicalities and details, PII is without doubt the most boring part of the Scott saga, but beneath its devilish detail lies a frightening picture of government secrecy, disregard for legal accountability, and ignorance of the law. Even if the discussion on PII has sometimes been obtuse, the underlying problem of government abuse of power remains acute.

What is PII?

PII is a doctrine of the law of evidence. A normal stage in pre-trial procedure is discovery and disclosure. Each side in litigation will disclose to the other the evidence on which it seeks to rely. There are several legal immunities which restrict the scope of the basic obligation to disclose, of which PII is one. The doctrine of PII allows for relevant and material evidence to be withheld if it would be contrary to the public interest for it to be disclosed. Initially this was a privilege granted only to the crown, as the crown was the constitutional guardian of the public interest. Indeed, before 1972 PII was known as crown privilege. Now PII is most frequently claimed either by a government minister or by the police, although claiming PII is not something which is limited

---

[1] Keith Dowding, *The Civil Service* (London: Routledge, 1995) n. 5 to ch. 8 (p. 182).

strictly to the state as such.[2] While the law of PII has a long history, its modern development can be seen to have commenced with the seminal war-time decision of the House of Lords in *Duncan* v. *Cammell, Laird & Co. Ltd.*[3] This case concerned a submarine, *Thetis*, which had been built by the respondent shipbuilders under contract with the admiralty. In tests, the submarine sank and flooded, killing ninety-nine men on board. A large number of actions for negligence were brought by various dependants of those killed. The plaintiffs requested discovery of documents from the shipbuilders, including the plans for the submarine, her hull, and machinery. The admiralty instructed the shipbuilders to refuse discovery and to object to the production of the plans on the ground that 'it would be injurious to the public interest that any of the said documents should be disclosed to any person'.[4] The case went to the House of Lords where the question to be determined was what the circumstances were in which it could be claimed on behalf of the crown that documents ordinarily required as evidence in a civil dispute could be validly withheld from production in court. The only speech in the House of Lords was delivered by Viscount Simon LC (although six other members of the House expressed their concurrence with him).[5]

Viscount Simon held that, as the admiralty had wished, the documents should not be disclosed. His reasoning was that it is the minister who is charged with the responsibility of safeguarding the public interest, and if the minister has certified (as the first lord of the admiralty had done here) that the production of the documents would endanger the public interest, then such an objection must be treated by the courts as being conclusive. The House of Lords in *Duncan* considered that the courts had no jurisdiction to go beyond the ministerial certificate: once a minister of the crown claimed PII, such a claim would, as a matter of law, be automatically upheld by the courts: 'the practice in Scotland, as in England, may have varied, but the approved practice in both countries is to treat a ministerial objection taken in proper form as conclusive'.[6] Having made this basic ruling, Viscount Simon went on to make two further points about PII which remain important. He stated first that PII could be claimed on two different bases: either because of the contents of a particular document or because of the class of documents into which the document concerned fell, irrespective of its actual contents. In

---

[2] In the 1970s the House of Lords held that the gaming board, a statutory body, and also the national society for the prevention of cruelty to children (NSPCC), a private, independent charity, could make claims to PII. See *R* v. *Lewes Justices, ex parte Home Secretary* [1973] AC 388 and *D* v. *NSPCC* [1978] AC 171.

[3] [1942] AC 624.   [4] [1942] AC at 626.

[5] There is clearly a separation of powers point here: was it appropriate, even in time of world war, for one cabinet minister (the lord chancellor) to adjudicate on the propriety of a claim made by another (the first lord of the admiralty)? This is a point which was not apparently considered in the House of Lords at the time.

[6] [1942] AC at 641.

other words, the claiming of PII, the withholding of documents from the court, may arise for either of two reasons: either because the contents of a document, if disclosed, would be damaging to the public interest or, more controversially, simply because, even though the contents of the document were harmless, the document was merely the sort of document which as a matter of general policy should not be disclosed. These types of documents would include cabinet papers, government departmental papers, and such like. These two different types of PII claims are known as contents claims and class claims. The importance and controversial nature of this distinction will become apparent as this chapter progresses. Viscount Simon also laid down an outline of the kinds of reasons why it would not be in the public interest for certain documents to be disclosed. In an important passage, he stated that:

it is not a sufficient ground that the documents are marked 'state documents' or 'official' or 'confidential'. It would not be a good ground that, if they were produced, the consequences might involve the department or the government in parliamentary discussion or in public criticism . . . Neither would it be a good ground that production might tend to expose a want of efficiency in the administration or tend to lay the department open to claims for compensation. In a word, it is not enough that the minister of the department does not want to have the documents produced. The minister . . . ought not to take the responsibility of withholding production except in cases where the public interest would otherwise be damnified, for example, where disclosure would be injurious to national defence, or to good diplomatic relations, or where the practice of keeping a class of documents secret is necessary for the proper functioning of the public service.[7]

Viscount Simon's speech might have laid down the legal foundations for the modern law of crown privilege (or PII) but it did not quieten the continuing political criticisms as to the government's use of the doctrine.[8] Indeed, much of Viscount Simon's approach was departed from as early as 1956—at least in Scotland[9]—and although English law was not formally changed for a further twelve years until 1968, the situation was so untidy that the lord chancellor felt compelled to make an important clarificatory statement in Parliament in 1956. In an attempt to pacify concerns that crown privilege was being claimed in respect of too wide a field of documents, Viscount Kilmuir LC stated that 'the proper way to strike a balance between the needs of litigants and those of government administration is . . . to narrow the class as much as possible by excluding from it those categories of documents which appear to be particularly relevant to litigation and for which the highest degree of confidentiality is not required in the public interest. We have carried

---

[7] [1942] AC at 642.

[8] One of the more controversial cases was *Ellis* v. *Home Office* [1953] 2 QB 135, on which even the conservative *Law Quarterly Review* was scathing: see C. K. Allen (1953) 69 *Law Quarterly Review* 449. See also, Devlin, 'The Common Law, Public Policy and the Executive' [1956] *Current Legal Problems* 1, at p. 4.

[9] See *Glasgow Corporation* v. *Central Land Board* [1956] SLT 41.

out an extensive survey of this field, and have certain proposals.'[10] The proposals included many which need not concern us here but, significantly for present purposes, Viscount Kilmuir stated that crown privilege would not be claimed in criminal proceedings—a matter to which we shall return shortly.

English law followed the Scottish example in moving further away from (parts of) *Duncan* when the House of Lords made its famous ruling in *Conway* v. *Rimmer*.[11] This case concerned an action for malicious prosecution brought by a former probationary police constable against his former superintendent. Relations between the two officers were clearly bad. When another constable lost his torch, Conway was suspected of having stolen it; during investigations into the missing torch the superintendent (Rimmer) told Conway that his probationary reports were adverse and advised him to resign from the police. Conway refused to resign. Rimmer then saw to it that Conway should be prosecuted for the theft of the torch (worth 15*s.* 3*d.*) but Conway's trial was stopped after the presentation of the case for the prosecution and a verdict of not guilty was returned. After the trial, Conway was dismissed from the police. He then brought his action for damages. Conway sought discovery of a number of documents which were in Rimmer's possession, including four probationary reports which Rimmer had made during Conway's probationary period with the police. It was admitted that these documents were relevant to Conway's action, but the home secretary objected to their disclosure, certifying that they fell within a class of documents the production of which would be injurious to the public interest. The question for the House of Lords, as it had been in *Duncan* v. *Cammell Laird*, was whether such a ministerial certificate was conclusive or not. All five Law Lords delivered speeches, and although in terms of the outcome they were unanimous, there are some important differences between them as regards the overall approach to PII.

The House of Lords decided that the rule in *Duncan's* case, that a ministerial certificate should be conclusive, should be overruled and that the court ought to be able to look behind such a certificate. Lord Reid held that although he had no doubt that *Duncan* was 'rightly decided', the House of Lords in 1942 was self-evidently preoccupied with cases where 'disclosure would involve a danger of real prejudice to the national interest'.[12] In times less driven by the emergency of war, a better approach, according to Lord Reid, would be for the court to accept that in cases where disclosure was resisted on public interest grounds there were two competing public interests at stake, and it was the court's role to balance them. On the one hand there is the public interest in ensuring the fair administration of justice, which would usually require full discovery and disclosure. On the other hand there is the public interest, as cited in the ministerial certificate, such as national security,

[10] HL Deb., Vol. 197, col. 743, 6 June 1956.   [11] [1968] AC 910.
[12] [1968] AC at 939.

confidentiality or the proper functioning of the public service, which would normally demand the withholding of the documents. The court's responsibility in such cases is to weigh these competing public interests and to determine, on the facts of the case, which one outweighs the other.[13] As to precisely how the courts are to do this—how are they to know (or judge) which public interest outweighs the other in any particular case—Lord Reid was silent. If the effect of *Duncan* v. *Cammell Laird* was to leave the question of PII entirely to the discretion of the minister, with no principles laid down as to how such discretion should properly be exercised, the effect of *Conway* v. *Rimmer* was to leave the issue as one for equally unguided judicial discretion.

During the course of his speech, Lord Reid, although he departed from Viscount Simon's speech in *Duncan* on the issue of the conclusivity of the ministerial certificate, echoed and supported many of the other things which had been said about PII in *Duncan*. For example, Lord Reid supported the notion that PII could be claimed on either contents or class grounds. He even went as far as to state that in his view there were 'certain classes of documents which ought not to be disclosed whatever their content might be. Virtually everyone agrees that cabinet minutes and the like ought not to be disclosed until such time as they are only of historical interest.' The most important reason for this, according to Lord Reid, was that, otherwise, disclosure would 'create or fan ill-informed or captious . . . criticism. The business of government is difficult enough as it is, and no government could contemplate with equanimity the inner workings of the government machine being exposed to the gaze of those ready to criticize without adequate knowledge of the background and perhaps with some axe to grind.'[14] *Conway* v. *Rimmer* may have been a reforming decision, but, as statements such as these make clear, it would be a mistake to parade the case as a great leap forward in the cause of open government and freedom of information. All *Conway* v. *Rimmer* did was to modify but the harshest effects of a rotten war-time precedent.

In addition to his support for Viscount Simon's approach to contents and class claims, Lord Reid also reinforced the spirit of *Duncan* v. *Cammell Laird* on the issue of the candour argument. As we saw above, Viscount Simon laid down a number of the situations in which it would be appropriate for a claim to PII to be made. This list of situations ended with Viscount Simon's statement that documents could be withheld where it was 'necessary for the proper functioning of the public service'. This is the so-called candour argument. The idea here is that civil servants and other government officials will only be frank and candid in their advice to ministers if they know that such advice is and will remain confidential and will not at some point in the future be open to criticism and review in a court of law. The threat of future judicial scrutiny,

---

[13] [1968] AC at 940 and 952.   [14] [1968] AC at 952. See also Lord Upjohn at 993.

it is said, is enough to inhibit the nation's civil servants and will result in advice which is somehow constrained and incomplete, rather than being full and free. This is a controversial argument, but it is one which Lord Reid had no trouble in supporting.[15]

The outcome of *Conway* v. *Rimmer*, as far as the House of Lords was concerned, was that after their ruling, the documents were privately inspected by the court, and, in the words of Lord Reid, nothing was found 'in any of them the disclosure of which would . . . be in any way prejudicial to the proper administration of the [police] or to the general public interest'.[16] The House therefore ordered their disclosure to Conway.

Many of these issues arose again in *Burmah Oil* v. *Bank of England*.[17] Unlike *Conway* v. *Rimmer*, *Burmah Oil* did concern high level government papers relating to the formulation of government policy on a sensitive issue: namely the rescue by the Bank of England of a troubled company. The rescue plan involved, among other things, the company (Burmah Oil) selling stock it had owned to the Bank of England. Some months after the rescue plan had been put into effect, the company commenced legal proceedings against the bank, arguing that it had been forced to sell its stock for an unconscionably and inequitably low price. The formulation of the rescue plan had involved weeks of sensitive negotiations between the bank, the treasury, the department of energy, and Burmah Oil. In the course of its action Burmah Oil sought discovery of a number of documents emanating from or relating to these negotiations, and the chief secretary to the treasury objected to the production of some of the documents on grounds of PII.

By the time the case reached the House of Lords, only ten documents remained subject to the claim to PII. These ten fell into two categories, known as category A and category B. The former consisted of 'communications between, to and from ministers . . . and minutes and briefs for ministers and memoranda of meetings attended by ministers. All such documents relate to the formulation of the policy of the government.'[18] Category B consisted of communications between, to, and from senior government officials. The PII claim in *Burmah Oil* was a class claim, based in the ministerial certificate on the candour argument: in the words of the certificate, 'it is, in my opinion, necessary for the proper functioning of the public service that the documents in category A and category B should be withheld from production. They are

---

[15] See his citing with approval the words of Viscount Simon: [1968] AC at 952. Other members of the House of Lords in *Conway* v. *Rimmer* were more critical of the candour argument. Lord Morris, for example, described it as 'a suggestion of doubtful validity' (at 957). Lord Morris thought that if civil servants feared the possibility of future judicial scrutiny of their advice, this would encourage them to be more rather than less candid. Lord Pearce echoed Lord Morris's doubts as to the validity of the candour argument (at 987).

[16] [1968] AC at 996–7.   [17] [1980] AC 1090.

[18] The words of the PII certificate signed by the chief secretary, quoted by Lord Wilberforce: [1980] AC at 1109.

all documents falling within the class of documents relating to the formulation of government policy.'[19]

The question for the House of Lords was whether, applying the balancing
exercise as described by Lord Reid in *Conway* v. *Rimmer*, the overriding public interest lay in the documents being disclosed or withheld. The majority of
the House held that they (the judges) should privately inspect the documents
in question in order to determine whether the interests of justice outweighed
those of confidentiality as outlined in the minister's certificate. Lord Keith,
one of four judges in the majority, held that even though the documents in
question in this case were high level government papers dealing with the formulation of government policy, this did not mean (contrary to what Lord
Reid had stated in *Conway* v. *Rimmer*) that the court could not authorize their
disclosure. In an approach significantly different from that which had been
adopted by Lord Reid, Lord Keith stated that 'it would be going too far to
lay down that no document in any particular one of the categories mentioned
should ever in any circumstances be ordered to be produced'.[20] Lord Keith
also poured scorn on the candour argument, on which the minister had relied
in his certificate in *Burmah Oil*, stating that:

the notion that any competent and conscientious public servant would be inhibited at
all in the candour of his writings by consideration of the off-chance that they might
have to be produced in a litigation is in my opinion grotesque . . . There can be dis-
cerned in modern times a trend towards more open governmental methods than were
prevalent in the past. No doubt it is for Parliament and not for courts of law to say
how far that trend should go. The courts are, however, concerned with the consideration that it is in the public interest that justice should be done . . . This may demand,
though no doubt only in a very limited number of cases, that the inner workings of
government should be exposed to public gaze, and there may be some who would
regard this as likely to lead, not to captious or ill-informed criticism, but to criticism
calculated to improve the nature of that working as affecting the individual citizen.[21]

While Lord Keith's views on open government and the 'grotesque' nature of
the candour argument were not shared by the other law lords in the majority,
the four majority judges did agree that they should privately inspect the documents in order to determine whether they should, on balance, be disclosed
or not. In the event, the four judges considered that although the documents
were relevant and material evidence in Burmah Oil's dispute with the bank,
they were not crucial and their absence from the litigation would not be unfair
to Burmah Oil. In Lord Scarman's words: 'their significance is not such as to
override the public service [i.e. candour] objections to their production'.[22]
The House of Lords therefore ordered that they should not be disclosed.

Despite the fact that Burmah Oil did not gain discovery of the documents it
had wanted, the majority view in the House of Lords in this case nonetheless

---

[19] Quoted by Lord Wilberforce: [1980] AC at 1110.   [20] [1980] AC at 1134.
[21] [1980] AC at 1133–4.   [22] [1980] AC at 1147.

represents the high-water mark of judicial willingness to countenance a degree of openness towards claims to PII, even at a relatively high level concerning sensitive government papers. The House was not unanimous, however, and the dissent of Lord Wilberforce is significant and merits examination because it was his dissent, rather than the position of the majority, which heralded the way the House would seek to develop the law in future cases. In Lord Wilberforce's view the claim to PII in *Burmah Oil* laid down in the ministerial certificate was *prima facie* a good one, and in the light of the concerns expressed by the minister in his certificate, before the court could privately inspect the documents concerned, the other side in the case (Burmah Oil) should first explain to the court exactly why it was in the public interest that the documents should be disclosed. Lord Wilberforce stated that 'a claim for PII having been made, on manifestly solid grounds, it is necessary for those who seek to overcome it to demonstrate the existence of a counteracting interest calling for disclosure of particular documents. When this is demonstrated, but only then, may the court proceed to a balancing process.'[23] This, he stated, Burmah Oil had failed to do. Thus, Lord Wilberforce refused even to inspect the documents privately, holding against Burmah Oil because it had failed to establish the grounds on which he as a judge could overturn the ministerial certificate: it had failed, in his view, to give him anything to weigh against the public interest in the proper functioning of the public service on which the minister had relied in his certificate.

Thus, in contradistinction to the views of Lord Keith, Lord Wilberforce had a good deal of sympathy with the candour argument. He stated of the candour argument that 'it seems now rather fashionable to decry this, but if as a ground it may at one time have been exaggerated, it has now, in my opinion, received an excessive dose of cold water. I am certainly not prepared— against the view of the minister—to discount the need, in the formation of such very controversial policy as that with which we are here involved, for frank and uninhibited advice from the bank to the government, from and between civil servants and between ministers . . . To remove protection from revelation in court in this case at least could well deter frank and full expression in similar cases in the future.' Lord Wilberforce summed up his views with the ringing phrase: 'I do not believe . . . that it is for the courts to assume the role of advocates for open government'.[24]

Lord Wilberforce's position, in dissent in *Burmah Oil*, was largely followed by the House of Lords as a whole three years later, on the next occasion when PII was considered by their lordships, in *Air Canada* v. *Secretary of State for Trade*.[25] The background to this case was that the British Airports Authority (BAA) was in the process of making major improvements at Heathrow. Under the Airports Authority Act 1975 the secretary of state had certain

---

[23] [1980] AC at 1113–14.   [24] [1980] AC at 1112.   [25] [1983] 2 AC 394.

supervisory powers over BAA, especially as regards finance. He required BAA to pay for the improvements at Heathrow from its own internal revenues. In order to afford this, BAA increased charges to airlines at Heathrow by some 35 per cent. Air Canada and seventeen other international airlines challenged the increases in charges levied on them. One of their main arguments in the litigation was that although the secretary of state did have certain statutory powers over BAA, these were powers which could only be exercised for legitimate purposes—i.e. the purposes which fell within the aims and objectives of the relevant Act. Here, they asserted that the secretary of state had exercised his statutory powers for an improper purpose: namely as a way of reducing the public sector borrowing requirement. Clearly, in order to determine whether this had indeed been the secretary of state's motivation, Air Canada needed access to documents containing communications between the secretary of state, his colleagues, and officials, and BAA. The government claimed PII for two categories of documents: first, for ministerial papers relating to the formulation of government policy (about 100 documents) and secondly, for interdepartmental communications between senior civil servants. Just as in the *Burmah Oil* case, these were class claims to PII based on the candour argument.

The judge at first instance decided that he should privately inspect the documents, but he stayed his order that the documents should be produced for his inspection, pending an appeal. The House of Lords unanimously dismissed Air Canada's appeal and held that the case even for private inspection, let alone public disclosure, had not been made out. Although unanimous as to this outcome, the House of Lords differed as to what precisely the test adopted should be to determine whether documents subject to a claim to PII should be privately inspected or not. Lord Fraser ruled that, while it was not possible to lay down any uniform test, the party seeking disclosure 'ought at least to satisfy the court that the documents are very likely to contain material which would give substantial support' to their case and that without it they 'might be "deprived of the means of . . . proper presentation" of' their case.[26] Lord Fraser stated that 'the test is intended to be fairly strict', as courts 'should not be encouraged to "take a peep" just on the off-chance of finding something useful'.[27]

Lords Scarman and Templeman[28] took a slightly different view. They felt that the documents should be privately inspected where they might assist either side in the litigation or where they were necessary for disposing of the matter fairly, rather than only where the party seeking disclosure had

---

[26] [1983] 2 AC at 435, citing *Glasgow Corporation* v. *Central Land Board* 1956 SC (HL) 1 at 18, per Lord Radcliffe.
[27] [1983] 2 AC at 436. Lords Wilberforce (at 438) and Edmund Davies (at 441) agreed with the approach of Lord Fraser.
[28] At 445 and 449 respectively.

established that the documents would assist them. On the facts of the present case, this different emphasis made no difference to the outcome: all five law lords were agreed that Air Canada had not demonstrated to the satisfaction of the court that the documents should be inspected by the judge. The rather obvious question to be asked here is, if the party seeking disclosure does not have the documents in its possession, how can it establish the ways in which those documents might be useful to its argument? It is somewhat of a catch-22 situation.

What do these cases tell us? One thing which is clear from this body of case-law is surely that, as was suggested in chapter three, the courtroom is not the most promising place to visit to secure a good view of open government. While there are occasional remarks of a positive and progressive nature (such as those of Lord Keith in *Burmah Oil*) the overall impression is one which gives little cause for believing that it is judges to whom we should turn if we are to push for more openness in central government. From the war time executive mindedness of *Duncan* v. *Cammell Laird* to the conservatism of Lord Wilberforce in *Burmah Oil* (to be followed by all their lordships in the *Air Canada* case) the picture painted by these authorities is of a senior judiciary which has done the barest minimum for freeing governmental information. Even supposedly liberal and reformist judges such as Lord Reid have happily endorsed the spectres of class claims and the spurious candour argument. Let us not forget that these are judicial creations: PII is royal prerogative power the boundaries of which are set by the courts and not by Parliament or government. As a basic framework this body of case-law is hardly a manifesto for openness. With that in mind, let us now turn to the ways in which PII became controversial in the Scott story.

PII in the Scott Report

If these cases form the basis of the modern law of PII as it stood in the period investigated by the Scott inquiry,[29] how was this general framework employed in the cases which Scott reviewed, and why was the government's use of PII so controversial? To take the Matrix Churchill case first. Three Matrix Churchill directors were prosecuted by customs and excise for an offence under the Customs and Excise Management Act 1979, section 68(2) of which provides that an offence is committed by any person who is 'knowingly concerned in the exportation . . . of any goods with intent to evade' export restrictions. Exports to Iraq were restricted under a number of Export of Goods (Control) Orders made pursuant to the Import, Export and Customs Powers (Defence) Act 1939, as amended in 1990. As we have seen in

---

[29] Subsequent cases such as *ex p. Wiley* are considered below.

previous chapters, these restrictions required the exporter to obtain a licence from the DTI. The case against the Matrix Churchill directors was that they had unlawfully obtained a licence by deceiving the DTI as to the true nature of the machine tools they were exporting to Iraq. The argument was that Matrix Churchill had claimed that their exports were for general civil engineering purposes, whereas in fact they were for the manufacture of weapons.

The Matrix Churchill directors proposed to run two arguments in their defence. The first was that they had told the UK's security and secret intelligence services exactly what they were exporting. Paul Henderson, one of the three defendants and Matrix Churchill's managing director, had been an SIS informer since at least 1976. Their second defence was that the government generally and Alan Clark in particular had encouraged them to export to Iraq and that dual-use goods such as machine tools should be presented on export licence applications as being for general civil use. In order to establish the truth of these arguments, the defence team was clearly going to need access to a large number of sensitive government documents. When discovery was sought, however, the government responded with PII certificates, at both the committal and full trial stages. Before the commencement of the full trial there were several days of argument in court on matters relating to discovery and PII after which the trial judge, Judge Brian Smedley, ordered the disclosure of many of the documents in respect of which PII certificates had been signed.[30] At the trial itself, defence counsel, led by Geoffrey Robertson QC used many of the disclosed documents to cross-examine prosecution witnesses. On the basis of this cross-examination Alan Clark, a key prosecution witness, appeared to concede that he had, as the defence alleged, encouraged the defendants to continue to export defence equipment to Iraq.[31] Once this central concession had been made it would have been exceptionally difficult for the prosecution to prove that the Matrix Churchill directors had deceived the government as to the nature of their exports. Therefore, leading counsel for the prosecution, Alan Moses QC, decided in consultation with Sir Brian Unwin, the chairman of customs, and Sir Nicholas Lyell, the attorney general, that the trial should not be continued and invited the court to acquit the defendants.[32]

Although it was the collapse of the Matrix Churchill trial in November 1992 that was the immediate reason behind the establishment of the Scott inquiry, the Matrix Churchill trial was not the only prosecution relating to exports to Iraq in which questions concerning PII were raised which was

[30] A full chronology is provided in the Scott report at para. G1.2. The PII hearings are considered in detail in the Scott report at ch. G14.
[31] Some of the exchanges between Geoffrey Robertson and Alan Clark are reproduced at para. G17.29.
[32] See para. G17.34.

investigated in the Scott report. At least two further cases require brief mention. At about the same time as customs commenced their investigations into Matrix Churchill (in early 1990) they also began investigations into a company called BSA Tools Ltd. In 1987 BSA had applied to the DTI for an export licence to export fifty lathes to the Iraqi armaments production centre at Nassr.[33] Customs charged BSA with offences contrary to section 68(2) of the Customs and Excise Management Act 1979 and were planning to use PII claims at the trial.[34] The case never came to trial, however, because customs took the decision to abandon the case in the light of the collapse of the (very similar) Matrix Churchill trial.[35] If it had come to trial, the BSA case might well have been even more controversial and even more embarrassing for the government than the Matrix Churchill case was. The government had clear intelligence on arms manufacture activities at Nassr from late 1987 onwards, and yet decided to allow the BSA licences to stand.[36] As the Scott report put it: 'the incongruity of a prosecution being brought, on the ground of an unlawful export of machinery intended for use in the production of shells, where government had consented to the export going ahead notwithstanding knowledge of that intended use is striking. This point had no parallel in the Matrix Churchill case.'[37]

The final case which should be considered is the Ordtec trial and appeal. A number of businessmen associated with Ordinance Technologies Ltd. (Ordtec) were charged with offences under section 68 of the Customs and Excise Management Act and with conspiracy under the Criminal Law Act 1977. The charges related to the exporting to Iraq of a fuse assembly line without a licence (where one was required) and the further attempted export of related sub-assemblies and components, again without the required licence. PII certificates were signed in respect of the Ordtec trial by Peter Lilley (secretary of state at the DTI) and by Kenneth Baker (home secretary) but they were not ultimately used. In February 1992 the defendants pleaded guilty. Three of them were sentenced to suspended terms of imprisonment for periods ranging from six months to one year and the fourth was fined £1,000. Even though the PII certificates were not used, the Scott report was extremely critical of them, arguing that they purported to claim PII in respect of documents for which there was no authority to claim PII even in civil cases, let alone criminal trials.[38] In April 1995 the defendants were granted leave to appeal principally on the basis that a number of relevant documents which had since come to light in the Matrix Churchill trial and at the Scott inquiry had not been disclosed to them by the prosecution. The defendants' appeal against conviction was allowed in November 1995.[39] A number of PII certificates were signed in respect of the Ordtec appeal. These certificates took

---

[33] See para. H1.1.   [34] See para. H1.31.   [35] See para. H1.33.
[36] See para. H1.3.   [37] See para. H1.21.
[38] See para. J6.66. This is discussed further, below.   [39] See para. J6.93.

a significantly different form from those which had been used earlier in these three cases. The Ordtec appeal PII certificates were not criticized in the Scott report and are considered further below.

The PII Certificates in Matrix Churchill

Four ministers signed PII certificates in respect of the Matrix Churchill trial: Kenneth Clarke, then home secretary, Tristan Garel-Jones, then minister of state at the foreign office, Malcolm Rifkind, then secretary of state for defence, and Michael Heseltine, then president of the board of trade.[40] The purpose of Mr Clarke's PII certificate, which was the first of the four to be signed, was to protect intelligence documents and information. By the time his PII certificate was signed (June 1992) the decision had already been taken that one of the witnesses to be called at trial by the prosecution would be a serving SIS officer, known in the Scott report as Mr T. Mr T's witness statement had been disclosed to the defence. Mr Clarke was informed of this in the submission put to him by his officials in connection with his signing the PII certificate.

There is an irony here. Mr Clarke signed a PII certificate which made a class claim protecting information and documents relating to the operations of the security and secret intelligence services yet there was no explanation as to how it was that the disclosure to the defence of Mr T's witness statement—which fell squarely within that class—was not likely to damage national security.[41] Paragraph 7 of Mr Clarke's certificate simply stated (without explanation) that he was satisfied that Mr T's evidence could be given. This irony is compounded and becomes downright inconsistent when Mr Clarke's certificate is compared to that which had been signed by Mr Baker for the committal which would have barred Mr T's evidence as being 'likely to cause serious and unquantifiable damage to the functions of the security and secret intelligence services'.[42] Inconsistency becomes dishonesty when this is

---

[40] Two cabinet ministers had signed PII certificates in preparation for the committal hearing in the Matrix Churchill case: Kenneth Baker, then home secretary, and Peter Lilley, then secretary of state at the DTI. Mr Lilley's certificate was designed to protect 16 DTI documents from disclosure. Mr Lilley's PII certificate was a class claim to immunity. In his evidence to the Scott inquiry Mr Lilley stated that he did not consider that any serious damage to the national interest would be done if the documents were disclosed and would not have made a contents claim in respect of any of them: see para. G13.4. Mr Baker's certificate was designed to cover documents and evidence concerning the security and secret intelligence services. He was advised that the purpose of his PII certificate was to 'ensure that PII is claimed for any information about [the work of SIS in relation to Matrix Churchill] on the basis that to give evidence about it would be likely to damage national security'.   [41] See para. G13.9.
[42] Para 6 of Mr Baker's certificate. See para. G13.12. Scott found this to be 'inconsistent' (para G13.14). A second officer from the intelligence services (Mr P) also gave evidence at the Matrix Churchill trial, yet no authority for this, from Mr Clarke or from any other minister, was ever given (see para. G13.17).

compared to the argument ministers and officials later put in evidence to the Scott inquiry to the effect that claiming PII is a matter of duty which cannot be waived, yet apparently it was waived here.[43]

As the secretary of state for foreign affairs was absent abroad at the relevant time, Tristan Garel-Jones, a minister of state at the FCO, signed a PII certificate in respect of foreign office papers. The certificate was required by 4 September 1992, yet Mr Garel-Jones did not receive his submission from his officials until the evening of 3 September, 'a time scale about which he was understandably aggrieved'.[44] Mr Garel-Jones was not told and did not know the anticipated defence case and was not told and did not know that one of the defendants was an SIS informer. The Scott report suggested that Mr Garel-Jones should have been informed of these matters, although it is unlikely that, had he been so informed, this would have prevented him from signing his PII certificate.[45] Mr Garel-Jones's certificate sought protection for three categories of document, known as categories A, B, and C. Category A contained two documents and was a contents claim in respect of the protection of the identity of informers. Category A is wholly unproblematic and no issue regarding it arose in the Scott inquiry or report: as the trial judge, Judge Smedley stated, 'this class of document has long been protected from disclosure save in the most exceptional circumstances'. Category B was a class claim in respect of 'minutes, notes and letters passing between ministers and ministers, ministers and officials and officials and other officials either within the FCO or interdepartmentally . . . all [of which] relate to the formation of the policy of HM Government'.[46] In respect of this category, Mr Garel-Jones stated in his certificate that:

I have formed the opinion that, for the reasons hereinafter set out, the production of such documents or any requirement of the witnesses to give oral evidence as to the meetings, discussions and deliberations would be injurious to the public interest and that it is necessary for the proper functioning of the public services that these documents be withheld from production. All these documents fall into a class of document which relate to the formulation of government policy and the internal dealings of government departments. Such policy was decided at a high level, for the most part by ministers of the FCO, MOD and DTI although the documents include documents preparatory to the advice given for the benefit of the ministers in office during the relevant period . . . It would, in my view, be against the public interest for documents or oral evidence relating to the process which provided for ministers honest and candid advice on matters of high level policy to be subject to disclosure or compulsion. Similarly records of discussions between ministers within or between departments should not be disclosed. In this connection I would respectfully pray in aid the reasoning of Lord Reid in *Conway* v. *Rimmer*.[47]

---

[43] This is examined in detail below.   [44] See para. G13.23.   [45] See para. G13.24.
[46] Para 3 of Mr Garel-Jones's certificate. See Scott, para. G13.25.
[47] Para 6 of Mr Garel-Jones's certificate. See Scott, para. G13.25. For the remarks of Lord Reid in *Conway* v. *Rimmer*, see [1968] AC 910 at 952, cited above. In his evidence to the Scott

Category C consisted of information relating to or emanating from the security and secret intelligence services. With regard to this information, Mr Garel-Jones stated that 'the very nature of the work of the security and intelligence services of the crown requires secrecy if it is to be effective . . . any evidence about the organisation of the security and intelligence services, their theatre of operations or their methods could substantially impair their operational efficiency . . . the disclosure of any sources or alleged sources of intelligence information, and any aspects of the means by which it was gathered . . . would cause unquantifiable damage to the functions of the security and intelligence services'.[48]

Let us pause a moment to consider Mr Garel-Jones's language and in particular his use of the term 'unquantifiable'. Presented with such forthright language, any judge would hesitate and think long and hard before releasing documents into open court. Indeed, Judge Smedley initially refused to order the disclosure of category C documents and only after considerable further argument was counsel for the defence able to persuade him to change his mind and authorize the disclosure of the heavily redacted category C materials.[49] At the inquiry, Mr Garel-Jones was asked to justify the use of the word unquantifiable. He stated that he thought that unquantifiable could mean either 'unquantifiably large' or 'unquantifiably small'.[50] In his report, Sir Richard Scott described this attitude as 'risible' and stated that 'if a PII claim is made in order to protect "apparently trivial information" the disclosure of which might in the event cause no more than "trivial" damage, it is difficult to understand why the judge should not be so informed'.[51]

The third PII certificate to be signed was that in respect of the MOD, which was signed by Malcolm Rifkind. This certificate was closely based on the FCO certificate signed by Mr Garel-Jones. It was designed mainly to protect some fifty-four category B documents. Mr Rifkind read these documents and duly signed the certificate. It is clear from evidence given by Mr Rifkind to the Scott inquiry that he did not consider that he had any discretion to decline to claim PII for documents which fell within the category B advice to ministers class. The claiming of PII protection for such documents did not depend on the minister actually forming the view that disclosure of documents would in fact damage the public interest.[52] Some of the category B documents were also included in category C because they raised intelligence concerns. Mr Rifkind's certificate illustrates the breadth of category C, however, in that it is clear from his evidence to the inquiry that category C (i.e. intelligence and

---

inquiry, Mr Garel-Jones reinforced these sentiments about the secrecy of government with the comment that 'almost any submission made to a minister, or in preparation for a submission to a minister, should, in principle, be confidential'. See Scott, para. G13.29.

[48] Paras 7–8 of Mr Garel-Jones's certificate. See para. G13.25.
[49] See paras. G14.11–19.   [50] See para. G13.32.   [51] See para. G13.32.
[52] See para. G13.46.

security) documents do not themselves have to raise intelligence matters as such in order to attract a claim to protection from disclosure. Rather, such documents merely have to mention intelligence: '*any* reference to intelligence matters is not normally disclosed unless the judge determines otherwise'.[53]

The fourth and final PII certificate signed in respect of the Matrix Churchill trial was that of the DTI, signed by Michael Heseltine. This was the certificate which was to give rise to the greatest controversy. Initially the FCO certificate was being taken as a model for the DTI certificate (as had been the case also in the MOD). A submission with a draft certificate was duly put up to Mr Heseltine, but when Mr Heseltine read the documents, he called a meeting of his officials and told them that even though he was satisfied that the DTI documents fell within categories B and C, he was not willing to sign the certificate. His unwillingness stemmed from his view that disclosure of the documents would not be injurious to the public interest[54] and that he was not prepared to assert a claim to PII in a manner that might damage the conduct of the defence in the Matrix Churchill case.[55] These views were communicated to the attorney general who replied by advising Mr Heseltine that 'once a minister accepts that documents fall within a class which should normally be immune from production in litigation as a matter of public interest, it is the duty of that minister to make the public interest immunity claim whatever his personal views about the desirability of disclosing the particular documents in question'.[56]

A redrafted certificate was enclosed with the letter containing the advice from the attorney general. The new draft stated that 'I emphasize that my concern is only with the question of whether the documents to which I have referred fall within classes of documents which are *prima facie* immune from production. Whether in fact all or part of any document or documents should be disclosed is a matter for the court.'[57] In the light of the attorney general's advice, Mr Heseltine signed the revised certificate. Mr Heseltine then wrote to the attorney general (on 11 September 1992) stating that 'I am glad that a way has been found of reconciling the fact that I am under a legal duty, which I cannot waive, to claim immunity from disclosure of certain documents on grounds of public interest with the fact that, in my view, *at least some of them ought to be disclosed in the public interest.*'[58]

The attorney general did not read this letter prior to the trial—that is to say, for at least three weeks. The Scott report described this failure as 'astonishing'.[59] The Scott report found, and it is clear that, Mr Heseltine only signed the PII certificate because he was of the belief that the trial judge would be made aware of his (Mr Heseltine's) view that some of the DTI documents

---

[53] See para. G13.49. Emphasis added.
[55] See para. G13.61.   [56] See para. G13.65.
[58] See para. G13.70. Emphasis added.

[54] See para. G13.59.
[57] See para. G13.66.
[59] See para. G13.70.

ought to be disclosed to the defence.[60] Yet Alan Moses QC, leading counsel for the prosecution in the trial, was never informed of this, and, therefore, Mr Heseltine's views were not in the event made clear to the court.[61] The Scott report made it clear that the 'major responsibility for the inadequacy of the instructions to Mr Moses must . . . be borne by the attorney general'[62] and went on to state that 'I do not accept that he [the attorney general] was not personally at fault.'[63] Sir Richard Scott concluded that he 'would have expected [the attorney general] to recognize that important constitutional and legal issues were raised by Mr Heseltine's stand and to have ensured that Mr Moses, whose responsibility was to place the issues fairly before the court, was adequately instructed so that he could discharge that responsibility'.[64]

The Government's Approach to PII

The senior government lawyer who settled the contents of the PII certificates used in the Matrix Churchill case was Andrew Leithead, an assistant treasury solicitor. His views of PII law and practice are revealing of the government's general attitude to state secrecy generally and PII in particular. In Mr Leithead's opinion, PII should be claimed for '*any documents relating to advice* given by an official to a minister, whether relating to formulation of policy or to the taking of an executive decision'.[65] In oral evidence to the Scott inquiry, Mr Leithead elaborated on this and argued that 'in practice, when one is dealing with PII claims, one tends to take a rather sort of generous view . . . generous to the government departments. *Anything* that involves advice to ministers or documents preparatory to such advice is considered to be within the class.'[66] When questioned on this, Mr Leithead conceded that this approach went well beyond what was sanctioned by the relevant legal authorities, such as Lord Reid's speech in *Conway* v. *Rimmer*[67] but stated that this

---

[60] See para. G13.71.

[61] Indeed, a note concerning Mr Moses' instructions from Mr Andrew Leithead (of whom more below) expressly stated that 'Mr Moses should be instructed to use such arguments as are available in respect of each document to persuade the judge that they are of *minimal relevance* to the issues in the case.' As the Scott report stated, there was 'no justification' for this comment: it was 'unacceptable'. See paras. G13.114–15. Emphasis added. A related problem is that even if Mr Moses had been properly briefed, he would have been placed in a difficult position in terms of addressing the court on this point, representing as he did not only the prosecutor (customs and excise) but also the various government departments involved. In the view of the Scott report, this potential for conflict of interest should be more openly recognized and in future different counsel should be appointed to represent the prosecution from those who represent government departments. See paras. G10.33, G14.2, and G15.25–8.

[62] See para. G13.123.   [63] See para. G13.125.   [64] See para. G13.125.

[65] See para. G13.95. Emphasis added.   [66] See para. G13.95. Emphasis added.

[67] [1968] AC 910 at 952. Lord Reid sanctioned the claiming of PII in respect of documents which were either concerned with policy making or which were deliberations about a particular case. He stated that the test should be whether the withholding of a document was '*really*

was 'the way PII tends to work', or the 'way the government tends to work PII' as it was later put.[68] When asked whether this was an approach which was bred of a desire for 'convenient administration', Mr Leithead answered 'Yes'.

This attitude to disclosure resulted in a vast breadth of documents being protected from discovery in category B in the PII certificates. This is a matter which was strongly criticized in the Scott report. When Judge Smedley refused to uphold the PII certificates, the various government departments in respect of which the certificates had been signed were asked if they would prefer to release the documents or to abandon the prosecution. The DTI stated that there were 'no documents dealt with by the existing PII certificate which the DTI would require not to be disclosed if the judge so ruled'.[69] The MOD stated that they could 'live with this level of release'[70] and that DIS 'have confirmed that there is . . . nothing that is thereby released [that is] of such a sensitivity that would cause us to consider asking customs to discontinue the prosecution'.[71] Similarly, the FCO stated that 'despite the fact that the disclosure of these documents will almost certainly cause embarrassment to the FCO and to the government as a whole, the minister thinks it would be prudent at this stage for the crown to persist with the prosecution'.[72] As the Scott report put it, 'the departmental reactions contrast . . . very strongly with the assertions in the PII certificates that it was "necessary for the functioning of the public service that the documents should be withheld from production" ' and further that 'the sensible pragmatic reactions of the departments to the judge's PII rulings go a long way . . . to deprive of credibility the basis on which the certificates had asserted the PII class claims'.[73]

It is not merely a question of credibility, however. It is also a question of legal authority. Even though the leading House of Lords cases make it clear that the claiming of PII in respect of category B style documents should be limited to documents concerning what can be summarized as high policy,[74] under the government's approach, as exemplified by Mr Leithead's evidence, '*any* communication between officials, between officials and ministers or between ministers dealing with the formation of policy *or with the application*

---

necessary for the proper functioning of the public service' (emphasis added). Under Mr Leithead's approach, this test appears to have been subverted so as to become one whereby any government paper concerning any advice to any minister is automatically withheld for reasons of candour and the proper functioning of the public service.

[68] See para. G13.95.   [69] See para. G14.21.   [70] See para. G14.25.
[71] See para. G14.26.   [72] See para. G14.28.
[73] See para. G14.30. In *Conway* v. *Rimmer*, Lord Morris stated that 'the court will accept . . . the truth of a minister's assertion that the production of a document will in some measure be detrimental to the public interest' [1968] AC 910 at 968. Perhaps the lesson of the Scott report in this regard is that the courts should not be so trusting.
[74] See the comments of Lord Reid in *Conway* v. *Rimmer* [1968] AC 910 at 952 cited above. See also *Burmah Oil* v. *Bank of England* [1980] AC 1090 where Lord Scarman stated (at 1144) that 'documents relating to the formulation of policy at a high level' may be withheld.

of policy should be the subject of a PII claim. In the case of any doubt, a PII claim should be made.'[75] As the Scott report concluded, although this approach constituted accepted practice in the treasury solicitors' department, it is an 'approach to disclosure of documents in a criminal trial [which] was, and is, contrary to principle and unacceptable'.[76] Further, it seems that during the period with which Scott was concerned the problem grew worse. Whitehall is so obsessed with secrecy, according to the Scott report, that it has gradually been including not only more documents but also a wider variety of documents in class claims to PII.[77] As the Scott report put it, 'experience suggests that if PII class claims are sanctioned, Whitehall departments will inevitably seek to bring within the recognized classes an increasing range of documents. I do not believe that the instinctive Whitehall reaction to seek to withhold government documents from public inspection is likely to change.'[78] This trend was most apparent in the category B class in respect of which PII was claimed. As regards this class, Scott ended his chapter of recommendations on PII with these comments: 'is it justifiable for the government to seek to protect . . . documents from disclosure on the ground that the protection of the class is "necessary for the proper functioning of the public service" or on the ground that the candour with which advice is given to ministers would otherwise be inhibited? I find it difficult to accept that these are satisfactory grounds for a class claim in the first place.'[79] We will examine the government's subsequent response to these conclusions later in this chapter.

Osman and the Question of Authority

In addition to the more general question of the government's overall approach to PII considered in the previous section, there are three narrower, more technical points raised in the government's use of PII in the Matrix Churchill case which call for some examination. The first is the question of authority; the second concerns the notion of the so-called balancing exercise; and the third concerns the question of whether ministers have a duty or a discretion to claim PII.

[75] See para. G18.49. Emphasis added.

[76] See para. G18.88. This view echoes that expressed (in a different context) by Lord Templeman in *R* v. *Chief Constable of the West Midlands, ex parte Wiley* [1995] 1 AC 274, where he stated that 'a rubber stamp approach to PII by the holder of a document is neither necessary nor appropriate'. In his article 'The Acceptable and Unacceptable Use of Public Interest Immunity' [1996] *Public Law* 427 (at p. 438) Sir Richard Scott confessed to feeling 'a sense of depression' over the government's attitude to secrecy and continued reliance on the candour argument.

[77] See, for example, the comment in the Scott report that 'the practice has, I believe, *grown* for government to seek to protect . . . documents by making a claim to PII' (at para. G18.55, emphasis added). In his lecture published in the *Web Journal*, Sir Richard echoed these comments with the statement that 'the existence of class claims has encouraged the government to seek protection for ever-expanding categories of documents'.

[78] See para. K6.16.   [79] See para. K6.25.

To turn first to the question of authority: under what legal authority may ministers make class claims to PII in respect of a criminal trial? The case most heavily relied on by the government in justifying its use of PII in Matrix Churchill was *R* v. *Governor of Brixton Prison, ex parte Osman*.[80] Osman had been in custody under the Fugitive Offenders Act 1967 awaiting extradition to Hong Kong. He brought a writ of habeas corpus, seeking to rely on nine items of correspondence between the British and Hong Kong governments which he alleged would show that his extradition was in bad faith. The disclosure of these nine documents was challenged and a claim for PII was made (the then minister of state at the foreign office, Francis Maude, signing the certificate). After finding that for present purposes habeas corpus actions were criminal proceedings[81] Mann LJ raised the question as to the applicability of PII in the criminal context. He recited the statement of Viscount Simon LC in *Duncan* v. *Cammell Laird*[82] where he had said: 'the judgment of the House in the present case is limited to civil actions and the practice, as applied in criminal trials where an individual's life or liberty may be at stake, is not necessarily the same'. Mann LJ then stated that as far as he was aware 'the matter rested there'. He continued that:

the seminal cases in regard to PII do not refer to criminal proceedings, but the principles are expressed in general terms. Asking myself why those general expositions should not apply to criminal proceedings, I can see no answer but that they do. It seems correct in principle that they should apply. The reasons for the development of the doctrine seem equally applicable to criminal as well as to civil proceedings. I acknowledge that the application of the PII doctrine in criminal proceedings will involve a different balancing exercise to that in civil proceedings . . . Where the interests of justice arise in a criminal case touching and concerning liberty or conceivably on occasion life, the weight to be attached to the interests of justice are plainly very great indeed.

Is this case sufficient legal authority to justify the government's use of PII class claims in the Matrix Churchill trial? In the view of the Scott report, it is not. Sir Richard Scott stated that he had 'very great reservations about the reliance placed on *ex parte Osman* by the treasury solicitors' department and by the attorney general . . . Whether or not *ex parte Osman* was rightly categorized as "criminal proceedings", it was certainly not a criminal trial'[83] and further that 'the Divisional Court decision in *Osman* stands as an authority for allowing PII class claims in habeas corpus applications. It is not an authority for allowing class claims in criminal trials.'[84]

[80] [1992] 1 All ER 108.
[81] On the ground that the direct outcome of the action would be a trial—see *Amand* v. *Secretary of State for Home Affairs* [1943] AC 147, per Viscount Simon LC.
[82] [1942] AC 624 at 633.   [83] See para. G18.76.
[84] See para. G18.84. Sir Richard Scott has used even more forthright language in public lectures he has delivered since the report was published. In Feb. 1996 he said that 'the application to criminal trials of PII principles derived from civil cases and designed for application in civil

The government published a robust defence of its position in the light of the criticisms contained in the Scott report in a paper placed in the House of Commons library in February 1996 entitled *Public Interest Immunity: Government Response to the Scott Report*. This paper was throughout wholly confrontational in content and in tone, admitting no wrong and containing not an ounce of contrition. It started with the exclamation that the Scott report 'expresses views on the law relating to PII which differ fundamentally from the generally accepted position'. On the question of the application of PII in criminal trials, the government's paper stated that 'the general principles of PII apply in the same way in criminal proceedings as they do in civil proceedings'. This was the starting point for Mann LJ in the *Osman* case. Unfortunately, this view is simply wrong. In civil cases, if a litigant seeking disclosure is to overcome a PII certificate, he or she must successfully jump two hurdles: first, he or she must persuade the judge to inspect the documents in question and secondly, if the judge has inspected the documents, the litigant seeking disclosure must persuade the judge to disclose them. In civil cases, even the first stage (inspection) is not automatic: the litigant seeking disclosure must explain in outline to the judge how the documents would help his or her case.[85] In criminal cases, inspection is automatic, even if ultimate disclosure is not. Authority for this is *R* v. *K*.[86] This is a point which is not made in the Scott report,[87] but is one which, nonetheless, marks a significant dent in the underlying reasoning of both the *Osman* case and of the government's subsequent reliance on it.

The government's paper in response to the Scott report continued by stating that the conclusions expressed in the report in relation to the *Osman* case 'are in conflict not only with the body of independent advice and case law upon which [the government's] views were soundly based, but also with the consistent line of subsequent authority and with the general practice in the

---

cases has been a mistake'. See Sir Richard Scott, 'The Use of PII Claims in Criminal Cases' (1996) *Web Journal of Current Legal Issues*. In a further article, Sir Richard provided extended analysis of the leading House of Lords civil PII cases which, in his view, do not support the use of PII in criminal trials: see 'The Acceptable and Unacceptable Use of Public Interest Immunity' [1996] *Public Law* 427, at pp. 429–32.

[85] See *Air Canada* v. *Secretary of State for Trade* [1983] 2 AC 394, discussed above.

[86] (1993) 97 Cr. App. R 342. Lord Taylor CJ held (at 346) in this case that 'when PII is claimed for a document, it is for the court to rule whether the claim should be upheld or not . . . [This] can only be performed by the judge himself examining or viewing the evidence, so as to have the facts of what it contains in mind.' In *R* v. *K*, a buggery case, a video tape was sought by the defence as evidence but a PII claim was made in respect of it. After hearing argument on the question of its disclosure, but without viewing the tape, the trial judge ruled that it should not be disclosed. On appeal by the defence, the Court of Appeal held that the exclusion of the tape without the judge having viewed it to test its relevance amounted to a material irregularity. The Court of Appeal then viewed the tape and further ruled that it would not have helped the defence, that accordingly the proviso to s. 2(1) of the Criminal Appeal Act 1968 should be applied. The appeal was therefore dismissed.

[87] *R* v. *K* is referred to in the Scott report (but not commented on) only at para. G11.17.

criminal courts'.[88] To support this view, the government relied on a number of counsel's opinions, among which was one written by Harry Woolf in 1978[89] in which it was stated that 'I have little doubt that the law must be the same in both civil and criminal proceedings.' A further opinion on this matter was received in January 1992 from Michael Kalisher QC, John Laws, and Nicholas Ainley in which it was asked 'does PII apply to criminal proceedings?' The answer was 'in our view it clearly does . . . there is now authority that this view is correct: see *ex parte Osman*'. An opinion sought in the light of the House of Lords decision in *R* v. *Chief Constable of the West Midlands, ex parte Wiley*[90] (i.e. in late 1995, after the Matrix Churchill trial but before the publication of the Scott report) stated that: 'it has been suggested that the principles of PII as developed in the civil context have been applied too readily to the criminal context . . . It is our view, however, that precedent and logic support the application of the same principles in both contexts, although there will be some differences between the two in practice.'[91]

The government also cited passages from recent case law in support of its position with regard to the relevance of PII to criminal trials. The government's paper claimed that in the Ordtec appeal, heard in November 1995, the Court of Appeal appeared to accept the validity of the class and contents claims to PII that had been made by government ministers in that case.[92] This claim is disingenuous. The Court of Appeal did state that there were some documents which 'were the subject of PII certificates signed by ministers, but only for the purpose of excising sensitive references and names which do not affect the issues in this case. With minor adjustments, we approved the disclosure of the documents as proposed in the PII certificates.' It would appear from this passage that the PII certificates signed in respect of the Ordtec appeal were contents rather than class claims to immunity.[93] This is the only reference to PII in the Court of Appeal's judgment in this case. This passage cannot possibly be taken as supporting the government's broad use of class claims to PII in the Matrix Churchill trial. To suggest that it is supportive of the government's line against the criticisms contained in the Scott report is positively misleading, to say the least. There is an irony here. The Scott inquiry heard very interesting evidence from a Mr David Bickford, formerly

---

[88] *Public Interest Immunity: Government Response to the Scott Report*, para. 3.3.
[89] Now Lord Woolf of Barnes MR.   [90] [1995] 1 AC 274. This case is discussed below.
[91] Opinion of A. W. H. Charles and Stephen Richards, Oct. 1995, para. 8.
[92] See *Public Interest Immunity: Government Response to the Scott Report*, para. 3.14. See *R* v. *Blackledge and others*, [1996] 1 Cr. App. R 326.
[93] See Scott, para. J6.84. In fact, of the four PII certificates in the Ordtec appeal, three were contents claims. Although the fourth, signed by Douglas Hurd, the foreign secretary, was presented as a class claim it concerned only a small number of documents whose contents would have made a contents claim possible, to say the least. Thus, the nature of the PII certificates in the Ordtec appeal and the nature, breadth, and importance of the documents in respect of which the PII certificates were made were significantly different from those concerning the Matrix Churchill trial. See Scott, para. J6.91. This is discussed further below.

legal adviser to the security and secret intelligence services, who stated that the services could and would quite happily rely on contents claims to protect sensitive information from disclosure and who argued further that 'I am convinced that the use of class claims undermines the credibility of the services.'[94] If even MI5 and SIS would be happy to abandon the use of class claims, why was the government so doggedly determined that they were such a good thing?

To conclude on this point, there does seem to be some authority for the use of PII in criminal proceedings, although it can hardly be said that the case law is exactly clear. Whether this authority extends to the use of broad claims to PII founded on a class rather than a contents basis as in the Matrix Churchill trial is highly doubtful.[95] Where there is significant doubt about the legality of a course of action, as there was and is here, the government is clearly right to seek legal advice and counsels' opinions. That advice suggested in this instance that the government could legally assert claims of PII on a class basis in a criminal trial. However, that advice (and the government's subsequent treatment of it, as well as the Scott report's examination of it) has all taken place in a curious constitutional vacuum. Constitutional law does have interesting things to say about government and law and about the lawfulness (and constitutionality) of government actions taken without clear legal authority. This is a point of constitutional dispute that was, according to the textbooks, settled some considerable time ago, in the celebrated decision in *Entick* v. *Carrington* in 1765.[96] British constitutional law states that government is subject to a principle of legality (even if that principle is not as strong as it might be). This means that the government is powerless to act unless it can point to clear, direct, legal authority which justifies its proposed course of action. Counsels' opinion does not constitute such legal authority and should indeed have gone further in recognizing its absence. The criticisms contained in the Scott report as to the applicability of class claims to PII in criminal trials are more than justified. Their only weakness is that they are not more firmly couched in the constitutional language which would have reinforced them.

The 'Balancing Exercise'

In civil cases, where a judge is presented with a PII certificate, his role in order to decide whether to uphold the claim to PII or not is said to be to balance the

[94] Sir Richard Scott, 'The Use of PII Claims in Criminal Cases' (1996) *Web Journal of Current Legal Issues*.

[95] As the Scott report put it, 'it cannot . . . possibly be supposed that the *dicta* regarding PII class claims to be found in *Duncan* v. *Cammell Laird*, in *Conway* v. *Rimmer*, in the *Burmah Oil* case, in *Air Canada* v. *Secretary of State for Trade*, were intended to have any application to criminal trials'. See para. G18.83.

[96] (1765) 19 St. Tr. 1030.

public interests identified in the PII certificate in favour of withholding the documents on the one hand against the public interest in the fair administration of justice and the private interests of the litigant seeking disclosure on the other. For criminal cases, the Scott report advocated a different approach. According to the Scott report, in criminal cases the only issue should be whether the documents in question might be of assistance to the defendant in defending himself. If they are, they should be disclosed.

Disclosure to the defence in criminal trials is governed by tests of relevance and materiality. The test is that material held by the prosecution should be disclosed to the defence if, on a sensible appraisal by the prosecution it appears (1) to be relevant or possibly relevant to an issue in the case; (2) to raise or possibly to raise a new issue whose existence is not apparent from the evidence the prosecution proposes to use; or (3) to hold out a real (as opposed to a fanciful) prospect of providing a lead on evidence which goes to (1) or to (2).[97] In a criminal trial, if documents exist whose potential to assist the defence is apparent, but a PII claim has been made in respect of them, could a situation arise in which their disclosure could properly be refused on PII grounds? According to the Scott report, the answer to this question ought to be no: 'for the purposes of criminal trials, the balance must *always* come down in favour of disclosure if there is any real possibility that the withholding of the document may cause or contribute to a miscarriage of justice. The public interest factors underlying the PII claim *cannot ever* have a weight sufficient to outweigh that possibility.'[98] If this is the approach which is to be adopted, it should not be referred to as a balancing exercise on the ground that, in a criminal trial, once it has been decided that a document might be of assistance to the defence, that should be the end of the PII claim. In this situation there is no real balance to be struck.[99] In a public lecture on PII which Sir Richard

---

[97] This test derives from *R* v. *Melvin* (unreported, judgment given by Jowitt J on 20 Dec. 1993); *R* v. *Keane* [1994] 1 WLR 746 per Lord Taylor CJ; and *R* v. *Brown (Winston)* [1994] 1 WLR 1599, per Steyn LJ. See Scott report, paras. K6.7–15. This approach is considerably narrower than that which had been adopted by the Court of Appeal in *R* v. *Ward* [1993] 1 WLR 619 per Glidewell LJ (see A. Tomkins, 'Public Interest Immunity after Matrix Churchill' [1993] *Public Law* 650, at pp 656–7). There are clearly some problems with the issue of disclosure to the defence, some of which are identified in the Scott report. There is insufficient space to examine these problems in detail here, but, briefly, one issue in both the Matrix Churchill and the Ordtec trials concerned information which various government departments held but which was not held by the prosecuting authority, customs and excise (see paras. J6.50–1). Another problem is the (over-?) reliance on prosecuting counsel who might erroneously decide that documents are not material when in fact they would have been. This was an issue in the Ordtec appeal: see Scott, paras. J6.32, J6.42, J6.71–4, and J6.90. On disclosure to the defence generally, see *Disclosure: A Consultation Document* (Cm. 2864, May 1995) and *Disclosure: The JUSTICE Response* (London: JUSTICE, Sept. 1995). See now also the Criminal Procedure and Investigations Act 1996, ss. 1–23. This Act makes substantial changes to the procedures dealing with disclosure in criminal trials, but does not affect PII, which is expressly excluded: see s. 21(2).

[98] See para. K6.12. Emphasis added.

[99] As the Scott report put it, 'there is, I believe, no reported criminal case in which the judge has concluded that documents would be of assistance to the defendant but has nonetheless

Scott delivered shortly after the publication of the report he stated that 'the suggestion that the public interest [that a defendant in a criminal trial should have a fair trial and that an innocent man should not be convicted] would ever have to give way in a balancing exercise is, to my mind, a grotesque one'.[100]

Sir Richard Scott admitted that this approach is not one which is shared in the relevant authorities (including *R* v. *Keane* and *R* v. *Brown (Winston)*)[101] but argued that despite judicial references in these cases to a balancing exercise, it is not actually apparent that in these cases the exercise by the judge can accurately or usefully be described as a balancing exercise.[102] In its response to the Scott report's conclusions regarding PII, the government contended that the report's views on the balancing exercise point run 'directly counter to the authorities'.[103] The government's paper argued that 'the authorities do not support the principle that documents protected by PII must be disclosed if they "might be of assistance to the defence", irrespective of the nature and strength of the PII claim. As the Scott report makes clear, such a principle is inconsistent with a true balancing exercise; yet the authorities show that a true balancing exercise is required.'[104] This inconsistency with the authorities was, as we have seen, conceded by Sir Richard Scott on the ground that in his view what the judges are doing and what they are saying they are doing in these cases (*Keane*, *Brown (Winston)*, etc.) are quite different from each other. It is interesting to note that the government's response focused solely on Scott's conclusions and not on his reasoning, which was wholly ignored. The plain fact that his views run counter to the authorities was enough for the government. The principled, fair, and sensible foundation upon which Scott's views were based was not addressed. The depth and sophistication of the legal analysis which is evident from the Scott report was plainly beyond the government, whose attempted rebuttal of Scott's conclusions with regard to PII entirely failed to dent the force of Scott's criticisms.

Makanjuola and the Question of Duty

In the political maelstrom that followed the collapse of the Matrix Churchill trial in November 1992 the government was roundly criticized for its use of PII certificates. The government sought to defend its actions by asserting that

declined, on PII grounds, to order them to be disclosed. The firm conclusion is . . . justified that in criminal cases the only question should be whether the documents might be of assistance to the defendant. This is not a "balancing exercise".' See para. G18.79.

[100] Sir Richard Scott, 'The Use of PII Claims in Criminal Cases' (1996) *Web Journal of Current Legal Issues*. Sir Richard provides further consideration of these issues in 'The Acceptable and Unacceptable Use of Public Interest Immunity' [1996] *Public Law* 427, at pp. 433–6.

[101] Cited *supra*, n. 97.   [102] See para. K6.14.

[103] *Public Interest Immunity: Government Response to the Scott Report*, para. 3.25.

[104] Ibid., para. 3.26.

the ministers who had signed PII certificates in the Matrix Churchill case had had no choice but to do so: the claiming of PII was a matter of duty, not discretion. During the Scott inquiry and following the publication of the report, the (Conservative) government never deviated from this line of argument. At the Scott inquiry, the attorney general, Sir Nicholas Lyell, argued that 'where documents or information fall into a class that has been recognized by the courts as attracting PII, the relevant minister is under a duty to make a claim . . . Ministers are not permitted to pick and choose when to make a claim. They must claim PII whether or not they would prefer (for whatever reason) to have the documents or information disclosed.'[105] The legal authority most heavily relied on by the attorney general in support of this position was *Makanjuola* v. *Commissioner of Police of the Metropolis*,[106] a Court of Appeal case decided in 1989 but not reported until 1992. *Makanjuola* was not a criminal case: it concerned civil proceedings arising out of complaints about the police. In the case, PII had been claimed in respect of documents concerning the investigation into the complaints and it was this claim to PII that Makanjuola had challenged. In the course of his judgment, Bingham LJ (as he then was) stated that:[107]

where a litigant asserts that documents are immune from production or disclosure on public interest grounds he is not (if the claim is well founded) claiming a right but observing a duty. PII is not a trump card vouchsafed to certain privileged players to play when and as they wish. It is an exclusionary rule, imposed on parties in certain circumstances, even when it is to their disadvantage in the litigation. This does not mean that in any case where a party holds a document in a class *prima facie* immune he is bound to persist in an assertion of immunity even where it is held that, on any weighing of the public interest in withholding the document against the public interest in disclosure for furthering the administration of justice, there is a clear balance in favour of the latter. But it does I think mean (1) that PII cannot in any ordinary sense be waived, since, although one can waive rights, one cannot waive duties; (2) that, where a litigant holds documents in a class *prima facie* immune, he should (save perhaps in a very exceptional case) assert that the documents are immune and decline to disclose them, since the ultimate judge of where the balance of public interest lies is not him but the court . . .

This has proved to be a difficult passage, capable of more than one interpretation. The key words are 'it is held'. Do these words mean 'held by the judge' (i.e. there is no duty to persist in any claim to PII after the court has ruled that the public interest lies in disclosure) or do they mean 'held by the minister claiming PII' (i.e. there is no duty to claim PII where the minister who has been asked to make the claim has decided that making the claim to PII would

---

[105] Oral evidence of Sir Nicholas Lyell, 24 Mar. 1994, opening statement, para. 8.
[106] [1992] 3 All ER 617.
[107] [1992] 3 All ER 617, at 623. Lord Donaldson MR expressly agreed with Bingham LJ on this point (at 621). This passage is cited in the Scott report at para. G10.12.

not be in the public interest)? The government, represented by the attorney general, favoured the former interpretation. The Scott report favoured the latter. Clearly this is more than a matter of legal nicety and linguistic semantics. If the second interpretation is preferred, the attorney general's advice to Michael Heseltine and his action in respect of Mr Heseltine's PII certificate was wrong and unlawful. If the first interpretation is preferred, however, the attorney general's advice and actions are less easy to criticize from a legal (if not a moral) point of view.

Academic and practising lawyers have disagreed ever since 1992 as to which interpretation of *Makanjuola* should be adopted.[108] That disagreement extended even to former and serving law lords and has carried on even after publication of the Scott report.[109] Although the decision of the House of Lords in 1994 in *R* v. *Chief Constable of the West Midlands, ex parte Wiley*[110] has clarified matters for the future, this case came too late to resolve the question of how the attorney general's advice and actions should be judged in the light of the law as it stood in 1992. The verdict of the Scott report, however, was unequivocal. According to the Scott report, 'nothing' in *Makanjuola* 'suggests that there is any duty to assert PII in circumstances where the disclosure to the defendant would not . . . be damaging to the public interest'[111] and further that 'the proposition that a minister is ever under a legal duty to claim PII in order to protect documents from disclosure to the defence notwithstanding that in the minister's view the public interest requires their disclosure to the defence is, in my opinion, based on a fundamental misconception of the principles of PII law'.[112] In the Matrix Churchill case, Mr Heseltine did not think such a claim would be in the public interest, but he was advised that he was nonetheless under a legal duty to claim PII. This advice, according to the Scott report, was wrong.

Needless to say, perhaps, the government subsequently attempted to refute the interpretation of *Makanjuola* contained in the Scott report. In its paper responding to the Scott report's analysis of PII, the government continued to defend its actions by repeating its argument that from *Conway* v. *Rimmer* in

---

[108] See, e.g., A. Tomkins [1993] *Public Law* 650, T. R. S. Allan [1993] *Criminal Law Review* 660, A. W. Bradley [1992] *Public Law* 514, A. T. H. Smith (1993) 52 *Cambridge Law Journal* 1, G. Ganz (1993) 56 *Modern Law Review* 564 and (1995) 58 *Modern Law Review* 417.

[109] In a letter to the editor of the *Daily Telegraph* published on 17 Feb. 1996, Lord Scarman stated that 'the crown does not have to exercise its privilege of non-disclosure'. Two days later Lord Lloyd of Berwick replied in the same newspaper arguing, contrary to Lord Scarman, that in 1992 it was clear that the law provided that claiming PII 'is not a privilege but a duty'. In the House of Lords debate on the Scott report, Lord Lloyd stated that 'the courts have held consistently that it is the duty of the minister to sign a PII certificate when the documents in question come within the class in question. That was certainly the law in 1992.' See HL Deb., Vol. 569, col. 1245, 26 Feb. 1996. The former lord chancellor, Lord Hailsham, endorsed this view (at col. 1246), as did Lord Simon of Glaisdale (at col. 1265).

[110] [1995] 1 AC 274. See further below.

[111] See para. G18.52.

[112] See para. G18.54.

1968 until *ex parte Wiley* in 1994, 'it was the general understanding of those advising government that, where a document fell within a PII class, the minister's duty was to assert the public interest in non-disclosure of that document'.[113] This 'general understanding' was described by the government as being 'an entirely reasonable approach' to have adopted.[114] In contrast, the government's paper described the views expressed in the Scott report as ones which 'differ fundamentally, and without a satisfactory basis, from the accepted position at the material time'.[115]

On the advice given by the attorney general to Michael Heseltine, the government contended in its paper that 'although Mr Heseltine considered that the overall public interest favoured disclosure and that the documents ought to be disclosed, the correct course was for him to sign a PII certificate and to leave it to the court to balance the competing public interests and to rule on disclosure'.[116] This continued uncompromising attitude of the government is far from helpful. As the Scott report made out, it is not at all clear that the course Mr Heseltine was advised to take was the correct one. And, as we have seen, it is even less clear that, to the extent that Mr Heseltine did take this recommended course of action, his views were adequately communicated to the court.

But Sir Richard Scott is not alone in his views. As mentioned above, in 1992 the government received legal advice on matters of PII in an opinion drafted by Michael Kalisher QC, John Laws, and Nicholas Ainley. This opinion played a significant role in the Matrix Churchill case and in the government's subsequent defence of its actions. Interestingly, however, this opinion does not justify the government's uncompromising stand on Mr Heseltine's PII certificate and the advice he received in respect of it. Paragraph 3.1 of the Kalisher, Laws, and Ainley advice states that 'in a clear case where no balance of the competing interests could realistically come down in favour of concealment the prosecution . . . need not keep the document to themselves but may reveal it without seeking leave of the court'. Does this not apply to the Heseltine certificate? Why was this view not explained to Mr Heseltine when he was instructed to sign a PII certificate in respect of documents he thought should be disclosed to the defence? Even the government's own legal advisers, cited by the government when it suited them, do not appear to support the government's actions with regard to Michael Heseltine's PII certificate in the Matrix Churchill case. The advice given by the attorney general to Mr Heseltine was based on a misinterpretation of Bingham LJ's judgment in *Makanjuola*, but worse, a misinterpretation which was not even clearly supported by the government's own legal advice.

---

[113] *Public Interest Immunity: Government Response to the Scott Report*, para. 2.1.
[114] Ibid., para. 2.2.   [115] Ibid., para. 2.35.   [116] Ibid., para. 2.25.

Wiley and New Directions for PII

Some of the difficulties discussed in the previous sections, and particularly those concerning the *Makanjuola* case, may well have been resolved, at least for the time being, by the decision of the House of Lords in 1994 in *R* v. *Chief Constable of the West Midlands, ex parte Wiley*.[117] Like *Makanjuola*, this was a civil case arising out of complaints against the police. The outcome of *Wiley* was that the decision of the Court of Appeal in *Neilson* v. *Laugharne*,[118] applied by the Court of Appeal in *Makanjuola*, that documents coming into existence in consequence of an investigation into a complaint about the police fell within a class which attracted PII, was overruled. What is of more interest, however, are the statements which Lord Woolf made in the course of his speech about Bingham LJ's approach to PII in the *Makanjuola* case as discussed above. After setting out the relevant passage from Bingham LJ's judgment Lord Woolf stated that:

> this is a very clear statement as to the nature of PII, most of which I would unhesitatingly endorse . . . However, [it . . .] may, I suspect, have been applied subsequently in a manner which goes beyond what Bingham LJ . . . may have intended . . . I would be surprised if Bingham LJ was intending by these remarks to extend principles of PII or to make their application any more rigid than was required as a result of the previous authorities. I would certainly not regard them as being of general application . . . It is to be noted that the *Makanjuola* case was not one involving a department of state. If a secretary of state on behalf of his department as opposed to any ordinary litigant concludes that any public interest in documents being withheld from production is outweighed by the public interest in the documents being available for the purposes of litigation, it is difficult to conceive that . . . the court would come to any different conclusion from that of the secretary of state.[119]

This passage clearly supports the interpretation of *Makanjuola* favoured by Sir Richard Scott and not that favoured by the attorney general. From 1994 onwards (at least) it is clear that where a minister who has been asked to sign a PII certificate considers that the documents in question should, in the public interest, be disclosed and not withheld, that minister is clearly *not* under a duty to claim PII. Thus the statement made by Sir Nicholas Lyell in his evidence to the Scott inquiry that 'ministers are not permitted to pick and choose when to make a claim. They must claim PII whether or not they would prefer (for whatever reason) to have the documents or information disclosed'[120] is, at least with regard to the law since 1994, wrong.[121]

---

[117] [1995] 1 AC 274.   [118] [1981] QB 736.

[119] [1995] 1 AC 274 at 296. The other members of the House of Lords (Lords Templeman, Bridge, Slynn, and Lloyd) all agreed with Lord Woolf on this point.

[120] See oral evidence of Sir Nicholas Lyell, 24 Mar. 1994, opening statement, para. 8.

[121] As the Scott report put it, 'Lord Woolf's judgment corrects and should prevent for the future an unjustified extended use being made of Bingham LJ's remarks in *Makanjuola* regarding the duty to claim PII.' See para. K6.4.

The government sought fresh legal advice as to PII law and practice in the light of the *ex p Wiley* decision. In October 1995 A. W. H Charles and Stephen Richards drafted an opinion on this matter which stated that although Lord Woolf's approach to PII in *ex parte Wiley* was not free from difficulty, his observations ought nonetheless to condition the future approach of government departments towards PII.[122] However, the advice was heavily coloured with the language of caution. For example, the opinion stated that although 'ministers are subject to understandable pressures to err on the side of disclosure in order to avoid suggestions of a cover-up . . . the freedom of action offered by the change of approach signalled in *ex parte Wiley* should be exercised with due restraint and care' and further that 'the minister may have to consider the issues of PII on the basis of an incomplete picture and may feel unable to reach a properly informed judgment on where the balance of public interest lies . . . in those circumstances we see no objection to the minister leaving the matter to the court and explaining why he has done so'.[123] The opinion suggested that there will be a 'need for safeguards to ensure that the public interest is not harmed by the greater freedom accorded to ministers . . . there should be some means of monitoring the extent to which voluntary and court-ordered disclosure has been made of documents falling within each class'.[124]

Despite this cautious tone, there is reason for some optimism that the future operation of PII post-*Wiley* may allow for a greater degree of governmental openness than had been evident beforehand. In *Bennett* v. *Commissioner of Police of the Metropolis*,[125] an extradition case which threw up a number of questions concerning PII, Rattee J held in December 1994, applying *Wiley*, that it is at least arguable that ministers are under a *duty* to consider, before objecting to disclosure on PII grounds, whether the balance of the public interest favours disclosure. In the light of this judgment, Charles and Richards advised that 'consideration should now be given *wherever possible* to the issue of voluntary disclosure and in any case where this is not done the court should be told why'.[126] Certainly, if this advice is adopted,[127] this will signal a considerably more open approach to disclosure of government documents than was apparent in the evidence given to the Scott report.

As to the future drafting of PII certificates, the Charles/Richards advice stated that after *Wiley* 'it will be necessary for future PII certificates to be considerably more informative than has been the practice hitherto. They will need to explain, for example, why it is that the minister has concluded that the

---

[122] *PII: Ex parte Wiley*, joint opinion of A. W. H. Charles and Stephen Richards, 9 Oct. 1995, para. 6.

[123] Ibid., paras. 18 and 33.   [124] Ibid., para. 43.   [125] [1995] 2 All ER 1, at 13.

[126] *PII: Ex parte Wiley*, joint opinion of A. W. H. Charles and Stephen Richards, 9 Oct. 1995, para. 13.

[127] In the government's paper, *Public Interest Immunity: Government Response to the Scott Report*, it was stated that the Charles and Richards advice 'has been accepted' (see para. 2.21).

overall public interest favours non-disclosure or why he felt unable to form a view on where the balance lies.'[128] The PII certificates signed in respect of the Ordtec appeal, heard in November 1995, are an example of this more fully informative approach. The PII certificate signed by the foreign secretary, Douglas Hurd, is a good illustration. Mr Hurd's certificate[129] sought to protect from disclosure five documents from FCO files and sought redactions to be made to a further twenty-four documents before they were disclosed. Paragraph 9 of his certificate was in quite different terms from the PII certificates which had been signed three years earlier for the Matrix Churchill trial. It stated that 'the duty to assert immunity on public interest grounds for information, including documents, the disclosure of which would damage national security, or would be of substantial value to terrorists and other criminals, does not require that in any case where such information forms part of a class of information a minister is bound to persist in the assertion of immunity if he is satisfied that having regard to the issues in the case there is an overall balance of public interests in favour of disclosure'.[130] Compare this to the robust and uncompromising language of 'unquantifiable damage' (Tristan Garel-Jones) and of 'any' documents concerning advice to ministers automatically attracting a claim to PII (Andrew Leithead) which was used in relation to Matrix Churchill.

Conclusion: The Attorney General's New Guidelines

Although Scott's criticisms of government malpractice as to PII were strong, his recommendations were comparatively limited. He recommended against legislation clarifying the principles of PII; he did not recommend that PII claims should only be permitted on a contents basis (although he did recommend that class claims should not be allowed in criminal cases); and he did not recommend that PII claims should in the future be based on something more compelling, and more exact, than the candour argument.[131] The Scott report made five main recommendations on PII. They were: first, class claims to PII should no longer be made in criminal cases;[132] secondly, material

---

[128] *PII: Ex parte Wiley*, joint opinion of A. W. H. Charles and Stephen Richards, 9 Oct. 1995, para. 37.

[129] In fact Mr Hurd signed two certificates for the Ordtec appeal. It is the main one that is considered here. A supplementary certificate was signed in respect of one further document, an intelligence report dating from 1990. See Scott report, para. J6.84.

[130] See Scott report, para. J6.85.

[131] Although Sir Richard did appear to suggest this in a subsequent public lecture: in 'The Acceptable and Unacceptable Use of Public Interest Immunity' [1996] *Public Law* 427 (at p. 444) Sir Richard stated that 'I hope that class claims will never be made if they cannot be based on something more substantial than the "candour" argument. If they are based solely on that argument I hope they will not be accepted.'

[132] See paras. K6.6 and K6.16.

documents whose potential to assist the defence is apparent should never be withheld on PII grounds from a defendant in a criminal trial—thus there is no real balancing exercise as such in criminal cases;[133] thirdly, in criminal cases (at least) PII claims made on a contents basis should not be made unless in the minister's opinion, 'disclosure will cause substantial harm';[134] fourthly, the same counsel should not represent both the prosecution and government departments—if a government department (rather than the prosecution) wishes to claim PII, the department and not the prosecution should make out its case in court;[135] and finally, PII certificates should be more informative— they should always describe, in as much detail as possible, the nature of the documents that are covered by the certificate. Details of this sort, including a schedule of the relevant documents, should enable the defence to present, on as informed a basis as possible, an argument opposing the PII claim.[136]

Depressingly, the government's initial reaction to the Scott report's findings on PII was defensive, unhelpful, and confrontational, and was no doubt informed primarily by the government's concerted attempt to avoid ministerial resignations, an attempt which was, of course, successful. The government simply brazened it out. It simply rejected Scott's views on PII law and continued to insist that in using PII claims in the context of a criminal trial, and in stating that ministers had been under a duty to claim PII, the government had done nothing wrong. However, the government did institute a short consultation process on PII law and practice after the Scott report was published, and in December 1996 the government made an important announcement in which it outlined a new approach to PII.[137]

While the government's new approach is limited to claims to PII made by the government itself (i.e. it does not extend to claims made by the police or by other non-departmental public bodies) and is limited to England and Wales, it does represent a significant and welcome step in the right direction. The new approach outlined in the government's paper applies equally to civil and criminal cases.[138] The central point of the new approach is the abolition of the distinction between class and contents claims. Government ministers will no longer make claims to PII based on the contents of a document or on the class into which a document falls. In its announcement the government stated that the distinction between class and contents claims was 'no longer helpful'[139] and had become 'obscure'.[140] The government's new approach is that PII can only be claimed 'where disclosure of material could cause real

---

[133] See paras. K6.12–14.

[134] These are Lord Templeman's words and represent his approach in *ex p. Wiley*. See para. K6.18(iv).

[135] See para. K6.19.   [136] See para. K6.23.

[137] See HC Deb, vol. 287, cols. 949–58, 18 Dec. 1996. The lord chancellor made a similar statement to the House of Lords: see HL Deb., vol. 576, cols. 1507–17, 18 Dec. 1996.

[138] *Attorney General's Guidelines on Public Interest Immunity*, Dec. 1996, paras. 1.7–9.

[139] Ibid., para. 2.3.   [140] Ibid., para. 3.3.

damage to the public interest'.[141] This obviously raises the question of what 'real damage' means. Is the new approach a change merely of words or will it also result in a change of practice? That the government chose late December to make its announcement (the day before the Christmas recess) and that the announcement was followed merely by placing a short document in the libraries of the Houses of Parliament (rather than by formally publishing a command paper, for example) might indicate that the government was anxious to minimize publicity for its new approach. This was hardly an exercise in genuinely open government! No doubt the government was mindful that after nearly eighteen years in power its new approach might be seen by some to represent an admission that past practice had been unacceptable.

However, even if the form of the announcement was flawed, its contents give cause for greater optimism. As for defining what the new test of 'real damage to the public interest' might mean, the government took the view that 'it is impossible to describe exhaustively what that damage might be'[142] although some examples were given. A claim to PII would be justified if, for example, it would prevent harm to an individual (such as an informant) or if it would prevent damage to what the government slightly mysteriously called the 'regulatory process' or to international relations or to the nation's economic interests.[143] This is not an exhaustive list: in the government's view no list could be complete—claims to PII would have to be considered on a case by case basis. As far as the candour argument is concerned the government stated that this would also now be governed by the 'real damage' test. In contrast to the previous position (as endorsed by such senior judges as Lord Reid) the government now 'accepts that an approach to PII which claimed a kind of blanket protection for pre-defined categories of document would be wrong in principle'.[144] Interdepartmental papers and other internal government documents 'will not be the subject of a PII claim unless the responsible minister is satisfied that their disclosure would cause real damage or harm to the public interest in good government'.[145] Again, however, even the government's new approach leaves unclear precisely what this 'real' harm might be.

Overall, the changes announced by the government in December 1996 represent a remarkable improvement on the the quite outrageous misuse of PII revealed by the Scott report. No longer will government ministers make PII claims automatically. No longer will claims to PII be made solely because a document constitutes high level advice to ministers.[146] Moreover, those PII certificates which are signed by ministers will now have to 'set out in greater detail than before both what the material in question is and what damage its disclosure would, in the opinion of the minister, do'.[147] Ministers will, in short, have to be a good deal more open about their reasons for not being open.

---

[141] Ibid., para. 4.2.   [142] Ibid., para. 4.3.   [143] Ibid.   [144] Ibid., para. 5.6.
[145] Ibid., para. 5.9.   [146] See ibid., para. 5.12.   [147] Ibid., para. 4.5.

Much of this chapter has been concerned with quite narrow, detailed, and technical (but nonetheless important) points of PII law and practice. In this legal focus on the detail of PII we should be careful not to lose sight of the fact that PII is but a part of a wider picture. Quite apart from PII the Scott report also chronicles in some detail other ways in which the flow of information in both the Matrix Churchill and Ordtec cases was far from free. In terms both of the disclosure by various government departments of relevant papers to the prosecution team[148] and in terms of the limited disclosure by the prosecution (in the Ordtec case) of material evidence to the defence even without a PII certificate,[149] the practices uncovered in the Scott report were seriously deficient. The government's attitude to PII whereby 'if in doubt, slap on a PII certificate' (a kind of factor 15 PII system) is but a symptom of the broader malaise of widespread government secrecy. Sunshine laws as far as the Conservative government was concerned related not to letting the sun in to shine on hitherto darkened corners of governmental practice, but rather concerned deliberate efforts to block the sun out, even at the cost of twisting or ignoring the law.

[148] See ch. G.9.
[149] This was, as we have seen, ultimately fatal to the Ordtec case: see ch. J.6, especially paras. J6.71–4.

PART IV

The American Connection

6

Iraqgate: The American Equivalent of Scott?

As indicated in the introduction, one of the reasons for studying the Scott story is that it lends itself very neatly to comparative analysis. This is unusual in political scandals, which are more often local and particular, rather than international, in character. But here again, Scott is different. There was an American twist to the Scott story, which this chapter will explore. The implications for American, and for British, constitutional law will be examined in the next chapter. The question which is addressed in these chapters is: what does the British constitution have to learn from recent American constitutional law and practice in the ways in which it responds to a major national security scandal?

Iraqgate was a major national security scandal in the United States. For reasons which we shall explore towards the end of this chapter, Iraqgate ultimately failed to make it as a full blown political crisis, or turning point, in the way that Watergate was in the 1970s or in the way that Iran/Contra was in the late 1980s, but nonetheless—or maybe even in part because of this—the story of Iraqgate is an illuminating one, which the British and American constitutions ignore at their peril. One of the reasons why Iraqgate is not as well known as it ought to be is that the facts and the background are complicated. This chapter spends some time attempting to set them out. This is important for a number of reasons: first, there is no single authoritative report which establishes the facts and which tells the story of Iraqgate in the way that large parts of the text of the Scott report do. Secondly, the fuller our understanding of the factual background, the easier it should be to appreciate the constitutional implications of the story. Thirdly, Iraqgate is a good story. It is an interesting one in its own right, and it is a useful one in terms of narrating, or viewing, the constitution.

The story which follows has been put together from a variety of sources. I do not pretend that what follows is in any sense complete—and that is in itself a part of the story, as we shall see. There is no single authoritative last word on Iraqgate in the US in the way that Scott is usually taken to have represented in Britain. In the American equivalent of the Scott story there is no equivalent of the Scott character. In Iraqgate there was no overall, independent investigation with a brief to look into the affair in the round. There were two internal department of justice reports, but they added little to the story. So in Iraqgate we have to look a little more widely, and dig a lot more deeply. The sources of this story are diverse and they are coloured. Everybody in Iraqgate speaks a political language—in Scott speak, we are in a different culture of truth from the one which Scott the judge and Scott the reporter tried to engender.

Fittingly, therefore, among our most important sources is a politician: Congressman Henry B. Gonzalez, the member of the House of Representatives for the district of San Antonio, Texas. Gonzalez has been in Congress for over thirty years, and was during the 104th Congress (1995–96) the third most senior member of the House. He is a Democrat, admiringly described in a recent exposé of political corruption in Washington as 'the last of the great Texan populists'.[1] He is a crusader, not known for toeing the party line for its own sake. He has, however, managed to climb up the congressional ladder, partly as a result of his being re-elected every other year by the people of San Antonio for the past three decades, and had become, by the beginning of the 1990s, the chairman of the powerful House banking committee. Gonzalez remained in this position until the Democrats lost control of the House of Representatives (for the first time in forty years) in 1994. He then became the ranking minority member on the committee.

Under Gonzalez' chairmanship, the banking committee was at the forefront of congressional investigations into the Bush administration's policies with regard to Iraq. Gonzalez himself made almost forty statements on the floor of the House about Iraqgate, all of which are printed in the *Congressional Record*, and in addition, the committee held a number of public hearings at which over one hundred witnesses were interviewed—much of this oral and written testimony is published.[2] This work provides a central source in the piecing together of Iraqgate. In addition, the two department of justice reports, referred to above, and the views of the judges involved provide useful starting points, but there is little other material as far as official sources are concerned. Beyond that, newspaper stories and interviews with various political players and academic and media commentators constitute the remainder.[3]

What do these sources tell us? In a nutshell, the Iraqgate story concerned the financing of the west's exports to Iraq before the Iraqi invasion of Kuwait

---

[1] A. Cockburn and K. Silverstein, *Washington Babylon* (London and New York: Verso, 1996) p. 71. *Washington Babylon* is one of those conspiracy-theories-running-amok accounts of the political scene in Washington, but the interesting thing about it is that Gonzalez is just about the only politician who comes out of the book well. That he is one of the politicians that conspiracy theorists can consider to be 'one of us' tells us a good deal about his public persona.

[2] There are seven sessions of hearings which form the basis of the banking committee's work: *The BNL Affair*, serial no. 101–178 (Oct. 1990); *The BNL Affair (part ii)*, serial no. 102–17 (Apr. 1991); *BNL and Eximbank*, serial no. 102–21 (Apr. 1991); *Regulatory Improvement*, serial no. 102–121 (May 1992); *USDA and the BNL Scandal*, serial no. 102–123 (May 1992); *The Rostow Gang*, serial no. 102–127 (May 1992); and *Testimony of Former BNL Employees*, serial no. 103–95 (Nov. 1993).

[3] Off the record interviews were conducted with a number of senior members and former members of Gonzalez' staff, as well as with various academic and media commentators in Washington in Sept. 1993 and Jan. 1997.

in August 1990. Where did Matrix Churchill and its competitors get the money from to trade with Iraq—and where did the heavily debt-laden Iraqi economy get the money from to pay for its arms procurement network, and for its economic rebuilding? Did the Reagan and even more so the Bush administrations either turn a blind eye to or even encourage banks' assistance to Iraq? If so, and this is what Gonzalez alleged, was the Bush administration later involved in a cover-up to attempt to prevent Congress—and the American taxpayer—from finding out about it? Again, it certainly appears so. Further, was the Bush administration trying to divert blame for this failed policy away from itself and towards the banks involved, just as the British government sought to blame not its own policies but the actions of exporters? Was it a part of this diversionary tactic to prosecute the middle man so as to provide a convenient scapegoat? Certainly there was a controversial prosecution to mirror the Old Bailey's Matrix Churchill trial. The defendant in the US prosecution was Christopher Drogoul. He was the manager of the Atlanta branch of an Italian bank known as the Banca Nazionale del Lavoro, or BNL, a branch which had lent extraordinarily large sums to the Iraqi government. Did Drogoul act alone, as the Bush administration always insisted? Or was he encouraged by the US secret intelligence community to bend the rules in Iraq's favour? These are the questions which make up the Iraqgate story, a picture which we can now begin to paint a little more fully.[4]

Background: US/Iraq Relations, 1979–1990

From the late 1960s onwards, relations between the US and Iraq were poor. In 1979, during the Carter administration, Iraq was officially labelled as a nation which supported international terrorism. This designation meant that Iraq was prohibited from purchasing many US goods, including civilian aircraft and military equipment. There were no diplomatic relations between the US and Iraq for seventeen years, until president Reagan restored them in 1984. At about this point—the mid 1980s—a remarkable turn-about started to occur. US/Iraqi trade grew fantastically, in just the same way as the British government warmed to Iraq as fears about Iran grew throughout the 1980s.

---

[4] Gonzalez himself was not equally concerned with all these various questions. As chairman of the banking committee, his focus was clearly on the banking aspects of the story. In an early floor statement, he outlined the issues which in his view were raised by Iraqgate. For him, the story raised six issues: first, it was another case study in bank regulatory failure; secondly, it raised the question of whether the US should allow financial institutions based in the US but owned elsewhere to be the conduit of US (or of others') foreign policy; thirdly, BNL loans were clearly linked to the build up of the Iraqi war machine; fourthly, much of the US assistance to Iraq in its military procurement may have been legal, as a result of the US having inadequate export control laws; fifthly, what did US intelligence agencies know, and when did they know it; and finally, why did the west appease and help to arm Iraq in the face of its repeated, grotesque human rights record? (*Congressional Record*, H 846, 4 Feb. 1991).

From 1985–90, for example, the US authorized over $4 billion in US govern-ment guaranteed agricultural exports to Iraq, the peak being $1.1 billion in 1988. Not only was this total exceptional, it also meant that at any one time, large amounts of money would be owed by Iraq to US institutions. At the time of the Iraqi invasion of Kuwait in 1990, for example, US banks had an exposure to Iraq of a little over $100 million. Yet Iraq was a nation which in 1988 at the end of the Iran–Iraq war, had debts of some $70–$80 billion.[5]

What was the US government's publicly stated policy on trade with Iraq during the period 1984–90? In testimony to Congress in June 1990 John Kelly, assistant secretary of state in the Bush administration, stated that US policy with regard to Iraq had five goals: 'first, maintaining the supply of oil from Iraq; secondly, maintaining stability in the entire Gulf and its oil supply; thirdly, ensuring Iraq's moderation in the Middle East peace process; fourthly, *preventing the proliferation of missiles* and nuclear, chemical, bio-logical weapons; and finally, promoting the improvement of Iraq's human rights record'.[6]

In October 1989 president Bush signed into effect national security direc-tive 26 (NSD-26). This directive marked a significant consolidation of the official US position with regard to Iraq and was classified as top secret.[7] It stated that 'normal relations between the US and Iraq would serve our long-term interests' and it mandated a series of moves to strengthen economic and military ties by stating that 'the US government should propose economic and political incentives for Iraq . . . to increase our influence with Iraq'. Specifically with regard to trade the directive stated that 'we should pursue and seek to facilitate opportunities for US firms to participate in the recon-struction of the Iraqi economy, particularly in the energy area . . . Also, as a means of developing access to and influence with the Iraqi defence establish-ment, the US should consider sales of non-lethal forms of military assistance.' The directive illustrated the Bush administration's policy of 'encouraging Saddam Hussein to join the family of nations'.

In the years following the Gulf war, when the House banking committee was scrutinizing the Bush administration's policies towards Iraq in the period before 1990, president Bush repeatedly claimed that 'we did not enhance Iraq's nuclear, biological or chemical weapons and missile capability'.[8] Bush stated that no US companies had exported 'bombs or something of that nature' to Iraq before the Gulf war. But clearly, while the policy as illustrated by NSD-26 might not have allowed things that could themselves blow up to

---

[5] *Congressional Record*, H 7139, 31 July 1992. Not all of this trade took the form of guaran-teed agricultural loans, of course. Between 1983 and 1990 the west exported to Iraq what Gonzalez described as 'sophisticated weaponry' worth a total of $47.6 billion. See *Congressional Record*, H 1112, 21 Feb. 1991.

[6] Cited by Gonzalez, *Congressional Record*, H 2939, 9 May 1991, emphasis added.

[7] Classification procedures are discussed in the next chapter.

[8] See, e.g., *Congressional Record*, H 6339, 21 July 1992.

be exported, 'it clearly allowed the sale of the equipment needed to make them'.[9] The reality was that under NSD-26 it quickly became the US government's practice routinely to grant licences for export to Iraq of dual use goods, as a direct result of which 'dozens of US firms, many of them receiving BNL financing, provided key technologies to Iraq's missile program'.[10] To support these allegations Gonzalez cited a classified state department memo dated November 1989 which stated that 'US policy, as confirmed in NSD-26, has been to improve relations with Iraq, including trade' and that went on to make clear that 'exports of dual use commodities for conventional military use may be approved'.[11] A further state department memo of early 1990 stated that 'an initial review of 73 cases in which export licences were granted . . . from 1986–89 shows that licences were granted for equipment with dual or not clearly stated uses' to be exported to Iraq.[12]

The figures unearthed by Gonzalez' researchers indicate just how routinely the process of export licensing was carried out. Out of 771 export licences granted by the commerce department for US trade with Iraq between 1985 and 1990, only one was ever checked to ensure that the equipment was actually being used for civilian purposes.[13] The role of the export licensing process is (ostensibly at least) to seek to prevent US exports and equipment from ending up in dangerous or undesirable hands.[14] Yet during the Reagan and Bush years, approximately two in every seven of these 771 export licences were granted for exports which went either directly to the Iraqi army or to Iraqi companies involved in the arms procurement network.[15] In this period over

[9] Gonzalez' words: *Congressional Record*, H 6339, 21 July 1992.

[10] *Congressional Record*, H 6340, 21 July 1992. In an earlier floor statement Gonzalez alleged that: 'our Government knew about the military uses of this technology and did nothing to stop it. The truth about the US export licensing process is that the N[ational] S[ecurity] C[ouncil], state department, and commerce department routinely ignored and actually encouraged the transfer of militarily useful technology to Iraq in violation of its public oath to prohibit such uses. On top of that they are now engaged in a comprehensive effort to cover up . . .' —*Congressional Record*, H 2939, 9 May 1991.

[11] *Congressional Record*, H 8821, 21 Sept. 1992.

[12] *Congressional Record*, H 8821, 21 Sept. 1992. The trade was not all one way. US purchases of Iraqi oil jumped from about 80,000 barrels per day in 1985–7 to 675,000 barrels per day in 1990, the 1990 figure constituting about 24% of Iraq's total oil exports, and about 8% of new US oil imports. (See *Congressional Record*: H 8822, 21 Sept. 1992.) By the time of the Iraqi invasion of Kuwait in Aug. 1990, US purchases of Iraqi oil had risen to over 1.1 million barrels per day.

[13] *Congressional Record*, H 6339, 21 July 1992.

[14] The relevant legislation includes the Arms Export Control Act, codified as amended at 22 USC §2751, and the Export Administration Act, 50 USC app. §2401. See J. D. Westreich, 'Regulatory Controls on US Exports of Weapons Technology', 7 *Admin. L J Am. U* 463 (1993); H. J. Berman and J. R. Garson, 'US Export Controls: Past, Present and Future', 67 *Colum. L Rev.* 791 (1967); M. W. Sawchak, 'The Department of Defence's Role in Free-World Export Licensing' [1988] *Duke LJ* 785; and J. I. Burkemper, 'Export Verboten: Export Controls in the US and Germany', 67 *S Cal. L Rev.* 149 (1993). See also, House Committee on Government Operations, *Strengthening the Export Licensing System*, HR Doc. 137, 102nd Congress, 1st session (1991).

[15] *Congressional Record*, H 634, 21 July 92. Of the 771 licences, 239 were granted under the Bush administration.

eighty export licences were approved for exports directly to the Iraqi armed forces.

Although the trade links were clearly important, they did not constitute the full extent of US/Iraqi relations in the late 1980s. During the Iran–Iraq war, for example, the US intelligence community, led by the CIA, embarked on a programme of intelligence sharing and co-operation with Iraq.[16] Indeed, Gonzalez asserted that US/Iraqi intelligence sharing was still operational even as late as May 1990: a national security council paper seen by the banking committee stated that in May 1990 intelligence sharing with Iraq had 'waned' since the end of the Iran–Iraq war, but had not stopped altogether.[17]

Yet despite this intelligence sharing with Iraq, it seems that, as in Britain, the US intelligence community failed to piece together the extent of the Iraqi arms procurement programme or the extent of US involvement in it until as late as 1990.[18] However, Gonzalez produced evidence indicating that the story could and should have been put together earlier. He cited, for example, an eximbank[19] memo of June 1989 which highlighted the dangers of trade with Iraq after the ending of the Iran–Iraq war. The memo stated that: 'the [Iraqi] government is planning to develop new state controlled industries to supply the military . . . these new industries will fashion products for the new arms industries . . .'.[20] Similarly, a federal reserve memo of September 1989 referred to 'allegations that BNL's funding was used at least in part to finance arms shipments to Iraq'.[21] That memo went on to cite Matrix Churchill as a leading front company in Iraq's arms procurement network. Yet two months later, another batch of Matrix Churchill export licence applications for shipments to Iraq was granted. The end-user for these shipments was cited by Matrix Churchill as TECO. The US government had information on TECO going back as far as the late 1980s, with one 1989 government report cited by Gonzalez stating that TECO was 'involved in high priority military projects that included chemical weapons, anti-missile programs, long-range missiles and nuclear weapons'.[22]

The background in terms of the development of relations with Iraq, and the lack of full intelligence about the consequences of that development, is remarkably similar in the US and in Britain. In Congress, Gonzalez was interested in this story not because he found in it examples of illegal or unconstitutional behaviour, but because he saw it is a profoundly misguided and

---

[16] *Congressional Record*, H 1109, 9 Mar. 1992.

[17] *Congressional Record*, H 1110, 9 Mar. 1992.

[18] Two US intelligence reports dated July 1990 entitled *Beating Plowshares into Swords: Iraq's Defence Industrial Program* and *Iraq's Growing Arsenal: Programs and Facilities* finally listed Nassr, Hutteen, and other places Matrix Churchill and others had cited as destinations, as armaments factories. See *Congressional Record*, H 6342, 21 July 1992.

[19] Eximbank, one of the key players in the Iraqgate story, is discussed below.

[20] *Congressional Record*, H 6699, 27 Sept. 1992.

[21] *Congressional Record*, H 6700, 27 Sept. 1992.

[22] *Congressional Record*, H 6701, 27 Sept. 1992.

disastrous policy.[23] Gonzalez' concerns were twofold—and were different from those in Britain which had given rise to the appointment of the Scott inquiry, where the focus had been more on allegations of improper, rather than merely unwise, policies. Gonzalez' concerns were first, that the Bush administration should be held accountable for its part in causing—or in contributing to the factors which caused—the Gulf war.[24] The Bush administration's policy of appeasing Saddam Hussein and of forging closer trade, political, diplomatic, and even intelligence links with Iraq, despite Iraq's human rights record and apparent foreign policy aspirations in the Gulf region, was one which served to encourage, rather than to warn Iraq away from, its action in August 1990. Secondly, Gonzalez, as chairman of the banking committee, was concerned with the apparent performance of the US federal banking regulation system which failed adequately to monitor or to control the vast amount of financial assistance which institutions in the US were lending to Iraq throughout the period 1985–90. For Gonzalez, this was the focal point of the committee's investigations, as constitutionally it had to be, as we shall see.[25]

Iraqgate's Main Players: Eximbank, the CCC, and BNL

We can now turn to the substance of the Iraqgate affair in a little more detail. First, we will examine the architecture of the affair itself—the ways in which US governmental and financial institutions helped to fund the Iraqi arms procurement network of which companies such as Matrix Churchill were a part. Then we will move on to examine the ways in which the Bush White House responded to congressional inquiries about Iraqgate: did the Bush administration unconstitutionally withhold information from Congress? Finally, we will look at subsequent developments, both with regard to the criminal prosecutions which were commenced and as regards the actions of the Clinton administration since 1993.

There were three main organizations involved in the financing of the Iraqi arms procurement network: the first was a government agency known as the

---

[23] On the policy failures of the US and the UN which contributed to the Gulf War, see generally, P. Salinger, 'The US, the UN and the Gulf War', 49 *Middle East Journal* 595 (1995) and J. E. Wilz, 'The Making of Mr Bush's War: A Failure to Learn from History?', 25 *Presidential Studies Quarterly* 533 (1995). Wilz argues (at p. 546) that the Bush administration was still trading in dual-use goods with Iraq even on the eve of the Kuwait invasion: on 1 Aug. 1990 the Bush administration approved the sale to Iraq of advanced data-transmission devices.

[24] These concerns were also explored in the US Senate: see Senate Banking Committee, *US Export Policy toward Iraq prior to Iraq's Invasion of Kuwait*, serial no. 102–996 (Oct. 1992).

[25] As is explained in the next chapter, congressional committees such as the House banking committee do not have unlimited powers to investigate for investigation's sake. Congressional investigations must be based on some potential *legislative* interest. Here, statutory reforms to the structure of banking regulation formed this all important legislative interest.

eximbank (export-import bank). Eximbank's role was to guarantee to cover loans granted by US exporters to Iraq if Iraq defaulted on its repayments. Eximbank operates by financing US exports by providing guarantees, insurance, and loan support which indemnify a party (either an exporter or a bank) against non-payment by a buyer (such as Iraq). Eximbank was created by statute in 1947. Its statutory objects and purposes are 'to aid in financing and to facilitate exports and imports and the exchange of commodities and services between the US . . . and any foreign country or the . . . nationals thereof'.[26] There is a statutory duty on eximbank to be competitive. Eximbank is also under a duty to comply with detailed reporting requirements to Congress. It is specifically prohibited from involvement with countries engaged in armed conflict with the US and it is further provided in the statute that 'eximbank shall not give approval to guarantee or insure a sale of defence articles or services unless (i) the president determines that it is in the national interest and (ii) such determination has been reported to the speaker of the House and to the House and Senate banking committees at least 25 days in advance'.[27] The president and vice-president of the eximbank are appointed by the president of the United States, by and with the advice and consent of the Senate.

Of the three main players in Iraqgate, eximbank was by far the most cautious when it came to dealing with Iraq, to such an extent that in March 1986 eximbank suspended operations with Iraq because of Iraqi repayment problems. Eximbank did not reopen for business with Iraq until July 1987. From then until August 1990 eximbank provided financial assistance to Iraq in 187 different projects, totalling $267 million.[28] Even Gonzalez had some praise for eximbank's approach with regard to Iraq.[29] However, Gonzalez did also state that eximbank money was directly used for the purchase by Iraq of military goods. As we have seen, if eximbank realized this, this would have been illegal. But Gonzalez did not allege that eximbank had behaved unlawfully: rather, his concern was that a commercial organization was being used by the Reagan and Bush administrations as a conduit for foreign and defence policy. In other words, eximbank's involvement with Iraq was being forced on them by the state department, which was leading the drive for closer links with Iraq. Gonzalez alleged that the state department repeatedly pressurized eximbank into being more generous with Iraq.[30] The largest transaction

---

[26] The eximbank statute, as amended, is now codified at 12 USC §635. It is reviewed in House Banking Committee, *US Export-Import Bank*, serial no. 103–91 (Nov. 1993) and House Banking Committee, *Eximbank Financing for Non-lethal Defence Articles and Defence Services*, serial no. 103–681 (Aug. 1994).

[27] 12 USC §635(b)(6)(D).

[28] Of these 187 transactions 'only a small handful' were checked to ensure that dual use goods were not being used for military purposes. See *Congressional Record*, H 2552, 25 Apr. 1991.

[29] *Congressional Record*, H 2548, 25 Apr. 1991.

[30] See, e.g., *Congressional Record*, H 513, 24 Feb. 1992.

involving Iraq which was approved by eximbank related to the Aqaba pipeline project. Eximbank guaranteed $484 million (out of a total of $1 billion required for the whole project). Gonzalez alleged that then vice-president George Bush personally intervened to persuade eximbank to support this project.[31] The project was never implemented. A note from eximbank which was cited by Gonzalez stated that the Aqaba project was being supported only because of pressure from the Reagan administration, and that 'under normal peaceful circumstances, this project would not be economically viable.'[32]

The second main player in Iraqgate was another government organization. This was an obscure US government credit-guarantee programme set up by the US department of agriculture (USDA) in the 1970s known as the CCC, or commodity credit corporation. Under the CCC programme the US government would promise exporters of US agricultural products that their bank loans would be covered in the event that the foreign buyer was unable to pay. CCC is authorized by statute to develop and administer programmes to expand US agricultural export markets. The relevant legislation provides that 'for the purpose of stabilizing, supporting, and protecting farm income and prices, of assisting in the maintenance of balanced and adequate supplies of agricultural commodities . . . and of facilitating the orderly distribution of agricultural commodities, there is created a body corporate to be known as the commodity credit corporation . . .'.[33] The CCC's programmes target countries that have potential for additional food purchases, but are short on cash and need credit. The CCC guarantee operates to attract credit from the private sector to finance sales of US agricultural commodities, rather than having the government provide credit directly. As far as Iraq was concerned, CCC appears to have operated two main programmes: GSM-102 in respect of which Congress had mandated CCC to make available no less that $5 billion annually, and GSM-103 in respect of which the figure was $1 billion. Iraq started using CCC credit in 1983 and by 1990 had received $5.08 billion worth under GSM-102 and GSM-103.[34] At the time of the Iraqi invasion of Kuwait, total CCC exposure to Iraq under these programmes was $2 billion.[35]

The sums dedicated to Iraq under the CCC programmes were huge. Indeed, the CCC was the largest single source of financial assistance which

---

[31] Ibid.

[32] Ibid. In an earlier floor statement, Gonzalez stated that: 'it took constant pressure from the state department and interventions from high level Reagan and Bush policy makers to get eximbank to permit Iraq to utilize its programmes to achieve policy objectives that were shifting, muddled, and ultimately that worked against [the United States'] own national interest'. See *Congressional Record*, H 513, 24 Feb. 1992.

[33] 15 USC §714.

[34] A table setting out the full figures is reprinted in the *Congressional Record*, H 848, 4 Feb. 1991.

[35] Of which CCC owed BNL between $347 million and $382 million, depending on whose figures you read. See *Congressional Record*, H 848, 4 Feb. 1991.

Iraq received from the west in the 1980s. Between 1983 and 1990 CCC granted credit guarantees which enabled Iraq to purchase a total of $5.5 billion worth of US farm products.[36] In 1988 and 1989 20 per cent of the total CCC programme was dedicated to Iraq. In 1989 Iraq received $1 billion in agriculture credit from the USA; and the USDA was in the process of granting the same amount again in 1990 when the BNL scandal began to break, and as a result of political pressure from Congress and elsewhere the USDA was forced to limit the 1990 amount of CCC assistance to Iraq to $500 million.[37] Despite the vast amounts involved, it appears that there was, at best, scant monitoring within the government as to the use Iraq was making of its CCC assistance.[38] In September 1989, for example, the USDA office of inspector general wrote that: 'the GSM program was operating without the benefit of a compliance review process or program to assess the direction and impact the program has had on US and foreign agricultural marketing activities. As a result, US exporters are participating in a $6 billion program without CCC conducting a review or periodic check to make sure the program is operating in accordance with applicable laws and requisitions.'[39]

This is not to say, however, that there were no doubts expressed by any government department about the extent of Iraq's involvement in the CCC programme. In 1985 the federal reserve, the department of the treasury, and eximbank all separately voted against increases in the CCC programme for Iraq, largely grounded on fears about Iraq's ability (or willingness) to pay its debts. Yet in this and following years not only did Iraq remain in the programme, but CCC exposure to Iraq continued to grow. As Gonzalez put it, it was clear that 'foreign policy drove the CCC program, not the Iraqis' ability to pay. Because the CCC program lacked tough standards for granting credit, the administration found it easier to use the CCC program for Iraq as a foreign policy tool at the expense of the US taxpayers.'[40]

That the CCC's exposure to Iraq was driven by foreign policy considerations is further illustrated by events in 1989. Even though Iraq's financial condition had deteriorated during that year, the USDA, at the state department's behest, proposed a $1 billion CCC programme for Iraq for fiscal year 1990. This proposal was put before the NAC: the national advisory council on international monetary and financial policies. This body is responsible for the policies and practices of agencies that make, or participate in making, foreign loans, including the CCC. The members of the NAC include the secretary of the treasury, the secretary of commerce, the chairman of the board of gover-

---

[36] *Congressional Record*, H 1111, 21 Feb. 1991.

[37] *Congressional Record*, H 1112, 21 Feb. 1991.

[38] For example, according to a report issued by the justice department in Jan. 1995 (the Hogan report, discussed further below) no commitment was obtained from Iraq or other countries that CCC commodities would not be resold or transferred even though this was required by law: see 7 USC §1707a(b)(7).

[39] *Congressional Record*, H 861, 2 Mar. 1992.   [40] Ibid.

nors of the federal reserve, and the chairman of the board of governors of the eximbank. The CCC was given to understand that it might be difficult to get the entire $1 billion 1990 budget for Iraq approved by the NAC, and so in September 1989 it approached the NAC with a modified proposal, the effect of which was to reduce the budget for Iraq to $400 million. In October 1989 this modified budget was unanimously approved by the NAC, but Iraq reacted angrily, regarding the new offer as an insult, a view Iraq was quick to press on the US embassy in Baghdad. Almost immediately, the secretary of state, James Baker, became personally involved, supporting Iraq's view. Despite Iraq's poor financial health and despite the Iraqgate scandal which was by then emerging in Congress, the state department successfully persuaded the NAC to reverse its earlier decision and by the beginning of November the NAC had met again and had approved the $1 billion credit in the CCC programme for 1990 that Iraq (and the state department, and the White House) had initially wanted.[41]

The third main player in Iraqgate was the most important one: the linchpin of the entire operation. This was the Atlanta branch of an Italian state-owned bank, the Banca Nazionale del Lavoro (BNL). BNL is one of the largest banks in Italy with assets of over $100 billion. It is 98 per cent owned by the Italian government. BNL has operations around the world, and has US branches in Chicago, Los Angeles, Miami, and in Atlanta, with its US headquarters located in New York. The Atlanta branch of BNL 'financed the sale [to Iraq] of chemicals, speciality steel products, sophisticated computer controlled industrial machinery, electronic components, computers and engineering and construction services. Much of this technology had civilian as well as military uses.'[42] BNL Atlanta financed the sale of over $850 million in US agricultural products to Iraq; $720 million of that amount was guaranteed by CCC.[43] 'During the latter half of the 1980s [Iraq] relied heavily on these BNL loans to finance the procurement of much of the western technology they were seeking. . . . But BNL loans were not ordinary financing . . .'.[44] In terms both of the economically unfeasibly low interest rates BNL were charging, and in terms of the extraordinarily generous repayment periods they were offering to Iraq, BNL was 'operating more like a charity than a

---

[41] *Congressional Record*, H 862–3, 2 Mar. 1992. In Apr. 1990 it was reported that USDA wanted to cancel Iraqi involvement in CCC because of numerous violations: the USDA had concerns, for example, 'about the diversion of US commodities for weapons for military purposes'. (*Congressional Record*, H 6238, 9 July 1992.) But pressure was put on Richard Crowder (USDA under-secretary, responsible for CCC) by secretary of agriculture Clayton Yeutter and by Brent Scowcroft to dissuade him from doing this. During his oral testimony before the banking committee, Mr Crowder was asked about NSC and White House involvement in CCC and the relationship between the operation of the CCC programme and US foreign policy, but in Gonzalez' words, Mr Crowder 'purposely failed to answer' the committee's questions. (*Congressional Record*, H 6238, 9 July 1992.) We shall return to this episode later when we discuss the Hogan report into Iraqgate issued under president Clinton's administration.

[42] *Congressional Record*, H 1111, 21 Feb. 1991.   [43] Ibid.   [44] Ibid.

bank'.[45] During 1987–9 BNL was the premier source of private western bank loans to Iraq. Gonzalez stated that:

BNL filled the void left by Iraq's inability to borrow by providing over $3 billion in loans that were not guaranteed by western governments. About one third of that amount went for food and freight charges while a little over $2 billion was earmarked for the ambitious Iraqi reconstruction programme. We have learned that a good portion of those funds were actually used to upgrade Iraqi military capability. BNL also provided almost $1 billion in US government guaranteed loans to Iraq. BNL was the largest single bank participant in the $5.5 billion USDA CCC programme with Iraq. Between $800 million and $900 million in BNL loans to Iraq were guaranteed by the CCC. BNL was also the second largest participant in the $267 million eximbank programme with Iraq. Over $50 million in BNL loans to Iraq were guaranteed by the eximbank.[46]

According to Gonzalez, four companies involved in the Iraqi arms procurement network received funding from BNL Atlanta. The first was Technology Development Group (TDG), Iraq's primary holding company in the UK. TDG received over DM81 million for a hot forging project at Nassr. Secondly, Technology Engineering Group (TEG) received over £1.6 million to export raw materials to Iraq. Thirdly, Matrix Churchill in Ohio and in Britain received £9 million to export sophisticated machined tools such as their high speed computer numerically controlled lathes to Iraq. Finally, the Italian front company, European Manufacturing Centre (Euromac) received over $50,000 in BNL funds to send small tools to Iraq.[47]

In addition to its agricultural business with Iraq, BNL Atlanta made over $2 billion in commercial loans to Iraq. These loans were used by the Iraqi ministry of industry and military industrialization (MIMI) to fuel the engine of Iraq's postwar reconstruction programme. Under the eximbank letter of credit programme with Iraq, for example, BNL was insured for fifty-one export transactions with a dollar value of $47 million, of which $43.8 million had been repaid by Iraq by 1990.[48] Further, while between 1985 and 1989 BNL had financed the sale of about $1.9 billion in CCC guaranteed sales to Iraq, BNL did little CCC business after the Iran–Iraq ceasefire in 1988. BNL's share of the CCC programme peaked at 92 per cent in fiscal year 1987. After 1988, BNL's business with Iraq concerned commercial loans (known as medium term loans, or MTLs) rather than agricultural loans. According to Gonzalez, BNL could afford to borrow the money to finance these loans 'because it had the backing of the Italian government which gave it a

---

[45] *Congressional Record*, H 1111, 21 Feb. 1991.

[46] *Congressional Record*, H 2548, 25 Apr. 1991. In addition, 'BNL was a main source of funds for Matrix Churchill and other members of the secret Iraqi technology' procurement network: see *Congressional Record*, H 2552, 25 Apr. 1991.

[47] *Congressional Record*, H 7139, 31 July 1991. On Euromac generally, see *Congressional Record*, H 704–7, 18 Feb. 1993.

[48] *Congressional Record*, H 7138, 31 July 1992.

topnotch credit rating'.[49] Gonzalez claimed that much of the $2.155 billion BNL provided in loans to MIMI was utilized to purchase military technology from the US: 'BNL funds were used to purchase equipment for the Condor II ballistic missile, the Scud missile modifications, the short-range Abadel rocket and the 210mm and the 155mm howitzer.'[50]

Clearly, the most important question concerning BNL's role in the financing of Iraq's military procurement network is whether it was acting alone or not. If it was not acting alone, who knew what BNL Atlanta was doing? Who supported or encouraged this vast business with Iraq? What did BNL Rome know? What did the Italian government know? What did the US intelligence community and the Reagan and Bush administrations know? As we shall see, it was always the government's line—duly echoed by the prosecutors who were brought in to prosecute not BNL itself, but six BNL employees who ran the Atlanta office—that BNL Atlanta was a lone wolf, acting without authority or encouragement. The six employees unsurprisingly took a different view. But before we can examine what was to become of them, we must consider first activities in Congress. We have seen that in large part the story of Iraqgate only became apparent because of the work of the House banking committee, led by Henry Gonzalez. What was the reaction of the Bush White House to Congress's growing interest throughout the early 1990s in Iraqgate? As ever in political scandals, it is not only the doing but also the attempt to hide what has been done which causes controversy and raises questions about constitutional propriety. Just as the Scott inquiry investigated not one but two scandals (the changing of policy and consequential misleading of Parliament on the one hand, and the prosecution and misuse of public interest immunity on the other) so too there are two parts to the Iraqgate story in the US. The first is the financing of the Iraqi arms procurement network, with or without the knowledge and encouragement of the US government, and the second is the White House's reaction when Congress started to ask awkward questions about the affair. It is this aspect of Iraqgate to which we can now turn.

Controlling Official Information: Congress and the Executive Branch

Gonzalez and the banking committee encountered opposition to their inquiries into BNL and Iraqgate right from the first moment. As early as September 1990 Bush's attorney general Richard Thornburgh wrote to Gonzalez urging him to drop the investigation.[51] Thornburgh's letter was written in strong terms, alluding threateningly to the BNL affair as being 'a

---

[49] Ibid.　　　　　　　　　　　　[50] *Congressional Record*, H 9505, 25 Sept. 1992.
[51] Thornburgh's letter to Gonzalez is reproduced in the *Congressional Record* at H 852, 4 Feb. 1991, and again at H 3370, 18 May 1992.

sensitive case with national security concerns' and stating bluntly that the banking committee's actions were in danger of 'significantly diminishing' the chances of prosecution success in the criminal proceedings against BNL employees that were under way in Atlanta. Gonzalez responded to Thornburgh's objections by citing US supreme court decisions upholding Congress's constitutional rights 'to know, seek and obtain information'[52] and by asking Thornburgh precisely which aspects of the congressional investigation were threatening the chances of success in the criminal proceedings, a question which Thornburgh was apparently unable to answer. Thornburgh had objected to the banking committee's hearing, *inter alia*, on grounds of national security. Gonzalez claimed that this was utterly disingenuous. He cited a letter from the state department to the justice department dated 18 December 1990 which he claimed made it quite clear that there were no real national security fears over Congress' growing interest in BNL. The letter stated that 'with respect to the national security aspects of the BNL investigation, we have determined that the state department does not have any concerns it wishes to raise at this juncture'.[53]

In 1991 Thornburgh resigned as attorney general (to run—unsuccessfully—for the Senate). His successor as attorney general, William Barr, also sought to dissuade the banking committee from continuing its investigations into the BNL affair. In May 1992, attorney general Barr sent a letter to Gonzalez in which he threatened to withhold classified documents relating to BNL from the committee on the ground that Gonzalez had read previous documents into the *Congressional Record*, which Barr alleged had jeopardized national security, an accusation Gonzalez condemned as 'ludicrous', especially as Barr's letter was not sent until four months after the date on which Gonzalez was alleged to have read the classified material into the *Record*.[54]

If these were among the threats that Gonzalez and the banking committee received over their interest in BNL and Iraqgate, what about actual attempts to withhold information from Congress? Certainly, Gonzalez made a number of allegations that various government departments and agencies had withheld relevant information from the committee. He alleged, for example, that the federal reserve withheld over seventy BNL-related documents from the banking committee[55] including a Bank of Italy report examining BNL Atlanta which had been sent to the federal reserve. He also cited the justice department, state department, treasury department, and the State of

---

[52] *Congressional Record*, H 850, 4 Feb. 1991. The relevant case-law is discussed in the next chapter.

[53] *Congressional Record*, H 2007, 30 Mar. 1992.

[54] See *Congressional Record*, H 3369, 18 May 1992. Gonzalez claimed that Barr's letter illustrated that the Bush administration had 'moved from foot dragging to outright obstruction' of the committee's work on BNL: see ibid.

[55] *Congressional Record*, H 1113, 21 Feb. 1991.

Illinois[56] as institutions which were unnecessarily obstructing the work of the banking committee. Gonzalez complained that: 'we are obstructed blatantly, pre-meditatedly and coldly, and in defiance of the plain constitutional prerogative of the Congress to know'.[57] Another example is provided by the evidence given to the banking committee by Paul Dickerson, a senior CCC official, who stated that the CCC programme for Iraq 'was a market driven agriculture-related program without reference to other issues'.[58] Yet we have already seen that the CCC programme with Iraq was heavily influenced by the national security council (NSC), the state department, and foreign and defence policy interests, facts which the Bush administration appeared to want to keep away from Congress.

Several documents seen by the banking committee were heavily blacked out (or redacted). One document sent by the justice department was redacted as the department claimed that it 'contained information, that, if it were released, would be harmful to its efforts to prosecute the BNL case in Atlanta'. It turned out that the redacted information was simply that the justice department had been ready to issue the BNL indictments in early 1990— which raises questions as to why the indictments were not actually issued until February 1991.[59] Why did the justice department want to keep this information away from Congress? Was it because the administration did not want Congress to know that the state department had pressured the justice department into delaying the BNL indictment until such time as it was more convenient *vis-à-vis* US foreign policy?

The executive branch does have the power to resist congressional subpoenas for documents in certain limited circumstances.[60] There was nothing *necessarily* wrong with these government departments and agencies attempting to resist the banking committees' subpoenas, even if less than full and frank reasons for doing so were provided. Much depends on what the motives for resisting the subpoenas were, and Gonzalez made a series of allegations in various floor statements in the House that the Bush White House's motives were not entirely above board. Gonzalez argued that one reason why the Bush administration wanted to keep Congress away from BNL was the number of distinguished Republicans and Republican advisers embroiled in the BNL story. Gonzalez stated that Henry Kissinger, for example, was a paid

[56] Illinois apparently investigated BNL Chicago, but filed a lawsuit preventing the federal reserve from showing the banking committee a copy of the report. See *Congressional Record*, H 1115, 21 Feb. 1991.

[57] *Congressional Record*, H 1114, 21 Feb. 1991. The justice department refused to supply the banking committee with documents the committee had subpoenaed mainly on the grounds that to do so would interfere with the ongoing criminal prosecution in Atlanta, although the justice department would not clarify exactly how this was the case.

[58] See *Congressional Record*, H 1278, 16 Mar. 1992.

[59] See *Congressional Record*, H 3369, 18 May 1992.

[60] Through the doctrine of executive privilege and through its ability to classify information. These are discussed in the next chapter.

member of BNL's consulting board for international policy and that BNL was a client of Kissinger Associates.[61] Lawrence Eagleburger, a member of Kissinger associates and Bush's deputy secretary of state, and formerly Carter's ambassador to Yugoslavia, had vast contacts in Yugoslavia especially in its banking world: Eagleburger helped to establish in the US a bank called LBS. LBS is a wholly owned subsidiary of Ljubljanska Banka, the second largest bank in the former Yugoslavia. The other party which according to Gonzalez was 'responsible for a significant amount of the growth' of LBS in the USA was BNL.[62] Eximbank exposure to Yugoslavia in March 1991 was $1.056 billion. Gonzalez does not produce much evidence that Eagleburger was influencing relations between LBS, BNL, and others, but he certainly implies that it was possible. Moreover, the Bush administration's overall lack of co-operation with the banking committee's attempts to uncover details of the working relationship between BNL and the US government obviously makes it more difficult to rule out all possibility of any such link.

Brent Scowcroft is another alumnus of Kissinger Associates. He was chosen by Kissinger to be president Nixon's deputy assistant on national security. He became national security adviser to president Ford, and regained this position under president Bush. According to Gonzalez, Scowcroft owned stock in some forty companies, including companies such as General Electric, one of America's largest defence contractors, and others such as AT&T, General Motors, and Mobil Oil, all of which routinely require export licences for large parts of their business. As head of the NSC, Scowcroft was responsible for advising president Bush and for implementing his national security directives. Under the National Security Act 1947 and subsequent legislation, the NSC also has significant powers *vis-à-vis* export licences and export controls. According to Gonzalez, companies in which Scowcroft owned stock together received one in every eight US export licences for sales to Iraq.[63]

The NSC functions as an advisory body to the president on national security issues and to improve co-ordination between the military services and other executive departments. The president is its head. Other members include the vice-president, the secretary of state, and the secretary of defence. The assistant to the president for national security (usually known as the national security adviser) has no statutory position and is therefore not a formal member of the NSC. It was in Nixon's (and Kissinger's) time in the early 1970s that the status of this post was transformed from a relatively low level co-ordinator and administrator into one of spokesman and negotiator on

---

[61] *Congressional Record*, H 2763, 2 May 1991. Kissinger was secretary of state in the Nixon administration in the early 1970s, and before that had been Nixon's national security adviser. Since he left government he has founded Kissinger Associates, a highly powerful Republican network and political consultancy.

[62] *Congressional Record*, H 2549, 25 Apr. 1991.

[63] *Congressional Record*, H 2764, 2 May 1991.

national security issues, extending to policy advocacy and the giving of personal advice. The national security staff serves the dual role of co-ordinating and monitoring the implementation of national security policy as well as providing independent advice, presenting options, and offering ideas to the president. The roles of the NSC staff of course became notorious with the Oliver North Iran/Contra scandal in the 1980s.

Although export licensing is ostensibly a matter for the commerce department, the NSC has considerable influence as regards export controls and can even direct the commerce department in sensitive cases. This is illustrated by evidence given to the banking committee by Paul Freedenburg, the chief export licensing official at the commerce department. He stated that in 1988–9 the commerce department was concerned about Iraqi use of poison gas (for example against its own Kurdish population) but that the NSC nonetheless encouraged the commerce department to grant export licences to Iraq allowing the export of significant technology transfer which was capable of having military uses.[64] The NSC was also involved in monitoring USDA internal reviews of the CCC programme, even going as far as to set the date for the publication of a USDA report on CCC (in May 1990).[65] Gonzalez described this NSC involvement in the USDA's affairs as 'highly unusual' and speculated as to why it might have been: 'could it be that the NSC's involvement in the USDA study of BNL was meant to cover up an awareness that CCC guaranteed commodities were being diverted to pay for Iraq weapons purchases?'[66]

So much for Kissinger, his associates, and the murky politics of the national security council. It was not only the NSC which was involved in the attempts by the Bush administration to control the information Congress was allowed to see on Iraqgate and BNL. In the autumn of 1991, president Bush presented a report to Congress pursuant to the Iraq Sanctions Act 1990 under which he was required to conduct a study and to report to Congress on the 'sale, export, and third-party transfer or development of nuclear, biological, chemical, and ballistic missile technology to or with Iraq'.[67] The report stated that no US company contributed directly to Iraq's conventional weapons capability. The report was classified as secret. President Bush's statement was misleading. In fact, as Gonzalez observed, 'Iraq operated an extensive clandestine procurement network that obtained critical financing through BNL and that operated in this country to procure US technology and know-how for Iraqi weapons programmes.'[68]

---

[64] Ibid.   [65] *Congressional Record*, H 2696, 28 Apr. 1992.
[66] *Congressional Record*, H 2697, 28 Apr. 1992.   [67] 50 USC §1701 note, s. 586J.
[68] *Congressional Record*, H 208, 3 Mar. 1992. Gonzalez had asked Bush for the report in Apr. 1991, but he did not receive it until Oct. of that year. Gonzalez stated that the 'secret' classification was misleading, as it turned out that 'there was no secret information in the report which had not previously appeared' in the media. According to Gonzalez the real reason for the report's classification was that it was 'a phoney . . . the president was misleading the Congress about the US role in arming Iraq'. See *Congressional Record*, H 6341, 21 July 1992.

Most significantly of all, in terms of executive attempts to shield Iraqgate from congressional scrutiny, however, was what Gonzalez labelled the Rostow gang. Nick Rostow was general counsel to the NSC. He chaired meetings of a group of White House lawyers and advisers who started to meet in April 1991 to 'oversee the collection and the submission of [all Iraqgate-related] information to Congress'.[69] Ostensibly the function of the group was to review documents and information applicable to congressional requests for Iraq-related information and to establish a co-ordinated approach to the dissemination of that information. A memorandum from the NSC seen by the banking committee stated that 'the NSC is providing coordination for the administration's response to congressional document requests for Iraq-related materials. The process is intended to be a cooperative one.'[70] Gonzalez saw things less congenially: he stated that the Rostow gang 'gave the White House a direct hand in regulating the flow of information to Congress, thus limiting oversight of Iraq policy'.[71]

The Rostow gang established a process whereby Congress had to hurdle a series of increasingly difficult barriers in order to obtain information from the government. First, the relevant government department or agency in-house lawyers would review and make an inventory of all congressional requests for information, in order to determine if documents could be denied on grounds of executive privilege. Secondly, documents would be denied to Congress and instead briefings would be offered to members of Congress and their staffs, thus enabling a department or agency to put its own spin on its actions, without Congress being able properly to question the veracity of the government's statements. Thirdly, if Congress insisted on access to the documents themselves, rather than the government's summary of the documents, this would have to be cleared by the full Rostow gang before access could be granted. This provided for delay, if nothing else. Finally, if access to documents was granted, then it would be granted only subject to certain conditions: the documents would be made available only to members, and not to their staffs; documents could be consulted, but not retained; any notes that were taken by the member of Congress would themselves be classified and therefore subject

---

[69] *Congressional Record*, H 1274, 16 Mar. 1992. Other members of the Rostow gang included Boyden Gray, president Bush's general counsel, and lawyers from the departments of state, justice, defence, the treasury, commerce, agriculture, energy, and the CIA. All of the these departments and agencies had received requests from Congress for documents and information concerning Iraq and BNL.

[70] Cited by Gonzalez: *Congressional Record*, H 1275, 16 Mar. 1992.

[71] Ibid. The Rostow gang did not operate independently or of its own accord. There was considerable high level White House involvement in it: extending as far up as the president himself, along with John Sununu (chief of staff), Brent Scowcroft, Robert Gates (CIA director), and Boyden Gray. According to Gonzalez, all these senior officials played 'direct roles in limiting congressional access to . . . information on Iraq'. See *Congressional Record*, H 6005, 7 July 1992.

to strict limitations as to access and distribution.[72] None of the procedures adopted by the Rostow gang could affect Congress's legal powers to sub-poena documents, but it is one thing to be able to demand a document, it is another thing to be able to read it.[73] The effect of the Rostow gang was significantly to delay and obstruct Congress's access to relevant documents: 'the NSC and members of the Rostow gang became directly involved in a scheme to mislead Congress and the American public . . . about the military nature of US technology transfers to Iraq'.[74]

Not content even with the strictures imposed on Congress by the Rostow procedures, in the summer of 1992 the Bush administration attempted to go even further in making life difficult for the banking committee. An attempt was made to deposit documents which had been subpoenaed by the banking committee not with the committee but with the House select committee on intelligence, with the minority (i.e. Republican) leader in the House, and with the speaker (Tom Foley). The intelligence committee had never asked for these documents. Speaker Foley wrote to the attorney general (William Barr) stating that the parliamentarian of the House knew of no precedent for the attorney general's request that the speaker should control access by a com-mittee to its own subpoenaed documents, and that he as speaker had no authority to impose on the committee the conditions that the justice depart-ment had wanted.[75] After this sound ticking off, the Bush administration did not try this trick again.

This is not a happy picture, and it raises important questions about the con-stitutional regulation of official information flowing—or not—between the executive and legislative branches in just the same way as the Scott report in Britain raises questions about parliamentary access to governmental infor-mation. The American constitutional framework which purports to govern these issues will be examined in the next chapter, when we will also be able to

---

[72] *Congressional Record*, H 1275, 16 Mar. 1992. The text of the key Rostow gang memo of Apr. 1991 which outlines their procedures is reproduced at *Congressional Record*, H 1279, 16 Mar. 1992. It was the systematic nature of the Rostow gang's procedures which more than any-thing else offended Gonzalez: he stated at one point that 'it used to be that cover-ups were sort of ad hoc events, a . . . scramble to provide damage control for the moment. The Rostow gang advance the notion that cover-up mechanisms have become an integral cog in the machinery of this administration.' *Congressional Record*, H 1276, 16 Mar. 1992.

[73] In Gonzalez' words: 'the strategy of the Rostow gang was to try to claim executive privilege or deliberative process over as many documents as possible . . . It was hoped that making these claims would work to deny Congress the most embarrassing and damaging information on Iraq . . . Congressional challenges to the fallacious executive privilege claims only worked to delay the submission of information' the aim being to delay things for so long that 'congressional sub-poena authority would lapse at the end of the first session of the 102nd Congress'. See *Congressional Record*, H 6005, 7 July 1992.

[74] *Congressional Record*, H 1275, 16 Mar. 1992. Gonzalez continued that, 'given that the NSC was instrumental in setting the export policy toward Iraq, it had a strong political motive to mis-lead Congress as to the military nature of the goods sent to Iraq'.

[75] See *Congressional Record*, H 8183, 9 Sept. 1992.

pose the question as to what British constitutional law has to learn from this American experience. Before we get to that stage, however, there are still some important aspects of the Iraqgate story that remain to be told. Let us switch our attention away from Washington and towards Atlanta, Georgia.

Criminal Proceedings against BNL Employees

Christopher Drogoul was not the only employee of BNL Atlanta to be prosecuted—five of his colleagues also faced criminal proceedings—but he was the only one to be jailed.[76] Drogoul was the manager of the BNL branch in Atlanta from 1984–9. The story of his criminal trial is an illuminating and worrying one, dogged by delays and controversy from Atlanta to Washington, and arguably never satisfactorily resolved. The proceedings started in August 1989 when the FBI raided BNL's Atlanta offices, putting a stop, at last, to BNL's financial assistance to Iraq. It was to take a further eighteen months before the indictments against Drogoul were announced, on 28 February 1991, the day the Gulf war ended. Yet the Atlanta prosecutors had been ready with the indictments in early 1990, so why did they not appear until the end of February 1991? In Congress, Gonzalez asserted that this was because the state department intervened to delay the prosecution of Drogoul on the ground that prosecution of the BNL affair in early 1990 would cause serious further damage to already worsening US/Iraqi relations.[77]

The appointed trial judge, Marvin Shoob, was informed in May 1992 that Drogoul would plead guilty to all 347 charges against him, which could leave him facing 390 years in prison and restitution of $1.8 billion. The plan was, however, that Drogoul would make a statement naming all the people in Washington and Rome who were involved, making clear that he was just a small fish in a larger operation. If he was not guilty, why did Drogoul agree to this plea bargain? He was asked this question when he gave evidence to the House banking committee in September 1993. He stated that his reasons were that he was in jail with no hope of bail; he owed his lawyers several hundred thousand dollars; and he had been assigned a federal public defender who, he thought, could not cope with the case (he recited the story of the occasion when she confessed to him, after having been on the case for a year, that she did not understand the significance of an international letter of credit).[78]

The judge set the plea hearing for 2 June while the Democrats in Congress waited impatiently for the revelations Drogoul would announce and hoped that the political damage to the Bush White House would be serious.

---

[76] Drogoul's five colleagues were sentenced to terms of probation in Aug. 1992.
[77] See *Congressional Record*, H 2008, 30 Mar. 1992.
[78] House banking committee record of hearings: *Testimony of Former Employees of BNL*, serial no. 103–95 (Nov. 1993) p. 16.

However, it was not to be: a new deal was reached between Drogoul and the prosecutors the day before the hearing was due to take place—the agreement being that Drogoul would plead guilty to only sixty of the charges, face a vastly reduced sentence, spend several weeks being debriefed by government officials, and abandon his plan publicly to name names.

At the hearing the following day a furious Judge Shoob bitterly complained that the case was being 'sealed, stonewalled [and] suppressed' by the government and called for the appointment of an independent counsel under the Ethics in Government Act.[79] The judge clearly felt that Drogoul was being made into a scapegoat, and stated to Drogoul that he did not 'believe for a minute that [he had been] able to do all this on [his] own'.[80] On the same day the House judiciary committee echoed the call for an independent counsel.[81] However, George Bush's attorney general, William Barr, refused to appoint an independent counsel. Instead he appointed a private investigator, Frederick Lacey, a retired (and staunchly Republican) judge. Lacey reported within seven weeks and concluded that 'all this stuff about there being a cover-up is arrant nonsense'.[82] Barr did later inform the House judiciary committee that he would decide in December 1992 whether to review his decision. The trick here was that the relevant law—the Ethics in Government Act—was to expire in December 1992 and would first need Congress to renew it, thus taking up more time.[83]

Drogoul's sentencing hearing started in September. After some days of argument, Judge Shoob informed the lawyers that he had been shown some CIA reports which he thought showed that BNL headquarters in Rome definitely knew exactly what Drogoul was doing in Atlanta—thus undermining the crux of the prosecution case. Drogoul wanted to change his plea to not guilty, but before he could the prosecution team abandoned their plans. The daily revelations coming out of the court had so undermined the

[79] The independent counsel provisions of the Ethics in Government Act 1978, as amended, are considered in the next chapter.

[80] A. Friedman, *Spider's Web: Bush, Saddam, Thatcher and the Decade of Deceit* (London: Faber, 1993) p. 231.

[81] House Committee on the Judiciary, *Need for an Independent Counsel to Investigate US Government Assistance to Iraq*, serial no. 102–43 (June 1992).

[82] See Friedman, *Spider's Web*, pp. 244–53. The full text of the Lacey report is reproduced in a House banking committee record of hearings: *Testimony of Former Employees of BNL*, serial no. 103–95 (Nov. 1993) pp. 337–677. The Lacey report entirely exonerated the justice department. Gonzalez was extremely critical of the report, on the following grounds: (1) it was limited only to the handling of the BNL affair by the justice department; (2) Lacey totally ignored the charges that the justice and commerce departments had altered export licence information before presenting it to Congress; (3) the whole thing was absurdly rushed; (4) the appendices containing the evidence on which Lacey reportedly based his findings were classified as top secret (the highest security classification in the USA) and were still secret even in 1993.

[83] The independent counsel provisions of the Ethics in Government Act did indeed expire at the end of the 102nd Congress, and were renewed in the 103rd Congress. It is highly likely that the present Congress (the 105th) will substantially amend or possibly even repeal the provisions. This is discussed further in the next chapter.

government's case that they cancelled the plea bargain agreement and decided they would prefer to go to full trial.

Drogoul's full trial was set down for 8 September 1993, but on 2 September president Clinton's attorney general, Janet Reno, stopped the clock. She approved (yet) another plea bargain and threw out all but three minor charges against Drogoul: two counts of bank regulatory violations and one of fraud. The latter was a charge under 18 USC §1341 which provides that 'whoever, having devised . . . any scheme or artifice to defraud . . . or to loan . . . for unlawful use any counterfeit or spurious . . . security', shall be guilty of an offence. Of the two bank regulatory offences, one related specifically to the CCC programme and the other was more general. As regards the CCC, 15 USC §714m provides that 'whoever makes any false statement knowing it to be false, or whoever willfully overvalues any security, for the purpose of influencing in any way the action' of the CCC shall be guilty of an offence. Finally, 18 USC §1001 provides that 'whoever, in any matter within the jurisdiction of any department or agency of the US knowingly and willfully falsifies, conceals or covers up any trick . . . or makes any false, fictitious or fraudulent statements', shall be guilty of an offence.

The trial judge, Marvin Shoob, remained persuaded that Drogoul was not the lone operator the prosecutors had made him out to be. In remarkably forthright language he had stated in court on 5 October 1992 that the prosecutors had 'not fully investigated whether Drogoul's superiors in the bank approved of and were aware of his activities'.[84] The judge declared that 'the court concludes that officials at BNL Rome were aware and approved of Mr Drogoul's activities. At the very least BNL Rome chose to ignore what were obvious signs of Mr Drogoul's extraordinary relationship with Iraq and his unusual lending practices.'[85] In support of this statement, Judge Shoob also cited an 'extensive report' of the Italian Parliament into BNL's involvement with Iraq which had concluded that 'Drogoul was not a lone wolf' and that BNL Rome's failure adequately to supervise the Atlanta branch 'permitted the continued illegal activity'.[86]

Perhaps even more damningly, Judge Shoob went on to criticize the way in which the Bush administration had attempted improperly to 'steer this case': citing meetings between the justice department and the Italian ambassador; the cancellation on the instructions of the state department of the Atlanta

---

[84] Judge Shoob's remarks are reprinted in a House banking committee record of hearings: *Testimony of Former Employees of BNL*, serial no. 103–95 (Nov. 1993) pp. 200–33.

[85] Ibid., p. 206. BNL had a close relationship with the former Soviet Union, which, if nothing else, ought to have warned US intelligence agencies to keep a close eye on it. Indeed, the banking committee was told in evidence by a former employee of the US national security agency, the body responsible for signals intelligence in the US, that 'the likelihood of a branch of an Italian bank in Atlanta dealing with the kind of sums that were involved not coming to the attention of the US authorities would be almost zero'. See *Congressional Record*, H 2938, 9 May 1991.

[86] Ibid., p. 208.

prosecutors' 'necessary' trips to Turkey and to Italy;[87] and the 'highly unusual and inappropriate telephone calls from the White House office of legal counsel [to the local prosecutors] indicating the potential embarrassment level of the case'.[88] In the judge's words, 'it is apparent that decisions were made at the top levels of the US justice department, state department, agriculture department and within the intelligence community to shape this case and that information may have been withheld from local prosecutors ... Furthermore, the attorney general's exceptional refusal to grant the congressional request for an independent counsel in itself raises concerns for the court about the government's impartiality in handling this case.'[89] Perhaps it is only to be expected that Judge Shoob's sentiments would be echoed and repeated by Democrats in Congress, but the then ranking minority member of the House banking committee (the respected Republican Jim Leach, who since the Republicans took control of the House in 1994 has replaced Gonzalez as chairman of the banking committee) also stated that while he had little doubt that Drogoul was individually responsible for some crimes, he equally had no doubt that Drogoul was being made a 'scapegoat for other banking authorities and possibly for the American foreign policy establishment'.[90]

After Drogoul's second plea bargain (to the three counts, in September 1993) Judge Shoob, at the request of the prosecution, recused himself from the case, and it was left to his colleague Judge G. Earnest Tidwell to sentence Drogoul. Judge Tidwell announced in December 1993 the sentences that were to be imposed on Drogoul: he received a thirty-seven month prison sentence. Drogoul had already spent twenty months in jail on remand and so with good behaviour could be out of jail within a year, which indeed he was.[91] At the sentencing hearing Judge Tidwell stated that he was sentencing Drogoul to a prison term shorter than that called for by federal guidelines in part because the US government had 'actually pursued a policy of economic support to Iraq even though the creditworthiness of Iraq would not have justified such credit' and that this policy 'clearly facilitated' Drogoul's activities.[92]

---

[87] In Congress, Gonzalez had already made similar allegations: see *Congressional Record*, H 2009, 30 Mar. 1992.

[88] Judge Shoob, *supra*, n. 84, p. 210. Gonzalez had also made this allegation: he had stated in Congress in July 1992 that assistant US attorney Gail McKenzie had taken the call from the White House, and she had recorded that she had the 'impression that [they were] concerned about the embarrassment level'. See *Congressional Record*, H 6005, 7 July 1992.

[89] Ibid., p. 214.

[90] House banking committee record of hearings: *Testimony of Former Employees of BNL*, serial no. 103–95 (Nov. 1993) p. 20.

[91] Drogoul was released in late 1994.

[92] See *Atlanta Journal and Constitution*, 12 Dec. 1993, story by Peter Mantius, p. A5. Mantius covered the entire Drogoul/BNL story for the Atlanta paper, and published a book on the affair: *Shell Game: A True Story of Banking, Spies, Lies, Politics and the Arming of Saddam Hussein* (St Martin's Press, 1996).

According to newspaper reports of the four-day sentencing hearing, Judge Tidwell was evidently impatient with all sides involved in the case and 'blasted nearly everyone concerned: the government, the defence, the bank, and Mr Drogoul'. He stated that the four-year case had been a waste of resources and that 'it has been blown way out of proportion to its real significance by everybody involved in it'.[93]

The Withering of Iraqgate

In the end, while Drogoul was always pretty good at threatening to name names, and was full of assertions that BNL Rome knew that the Atlanta branch was lending such vast sums to Iraq, and that BNL was engaging in this activity not as a bank but as an innocent tool of US and Italian foreign policy, he remained short on details, evidence, and proof. Even in his extensive testimony before the House banking committee in September 1993[94] he failed to deliver the goods. For example, when Drogoul was asked by a committee member what his motivation had been in making the $5 billion loans to Iraq, Drogoul replied that he was not making the loans: BNL and the Italian government were. When he was asked what evidence he had to support this claim, Drogoul replied that he would produce it at his sentencing hearing, in three months' time.[95] Yet, when it came to the sentencing hearing in December 1993 Drogoul did not supply the evidence then either.

Just as, during his testimony to Congress, the initially packed committee room quickly emptied out once it became clear that Drogoul was not going to give details of what he alleged had been the Bush administration's daily involvement with BNL, so too did press and congressional interest in the scandal that during the 1992 presidential election campaign Al Gore had described as 'a bigger cover-up than Watergate'[96] start to wane. The reasons for this loss of interest spread beyond Drogoul's personal failure to live up to Democrat and media expectations: the fact that by then Clinton had beaten Bush may also have had something to do with Congress's loss of political stomach for another round of frustrating and time consuming (not to say expensive) investigations. What was the point now that Bush was no longer in the White House? Iraqgate, unlike the better known but probably less serious Iran/Contra scandal that had preceded it, had worked politically—there was now a Democrat in the White House, albeit one who did not share all the liberal tendencies of the Democrats on the Hill. Iran/Contra was probably

   [93] *American Banker*, 13 Dec. 1993, p. 5.
   [94] House banking committee record of hearings: *Testimony of Former Employees of BNL*, serial no. 103–95 (Nov. 1993) pp. 1–147.
   [95] Ibid., pp. 34–5.
   [96] Speech of (then) vice-presidential candidate Al Gore, 25 Oct. 1992.

another contributory factor in the withering away of Iraqgate: the American political community has a limited appetite for complex foreign policy scandal. Iran/Contra had been exhausting and almost as complicated as Iraqgate. Perhaps if Bush had won a second term in 1992 there would have been sufficient media interest in Iraqgate to sustain the investigation, but as it was there were simply too few people both within Congress and throughout the hordes of political commentators who observe and broadcast from Washington who had the energy to unravel (never mind explain) the unusually complicated factual relationship between eximbank, the CCC, BNL, and the Bush administration.

The final reason lying behind the withering of Iraqgate concerns congressional personnel. Henry Gonzalez may be a long-serving member of the House of Representatives but he is regarded by some, even from within his own party, as a marginal, somewhat idiosyncratic figure. Members of Gonzalez' staff felt that other interested House Democrats were slow to join in the banking committee's BNL investigations because of the political profile of Gonzalez. Eventually, they were able to persuade the House agriculture committee and the House judiciary committee to take a more active interest—and both of these committees held hearings into, respectively, the CCC and the justice department's involvement in the affair.[97] But there was another, more dangerous, aspect of congressional personality that played a part in the collapse of Iraqgate: namely, secret intelligence. The investigation came to an end before the Democrats lost control of the House (in the 1994 elections) because the banking committee's staff did not enjoy security clearance, and by that stage it had become quite clear that Iraqgate was about more than just banking—it involved secret intelligence and national security. Unless Congress could subpoena the papers of the CIA,[98] the NSA,[99] and the NSC,[100] the investigators knew that they would be unable to get to the bottom of the story. There is, of course, a committee in the House and a committee in the Senate, both of which are entrusted with the responsibility of intelligence oversight (the House permanent select committee on intelligence and the Senate select committee on intelligence) but neither of them could be

---

[97] See, for example, House agriculture committee record of hearings: *Iraq's Participation in Agricultural Guaranteed Loan Programs*, serial no. 102–96 (July and Sept. 1992); and House judiciary committee: *Need for an Independent Counsel to Investigate US Government Assistance to Iraq*, serial no. 102–43 (June 1992).

[98] Central Intelligence Agency, responsible for human intelligence: National Security Act 1947, 50 USC §§401–5.

[99] National Security Agency, responsible for signals intelligence: National Security Agency Act 1959, 50 USC §402 note.

[100] National Security Council, the President's advisers on national security, discussed in relation to the so-called Rostow gang, above. The NSC also has statutory provision in the National Security Act 1947: 50 USC §402 provides that its functions are 'to advise the president with respect to the integration of domestic, foreign and military policies relating to the national security'.

persuaded to open a formal investigation into Iraqgate.[101] This was the real killer: no national security scandal involving matters of secret intelligence can be successfully or fully investigated by Congress without the active support of one of the intelligence committees, and as regards Iraqgate, for reasons which only those committees know, such support was never forthcoming.

Actions under the Clinton Administration

By the time the Clinton administration arrived in Washington in January 1993 Iraqgate had fallen considerably down the agenda. Its diminishing importance was only exacerbated by the delays in appointing the new attorney general and by the consequent limbo in which the justice department found itself after the election. When Janet Reno's appointment was eventually ratified by the Senate—Reno was Clinton's third choice as attorney general[102]—one of her first tasks was to decide what to do about the continuing, if by now rather more background, noise emanating from Congress on Iraqgate. She appointed a former colleague of hers from the Miami prosecutors' office in Florida, John Hogan, to look into the justice department's BNL investigations and to report back to her as to how, if at all, the justice department should now proceed. Hogan spent four months on this task and in August 1993 informed Judge Shoob in Atlanta that he had found no evidence of any conspiracy involving anyone other than the six employees of BNL Atlanta who had already been prosecuted. The judge, whose views on the BNL affair we have already seen, predictably responded that Hogan's conclusion was one which could only be reached in 'never-never land'.[103] Hogan then closed the justice department's file on BNL.

Congress was not entirely placated, however, and, although no new evidence was produced, the mutterings refused to go away completely. As

---

[101] The only Iraqgate paper from either of these committees is a little known staff research paper written for members of the Senate intelligence committee in Feb. 1993. According to the government printing office's catalogue this report was published, but finding a copy, either on paper or on microfiche, is another story(!) There is a copy of it on microfiche in a collection published by the national security archive, a charitable organization based in the George Washington University library in Washington DC. The collection (which is available for purchase if you have $4,000 to spare) is entitled *Iraqgate: Saddam Hussein, US Policy and the Prelude to the Persian Gulf War*. The Senate staffers' report is mainly concerned with relations between the CIA and justice department prosecutors stating that the present relationship is unclear both in law and in practice—an issue which was echoed in the Scott report (see above, ch. 5). The report makes several recommendations. It does not deal with the substantive issues of CIA involvement in encouraging/orchestrating BNL Atlanta loans to Iraq, but it does reveal that there was an apparent absence of intelligence awareness of the full extent of the Iraqi procurement network until 1989–90. Again, this is reminiscent of findings made in the Scott report.

[102] The story of Clinton's difficulties in appointing an attorney general is told in P. Anderson, *Janet Reno: Doing the Right Thing* (New York: John Wiley, 1994).

[103] Ibid., p. 222.

pressure continued to build up during late 1993 and early 1994 on the Clinton administration to do more to find out what the full extent of the involvement of the Bush White House had been, it was eventually decided that Hogan would reopen the file and compile a full report, which this time would be published so as to attempt to silence any ongoing congressional criticism of the justice department. This report was finished in October 1994 and released in January 1995.[104] The Hogan report was not a complete investigation into all the allegations that had been made by Drogoul, Gonzalez, and Judge Shoob, but was confined merely to determining whether chargeable crimes could be proved beyond a reasonable doubt. It was expressly not designed to be a critique of the policy decisions taken by the Bush administration. The Hogan report stated that 'no evidence of corruption or incompetence in the conduct of the BNL investigation' had been found and that the department 'did not find evidence that US agencies or officials illegally armed Iraq or that crimes were committed through bartering of CCC commodities for military equipment'.[105]

Hogan considered several specific allegations against various officials in the Bush administration. The first set of allegations concerned misleading or obstructing Congress. The report concluded that only one instance of misleading Congress had been established (concerning the manipulation of commerce department licences for exports to Iraq) but that even here there was insufficient evidence to establish criminal intent, and so the justice department was justified in not bringing criminal proceedings.[106] Four named individuals from the Bush administration were investigated in respect of allegations of misleading Congress: in all four cases Hogan concluded that no prosecution should be brought. Kevin Brosch, former deputy assistant general counsel at the USDA, had been accused of having made misleading statements to congressional committee staff. Hogan found that there had been 'miscommunication' but that there was no evidence of 'intentional falsification' and that therefore no prosecution should be brought.[107] Richard Crowder, former under-secretary at the USDA, had been accused of having committed perjury in his testimony to the House banking committee in May 1992. Hogan found that while Crowder's answers were not entirely true (in Scott language, they did not reveal the whole picture) they were not entirely false either, and under these circumstances a criminal prosecution would be

---

[104] This report does not appear in the government printing office catalogue, but is reproduced in the collection published (on microfiche) by the national security archive, *Iraqgate: Saddam Hussein, US Policy and the Prelude to the Persian Gulf War* (op. cit., n. 101). There is also an addendum to the final Hogan report, concerning CIA involvement and co-operation with Hogan's investigations. This addendum was initially classified as top secret but has since been declassified and is also available on the national security archive microfiche collection.

[105] *BNL Task Force: Final Report*, ibid., p. 119.   [106] Ibid., p. 6.

[107] Ibid., pp. 92–8. The statutes governing misleading of Congress are considered in the next chapter.

inappropriate.[108] Iain Baird, former director of the commerce department's office of export licensing, had been accused of having hosted a 'party' at which relevant documents which were sought by Congress were shredded. Hogan's report is heavily redacted in the passages considering these allegations, and it is consequently impossible to know the reasons for Hogan's recommendation that no further action needed to be taken.[109] Finally, Dennis Kloske, former under-secretary at the commerce department, had been accused of manipulating written evidence given by his former department to Congress. The evidence concerned the descriptions of US goods which had been shipped to Iraq under export licences granted by the commerce department. Kloske had changed the phrase 'military vehicles' on one of the export licences to 'vehicles designed for military use' and then he had further changed that phrase to the sole word 'vehicles' and the phrase 'commercial utility cargo vehicles'. The inspector-general of the commerce department had described these changes as 'unjustified and misleading' but Hogan concluded—rather mysteriously—that because Kloske appeared to be acting alone, and not on the instructions of the White House or of the Rostow gang, that the changes he had made did not constitute 'corrupt behaviour' and therefore no criminal proceedings should be commenced.[110]

The second main issue considered in the Hogan report was the role that had been played by the intelligence community, and in particular by the CIA. This issue was dealt with in a carefully worded addendum to the main report, in which it was stated that:

while we benefited from extensive co-operation and assistance from the CIA . . . the CIA's ability to retrieve information is limited. Records are 'compartmentalized' to prevent unauthorized disclosure; only some of these records are retrievable through computer databases . . . not all information is recorded. In the course of our work we learned of 'sensitive compartments' of information not normally retrievable and of specialized offices that previously were unknown to the CIA personnel who were assisting us. In one instance it took the CIA two months to identify the intended recipient country of weapons shipped at the CIA's request. Limitations on the CIA's ability to retrieve information preclude complete confidence that we have seen all relevant records. I do not believe this uncertainty severely undermined our investigation.[111]

---

[108] *BNL Task Force: Final Report*, pp. 98–101. Crowder had been asked whether he had had any information indicating that he should not proceed with CCC sales to Iraq in 1990. He replied, 'No'. According to Hogan, this answer ('No') was ambiguous. It could have meant that Crowder did not have any *official* information, or it could have meant that Crowder had heard nothing to raise his suspicions, whether from official sources or not. In fact, Crowder had heard (unofficial) gossip that Iraq was misusing its CCC resources, but he evidently did not consider such gossip to be 'information'.

[109] See ibid., pp. 101–2.   [110] Ibid., pp. 103–12.

[111] Declassified addendum to Hogan report (available on the national security archive microfiche collection, *Iraqgate: Saddam Hussein, US Policy and the Prelude to the Persian Gulf War*), pp. 2–3.

Again, this indicates that even in a culture of (relatively) open government, and even when it is merely another government department, not a hostile, alien body such as Congress or an independent judicial inquiry, it is still difficult authoritatively to establish what members of the intelligence community knew, when they knew it, and who they told.[112]

The Hogan report was the penultimate chapter of the Iraqgate affair in the USA. The final chapter came the month following the release of the report. On 15 December 1992 BNL had filed a lawsuit in the US court of federal claims in Washington DC, seeking recovery of over $340 million on defaulted loans to Iraq that were guaranteed under the CCC programme.[113] After the Hogan report had been published, the justice department announced in February 1995 that the US government would pay almost $400 million to BNL. Gonzalez issued a critical press release on behalf of the American taxpayer who was to foot the bill,[114] the usual handful of political columnists inserted a small piece in their respective papers low down on a page well into their news sections, and that was that: the end of an affair.

It is important to stress that Iraqgate did not collapse as a political scandal because it was established by the executive branch that the allegations that Gonzalez, Shoob, and others had made had been proved to be unfounded. Neither the Lacey nor the Hogan reports even addressed, never mind dismissed, the bulk of the allegations as outlined in this chapter about either the merits of the policy of allowing financial institutions in the US to support Iraq's arms procurement network; or what the position of the US intelligence community was; or the constitutional questions which were raised by the affair in terms of executive information and Congress, and so on. A former senior adviser to the deputy secretary of state in the Bush administration published a short article in *Foreign Policy* in 1994 entitled 'The Myth of Iraqgate' in which he sought to dismiss the idea that there had ever been either a failure of policy before 1990 or an attempted cover-up after 1990.[115] Yet the only substantive point that the author is able to make is that some commentators misconstrued the mechanisms of the CCC programme and alleged— wrongly—that CCC granted loans to Iraq, when in fact it did not: it granted credit to Iraq. This is an important detail, but it is only a detail. Surely the main point is that the vast amounts of CCC credit that were awarded to Iraq allowed the desperate Iraqi economy to free up resources (i.e. cash), that would without CCC assistance have had to have been spent on food, to be

---

[112] This is also reminiscent of Scott's concerns that his inquiry had not got to the bottom of certain aspects of the story it was investigating, especially with regard to supergun.

[113] See *Congressional Record*, H 134, 21 Jan. 1993.

[114] Gonzalez' press release stated that 'this enormous taxpayer loss is yet another sad and costly illustration of the Reagan and Bush administrations' policy of coddling Saddam Hussein . . . [The BNL] guarantees would never have been made if Iraq's credit worthiness had been honestly considered, or even if the administration had cared about the brutality of the Iraqi regime.'

[115] Kenneth I. Juster, 'The Myth of Iraqgate', 94 *Foreign Policy* 105 (1994).

spent instead on arms procurement. Is that not the nature of credit? Just because the terms 'credit' and 'loans' were confused does not mean that Iraqgate was a myth. Neither Hogan, nor Lacey, nor the *Foreign Policy* article have been able to establish that the story of Iraqgate was a fictional one.

But despite the fact that Iraqgate ultimately failed to make it as a grade one political scandal in the USA, from the perspective of British constitutional law there is still much to learn both from the story of BNL and from the American constitutional reaction to the story, matters which are dealt with in the next chapter.

7

Implications of the Iraqgate Story

THERE are a number of issues of American constitutional law and practice which are called into question by the story of Iraqgate. These issues are examined in this chapter; and in the last section of the chapter, we will turn to what it is that the British constitution might learn from this American experience. The substantive issues raised in this chapter revolve around the following questions: what powers does Congress have to investigate the executive branch? What constitutional powers does the executive branch have to protect itself from congressional investigation which it deems to be either unnecessary, unconstitutional, or undesirable? If the constitutional answer to these questions leaves the delicate issue of executive oversight on national security matters in a state of unresolved 'balance' between the branches, what role does that leave for the third branch—the judiciary and what further, independent or autonomous, institutions are involved?

Congressional Investigations

Nowhere in the United States constitution is it expressly provided that Congress has the authority to investigate, yet congressional investigations have become a central feature of the contemporary American political landscape, and they have a long history—dating back as far as 1792. The authority which Congress does enjoy under the constitution is the power to legislate: the opening words of the first section of the first article of the US constitution provide that 'all legislative powers herein granted shall be vested in a Congress of the United States, which shall consist of a Senate and House of Representatives'. Article I then goes on to make provision for the composition and election of the Senate and the House, and as to legislative procedure. Section 8 of article I contains a list of matters on which Congress (rather than the States) has the power to legislate, ending with the clause: 'Congress shall have the power . . . to make all laws which shall be necessary and proper for carrying into execution the foregoing powers . . .' but even this clause is still referring only to legislative powers, not expressly to investigatory powers.[1]

---

[1] In his floor statements on Iraqgate Henry Gonzalez would occasionally refer to Congress's constitutional powers. His view was that Congress had three great constitutional powers: the power to declare war, the power of the purse, and the right to know, and that of these only the third now remains in Congress's hands. Gonzalez described it as 'the power to know, the power

From a modern perspective this looks like a considerable omission, for, as former US president Woodrow Wilson argued, legislative oversight of the executive branch is just as important in a presidential system as it is in a parliamentary one.[2]

It has taken the supreme court to provide authority for congressional investigations—or rather to clarify that the constitution does in law provide such authority even though it does not say so expressly. The leading case is *McGrain* v. *Daugherty*.[3] This case concerned a congressional investigation into the conduct of the justice department under attorney general Daugherty, who challenged the constitutionality of the investigation. The court unanimously held that the investigation fell within Congress's constitutional authority, as 'power of inquiry . . . is an essential and appropriate auxiliary to the legislative function' and further that, in pursuit of its investigations, Congress may 'compel a private individual to appear before it or one of its committees and give testimony needed to enable it efficiently to exercise' its legislative constitutional role.[4] This case makes it clear that although Congress does have extensive constitutional powers to investigate, powers which include the right to compel oral and written testimony, these powers are not unlimited. They must be exercised in accordance with some notion of legislative need. Thus, when a legal challenge is made to the constitutionality of any particular congressional investigation, that challenge will focus on the question of whether, in its investigation, Congress was inquiring into something on which it had a potential legislative interest. Congress has no power to inquire for inquiry's sake, unlike departmental select committees of Parliament, which may inquire into any aspect of the 'expenditure, administration or policy' of the relevant government department.[5]

In *McGrain* v. *Daugherty*, the court held that the investigation (into whether the attorney general and the department of justice were properly directing themselves) did concern a subject on which legislation could be enacted and whose formulation would be materially aided by the information

to search out and get the information that a wise lawmaker and a just lawmaker and an honest lawmaker must have in order to render a judgment in the perfecting of the rules and the laws that will make the policy for our constituents'. See *Congressional Record*, H 2007, 30 Mar. 1992. See also Gonzalez, 'The Relinquishment of Co-Equality by Congress', 29 *Harv. J Legis.* 331 (1992).

[2] In *Congressional Government* (first published in 1885) Wilson stated that in a system of government based on the separation of powers, quite 'as important as legislation is vigilant oversight of administration'.

[3] 273 US 135 (1927).   [4] Ibid., pp. 174–5.

[5] In Congress there is no formal distinction between legislative committees and investigatory committees to mirror the distinction in Parliament between standing and select committees. That is not to say, however, that all congressional committees are identical: some (e.g. the budget committees) will in practice have more legislating and less investigating to do than others (such as e.g. the controversial House Committee on Un-American Activities (HUAC) in the 1950s, on which more below). See generally, C. Tiefer, *Congressional Practice and Procedure* (Westport: Greenwood Press, 1989) and L. N. Rieselbach, *Congressional Politics: The Evolving Legislative System* (Boulder: Westview, 2nd edn., 1995) esp ch. 4.

which the investigation was designed to elicit. The court stated that it was to be presumed that the object of Congress in ordering an investigation is to aid it in legislating. It is not a valid objection to such investigation that it might disclose wrongdoing or a crime by a public officer. The resolution of the Senate which had authorized the establishment of the investigation had stated that testimony from witnesses would be sought with the purpose of obtaining 'information necessary as a basis for such legislative and other action as the Senate may deem necessary and proper'. This resolution was taken by the court to support its inference of a legislative object. In delivering the judgment of the court, Van Deventer J ruled that: 'a legislative body cannot legislate wisely or effectively in the absence of information respecting the conditions which the legislation is intended to affect or change; and where the body does not itself possess the requisite information—which not infrequently is true—recourse must be had to others who do possess it. Experience has taught that mere requests for such information often are unavailing . . . so some means of compulsion are essential.'[6] Thus, even though the text of the constitution is silent on the question of congressional powers to investigate and to call witnesses, Congress possesses 'not only such powers as are expressly granted to [it] by the constitution, but such auxiliary powers as are necessary and appropriate to make the express powers effective'.[7] Even in the written constitution, not everything constitutional is written down in the constitution.

The limitations on these congressional powers, limitations which can be enforced by the courts (these are not 'political questions' within the meaning of *Baker* v. *Carr*[8]), are exemplified in the early case of *Kilbourn* v. *Thompson*,[9] a case which remains important even though more recent decisions have raised questions about aspects of the court's approach.[10] Kilbourn had refused to answer questions put to him by a House committee which was investigating a real estate partnership in which Kilbourn was involved. He had also refused to provide the committee with certain books and papers which the committee had requested. The House imprisoned Kilbourn for forty-five days. He sued for damages. The supreme court held that although the House has the power to punish its own members for disorderly conduct and although it may fine or imprison contumacious witnesses,[11] there is no constitutional power vested in either the House or in the Senate generally to punish for contempt. In reaching this decision the court looked at the English position (where Parliament does have such a power) but found that Parliament's powers were unique to it and stemmed from its unusual history

---

[6] 273 US 135 at p. 175.   [7] Ibid., at p. 173.   [8] 369 US 186 (1962).
[9] 103 US 168 (1880).
[10] See, for example, Frankfurter J in *US* v. *Rumely* 345 US 41, at p. 46 (1953), discussed below.
[11] Contumacious means deliberately or wilfully uncooperative. Contumacious witnesses and contempt of Congress are considered further below.

as a court of judicature and that these were not general powers of legislatures shared by Congress.

The committee which had called Kilbourn as a witness was investigating a real estate pool in the District of Columbia the affairs of which were in litigation before the bankruptcy court. The court ruled that the subject-matter of the investigation was judicial and not legislative. It was pending before the proper court and there existed no power in Congress, on the allegation that an insolvent debtor of the United States was interested in a private business partnership, to investigate the affairs of that partnership, and consequently there was no authority to compel the witness to testify on that subject. Congress could not constitutionally inquire into the private affairs of individuals where the investigation could result in no valid legislation on the subject. Therefore the order of the House compelling imprisonment was void.

In the context of the banking committee's investigations into Iraqgate, Gonzalez was fully aware of these constitutional limitations on his committee's powers of inquiry, and in his floor statements he frequently stressed that, contrary to popular Republican opinion, his interest in BNL was not merely a partisan attempt to undermine the credibility of the Bush White House but was properly underpinned with legislative interest. This is borne out by the passage in December 1991 of the Foreign Bank Supervision Enhancement Act, a piece of legislation which amended and strengthened the powers of the US banking regulatory system under the International Banking Act of 1978, amendments which the banking committee saw fit to promote as a result of its investigations into BNL Atlanta.[12]

Congressional Committees, Reluctant Witnesses, and Constitutional Rights

Kilbourn v. *Thompson* concerned a congressional investigation which was held not to be for a legislative purpose. What of the case where Congress is investigating a matter which falls within its legislative agenda, and thus the investigation is itself constitutional, but where the witness does not cooperate? One of the most important sanctions which Congress has is that both Congress and its committees may issue subpoenas compelling the attendance of witnesses. Although the text of the constitution itself is again silent on this point the supreme court has found that the power to subpoena is an 'indispensable ingredient' of the legislative powers granted to Congress by the constitution.[13] Failure to comply with a subpoena will amount to a contempt. But how can this sanction be enforced? How can its enforcement be balanced against the witness's constitutional rights, most notably the protection

---

[12] This legislation is codified at 12 USC §3101.
[13] *Eastland* v. *US Servicemen's Fund* 421 US 491, at p. 505 (1975), discussed further below.

guaranteed in the fifth amendment's privilege against self-incrimination clause?[14]

There are a number of various legal provisions which may apply. Three statutes apply specifically to Congress and its rights to information. First, under the law of perjury it is a felony to lie to Congress under oath.[15] Secondly, it is a misdemeanour improperly to withhold testimony or papers in 'any matter under inquiry before either House' or any committee of either House of Congress.[16] This is the criminal contempt of congress statute, first enacted in 1857. It provides that 'every person who having been summoned as a witness by the authority of either House of Congress to give testimony or to produce papers upon any matter under inquiry before either House . . . or any committee . . . wilfully makes default, or who, having appeared, refuses to answer any question pertinent to the question under inquiry' is guilty of an offence, for which the maximum punishment is a fine of $1,000 and/or one year's imprisonment. Thirdly, it is an offence to endeavour corruptly to obstruct the proper exercise of Congress's powers of inquiry.[17] In addition, the false statement statute prohibits the making of materially false statements and the wrongful concealment of material facts in 'any matter within the jurisdiction of any department or agency of the United States'.[18] In addition to these statutory provisions, Congress also enjoys inherent powers of contempt of Congress. These powers were widely used historically, although they have not been employed since 1932. Under this procedure a committee may adopt a resolution requesting the presiding officer of the chamber to issue an arrest warrant, to be executed by the serjeant-at-arms. A witness failing to comply with this warrant may be imprisoned if the full chamber adopts a resolution to that effect. The witness must be released if he complies with the subpoena.[19]

[14] 'No person . . . shall be compelled in any criminal case to be a witness against himself.'

[15] 18 USC §1621.

[16] 2 USC §192. Under this Act Congress may seek judicially imposed sanctions. The procedure is for the relevant committee to report on the witness's failure to comply with a subpoena to the full chamber, which then votes on whether to cite the witness for contempt.

[17] 18 USC §1505. See *US* v. *Mitchell* 877 F 2d 294 (4th Cir., 1989) in which it was held that corruptly was to be broadly interpreted, as the statute was drafted with an eye to the variety of corrupt methods by which the proper work of Congress may be impeded or thwarted—the means of corruption do not themselves need to be illegal for the behaviour to fall within the statute.

[18] 18 USC §1001. In *US* v. *Barenblatt* 348 US 503 (1955), discussed below, the supreme court held that 'department' was not confined to the executive branch but included the legislative and judicial branches as well. As a result of this ruling, the more specific statutes have been used much less frequently since 1955. It has been argued that *Barenblatt* was a mistake, as it has rendered §1001 too open-ended and uncertain in scope: for a lengthy analysis, see Peter W. Morgan, 'The Undefined Crime of Lying to Congress: Ethics Reform and the Rule of Law', 86 *NWU L Rev.* 177 (1992).

[19] See generally Todd T. Peterson, 'Prosecuting Executive Branch Officials for Contempt of Congress', 66 *NYU L Rev.* 563 (1991) at p. 566. As a final alternative, Congress may file a civil action in the federal district court to enforce subpoenas issued by the Senate (but, oddly, not by the House): the Ethics in Government Act (28 USC §1365) empowers the congressional offices of legal counsel to do this. If the witness refuses to comply with the court order, this is a contempt of court. This provision does not apply, however, to officers or employees of the federal government acting within their official capacities: 28 USC §1365(a).

An early example of Congress's inherent contempt power is the case of *Anderson* v. *Dunn*.[20] Anderson had been arrested and brought before the House to answer contempt charges. He sued the serjeant-at-arms for assault and battery and false imprisonment. The supreme court upheld the trial court's dismissal of the case, ruling that Congress had inherent constitutional authority to punish contempts in order to protect its ability to carry out its legislative function. The court stated that the argument that Congress lacked power to punish contempts 'leads to the total annihilation of the power of the House . . . to guard itself from contempts, and leaves it exposed to every indignity and interruption that rudeness, caprice, or even conspiracy may mediate against it. . . . That a deliberative assembly, clothed with the majesty of the people, and charged with the care of all that is dear to them . . . should not possess the power to suppress rudeness, or repel insult, is a supposition too wild to be suggested.'[21]

The limitations on this power are illustrated by *Marshall* v. *Gordon*.[22] Here, the House sought to punish an individual (who was not a member of the House) for contempt after he had published a letter which he had sent to a House committee chairman. The chairman, and the House, considered the letter to be 'ill-tempered and irritating'. The supreme court ruled that although the House does have the power to punish non-members for contempt, its actions here were 'without constitutional justification'. While the letter was 'offensive and vexatious' it was not 'calculated or likely to affect the House in any of its proceedings or in the exercise of any of its functions'.[23] This case illustrates that Congress's contempt powers are not to be used frivolously: they are severe measures, and are designed only as a means of institutional self-preservation.[24]

Of greater practical importance than these inherent powers, especially in more recent times, has been the statutory offence of criminal contempt of congress. A number of cases from the 1950s arising out of the infamous investigations into so-called 'un-American activities' illustrate the extent of Congress's powers under this statute. In *Quinn* v. *US*[25] Quinn had been summoned to testify before a congressional committee where he was asked whether he was or had been a member of the communist party. He refused to answer, citing generally the first and fifth amendments as justifications for his silence (admitting membership of the communist party could have incriminated Quinn). The committee did not ask him to specify or to state more clearly the precise ground for his refusal to answer and did not overrule his objections to the questions. Quinn was not directed by the committee to

---

[20] 6 Wheat. (19 US) 204 (1821).
[21] Ibid., at pp. 228–9. As Peterson points out, the Court cited no constitutional or common law to support this conclusion. See *supra* n. 19, p. 609.
[22] 243 US 521 (1916).
[23] Ibid. Cited in *McGrain* v. *Daugherty* 273 US 135 at p. 173.   [24] Ibid., at p. 542.
[25] 349 US 155 (1955).

answer its questions. Yet he was tried for contempt of congress.[26] The case reached the supreme court, which ruled that Quinn should have been acquitted. The court based its decision on two grounds. The first concerned Quinn's 'claiming of the fifth': it had been argued that Quinn had not done enough to establish what precisely it was in respect of which he was claiming the privilege against self-incrimination, and that neither had he explained why he was claiming the fifth. Rejecting these arguments, the court ruled that no special form of words was required and that by citing the fifth amendment Quinn had done enough to protect himself. The court stated that the amendment should be construed liberally in favour of the right it was intended to secure. The court's second ground for ruling in Quinn's favour was that on the facts there was insufficient evidence that Quinn had had a deliberate intention of refusing to answer—such an intention being an essential element of the offence under §192. The committee had not made it clear to Quinn that it considered that he had not sufficiently answered its questions: a committee must fully apprise a witness of its views before a §192 offence can be committed. In giving this ruling, the Warren court (Warren CJ delivered the opinion of the court) was anxious to make it clear that the judgment in this case did not mean that congressional committees would be left defenceless in the face of a devious scheming witness, but, before a committee could seek to rely on criminal provisions, it had to do more to inquire into the basis of a witness claiming the fifth, which this committee had not done.[27]

In *Watkins* v. *US*[28] Watkins, like Quinn a former witness before the House committee on un-American activities (HUAC), was convicted of an offence under §192. Before HUAC Watkins had testified freely about his own activities and associations, but had refused to answer questions as to whether he had known certain other persons to have been members of the communist party, on the ground that such questions were outside the scope of the committee's brief. This was found to be a contempt under §192. Watkins challenged this finding, arguing that he could not be found to be in contempt of Congress if Congress had failed to make sufficiently clear what the legislative purpose of the committee's hearings was. Thus the question for the court became: how was the scope or legislative purpose of the committee's work to be determined? Each committee, whether of the House or of the Senate, is established by a resolution of the full chamber. The court found that in this case, the House resolution establishing HUAC was vague and did not clearly outline the committee's tasks with precision.[29] Neither were the committee's

---

[26] Under 2 USC §192.   [27] 349 US 155 at pp. 164–5.   [28] 354 US 178 (1957).
[29] The *Watkins* Court was very critical of this, stating that in authorizing an investigation by a committee it is essential that the Senate or House should spell out the committee's jurisdiction and purpose with sufficient particularity to ensure that compulsory process is used only in furtherance of a legislative purpose. The importance of the resolution establishing the committee's investigations is illustrated by *US* v. *Rumely* 345 US 41 (1953). In this case, Rumely was the secretary of an organization which sold political books. He refused to disclose to a congressional

past practices or the statements of its chairman of any help. As a result, the supreme court held that Watkins had not been given a fair opportunity to determine whether he had been within his rights to refuse to answer the committee's questions and his conviction was therefore invalid under the due process clause of the fifth amendment.[30] In coming to this conclusion the court ruled that it cannot simply be assumed that 'every congressional investigation is justified by a public need that overbalances any private rights affected, [since to] do so would be to abdicate the responsibility placed by the constitution upon the judiciary to ensure that Congress does not unjustifiably encroach upon an individual's right of privacy nor abridge his liberty of speech'.[31] In an important passage, the court further stated that 'there is no congressional power to expose for the sake of exposure'. Congress's legitimate powers 'cannot be inflated into a general power to expose where the predominant result can only be an invasion of the private rights of individuals'.[32]

Watkins was distinguished in *Barenblatt* v. *US*, another HUAC-related supreme court decision.[33] Barenblatt was another HUAC witness. He had been a teaching fellow at the University of Michigan (by the time he appeared before HUAC his four-year fixed term contract had expired and had not been renewed). Barenblatt refused to answer questions as to whether he was or had been a member of the communist party. He did not seek to rely on the privilege against self-incrimination but objected generally to the committee's inquiries into his 'political and religious beliefs [and his] personal or private affairs or associational activities'.[34] Barenblatt was convicted of contempt of Congress under §192, and the supreme court (by five votes to four) upheld his conviction. He was jailed for six months and fined $250. In upholding Barenblatt's conviction, the majority of the supreme court held that the committee's long history had made clear by the end of the 1950s what it was for: its legislative purpose could no longer be regarded as vague. The rules of the House of Representatives[35] stated that the committee was concerned with national security and with the implications for national security of communist activity in the US, including in educational circles. Unlike Watkins,

---

committee the names of those who made bulk purchases. He was convicted under §192. On appeal, the supreme court ruled that the committee had had no authority to seek this information: the resolution establishing the work of the committee was concerned with 'political lobbying' which was materially different, the court ruled, from selling books, or attempting 'to saturate the thinking of the community', as it was put in the case (at p. 47).

[30] 'No person . . . shall be deprived of life, liberty or property, without due process of law.'
[31] 354 US 178 at pp. 198–9.   [32] Ibid., p. 200.   [33] 360 US 109 (1959).
[34] Barenblatt based his objections on the first, ninth, and tenth amendments. The first amendment provides, *inter alia*, that 'Congress shall make no law . . . abridging the freedom of speech . . . or the right of the people peaceably to assemble.' The ninth amendment provides that 'the enumeration in the constitution of certain rights shall not be construed to deny or disparage others retained by the people'. The tenth amendment provides that 'the powers not delegated to the United States by the constitution . . . are reserved to the States respectively, or to the people'.
[35] The court relied on rule XI, 83rd Congress.

Barenblatt had been fully apprised of the pertinency of the committee's questions to its constitutional function. Further, the committee was not questioning the contents of academic lectures: it was merely trying to establish the extent of communist activity on campus. This was a valid legislative purpose, according to the majority: this was not a case of exposure for the sake of exposure. On these facts, the balance between individual rights and government interests had to be struck in favour of the government—the first amendment had not been transgressed.

The proper constitutional relationship between the court and Congress was further delineated in *Eastland* v. *US Servicemen's Fund*[36] in 1975. The Senate subcommittee on internal security had been reviewing the Internal Security Act 1950. During the course of its investigations, the subcommittee had inquired into USSF activities to determine whether they were potentially harmful to the morale of the US armed forces (the USSF was a focus for expression of dissent concerning US involvement in South East Asia; it organized 'coffeehouses' near military bases in the US and published a newspaper). The subcommittee issued a subpoena to the USSF's bankers, ordering production of all the bank's records involving the USSF's accounts. The USSF brought an action to have the subpoena overturned. The court of appeals stated that although the court should hesitate to interfere with congressional actions even where first amendment rights were implicated, such restraint should not preclude judicial review where there were no alternative means of relief available. Here, as the USSF's rights under the first amendment would be violated if the subpoena were obeyed, the court would intervene. The supreme court reversed, holding that the subcommittee's activities fell within the 'legitimate legislative sphere' and were therefore protected under the speech and debate clause[37] from being questioned in any place other than Congress. The committee's activities were therefore immune from judicial interference. Burger CJ, giving the opinion of the court, stated that 'the wisdom of congressional approach or methodology is not open to judicial veto . . . Nor is the legitimacy of a congressional inquiry to be defined by what it produces. The very nature of the investigatory function—like any research—is that it takes the searchers up some "blind alleys" and into non-productive enterprises. To be a valid legislative inquiry there need be no predictable end result.'[38]

---

[36] 421 US 491 (1975).

[37] US constitution, art. 1, s. 6: 'the Senators and Representatives . . . for any speech or debate in either House . . . shall not be questioned in any other place'.

[38] Ibid., at p. 509. The same is generally true for State legislatures. State legislatures in the US are governed by their own State constitutions, but there is some supreme court case-law which seeks to lay down some general principles. These, for the most part, echo the court's jurisprudence on the constitutional authority and rights of Congress: see, e.g., *Tenney* v. *Brandhove* 341 US 367 (1951); *Sweezy* v. *New Hampshire* 354 US 234 (1957); and *Uphaus* v. *Wyman* 360 US 72 (1959).

In addition to the various contempt powers vested in Congress, either inherently or by statute, Congress also enjoys one further power to secure testimony from reluctant witnesses. If a witness claims protection under the fifth amendment, that is not necessarily an end to the matter. A 1970 enactment provides that where a witness claims the fifth before a congressional committee, the chairman of that committee may order the witness to answer, and the witness may not then refuse, although 'no testimony or other information compelled under the order . . . may be used against the witness in any criminal case, except a prosecution for perjury'.[39] The constitutionality of this provision was challenged in *US* v. *Kastigar*[40] but the supreme court found that the enactment did not violate the constitution. This provision was central to the criminal prosecution of Oliver North in the Iran/Contra scandal. North challenged some of the evidence on which the independent counsel[41] prosecuting him was seeking to rely, on the ground that some of it derived from testimony he had been forced to give before Congress. The court of appeals for the DC circuit, in a controversial judgment,[42] held that *Kastigar* requires the independent counsel to establish that 'all the evidence it proposes to use was derived from legitimate independent sources'.[43] To allow this to be demonstrated, courts should hold a '*Kastigar* hearing' at which the prosecutors can establish an independent source for each item of evidence. As this had not occurred in North's case, his convictions could not stand and the court of appeals remanded the case to the district court. Wald CJ dissented from this judgment, arguing that the insistence on a 'line by line, item by item' *Kastigar* hearing 'represents an overblown interpretation of the *Kastigar* case'.[44]

Congressional Committees and the Executive Branch: Executive Privilege

For our purposes these cases establish two basic aspects of the constitutional backdrop to congressional investigations. On the one hand, they make it clear that when conducting their investigations, congressional committees must act in accordance with the constitutional rights of individual witnesses. On the

---

[39] 18 USC §6002.   [40] 406 US 441 (1971).

[41] The independent counsel is a prosecuting authority which is independent of executive branch (justice department) prosecutors. Independent counsel are appointed under the Ethics in Government Act 1978 (28 USC §591) to investigate and if appropriate to prosecute high-ranking government officials. The independent counsel is discussed further, below, as is the Iran/Contra affair.

[42] *US* v. *North* 910 F 2d 843 (1990); modified in part at 920 F 2d 940 (1991).

[43] Ibid., at p. 854.

[44] Ibid., at p. 924. Wald CJ stated that the requirement was that trials should be fair, not perfect. For conflicting arguments about *Kastigar* and *North*, see R. S. Ghio, 'The Iran/Contra Prosecutions and the Failure of Use Immunity', 45 *Stan. L Rev.* 229 (1992) and M. Gilbert, 'The Future of Congressional Use Immunity After US v North', 30 *Am. Crim. L Rev.* 417 (1993). See also Akhil Reed Amar, *The Constitution and Criminal Procedure: First Principles* (New Haven: Yale UP, 1997) ch. 2, esp. pp. 57–61.

other hand, it is also clear that the judicial branch has a significant role to play in setting the boundaries of Congress's powers. Most of the cases considered in the previous section, however, concerned private individuals rather than members of the executive branch. What of the situation, more closely associated with the circumstances surrounding the Scott and Gonzalez stories, where the government (executive branch) is directly involved? If the fifth and sometimes also the first amendments can be seen on occasion to protect reluctant individual witnesses, what constitutional or other protection is accorded to the executive branch? There is less case-law on this issue than there is on the question of Congress and individual rights[45] but there are two main constitutional developments to address: first the question of executive privilege, and secondly the issue of classification of documents and freedom of information.

The concept of executive privilege is similar in effect, but broader than, the doctrine of public interest immunity in English law. Executive privilege relates not only to government information in court, but also to government information and Congress. The executive branch in the US can claim executive privilege in response to and as a means of avoiding compliance with a congressional subpoena for written documents or oral testimony. Among the more common grounds on which executive privilege is claimed in response to congressional subpoenas are national security, confidentiality of presidential communications, protection of provisional governmental opinions, and the secrecy of the files of law enforcement agencies (such as the department of justice and the FBI).[46]

Although there are some judicial precedents on executive privilege and Congress—which we shall examine in a moment—at least until recently executive privilege disputes between the executive and Congress were more normally resolved through political means rather than in court. The lack of clear legal procedures for resolving claims of executive privilege made in response to congressional demands for information may call into question the customary belief that the US government is one of laws: as Peter Shane has written, 'the more Congress's access to information about the executive branch seems subject to vagaries of politics, rather than to processes of law, the greater the apparent gap between our ideals of government accountability

[45] Which itself is interesting. On the one hand this is indicative of American constitutional law in general: the overall trend being one of greater judicial involvement in matters of the individual and the state as opposed to questions of the structure of government. But in this instance, it may also mark a reluctance on the part of the legislative and executive branches to involve the judges. Such a reluctance is not so widely shared with private individuals, who may be readier to use the courts in political battles with branches of the state. We will return to this point later.

[46] See generally, R. Berger, *Executive Privilege: A Constitutional Myth* (1974); Cox, 'Executive Privilege', 122 *U Pa. L Rev.* 1383 (1974); Freund, 'Foreword: On Presidential Privilege', 88 *Harv. L Rev.* 13 (1974); Sofaer, 'Executive Privilege: An Historical Note', 75 *Colum. L Rev.* 1318 (1975).

and the reality of government practice'.[47] We will return to this point and to its implications a little later. In the meantime, we should first examine how the politics of executive privilege claims against Congress have in practice worked themselves out. One leading example occurred in 1975, when president Nixon's secretary of state, Henry Kissinger, became the first cabinet member to be cited by a congressional committee for contempt of Congress. This involved a row over access by the House committee on intelligence to papers from the state department concerning covert activities sponsored by the national security council. Before the full House could vote on the contempt charge, however, the disagreement had been resolved through a negotiated compromise between Kissinger and the committee. Similarly, in 1981 secretary of the interior James Watt was subpoenaed to provide the House energy and commerce subcommittee with documents relating to Canadian companies' allegedly discriminatory practices under the Mineral Lands Leasing Act. President Reagan invoked executive privilege, and the committee held two days of hearings on the matter before a compromise agreement was reached whereby committee members could see the relevant papers for a short time and take notes from them, but not photocopy them. There are many further similar stories—other examples of congressional committees making a provisional citing of contempt in response to a claim of executive privilege, only for a negotiated settlement to be reached before the contempt citation can be voted on by the full House.[48]

Confirmation hearings in the Senate can also turn into battles between the legislative and executive branches over access to information and executive privilege. In 1986, for example, president Reagan nominated William Rehnquist to become chief justice of the supreme court. In its confirmation hearings, the Senate judiciary committee wanted access to papers concerning Rehnquist's position in the Nixon administration at the department of justice. Reagan claimed executive privilege, and the committee threatened to delay the hearings. The two sides negotiated and reached a compromise settlement: the Reagan administration conceding to a more narrowly focused request for documents. The hearings progressed and Rehnquist was later duly confirmed as chief justice. Similar problems, with similar solutions, were encountered by Reagan's successor in the White House, George Bush. Bush was concerned, for example, about the adverse publicity surrounding the lengthy confirmation hearings in the Senate of his nominee to the supreme court, Clarence Thomas, and his nominee as director of central intelligence at

---

[47] Peter Shane, 'Legal Disagreement and Negotiation in a Government of Laws: The Case of Executive Privilege Claims against Congress', 71 *Minnesota Law Review* 461, at p. 462 (1987).

[48] Other episodes involved the secretary of commerce, Roger Morton, in 1975; the secretary of energy, Charles Duncan, in 1980; and the secretary of energy, James Edwards, in 1981. See generally J. D. Bush, 'Congressional-Executive Access Disputes: Legal Standards and Political Settlements', 9 *J L & Politics* 719, at pp. 736–8 (1993).

the CIA, Robert Gates, as a result of which he proposed to limit Senators' access, among other things, to FBI files they were using. The Senate committees consequently resolved to conduct their own background investigations, which would have the effect of considerably slowing down the confirmation process, as a swift result of which Bush reversed his policy, and both Thomas and Gates were duly confirmed.[49]

So much for the politics. Although this might be the preferred approach to solving disagreements between Congress and the executive branch there have been occasions when the courts have been called in to adjudicate, although the supreme court has not (yet) adjudicated an executive privilege claim directly involving Congress. Such judicial precedents as there are 'set forth no bright-line rules of law, but they do provide some general guidelines for consideration of the constitutional issues' involved.[50] In *Senate Select Committee on Presidential Campaign Activities* v. *Nixon*,[51] a subpoena for the so-called Nixon tapes had been issued by the Senate Watergate committee. The tapes were recordings of five conversations between Nixon and his former counsel, John Dean. Executive privilege was claimed in support of the administration's decision not to provide the committee with the tapes. The Nixon administration argued that for the recordings to be made public would be inconsistent with 'the confidentiality essential to the functioning of the office of president'.[52] The committee challenged this use of executive privilege on the basis that the tapes were 'vitally and immediately needed if the select committee's mandate and responsiblities . . . are to be fulfilled'.[53] The court of appeals of the DC circuit ruled that the presumptive privilege of presidential communications 'can be defeated only by a strong showing of need by another institution of government—a showing that the responsibilities of that institution cannot possibly be fulfilled without access to records of the president's deliberations'.[54] On the facts, the court found that the need demonstrated by the committee was too tenuous and too tangential to its functions to satisfy this strict test: the committee could point to 'no specific legislative decisions' which were affected.[55] The committee did not appeal the court's decision, but noted in a report that the case had rested on its facts and 'should not necessarily prevent legislative committees in the future from obtaining materials relating to presidential communications'.[56]

---

[49] J. D. Bush, ibid., pp. 738–9. See also Louis Fisher, *Constitutional Conflicts between Congress and the President* (University Press of Kansas, 3rd edn., 1991) p. 173. More recent developments which may have affected this traditional preference for political compromise rather than judicial resolution are considered later in this chapter, below.

[50] John C. Grabow, *Congressional Investigations: Law and Practice* (Clifton, NJ: Prentice Hall, 1988) p. 170.

[51] 498 F 2d 725 (DC Cir., 1974). See also *United States* v. *Nixon* 418 US 683 (1974).

[52] Ibid., at p. 727.   [53] Ibid.   [54] Ibid., at p. 730.   [55] Ibid., at p. 733.

[56] *Senate Select Committee on Presidential Campaign Activities, Final Report*: S Rep. No. 981, 93rd Congress, 2nd Session, 1083 (1974).

Two years later, in *United States* v. *American Telephone & Telegraph Co.*,[57] the subcommittee on oversight and investigations of the House committee on interstate and foreign commerce, as part of its investigation into warrantless wire-tapping in the US for national security purposes, subpoenaed from AT&T copies of FBI national security 'request' letters identifying telephone lines to be tapped. Although AT&T was willing to comply with the subpoena the Ford administration objected to the disclosure on national security grounds. Negotiations between AT&T, Congress, and the department of justice broke down and the department of justice brought an action to prevent AT&T from providing Congress with the subpoenaed documents. The district court granted the department's motion for summary judgment and enjoined AT&T from complying with the subpoena. Reviewing this decision, the court of appeals held that in light of the 'nerve-center constitutional questions' raised in the case, it would refuse to balance the asserted constitutional interests and that instead the case should be sent back to the district court for further supervised negotiation. These negotiations proved unsuccessful but in its second opinion the court of appeals once again refused to rule on the merits of the executive privilege claim, stating merely that: 'the degree to which the executive may exercise its discretion [in the area of national security] is unclear when it conflicts with the equally legitimate assertion of authority by Congress to conduct investigations relevant to its legislative functions'.[58] The case was eventually resolved in late 1978 after an agreement for congressional access was reached, but for more than two years previously Congress had been effectively frustrated in its investigation because of the initial summary judgment obtained against AT&T by the department of justice.

This case neatly illustrates the pitfalls of involving the judicial branch (most obviously, delay) and the court was itself conscious of this. While the court was anxious to stress that in its view complete judicial abstention from the issues raised in the case was not warranted on political questions grounds,[59] it nonetheless made the following important ruling: 'the framers, rather than attempting to define and allocate all governmental power in minute detail, relied . . . on the expectation that where conflicts in scope of authority arose between the coordinate branches, a spirit of dynamic compromise would promote resolution of the dispute in the manner most likely to result in efficient and effective functioning of our governmental system' and further that 'each branch should take cognizance of an implicit constitutional mandate to seek optimal accommodation through a realistic evaluation of the needs of the conflicting branches'.[60]

This constitutional and judicial preference for politically negotiated settlement of these disputes was reflected in the following important episode,

---

[57] 551 F 2d 384 (DC Cir., 1976) and 567 F 2d 121 (DC Cir., 1977).
[58] 567 F 2d 121, at p. 128 (DC Cir., 1977).   [59] See *Baker* v. *Carr* 369 US 186 (1962).
[60] *US* v. *AT&T* 567 F 2d 121, at p. 127 (DC Cir., 1977).

although the courts were peripherally involved. In 1983 Ann Gorsuch Burford was cited for contempt of Congress. Burford was an administrator at the environmental protection agency. This was the first time in US history that Congress had held the head of an executive agency in contempt. Burford had refused to comply with a subpoena from the subcommittee on investigations and oversight of the House committee on public works and transportation for documentation concerning the EPA's enforcement of the so-called superfund statute.[61] When the contempt charges were certified before the attorney general for the District of Columbia (in accordance with the contempt statute, discussed above) the department of justice brought an action against the House of Representatives seeking a declaratory judgment that Burford had acted lawfully in refusing to comply with the subpoena on executive privilege grounds. In the ensuing case, *United States* v. *House of Representatives*,[62] the district court dismissed the justice department's action on the ground that Burford's constitutional and other objections to the committee's investigation should be raised as a defence to the contempt charge, stating that 'courts have been extremely reluctant to interfere with the statutory scheme by considering cases brought by recalcitrant witnesses seeking declaratory and injunctive relief . . . [When] constitutional disputes arise concerning the respective powers of the legislative and executive branches, judicial intervention should be delayed until all possibilities for settlement have been exhausted . . . Judicial restraint is essential to maintain the delicate balance of powers among the branches established by the constitution.' The executive privilege claim was not ultimately judicially resolved. After the suit was dismissed the Reagan White House agreed to provide Congress with access to the subpoenaed material under special procedures designed to ensure the secrecy of certain 'enforcement sensitive' documents. In return Congress purged Burford of the contempt charge. This is exactly the kind of political result that the court in AT&T advocated and that it is assumed is imagined in the constitution.[63]

To conclude on executive privilege, although there are some lower court precedents, and although the supreme court has upheld the constitutionality of at least some notion of executive privilege in *US* v. *Nixon*,[64] the court in

[61] This involved a $1.6 billion programme established by Congress to clean up hazardous waste sites and to prosecute companies responsible for illegal dumping.

[62] 556 F Supp. 150 (DDC, 1983).

[63] On the Gorsuch controversy, see Ronald L. Claveloux, 'The Conflict between Executive Privilege and Congressional Oversight: The Gorsuch Controversy' [1983] *Duke Law Journal* 1333; Peter M. Shane, 'Legal Disagreement and Negotiation in a Government of Laws: The Case of Executive Privilege Claims against Congress', 71 *Minnesota Law Review* 461 (1987); and Louis Fisher, *Constitutional Conflicts between Congress and the President* (University Press of Kansas, 3rd edn., 1991) ch. 6. Peter Shane's important article provides a lengthy analysis of the processes of political negotiation in the context of executive branch reluctance to provide materials requested by Congress.

[64] 418 US 683 (1974).

Nixon expressly reserved any question concerning the balance between the president's 'generalized interest in confidentiality . . . and congressional demands for information'.[65] The extent to which the supreme court would now recognize as constitutionally based a claim to executive or presidential privilege against Congress therefore remains unclear. The crux of the judicial doctrine, such that it is, appears to be as follows: on the one hand, Congress has a constitutionally based power to demand information pursuant to investigations which can be shown to have a potential legislative interest at their core. On the other hand, the executive branch has a limited constitutional privilege to withhold information the disclosure of which would impair or impede the constitutional functions of the executive branch. If the legislative and executive branches cannot or will not resolve any such dispute between themselves, then there is a role for the courts, but resort to the courts does not appear to be the preferred option for any of the three branches, at least not for the time being.

To place this analysis alongside the events of Iraqgate, it is unclear quite what the courts would make of the attempts by the Bush White House (and especially by the Rostow gang) to control and limit congressional access to governmental papers. Would the courts share Gonzalez' view that such a systematic approach to the control of information demonstrated an overly dismissive and unconstitutional attitude to Congress's legitimate authority, or would a court regard the activities of the Rostow gang merely as an efficient means of ensuring that the position of the executive branch was not unduly undermined? On the strength of existing precedents, there can be no certain answer to these questions: not only have courts not addressed these issues, but, as we have seen, they have made it clear that they would prefer these problems to be resolved by way of political negotiation rather than by judicial decision. We will consider whether this approach represents an unreasonable abdication of judicial responsibility later in this chapter.

Classification of Documents and Freedom of Information

If making a claim of executive privilege is the first tactic that the executive branch can employ in an attempt to avoid producing documents (or giving oral testimony) for Congress, then the second is the executive's overall control of sensitive information through the classification system. Since 1966 the starting point in understanding the American legal position with regard to government and official information has been the Freedom of Information Act, now codified at 5 USC §552. This is a broad piece of legislation, which makes provision for the automatic publication of certain details of govern-

---

[65] Ibid., at p. 710.

ment functions, organizations, and rules of procedure as well as providing for certain (qualified) rights to seek access to government information. The Act[66] provides that: 'each agency, upon any request for records which (a) reasonably describes such records and (b) is made in accordance with published rules stating the time, place, fees (if any), and procedures to be followed, shall make the records promptly available to any person'. The government's application of these provisions is judicially reviewable.[67] In §552(b) the Act provides for a series of exemptions. The first exemption relates to 'matters that are specifically authorized under criteria established by an executive order to be kept secret in the interest of national defence or foreign policy and [which] are in fact properly [so] classified'.[68] Other exemptions include internal personnel rules; matters specifically exempted from disclosure by statute;[69] trade secrets and confidential commercial information; inter- or intra-agency memorandums or letters;[70] personnel and medical files; records kept for law enforcement purposes; and certain geological and geophysical information and data.[71] Although FOIA may not be used by the executive to withhold records from Congress,[72] the classification system which Congress implicitly recognized in exemption one has been widely used effectively to limit congressional access to sensitive information.

The House banking committee's investigation into BNL was, according to Gonzalez' floor statements, repeatedly delayed and obstructed by the committee's inability to access documents which had been classified by the Bush administration. How can a system of security classification sit happily in a

---

[66] 5 USC §552(a)(3).

[67] 5 USC §552(a)(4)(B). If a FOIA request is turned down, this can be appealed first within the department or agency concerned and can then be reviewed by the courts under the administrative appeal procedures provisions.

[68] 5 USC §552(b)(1). Some judicial decisions relating to this provision are discussed below. Among the many illuminating instances where this provision has been applied are: *Knopf* v. *Colby* 509 F 2d 1362 (4th Cir., 1975); *Assassination Archives and Research Center* v. *CIA* 720 F Supp. 217 (DDC, 1989); *National Security Archive* v. *FBI* 759 F Supp. 872 (DDC, 1991) and *Public Citizen* v. *US Trade Representative* 804 F Supp. 385 (DDC, 1992).

[69] For example, the Atomic Energy Act 1954 (42 USC §2162) prohibits the disclosure of 'restricted' nuclear weapons data unless there is no risk to common defence in releasing the data. Similarly, the Intelligence Identities Protection Act 1982 (50 USC §421) criminalizes the disclosure of classified information which identifies a covert agent.

[70] This is much more narrowly construed in the US than the related candour argument is in English law. The *Citizen's Guide on Using FOIA* (6th edn., 1995) states that 'the purpose of [this] exemption is to safeguard the deliberative policy-making process of government. The exemption encourages frank discussion of policy matters between agency officials by allowing supporting documents to be withheld from public disclosure . . . Protection for the decision-making process is appropriate only for the period while decisions are being made . . . Once a policy is adopted the public has a greater interest in knowing the basis for the decision' (pp. 13–14). It will be recalled that there is no similar time limit on the candour argument in English law. The *Citizen's Guide on Using FOIA* is published periodically by the House committee on government reform and oversight and is distributed widely and sold cheaply by the government printing office. The most recent edition is the 6th, which was published in June 1995 as House report 104–156. It costs $3.00.

[71] 5 USC §§552(b)(2)–(9). [72] See §552(c).

framework which is now dominated by the Freedom of Information Act, when the constitution nowhere mentions any executive authority to classify documents, and when the courts have repeatedly interpreted the constitution to grant Congress powerful authority to investigate matters which fall within its legislative purview?[73] This is of course one of those famed American constitutional checks, or balances. The contemporary practice of American separation of powers doctrine seems to provide not only for formal checks and balances in the sense that each branch can limit or oversee certain activities in the other branches, but it also appears to extend to a situation whereby each branch quietly accepts that the other branches have certain unwritten, rarely spoken but still constitutional, privileges which will, in their mutual interests, not be challenged. In this way, Congress allows the executive to classify documents on the understanding that the executive branch will usually cooperate with (genuine) congressional investigations, while the court is happy to stay out of it, thereby minimizing the otherwise considerable risk of being heavily criticized for unwelcome political involvement. It is important to remember that written constitutions work in this way just as much as unwritten ones do. The written constitution can only ever be a partial constitution.[74]

Classification procedures are set out in executive orders, which are promulgated and signed by presidents. The first executive order to deal with classification of documents was signed in 1940 by president Roosevelt. Executive order 8381 authorized government officials to classify military and naval information to protect national security. Roosevelt claimed that the authority under which the order was signed was not the constitution but the Espionage Act 1938.[75] After the second world war president Truman granted classification authority to non-military national security agencies in executive order 10290, under the authority, he claimed, of the constitution. In the 1950s president Eisenhower limited the effect of Truman's order, by defining national security agencies and the scope of classification more narrowly. Before Eisenhower's amendments there had been rumblings in Congress critical of the regime for classifying documents, and formal hearings were held

---

[73] We are back in the realm of the unwritten part of the written constitution, or what Henry Monaghan has called 'constitutional common law': see 'The Supreme Court, 1974 Term— Foreword: Constitutional Common Law', 89 *Harv. L Rev.* 1, at pp. 10–17 (1975). Constitutional common law can be described as judicially recognized principles which are deemed to be deducible from the constitution and which are designed to implement the constitution's structure and to fill its gaps. Such principles may be subject to statutory modification. See Akhil Reed Amar and Neal Kumar Katyal, 'Executive Privileges and Immunities: The *Nixon* and *Clinton* Cases', 108 *Harv. L Rev.* 701, at p. 704 (1995).

[74] See generally, Cass R. Sunstein, *The Partial Constitution* (Cambridge: Harvard UP, 1993). At p. vi, Sunstein argues that 'the constitution does not mean only what the judges say it means. On the contrary . . . its meaning to Congress, the president, state government and citizens in general has been more important than its meaning within the narrow confines of the supreme court building.'

[75] See Note, 'Keeping Secrets: Congress, the Courts and National Security Information', 103 *Harv. L Rev.* 906 (1990).

even after Eisenhower's revisions, in 1955 and 1957.[76] In 1966, Congress allowed for classified documents to constitute a class of exempted material under FOIA which was enacted in that year.

The clause of the constitution which is relied on in this context is the commander in chief clause of article II, which simply provides that the 'president shall be commander in chief of the army and navy of the United States, and of the militia of the several States, when called into the actual service of the United States'.[77] Does this clause provide authority for classification powers, as presidents since Truman have claimed? There is virtually no case law on this point, but in *Department of the Navy* v. *Egan*,[78] the supreme court did suggest in *obiter dicta* that the president's 'authority to classify and control access to information bearing on national security . . . flows primarily from this constitutional investment of power in the president and exists quite apart from any explicit congressional grant'.[79] Thus, as the formal legal position presently stands, the constitution 'does not expressly allocate classification authority among the branches, and nor have the courts ever articulated a rigorous constitutional framework to justify the executive's national security secrecy privilege'.[80]

Until recently the law was based on an executive order signed by president Reagan early in his first term: executive order 12356 of 1982. Reagan's order was the most sweeping classification order since FOIA was passed. It eliminated president Carter's requirements (in executive order 12065) that 'the public interest in disclosure' be balanced against 'the need to protect the information'. The Reagan order reversed Carter's presumption of non-classification with the stipulation that the information 'shall be classified [if it] reasonably could be expected to cause damage to national security'.[81] Three tiers of classification are provided for: confidential, secret, and top secret. Documents are classified as falling within one of these categories if their contents, if released, could reasonably be expected to cause damage, serious damage, or exceptionally grave damage to US national security interests.

Reagan's order, like its predecessors, also provided for the declassification of classified material, which should occur as soon as national security considerations permit. Declassification is, if anything, more controversial in the US than classification, as commentators are fearful of the significant degree of 'spin control' it gives to the executive branch in that useful (good) information can be selectively declassified as it suits the political interests of the party

---

[76] See ibid.   [77] US constitution, art. II, s. 2.   [78] 484 US 518 (1988).

[79] Ibid., at p. 527. See S. Dycus, A. Berney, W. Banks and P. Raven-Hansen, *National Security Law* (Boston: Little Brown, 2nd edn., 1997) p. 754.

[80] Note, 'Keeping Secrets: Congress, the Courts and National Security Information', 103 *Harv. L Rev.* 906 (1990), at pp. 918–19.

[81] See J. A. Goldston, J. M. Granholm and R. J. Robinson, 'A Nation Less Secure: Diminished Public Access to Information', 21 *Harv. CR-CL L Rev.* 409, at p. 483 (1986).

in power.[82] As far as classification (rather than declassification) is concerned, most commentators in the US seem to be more concerned with the quantity of classified material as opposed to the fact of classification or the dubious (or silent or invisible) constitutional foundation for it. We have already seen that Gonzalez complained that the Bush administration was classifying over seven million documents yearly.[83] In 1982 under the Reagan administration there were 17,505,000 documents classified; in 1983, 18,005,000; and in 1984, 19,608,000—an average rise of 6 per cent per annum.[84] Even the government's own information security oversight office has stated that the US federal government over-classifies its documents—for the reason, apparently, that officials are under the impression that if a document they have worked on receives a security classification, this will enhance the status of their work, of the documents they create, and ultimately of the officials themselves.[85]

In April 1995 president Clinton replaced Reagan's order with his own version: executive order 12958.[86] Clinton's order reverses many of the strictures of the Reagan order and returns to the trend, which Reagan had bucked, towards less government secrecy. Clinton's order, for example, contains a new instruction that any doubts about the need to classify a document should be resolved by deciding against classification.[87] There are also new provisions concerning the duration of classification[88] and automatic declassification, as well as new protection for whistle-blowers.[89] Further, president Clinton has altered the test for classification: whereas Reagan's order had stipulated that information '*shall* be classified [if it] reasonably could be expected to cause damage to national security', Clinton's order requires only that information '*may*' be classified if its unauthorized disclosure 'reasonably could be expected to result in damage to national security *and the original classification*

---

[82] See, e.g., ibid.   [83] See *Congressional Record*, H 8182, 9 Sept. 1992.

[84] See Goldston, Granholm and Robinson, *supra* n. 81, at p. 484. Arthur Goldberg, former supreme court justice and UN ambassador, stated in testimony to Congress during the Vietnam war that 'in my experience, 75% of [the classified] documents [I have read] should never have been classified in the first place; another 15% quickly outlived the need for secrecy; and only about 10% genuinely required restricted access over any significant period of time'. Cited by Harold Koh, *The National Security Constitution: Sharing Power after the Iran-Contra Affair* (New Haven: Yale UP, 1990) p. 201.

[85] Ibid., at p. 485.

[86] Published at 60 *Fed. Reg.* 19825 (1995); reprinted in part in S. Dycus et al., op. cit. n. 79, pp. 748–52.

[87] §1.2(b) of Clinton's order provides that 'if there is significant doubt about the need to classify information, it shall not be classified'.

[88] §1.6 of the order provides that 'at the time of original classification, the original classification authority shall attempt to establish a specific date or event for declassification based upon the duration of the national security sensitivity of the information. The date or event shall not exceed . . . 10 years from the date of the original classification' unless certain narrow circumstances are met, such as, for example, that the document would reveal intelligence methods, or intelligence officers' identities.

[89] See S. Dycus et al., op. cit. n. 79, p. 753.

authority is able to identify or describe the damage'.[90] In addition to these new features, Clinton's order has reintroduced some of the aspects of president Carter's order which the Reagan order had removed. One example of this is the provision that in some cases the need to protect classified information 'may be outweighed by the public interest in disclosure of the information, and in these cases the information should be declassified'.[91]

What then is the relationship between the various competing executive and legislative interests, both under the constitution and under FOIA? If an individual, or a member of Congress, wants or needs information which has been classified, what can be done to secure access to that material? What if the executive branch claims that the information is classified, but there are strong grounds for suspecting that this is untrue? Alternatively, what if the information has been erroneously classified? Is classification, or apparent classification, always the last word, the trump card that the executive can deploy to put an effective stop to inconvenient congressional inquiry? As ever, there are two answers: one political, the other juridical. Let us look at the juridical approach first. The FOIA provisions are widely used by Congress in seeking access to government information, and from time to time such FOIA requests result in litigation. One such case was *Environmental Protection Agency* v. *Mink*.[92] This case remains a leading supreme court authority on the relationship between Congress's constitutional rights to subpoena documents, its statutory rights under FOIA, and the executive's unwritten constitutional right to classify information. Mink and several other members of Congress brought an action under FOIA to compel disclosure of nine documents that various officials had prepared for the president concerning underground nuclear testing. All but three of these documents were classified as secret or as top secret. According to the environmental protection agency all nine were being used in executive decision making (and were therefore exempt from disclosure under FOIA exemption five). The court of appeals had held that the classified material exemption (exemption one) applies only to the secret portions of classified documents and requires disclosure of non-secret parts where these are severable. It had further held that exemption five does not shield factual information unless it is inextricably intertwined with policy-making processes. It ruled that the district court should examine the nine documents in camera in order to determine whether they fell within these categories.

The EPA's appeal to the supreme court was successful. The majority of the supreme court[93] took a view which was much less favourable to Congress's position. The majority held that exemption one did not permit compelled

---

[90] Emphasis added. See §1.2(4) of Clinton's order.
[91] See §3.2 of Clinton's order.   [92] 410 US 73 (1973).
[93] Brennan and Marshall JJ dissented from the court's holdings on exemption one; and Douglas J dissented altogether.

disclosure of the six classified documents, and nor did it allow in camera inspection to sift out non-secret components. The court further held that exemption five did not automatically require in camera inspection—the lower courts had been wrong not to have permitted the EPA to demonstrate that the documents should not be disclosed without the court having to inspect. In the course of its judgment the supreme court laid down what lower courts have subsequently regarded as general principles to be adopted in resolving access-to-information disputes between the legislative and executive branches. Among the more important subsequent decisions which illustrate how the *Mink* approach has been put into effect is *Schaffer* v. *Kissinger*.[94] This was a case brought under FOIA to require Kissinger, then secretary of state, to disclose reports concerning conditions in prisoner of war camps in south Vietnam. Kissinger resisted disclosure under exemption one, claiming that the reports were required by executive order to be kept secret in the interests of national defence and foreign policy. The court of appeals for the DC circuit held that, following *Mink*, the test to be applied was 'whether the president has determined by executive order that particular documents are to be kept secret' and that the courts are not free to inquire into 'the soundness of executive security classifications'.[95] The court ruled that although there can be no judicial examination of the reasons or motives behind an executive security classification, the burden is on the agency to demonstrate to the court that the documents were in fact properly classified pursuant to the executive order.

Thus, the law appears to be that, on the condition that the executive can demonstrate to the court that the documents have been properly classified, there is nothing Congress (or anyone else seeking information) can do. Moreover, the executive branch retains control of the effective meaning of the crucial phrase, 'properly classified', as it is the executive branch in its executive orders which apparently has the unwritten constitutional power to set out what information can be classified, by whom, under what circumstances, and for how long. Even in a formal constitution based on checks and balances and the separation of powers, the executive branch still holds, if not all the cards, then at least the upper hand—and it is a hand which does not always have to be disclosed. Perhaps then it is not surprising that when the banking committee's BNL investigation ran into questions of secret intelligence and national security it ground to an inconclusive halt. Certainly without the support of the intelligence committees, other members of Congress are in a far weaker legal position than the executive branch when it comes to the constitutional regulation of national security information.

---

[94] 505 F 2d 389 (DC Cir., 1974).   [95] Ibid., at p. 390.

The Changing Constitutional Politics of Washington

So much for the legal answer. It has already been noted that the political branches may not always prefer to travel down this legal route. Some kind of politically negotiated settlement might sometimes be preferred. This now calls for further examination. The political approach encourages Congress and the relevant agency or department of the executive branch to negotiate a compromise, such that members of Congress or their staffers will be permitted to consult the classified documents, but not to remove them; or that some portions of the documents could be released but only in some kind of redacted form, and so on. Until recently, these political solutions were generally seen to be working satisfactorily, but they clearly depend on one crucial ingredient: that is, co-operation between the parties. To say that it is an often repeated observation in Washington that the once-good relations between the parties are now in an advanced stage of breaking down would be a vast understatement. In the 104th Congress (1995–6) relations between the Republican House, led by speaker Newt Gingrich and the Clinton White House were very poor. Since the 1996 elections (which resulted in the Republicans' majority in the House being vastly reduced) and Gingrich's own personal difficulties with the ethics committee in January 1997 Gingrich seems to have cast himself in a new, less confrontational, light. On the other hand, this may be just so much post-inauguration posturing. In any case, even if Democrat/Republican relations do improve from the low ebb of the 104th Congress, while the Whitewater, Travelgate, campaign finance, and various other controversial investigations into the Clintons continue, they are likely to remain generally poor.

As to when all this began, various suggestions have been made. It may be that the widespread feeling that relations were less hostile twenty years ago is but another manifestation of the general life-was-more-secure-twenty-years-ago mood that every generation passes through and that no generation remembers the previous generation experiencing.[96] But it may be that Watergate, or the Church committee,[97] or the Bork nomination, or the Iran/Contra affair, or the New Republicans' electoral success in the House in 1994 was the trigger which started the race down the slippery slope. For our purposes, none of this really matters. What is of some importance is that if the

---

[96] For what remains a seminal exposure and analysis of this phenomenon, see G. Pearson, *Hooligan: A History of Respectable Fears* (London: Macmillan, 1983).

[97] In 1975 the Senate created a committee to study governmental operations under the chairmanship of Senator Frank Church of Idaho. The committee's task was to determine 'the extent, if any, to which illegal, improper, or unethical activities were engaged in by the intelligence agencies'. See S. Dycus, A. Berney, W. Banks and P. Raven-Hansen, *National Security Law* (Boston: Little Brown, 2nd edn., 1997), at p. 432. Dycus et al. suggest that the Church committee significantly contributed to the 'changed climate' in Congress.

104th Congress is anything to go by—and it is still too early to know whether
it was the beginning of a lasting and disturbing trend or merely a blip which
now looks more sinister than it really was—the traditional preference among
the branches for political negotiation rather than legal battles to resolve inter-
branch disputes is changing.

Both the Clinton White House and the Gingrich led House are prepared to
reach for the rule book and for their constitutional powers more quickly than
their predecessors were. The contemporary equivalents of the Henry
Kissinger, James Watt, and William Rehnquist controversies (which were all
resolved by political compromise) are no longer being resolved in the same
way. In the ongoing travel office investigation, for example, which concerns
the controversial dismissal of personnel from the White House travel office,[98]
legal counsel within the Clinton administration have been provisionally cited
for contempt of Congress for claiming executive privilege in response to congressional subpoenas for documents.[99] Similarly in the investigation into
whether (or when) the Clinton White House knew that security agents of
Haiti's US-backed government had murdered political opponents, president
Clinton has again made controversial claims to executive privilege, described
in Congress as a 'blatant abuse of power to cover-up a massive foreign policy
failure'.[100] Charles Tiefer, a leading authority on the law of Congress,[101] has
suggested that president Clinton's use of executive privilege during the 104th
Congress was 'record-setting'. Whereas Clinton formally claimed executive
privilege three times in the 104th Congress, Bush formally invoked it only
once, Reagan only twice (in eight years), and Carter never claimed executive
privilege at all.[102]

What is going on in these cases is that the normal processes of behind the
scenes co-operation, negotiation, and compromise are breaking down, and
the argument is taking place much more in the open, with a formal (public)
claim of executive privilege being met by an equally formal (and public) provisional citation by a committee of contempt. Then, some time later but
before the full House has voted on the contempt charge (which it must do
before the issue can go to court) the White House hands over some of the documents, albeit heavily redacted, and asks for more time on others, leading to
more delay and more ill will between the parties, but still avoiding the courts.
As Tiefer has argued, 'what has happened is that both the president and the
speaker have evidently detected a change in the costs and benefits of escalat-
ing an oversight dispute'. Analysing the dispute over Haiti, for example,

---

[98] Seven employees were fired, according to the Clinton White House because of allegations
of misconduct. All seven have since been exonerated and most have been offered other jobs
within the administration.

[99] *Washington Post*, 15 Dec. 1996, p. A16. See also, *Washington Post*, 31 May 1996, p. A10.

[100] As reported in the *Washington Post*, 26 Sept. 1996, p. A20.

[101] See, e.g., his *Congressional Practice and Procedure* (Greenwood Press, 1989).

[102] See *American Lawyer*, 18 Oct. 1996.

Tiefer has concluded that 'given a choice between compromising on fairly generous access terms that would have amounted to a House victory or pushing the President into a successful invocation of privilege' speaker Newt Gingrich prefers the latter outcome. In a passage entitled 'no more quiet compromises' Tiefer wrote that whereas 'both sides used to count compromise of one kind or another as the best outcome, now both sides seem to prefer an outcome in which the President is forced to assert privilege, and the House leaves that invocation unchallenged'.[103] Why is this happening, and what does it mean for our constitutional analysis?

There are as many theories as to why normal service has been interrupted as there are people in Washington who can talk of nothing else. One theory has it that it is all tactical. President Clinton, the inveterate and permanent campaigner, is of the view, according to this theory, that although claiming executive privilege in response to congressional subpoenas is bad publicity, it is only news for a day, as the media soon lose interest in the absence of hard evidence. A second theory, favoured by Democrats (especially those in minority in the House), is that what we are witnessing is the Republicans' revenge. This goes back to Church, Bork, and Iran/Contra. During the 1980s, and especially over the Iran/Contra scandal, Republicans (especially New Republicans of the Gingrich variety) were deeply offended by the Democrats in Congress who kept giving the Reagan and Bush White Houses such a hard time for so long over what they felt was so little. Iran/Contra was seen by many Republicans in Congress as nothing but a short-term partisan attack on President Reagan and his staff. The length of independent counsel Lawrence Walsh's investigation, and the paucity of charges that he was ultimately able to make stick, were illustrations for these Republicans that the whole thing was all part of a big Democrat conspiracy. Most independent commentators have dismissed this view, and rightly so too. Iran/Contra was not as big a politcal scandal as some Democrats would have liked, but it was serious and raised important constitutional questions, as subsequent work has shown.[104] Irrespective of this, however, the second theory as to the changing political climate in Washington is that now that the Republicans have won control of the House, they are getting their own back, and using congressional authority to score political points and to investigate political controversy implicating the Clintons for its own sake, and are generally misbehaving in the way they felt the Democrats did before 1992. The third theory builds on the

---

[103] Ibid.

[104] For an outline of the Republican view of Iran/Contra (which is then quickly dismissed), see Harold Koh, *The National Security Constitution: Sharing Power after the Iran-Contra Affair* (New Haven: Yale UP, 1990) p. 2. Koh's work is considered further, below. In addition to Harold Koh's work, Dycus, Berney, Banks and Raven-Hansen (*National Security Law*, 2nd edn.) devote 96 pages to a thorough analysis of the grave importance of Iran/Contra. See also Lawrence Walsh, *Firewall: The Iran/Contra Conspiracy and Cover-Up* (New York: Norton, 1997).

second one: this is that Clinton realizes exactly what the Republicans are doing and thinks (hopes?) that it will not stand up in court, should it ever get there, on grounds of an absence of legislative purpose. Thus, Clinton does not take Congress's investigations into his affairs very seriously and sees no need to play the usual political game of behind the scenes compromise.[105]

Reworking the National Security Constitution?

The more important question, whatever the reasons for the changing relationship between Congress and the White House, is what these developments might mean for our constitutional analysis. To understand what Iraqgate and what the contemporary political scene in Washington tells us about the constitution and why these issues are important we must rewind the clock slightly, to Iraqgate's immediate predecessor (and in some ways, direct parent): namely, the Iran/Contra scandal of the late 1980s. Unlike Iraqgate, Iran/Contra did receive widespread media coverage and became arguably the biggest political story of president Reagan's second term (1984–8). This is not the place to go into a full account of what happened and why it mattered, but a brief outline is necessary. We will then be able to see more clearly how Iraqgate built on where Iran/Contra left off, and what this means for contemporary constitutional law and politics.

The essence of Iran/Contra is that a team of White House staff in the Reagan administration conspired to support a covert war in Nicaragua (the Contras against the Sandinistas). They did so by diverting proceeds from illegal arms sales to Iran to the Contras. This was a case, like Watergate had been in the 1970s, of the mixture of funds of unaccountable origin along with private agents being used to direct covert actions directly from the White House with little if any regard for other government departments or Congress.[106] At the heart of the White House team responsible for Iran/Contra was Oliver North, although other senior members of the Reagan administration were also implicated, to varying degrees.[107] Ultimately, like Iraqgate, Iran/Contra failed to deliver the Republican scalps that the Democrats had predicted and

---

[105] To which can be added the further element that the Republicans' attacks are focused on the *Clintons*, as opposed to the Democrats generally (Whitewater is a good example). President Clinton has been elected twice and cannot be again, and so for as long as he and his family remain the focus of attention, the Democrats are not particularly worried about any electoral implications, which they think will be minimal. The key for the Democrats is to keep the current vice-president and front runner for the 2000 ticket, Al Gore, away from the sleaze allegations.

[106] See Harold H. Koh, *The National Security Constitution: Sharing Power after the Iran-Contra Affair* (New Haven: Yale UP, 1990) p. 11. Koh's book contains a full analysis of the implications for American foreign policy and constitutional law of the Iran/Contra affair.

[107] See Koh, ibid., ch. 1, in which the findings and failings of the various Iran/Contra investigators are discussed.

hoped for—even North escaped jail.[108] Again, like Iraqgate, the Iran/Contra
affair ended in political acrimony as one side considered that the scandal had
been a failure of people not of laws, and the people had been caught (even if
they had not been punished as much as some would have liked); whereas the
other side felt that the scandal was not a scandal at all and that there had been
no failure either of people or of laws: merely a prolonged exercise in congressional folly.[109] Harold Koh has shown that with regard to Iran/Contra both
these popular Democrat and Republican views are misguided and misleading. In Koh's view, the tragedy of Iran/Contra was not only that it was a 'fundamental failure of the legal structure that regulates the relations among the
president, Congress and the courts'[110] in national security but also that
neither Congress nor the executive branch recognized that this was what
Iran/Contra was about.

Koh warned that to treat the Iran/Contra affair 'solely as an exercise in
executive hubris or congressional folly is to ignore its historical significance:
as an uncured constitutional crisis in national security decision making that
waits to afflict us anew'.[111] Quite so, and Iraqgate was just that—a repeated
constitutional crisis in national security decision making which was caused by
exactly the same factors as Koh identified as having caused the Iran/Contra
affair. These factors are: executive empire-building, congressional acquiescence, and judicial tolerance. Koh's argument is that the national security
constitution which was developed in the century following the civil war has
been gradually worn down (or 'assaulted') in the fifty years since the end of
the second world war.[112] All three branches have been responsible: the executive has been allowed to take the initiative without sufficient checks being
imposed on its growing power. As far as Congress is concerned this is because
of a combination of legislative myopia, inadequate drafting, ineffective legislative tools, and sheer lack of political will.[113] As far as the supreme court is
concerned this is because of a reluctance to grant standing in national security cases coupled with a tendency merely to support the executive branch on
the merits should a case progress that far.[114]

[108] North was convicted on three counts of obstructing Congress by creating false and illegal
chronologies; of altering, concealing and destroying documents; and of receiving a residual security system as an illegal gratuity, for which he received a suspended sentence, civil fines, and community service. The failure of the independent counsel successfully to prosecute North and others
on the more serious offences was in large part due to a remarkably generous (i.e. generous to
North) decision of the US court of appeals for the District of Columbia circuit which significantly
restricted the prosecutorial use that could be made of North's testimony before Congress: see *US
v. North* 910 F 2d 843 (1990), discussed above, n. 43 and associated text.

[109] See Koh, p. 2.   [110] Ibid., p. 3.   [111] Ibid., p. 2.

[112] Koh's analysis of what he calls the national security constitution, its development up to the
National Security Act 1947, and the subsequent assault on it can be found in chs. 3 and 4 of his
book.

[113] Koh, ibid., ch. 5. Koh provides details of his charges against Congress at pp. 123–33.

[114] Koh, ibid., ch. 6. Among the standard US national security cases Koh discusses in this
chapter are *Snepp* v. *US* 444 US 507 (1980) (which could be compared to the *Spycatcher*

The lesson of Iraqgate is that the lessons of Iran/Contra have not been learned. Most people in Congress were not interested in pursuing the Bush White House on its policies with regard to Iraq before August 1990 even though subsequent work has shown that it was clear to foreign policy experts at the time that US policy was in part responsible for Saddam Hussein's decision to invade Kuwait. Gonzalez was of course an exception to this and the reactions of the Bush White House, and of the Rostow gang, of attorney general Thornburgh's attempts to dissuade the House banking committee from looking into the BNL affair all illustrate what a thorn Gonzalez was in Bush's side. But one Congressman, even in the company of a handful of colleagues and with the support of an influential committee, cannot without more help bring about a halt to the collapse of the national security constitution, especially when the intelligence committees of the House and of the Senate refuse to co-operate. For all Gonzalez' efforts, Iraqgate represents another chapter in the sorry saga of congressional acquiescence in the executive's domination of the national security agenda. Similarly, while the Atlanta trial judge, Judge Shoob, did what he thought was appropriate to express his fears that the defendants before him were being made into scapegoats for more serious offences, he was ultimately removed from the case, and no higher court was ever involved in any substantive matter emanating from the Iraqgate story.

What then should be done? In his analysis of Iran/Contra, Koh argued that a relatively straightforward package of reforms could be adopted to encourage a return to the desired goal of more 'balanced institutional participation' in the national security constitution. In particular, he suggested three improvements which would limit (if not cure) the present sources of congressional acquiescence: first, the creation of a centralized foreign affairs expertise within Congress; secondly, the building of a central repository of legal advice within Congress concerned with foreign policy; and thirdly, the improving of congressional access to sensitive information by reforming the ways in which information is classified, which should not be a matter exclusively for the executive branch.[115] Certainly these small measures would constitute a valuable step in the right direction, but, for all Koh's good intentions, is there not a deeper point here, and one which it is much harder to touch through law or through law reform? While small law reforms such as those Koh has recommended might change slightly the quality of the pitch on which the game is played, they will not affect the rules of the game itself nor the tactics that are employed in trying to win it.

litigation in Britain, and elsewhere) and *Dames and Moore* v. *Regan* 453 US 654 (1981) (which could be compared to the *GCHQ* or *Malone* cases in Britain in that all these cases illustrate a general judicial reluctance to find that the executive has acted illegally in a national security context despite the absence of clear legal authority to support the government's action).

[115] Koh, *supra* n. 106, ch. 7.

The game, of course, is the deadly serious one of politics. Just as it is politics that has assaulted the national security constitution since 1947 so too will it be politics that reaches a new settlement—if one is to be reached at all—which may or may not return the American polity to Koh's dream of more balanced institutional participation. This is why the contemporary Washington climate is important. If in 1990 Koh was pessimistic as to the chances of making progress with his agenda for reforming the national security constitution, at the other end of the decade things look rather different. Relations between the Clinton White House and the Gingrich led House of Representatives are forcing both the executive and legislative branches to reassess the way they have traditionally played the national security game of politics. There is not much yet to suggest that this period of reassessment will necessarily lead America in the direction Koh would like, but there is a good chance, for three reasons. First, Clinton is primarily, indeed overwhelmingly, a domestic president. He was elected on a domestic agenda, beating George Bush, that most successful of foreign policy presidents.[116] The greatest triumphs of Clinton's first term were domestic, not foreign.[117] Clinton as president has the loosest relationship with the intelligence community since at least Carter. For all these reasons, Clinton's commitment to continuing the executive's half century of empire building in the national security field may be significantly less enthusiastic than that of his two Republican predecessors.

Secondly, if our analysis above to the effect that the traditional forms of political negotiation are breaking down and are being replaced by more confrontational and legal language and tactics is right, this may eventually lead to further judicial involvement in national security relations between Congress and the White House. Clinton and Gingrich are not exactly rushing to get to court to battle it out, but if they continue as they left off in the 104th Congress to bounce ever more tetchy subpoenas and claims to executive privilege off each other, the chances are that something will end up in court. Even if the supreme court did have the opportunity to move in the direction Koh has advocated, there must however be some doubt as to whether the present somewhat conservative court would want to take it. But if the right case were to come before the court, it might decide that the time was ripe for a reassessment of the political negotiation which previous courts (in the *AT&T* case, for example) have assumed was the proper constitutional basis for these issues. If the court took the view presented here, that the tradition of political compromise in disputes over access to sensitive government information was

---

[116] See, for example, Charles O. Jones, 'Campaiging to Govern: The Clinton Style', in Colin Campbell and Bert A. Rockham (eds.), *The Clinton Presidency: First Appraisals* (Chatham, NJ: Chatham House, 1996) ch. 1.

[117] Discussed, for example, in Colin Campbell, 'Management in a Sandbox', in Campbell and Rockham, ibid., ch. 2.

breaking down, then that might encourage even a conservative court to provide some firmer juridical underpinning to at least this aspect of the national security constitution in the way that Koh has advocated.

Finally, and most significantly, Congress is tired of its failure to get the results it wants with the information it has. While this has been true of the Democrats for some time, it is now a view widely shared across both political parties, as the Republicans in Congress are now experiencing the same difficulties as regards the White House as the Democrats did in the 1980s. Congressional tiredness in this context is best seen in the ongoing debate about the future of the independent counsel provisions of the Ethics in Government Act.[118] Congress passed this legislation in response to the Watergate affair, as it was felt that there ought to be a statutory framework for the appointment of some kind of special prosecutor or independent counsel to investigate and if necessary to bring criminal proceedings against senior government officials suspected of criminal wrongdoing. An independent counsel was appointed in the Iran/Contra affair, and the House called for one to be appointed in Iraqgate, although Bush's attorney generals refused. Under the Clinton administration independent counsel have been appointed not only to look into Whitewater but also to investigate other minor scandals such as those involving the White House travel office, policy over Haiti, and so on.

While the independent counsel provisions are in theory a great idea (in that they prevent the department of justice from investigating its own governmental colleagues, and thereby provide an essential degree of distance and credibility in times of political controversy) they have become in practice an expensive disappointment. What has tended to happen is that Congress finds a cause to battle, or a scandal to investigate, and after a period of political investigation, the issue is handed over to an independent counsel. After years of criminal investigation, either very little is brought before the courts, or no prosecution is brought at all, leading to disappointment among the executive's political opponents and allegations of time- and money-wasting among the executive's political allies.[119] As recent years have seen each of the two

---

[118] Codified at 28 USC §591. These provisions provide that when the attorney general receives sufficient information such as to constitute grounds for an investigation, he shall, if the evidence is sufficiently specific and comes from a suitably credible source, within 90 days apply to the court for the appointment of an independent counsel. If the attorney general receives a request for the appointment of an independent counsel from certain specified groups in Congress, he must reply within 30 days, giving reasons for his decision. Once appointed, the independent counsel has 'full power and independent authority to exercise all investigative and prosecutorial functions and powers of the department of justice' (§594(a)). The independent counsel can only be removed by the attorney general for good cause. The constitutionality of these provisions was upheld by the supreme court in *Morrison* v. *Olsen* 487 US 654 (1988).

[119] Iran/Contra and Whitewater both followed this basic pattern. The investigation by Lawrence Walsh, the independent counsel in Iran/Contra, lasted for five years and cost $32.5 million.

parties in control of both the executive and the legislative branches, both parties have now experienced both sets of reactions. This should allow Congress sensibly to debate the future of the independent counsel provisions without either side making the usual unhelpful accusations to the effect that one side only wants to repeal the provisions because of present political discomfort as a result of ongoing independent counsel investigations. Congress will have an opportunity to conduct this debate formally, as the independent counsel provisions of the Ethics in Government Act are not permanent: they require congressional renewal from time to time.[120]

Whether this actually happens or not it provides the executive and legislative branches with an opportunity to begin to reassess the balance between them as to their respective roles and participation in the national security constitution, hence the potential significance of the independent counsel debate to our analysis. Because of the widespread political dissatisfaction with the results achieved by various independent counsel and because both parties have resented the appointment of some independent counsel in what they see as inappropriate (i.e. not sufficiently serious) circumstances,[121] a new approach is likely to have to be taken. Congress is of course highly unlikely simply to repeal the provisions without replacement—handing over independent counsel investigations to the department of justice would not be something Congress would rush to embrace. Quite what the new settlement will involve, however, is not clear. But it may well be that along the way to reaching the new settlement, Congress will take the opportunity to move in the direction that Koh has urged. If the lesson of Iran/Contra was that the national security constitution had broken down, the hope after Iraqgate must be that the legislative and executive branches now realize this and are, as a result, beginning to conduct themselves differently, even if this is happening more by luck than judgement. The question which remains for us now is not what the American political establishment is going to do next, but what these various American experiences mean for Britain, and for the British constitution.

Conclusion: Lessons for the British Constitution?

There are clearly a number of issues which arise in both the Scott saga and in the American story related in this chapter. The stories are not identical, but they are similar. The most obvious difference between Iraqgate in the USA and the Scott saga in Britain is one of outcome. The American constitution did not come out of Iraqgate in a particularly healthy state. Neither Congress

---

[120] Indeed, the independent counsel provisions of the Ethics in Government Act lapsed in Dec. 1992 at the end of the 102nd Congress, but were renewed in the 103rd Congress: see Independent Counsel Reauthorization Act 1994, Pub. L No. 103–270; 18 Stat. 732 (1994).

[121] Again, both Iran/Contra and Whitewater are good examples.

nor any court was able satisfactorily to resolve the questions of constitutional behaviour which arose in Iraqgate. Subsequent reforms have been limited and have affected banking law more than constitutional law. In Britain, on the other hand, the old British constitution did manage to uncover much more, and despite the absence of ministerial resignations, significant constitutional changes (as regards PII, ministerial responsibility, parliamentary questions, and so on) have occurred. And yet, when serious and difficult questions are raised about the old British constitution, a common reaction in both the media and the academic constitutional community is to call for constitutional reform. Constititutional reform—a vibrant political issue at this time—has taken on a momentum of its own. There is a danger that constitutional lawyers may have focused with such intensity on questions of constitutional reform for so long that issues of current constitutional law and constitutional practice have been relatively neglected. This danger is compounded by the fact that when it comes to the reform question, there is now little room for debate—it is as if the package has already been sealed, if not yet delivered. All the items contained in the package are familiar: a Bill of Rights, a Freedom of Information Act, devolution, reform of the House of Lords, electoral reform for the House of Commons, and eventually a written constitution. The question which the Scott story raises, especially when studied in comparative perspective in the way in which we have done here, is what these episodes tell us about this constitutional reform package. Would the items on this constitutional reform agenda have made a difference? Is it the case that if Britain had a written constitution with a bill of rights and a freedom of information act (as the US has) the scandals that gave rise to the Scott inquiry could not have happened?

Of course not. In the USA there was throughout the period we have considered a written constitution with a bill of rights and a freedom of information act. Yet these constitutional features (which figure so prominently in the constitutional reform package) did not seem to prevent American involvement in Iraq's military procurement network, and nor did they appear to assist in the uncovering—or discovering—by Congress and by the media of the real nature of the Bush administration's policy with regard to Iraq before August 1990. This is an important issue, because if it is the case that these constitutional reforms would have made no substantial difference to the events discussed in this book, does that not raise very difficult questions for the advocates of the standard constitutional reform package? Scott was the most important constitutional crisis of the long Conservative period in office. Surely any package of constitutional reform should be able to address what went wrong in that period, as exemplified by the events which gave rise to the Scott inquiry, and any constitutional reform package which does not do so is not worthy of the name and should be rejected as inadequate or misguided or both. It is the task of the conclusion which follows this chapter to attempt to identify the direction in which the old British constitution should be moved as a response to Scott and to articulate a vision of constitutional reform which is based on an understanding of basic constitutional needs rather than on liberal political dogma.

Conclusion:
Reforming the Parliamentary Constitution

Two constitutional themes run throughout the events on which this book has focused: namely, secrecy and accountability. Whether it is ministers or the civil service, Congress or Parliament, the secret intelligence services or the courts, all of these institutions suffer in one way or another from too much of one and not enough of the other. The question remains, however, what then should be done?

Britain has now entered a period of wide-ranging constitutional debate and, probably, of significant constitutional change. The Labour government was elected in 1997 on a manifesto which included a considerable commitment to constitutional reform, most notably as regards devolution of power to Scotland and to Wales (subject to referendums). As well as devolution, however, the incorporation of the European Convention on Human Rights into domestic law, the enactment of a Freedom of Information Act, and the abolition of voting rights for (most) hereditary peers in the House of Lords were all promised in the Labour party's manifesto.[1] In addition, a number of potential changes to the House of Commons were highlighted. The manifesto stated that 'the House of Commons is in need of modernization' and that a special select committee of the House should be set up to look into its procedures. Further, 'prime ministers questions will be made more effective [and] ministerial accountability will be reviewed so as to remove recent abuses'.[2] Indications were also given that the Nolan committee would be invited to conduct an inquiry into the funding of political parties, and that a referendum would be held on the voting system for the House of Commons.[3] This is an ambitious programme, but the question for us is: what do the Scott and Iraqgate stories tell us about how this agenda should be realized? Will the new government's plans reduce state secrecy and enhance public accountability in the way in which the Scott saga suggests is necessary, or are they aimed to achieve slightly different goals?

First impressions of the Labour government suggest that the centre of power—the prime minister's office—intends to keep as tight a rein on the political machine as possible. Tony Blair has repeatedly indicated since he became prime minister that he believes that it was his programme which was elected on 1 May 1997, and woe betide anything or anyone that gets in the way of the government's implementation of its programme, including

---

[1] *Because Britain Deserves Better* (London: Labour Party, 1997) pp. 32–5.
[2] Ibid., p. 33.   [3] Ibid.

Parliament. When the Referendums (Scotland and Wales) Bill was introduced in the first weeks of the new Parliament, its second reading took place before the usual ten-day period between the publication of a bill and the date of its second reading had elapsed. When the government saw the numbers and extent of the amendments which had been put down in respect of the bill, it lost no time in declaring that guillotine motions would be used to curtail debate at committee stage, despite the fact that the bill was a hotly contested (and constitutional) matter. When challenged about these moves at question time, the prime minister seemed angry that anyone could object to the government seeking to ensure that its legislative agenda was pushed through Parliament as smoothly and swiftly as possible, repeating his view that it was the government which had won the election, and it was Parliament's responsibility not to obstruct the government in carrying out its democratic mandate.[4] Even the format of prime minister's question time was changed by Mr Blair from twice-weekly sessions of fifteen minutes to a weekly session of half an hour. The change was no doubt designed to move away from the pettiness of the point-scoring, soundbite-dominated punch and judy show which prime minister's question time had become during the Thatcher/Kinnock years, but the point here is that irrespective of the prime minister's motives, the change should not have been one for him to make. It should be for Parliament to decide when and how frequently and for how long the prime minister should be compelled to give an oral account to the House of the government's actions and policies, not for the prime minister to dictate. No doubt the government would have managed to convince a majority of MPs to sanction such a change.

The Parliamentary Constitution

Britain's constitution takes an unusual form in that it is unwritten. This does not mean, of course, that none of Britain's constitutional rules are written down—increasingly, they are.[5] But it does mean that there is no single, formal document which can be identified as The Constitution. The distinction

---

[4] See HC Deb., Vol. 295, col. 389, 4 June 1997 when the prime minister asked, 'which is undemocratic—a government using their mandate' to ensure that legislation is passed or the opposition complaining in Parliament about the guillotine? Mr Blair asserted that 'we are implementing the policies upon which we were elected' as if that somehow justified the government acting without regard for Parliament's position. The prime minister's point is not entirely without foundation: to the relatively simple 6 clauses and 2 schedules of the Referendums (Scotland and Wales) Bill the Conservatives (who of course since 1997 have had no MPs in either Scotland or Wales) had tabled some 250 amendments, including 21 new clauses and 12 new schedules. The opposition's actions were hardly designed to enhance constructive debate.

[5] The resolutions on ministerial responsibility passed by the House of Commons and the House of Lords discussed in ch. 1 constitute one example of the writing down (even codification) of one previously unwritten so-called constitutional convention.

between written and unwritten constitutions is primarily one of form, but it does have some important substantive consequences. One of the most notable things about written constitutions is the style of language which they adopt. They are not written as if they were essays in political philosophy or as if they were politicians' speeches. Rather, they tend to be written as if they were legal documents, with numbered articles, sections, clauses, and so on. This is no accident. One of the most striking features of written constitutions, especially (but not only) in the modern western world, is the high profile given in them to the law, and to those who enforce the law: lawyers, judges, and courts. A lawyer reads a written constitution, whether it be that of the USA, of France or of Ireland, and he or she feels a kind of reassuring familiarity. Lawyers recognize written constitutions as part of their jurisdiction—as belonging to their world. The legal form and juridical language of the written constitution lend support to the view that constitutionalism and constitutional governance are matters for the law and for legal institutions. This is as evident in Marshall's famous hijacking on behalf of the judiciary of supremacy under the US constitution in *Marbury* v. *Madison*[6] as it is of more recent attempts to judicialize constitutional politics in Canada, in Australia, and by the European Court of Justice.[7]

The tendency towards judicialization has thus far been limited in Britain, in part because of the unwritten nature of the constitution. There is no legal document by which judges can feel entitled to claim the constitution as theirs for the making. The British constitution, as has been famously remarked before, is a political constitution.[8] In the absence of a constitutional court adjudicating on constitutional law, in Britain, it is the political rather than the legal institutions which play the leading roles on the constitutional stage. Thus, Parliament is not only the national legislature, it is also the primary forum in which the government is held to account. The constitutional accountability of the government takes a political form (and takes place in a political arena) under the unwritten British constitution—the courts play only a secondary role. In this way, great trust and great hope are placed at Parliament's door. The British constitution is, above all, a parliamentary constitution. Governments are created out of Parliament. Ministers are respon-

---

[6] 5 US (1 Cranch.) 137; 2 L Ed. 60 (1803).

[7] On Canada, see M. Mandel, *The Charter of Rights and the Legalization of Politics in Canada* (Toronto: Wall and Thompson, 1989); on Australia, see *Australian Capital Television Pty. Ltd.* v. *Commonwealth of Australia (No. 2)* (1992) 108 ALR 577 and *Nationwide News Pty. Ltd.* v. *Wills* (1992) 108 ALR 681, discussed by K. D. Ewing, 'New Constitutional Constraints in Australia' [1993] *Public Law* 256 and H. P. Lee, 'The Australian High Court and Implied Fundamental Guarantees' [1993] *Public Law* 606; on the ECJ see *Costa* v. *ENEL* (Case 6/64) [1964] ECR 585 and *Amministrazione delle Finanze dello Stato* v. *Simmenthal SpA* (Case 106/77) [1978] ECR 629.

[8] See J. A. G. Griffith, 'The Political Constitution' (1979) 42 *Modern Law Review* 1.

sible not to courts or to commissioners but to Parliament.[9] Contrary to Tony Blair's erroneous view, it was not his government, but a new Parliament, which was elected on 1 May. It is because and only because Parliament allows it and wants it (for the time being) that he and his ministers hold office. That is why they are constitutionally responsible *to Parliament*. It might be the queen who confers the keys of office onto her ministers, but in modern times it is Parliament which determines to whom she may offer those keys. Without the authorization and approval of Parliament, the crown's ministers would be constitutionally and practically powerless.

It is easy to overlook this. The power of the party machines and the scourge of the whips have successfully managed to blur the formal distinction between Parliament and government. But they have not completely erased it. In the context of the Scott debate in the House of Commons on 26 February 1996, Quentin Davies and Richard Shepherd demonstrated that even when the government is desperate it cannot always rely on 'its' MPs to toe the line. No doubt when the party in government enjoys a majority in the House of Commons of the magnitude which the electorate returned in May 1997 the effect of such 'independently minded' MPs will be much reduced, which is part of the reason why we should perhaps remain sceptical as to the ability of the new regime to learn all of the uncomfortable lessons of the Scott report.

The other part of the reason is those words in inverted commas. We constantly hear of the 'government majority' in the House of Commons being 179 MPs. This phrase is inaccurate but symptomatic of the contemporary malaise of British constitutional politics. The government has no majority in the House of Commons. Approximately ninety MPs are members of the government: ninety out of 659. The government is always in the minority in the House of Commons.[10] The majority is composed of Labour party MPs. Labour party MPs and the government are not synonymous. No government should regard MPs from the same party (or parties) which form the government as 'its' MPs, just as MPs who refuse to toe their party line should not be termed 'independently minded' as if they are somehow uncontrollable, wild animals. They should be praised for their parliamentary-mindedness, not patronized and denigrated as mavericks engaged on a frolic of their own.

In a political climate which is dominated by party control freaks (the Peter Mandelsons and Alan Duncans of this world) these views are no doubt absurdly unrealistic. Yet they do constitute a constitutional ideal towards which it is not only desirable but essential that we move. The single most important weakness of Britain's constitutional structures which the Scott

---

[9] This is not to deny that large and important areas of Britain's public law take place well away from Parliament. Regulation of privatized utilities is but one field of growing significance to public law where Parliament plays a minimal role. The point here is simply that in the field of ministers' accountability it is Parliament, rather than the courts, which takes the lead.

[10] See House of Commons Disqualification Act 1975, s. 2, which provides that no more than 95 sitting MPs may hold ministerial office at any one time.

story identified was the present inability of the parliamentary constitution to act as a sufficiently powerful check on executive power. That inability is caused not as much by any systemic failing as it is by a political unwillingness on the part of those who matter: namely, parliamentarians. The problem is not so much that the executive dominates Parliament. Rather, it is that political parties dominate members of Parliament. Whether in government or in opposition it is extremely difficult for individual MPs to progress as professional parliamentarians without first receiving the approval of their party managers. There is no parliamentary career structure other than the hope of ministerial office. This is just as true of opposition as it is of government. This means that, at the same time as the parties gain more and more central control over the choice of candidates which ostensibly autonomous local parties adopt (especially in the Labour party), the variety of people putting themselves forward is lessening, as it becomes ever clearer that once you enter the House of Commons your choices are extremely limited. Either you will toe the line on the promise of the potential of ministerial power, or you will forever remain on the back benches, anonymous, ignored, unpromoted, and unpromotable (as there is nowhere for you to be promoted to) irrespective of your interests and of your expertise. It is that the second option is so unattractive to most of those who become MPs that is the real cause of the problems of accountability which Scott encountered.

Scott was evidently a believer in the parliamentary constitution. Instead of making sweeping recommendations for reform of such constitutional essentials as the practice of ministerial responsibility, the provision by the government of information to Parliament, or the future regulation of the civil service and of the security and secret intelligence services, he left these next steps largely to Parliament. As we have already seen, Scott saw his task primarily as one of fact-finding. Once he had found the facts he left it to others who were better placed and more experienced to work out what should be done in the light of the account Scott provided. This approach resulted in the admirable work of the public service committee, the ground-breaking resolutions on ministerial responsibility, the new guidelines on answering parliamentary questions, the new guidelines on PII, and so on. Only in the field of secret intelligence did the parliamentary constitution really let Scott down. That area aside, however, Scott's faith in the parliamentary constitution has been justified, despite its being initially attacked by lawyers' reviews of the Scott report.[11] Certainly, when compared with the uninterested way in which the US constitutional authorities reacted to Iraqgate, indifferent to successive administrations merely sweeping the scandal under the carpet, the unfashionable British parliamentary constitution has emerged from the Scott saga with a good deal of credibility. This is not to say that the Scott story is a total

---

[11] See I. Leigh and L. Lustgarten, 'Five Volumes in Search of Accountability: The Scott Report' (1996) 59 *Modern Law Review* 695 at pp. 706–7.

vindication of the present parliamentary constitution. On the contrary, there were some major disappointments, including the House of Commons' predictable set-piece debate on the report on 26 February 1996—a mere pair of MPs voting contrary to their party line on a matter which so clearly concerned Parliament as an institution separate from government is hardly a shining record.

How to Combat Failure and Rekindle Hope in the Parliamentary Constitution

The great strength of the parliamentary constitution is that it recognizes the essential truth that ministers will try to do anything which they think they can politically get away with. This is a principle the full force of which most constitutions of the written, juridical, variety fail to acknowledge, and it is an unusual advantage of the British constitution that it does not have to rely on the mechanisms of judicial accountability and the rule of law to control the exercise of executive power but can instead place its faith in the more potent political processes of Parliament to play the leading role in that task. The weakness of the parliamentary constitution is that, despite the efforts of the public service committee, it is not working as well as it should. This presents us with a choice. Should we throw away the British parliamentary constitution, give up on Parliament, and turn instead to the courts; or should we seek to mend it and to find ways of rejuvenating Parliament so that its place at the heart of the constitution control room can be restored?

In times of popular disillusionment with politics generally and with Parliament in particular, it is commonplace to find advocates of constitutional change taking the former approach, especially when they happen to be lawyers. The judges have, after all, worked hard to improve their image after some difficult years, with prominent miscarriages of justice which dogged the late 1980s and early 1990s now firmly in the past (we hope). Scott himself, along with Lord Nolan (on public standards) and Lord Woolf (on prisons and then on civil justice) and the late Lord Taylor (on football grounds) have all contributed to the restoration of the judiciary's public relations over the past decade. The mood of renaissance has led some among the judiciary to go a good deal further, and to begin to sketch out in a series of public lectures a new constitutional deal whereby the courts would play a much bigger role in checking the constitutionality of the actions of Britain's parliamentary government. Even such sacred cows as the legislative supremacy of Parliament seem to be within at least some of these judges' sights.[12] However, in the

---

[12] See among many examples, Sir John Laws, 'Is the High Court the Guardian of Constitutional Rights?' [1993] *Public Law* 59, 'Law and Democracy' [1995] *Public Law* 72, and 'The Constitution: Morals and Rights' [1996] *Public Law* 622; Sir Stephen Sedley, 'The Sound of Silence' (1994) 110 *Law Quarterly Review* 270 and 'Human Rights: A 21st Century Agenda'

contexts of accountability and information, as the history of public interest immunity law illustrates (especially when compared with the relative freshness of the ombudsman's approach under the Code of Practice on Access to Government Information), the courts do not have a particularly shining record in securing greater accountability and less government secrecy. Of course there have been good decisions, but let us not forget that it was a judicial (not statutory or royal prerogative) doctrine on which the Thatcher government relied in the *Spycatcher* cases;[13] it was the jury which acquitted Clive Ponting despite rather than because of the trial judge's summing up;[14] it was the courts and not the government which gave voice to the candour argument and to the prospect of class claims in the law of PII; and even relatively open decisions such as *ex parte Wiley* have been limited by subsequent decisions such as *Taylor* v. *Anderton*.[15] It is far from clear that the case has been made out to transfer the constitutional functions of checking the executive from Parliament to the courts.

This is not to suggest, however, that things should be left as they are. On the contrary, the argument here is that the longer-term lesson of the Scott report is that Parliament must change. The failure to find out what the government's policy on trade with Iraq was; the failure to find out exactly what the DTI knew and when it knew it about supergun; the failure to establish when the government realized that it was abusing the law of evidence to ease the prosecution of men who had risked their lives to inform the security and secret intelligence services about Iraq's arms procurement network. All of these were parliamentary failures, and they all cry out for wide-ranging parliamentary reform. We have already seen how several small reforms have been made to parliamentary government in the light of the Scott report, ranging from new guidelines on answering parliamentary questions to written statements of the meaning and extent of ministerial responsibility. The Code of Practice on Access to Government Information has also made an important contribution, even if it is limited by the continued existence of the Osmotherly rules and by the continued insistence on the part of the government that civil servants are there to serve them, not the public. But there is a need, in addition to the various piecemeal reforms which have taken place, for a broader reappraisal of the ways in which Parliament fulfils its constitutional role of keeping the executive in check.

[1995] *Public Law* 386; and Lord Woolf, 'Droit Public—English Style' [1995] *Public Law* 57. See also the troika of essays by Sedley J published in the *London Review of Books*, vol. 19, nos. 9–11 (May and June 1997).

  [13] Breach of confidence: see *Attorney General* v. *Guardian Newspapers* (No. 1) [1987] 1 WLR 1248 and (No. 2) [1990] 1 AC 109.

  [14] *R* v. *Ponting* [1985] Crim. LR 318.

  [15] [1995] 2 All ER 420, in which the Court of Appeal held that although the House of Lords had ruled in *Wiley* ([1995] 1 AC 274, see ch. 5 above) that PII does not attach to a class comprising witness statements concerned with police disciplinary hearings, reports of such investigations could still attract PII on a class basis.

The work of select committees, the roles of the commissioners (on admin-istration and on standards), and the procedures in the chamber, concerning debates and question time, all demand attention and renewal. One of the first actions of the Labour government's leader of the House, Ann Taylor MP, was to institute a wide-ranging inquiry under the auspices of a new modern-ization committee into many of the issues which have been raised here, although it is still too early to evaluate the work of that committee. Although the first items on the committee's agenda related to legislative procedure rather than to the ways in which Parliament holds the government to account, it is expected (and to be hoped) that the committee will move on to these mat-ters in due course. The first areas to be investigated by the committee were procedures for examining legislative proposals; methods of voting in the House; and the layout of the Order paper.[16]

When she was shadow leader of the House Ms Taylor indicated that Parliament was failing in both of its main tasks (of legislating and of holding the government to account). She suggested first that a number of moderniz-ing changes designed to ease MPs' working lives could be relatively easily implemented, concerning such practical matters as 'sitting hours, proxy voting, Bill timetabling and office accommodation'.[17] While the Jopling reforms introduced during the previous Parliament had gone some way to improve matters by cutting down on the numbers of late sittings (beyond 10 p.m.), by introducing more Wednesday morning sessions for back-bench business (including, very often, debates on select committees reports), and by helping to free up Fridays for constituency work, these changes had not been designed to enable Parliament either to produce better legislation or to hold the government more effectively to account. Despite the changes which Jopling had ushered in, these big issues remained.

On these big issues, however, Ms Taylor was less clear as to what should be done. She suggested that question time should be reformed but stated that this was 'not something for the government to decide' as the government could not 'dictate change: Parliament must own its process',[18] which in the light of the Blair government's decision to change the format of prime minis-ter's question time now seems rather quaint. On select committees, Ms Taylor stated that in her view the two most significant problems which the commit-tees faced were that there was insufficient time for their reports to be properly debated in the chamber, and that their work was usually an assessment of events which had already happened, rather than of matters which were currently facing, or which were likely to face, departments. To ameliorate the

[16] See the committee's press notice issued on 12 June 1997. This can be found on Parliament's web site: www.parliament.uk/commons.

[17] See, for example, the speech entitled *New Politics, New Parliament* given by Ann Taylor MP (when shadow leader of the House) to Charter 88's seminar on the reform of Parliament, 14 May 1996.

[18] Ibid., pp. 4–5.

situation, she suggested that among the issues which could be considered, select committees might be given greater responsibilities by subjecting some senior public appointments to prior ratification by the appropriate committee, and additionally that government agencies and non-departmental public bodies should be required to report annually to select committees. These are strange suggestions which appear to be more concerned with giving select committees more diverse things to do rather than with enhancing the ways in which they perform their central task of holding government departments to account for their policies, decisions, and actions. We can only hope that it is not part of the Labour government's agenda to water down the effectiveness of select committees by overloading them. As we saw in chapter three the changes which recent events such as the Scott story suggest would be more valuable to select committees are more help from such bodies as the national audit office with fact-finding; the institution of parliamentary commissions to investigate matters of political controversy or pressing public concern; and, most importantly, abolition of the Osmotherly rules. From the point of view of revitalizing the parliamentary constitution, it is reforms such as these which the present Parliament should be pressing for.

The Liberal Democrats have advocated a more ambitious approach. In a policy paper published in 1996, they suggested that select committees should appoint rapporteurs to carry out investigations on the committee's behalf and to draw up reports for the committee's consideration.[19] The Liberal Democrat paper was based on the argument that what is really needed if we are genuinely to rejuvenate the parliamentary constitution is a greater degree of separation between Parliament and government. Unusually (and boldly) for a political party, the paper welcomed what it described as the 'increasing willingness of MPs to exercise their independent judgement and to vote from time to time against their party line'.[20] To this end, the paper recommended that a career structure should be established in the House of Commons which is separate from that of the government payroll. Those who serve on select committees should be paid for their services. Those who chair committees or who perform special functions for committees (such as acting as rapporteurs, should this proposal be adopted) should be paid more, and so on. These would be extremely valuable reforms, and should be embraced by Parliament. While the mere existence of a pay structure in the House of Commons which is separate from that of ministers will not guarantee that Parliament will learn to grow more independent of government or of the party machines, its introduction would be a useful first step in encouraging such a development.

---

[19] *A Parliament for the People: Proposals to reform the House of Commons* (policy paper no. 20, Sept. 1996, p. 15).
[20] Ibid., p. 14.

Conclusion

While attention is focused on the role of the judiciary in Britain's changing constitution, with the ongoing debates on the Bill of Rights, the lesson which Scott and Iraqgate demonstrate is that it is the strengthening of Parliament which is most urgently required. The dogma of the liberal constitutional reformers (especially the lawyers among them) may insist that the British constitution should be judicialized, but the experience of the most important constitutional event of the long Conservative period in office suggests that other concerns may in fact be more pressing. Just as 'law is not and cannot be a substitute for politics',[21] judicial mechanisms of accountability are not and cannot be a substitute for Parliament. While the Blair government's constitutional reforms will no doubt enhance the judiciary's role in holding the executive to account, this will only result in the genuine rejuvenation of constitutional accountability if it is accompanied by parliamentary reform. Parliament is and will remain the key to the issues of accountability and secrecy in central government. But the parliamentary key will only be able to unlock British government if Parliament is extensively reformed. Separate pay scales and career structures will help, as would better offices, more support staff, and wider research facilities. The *ad hoc* changes which have followed Scott (as regards ministerial responsibility, answers to parliamentary questions, and public interest immunity) will also make an important contribution. But for these various improvements to have full effect they will have to be reinforced by significant cultural change in Parliament away from the domination by party machines. This seems to be as far from Tony Blair's intentions as it was from those of his predecessors. It might not even be achievable (whoever the party leaders are) as long as the House of Commons is elected under its present first-past-the-post system.

The Scott report made an unprecedented contribution to constitutional understanding in modern Britain. The secretive practices of central government which Scott was uniquely able to unwrap have been subjected to the public gaze as never before. In many areas, despite the report's lack of immediate political bite, the Scott inquiry has resulted in significant and welcome reforms. But its most important constitutional lesson is that there can be no substitute for enhanced parliamentary accountability. The legacy of the Scott report is that more than anything else the British constitution urgently needs to find some way of driving a wedge between the interests of Parliament, government, and party. In this way, Scott has taught us not to forget what we already suspected but did not like to admit: namely, that if ministers will do whatever they can politically get away with, we have to find ways of allowing them politically to get away with less.

[21] Griffith, op. cit. n. 8, p. 16.

Index